LGAA

MAKING SOCIAL POLICY

MAKING SOCIAL POLICY

The mechanisms of government and
politics, and how to investigate them

PETER LEVIN

Open University Press
Buckingham · Philadelphia

Open University Press
Celtic Court
22 Ballmoor
Buckingham
MK18 1XW

and

1900 Frost Road, Suite 101
Bristol, PA 19007, USA

First Published 1997

A catalogue record of this book is available from the British Library

ISBN   0 335 19084 7 (pbk)   0 335 19085 5 (hbk)

Library of Congress Cataloging-in-Publication Data
Levin, Peter, 1936–
    Making social policy : the mechanisms of government and politics,
    and how to investigate them / Peter Levin.
        p.   cm.
    Includes bibliographical references and index.
    ISBN 0–335–19085–5 (hbk). — ISBN 0–335–19084–7 (pbk.)
    1. Great Britain—Social policy—1979–   . 2. Policy sciences—
Methodology. I. Title.
HN383.5.L48   1996
361.6'1'0941—dc20
                                                                                        95–50905
                                                                                              CIP

Typeset by Dorwyn Ltd, Rowlands Castle, Hants
Printed in Great Britain by Redwood Books, Trowbridge

For the alumni of SA5620,
with love and gratitude

CONTENTS

Chapter one

INTRODUCTION

What this book is about

This book is about two things. First, it is about the phenomenon known as 'policy making'. It examines the mechanisms by which the government of the United Kingdom (and in one case the governing institutions of the European Union) makes 'policy', and by which legislative and other measures come into being, especially in 'social policy' fields like education, housing and social security. Second, it is about how to study those mechanisms. It offers a methodology: it suggests where we can find useful material, how we can 'interrogate' that material for relevant evidence, and how we can interpret that evidence and draw reasoned conclusions from it.

The role of central government in the social policy fields is a particularly interesting one to study, because it allows us to explore the interaction between government and society, to see how ministers and officials perceive and respond to circumstances in the 'real world'. It is interesting also because people in central government depend on other people, in other organizations, actually to undertake education, provide and manage housing, deliver social security benefits etc., and so we have an opportunity to explore the consequences of this dependence too.

The material that I use is presented in the form of five 'case studies' of policy making in the 1980s and early 1990s, under the Conservative governments led by Margaret Thatcher and latterly John Major. The case studies are of very different kinds. The first is a case study in the formulating of intentions: it deals with the far-reaching proposals on education and housing that were published in the Conservative election manifesto of 1987, after Thatcher had turned her attention to the reform of the 'welfare state'. The second is a case study in the

poll tax
= LA reduce spending

dependence of the then Prime Minister as well as her power: it deals with the invention, introduction and eventual abandonment of the Community Charge, better known as the 'poll tax', a measure intended to exert pressure on local authorities to hold down their spending. The third deals with the formulating and putting into effect of the 'Fowler' reforms of social security in the mid-1980s: this is a case study in the strategies used by ministers and pressure groups. The fourth case study is a 'composite' one, of a recurring process, the annual spending round, in which the Government plans public expenditure in the years immediately ahead: this is a case study in the interaction between the Treasury and the spending departments and the obstacles to 'rational' decision making. The fifth is the adopting of the European Social Charter by eleven of the twelve heads of state or government of the then European Community and the translating of some of its aspirations into the law of the UK, despite the UK Government's refusal to endorse the Charter and its opposition to some of those legislative provisions.

Although many studies have been made of policy making, and much has been written on the subject, there is very little guidance available on *how* to study it. One of my aims in writing this book has been to fill some of that gap, by presenting as much as possible of the 'raw material' that I have used and by making as explicit as I can the conceptual 'tools' that I have applied to it. The most appropriate tools, it seems to me, are incisive questions derived from conceptual frameworks that are 'rooted' in the experiences of those whose behaviour we are studying. I make use of four such frameworks. They involve viewing policy as, respectively, the product of a rationale, a selective response to interests, the outcome of a process, and a reflection of the 'power structure'. I have selected these on the basis that they can readily be applied to the 'raw' material that we encounter (i.e. to descriptions of what actually took place, and what politicians and officials and other participants were thinking and feeling); that they help us to do the detective work that enables us to find out what went on in a particular case; and that they help us to gain some insight into the mechanisms at work.

My approach differs from that of most other compilers of case studies of policy making, who tell us that they set out to generalize from their findings. Their approach is thus based on the presupposition that there are generalizations to be found. It seems to me that this is not a realistic presupposition: when we look at actual cases we find that every one is unique: one might almost say that the only safe generalization in this field is that there are very few safe generalizations,[1] especially 'high-level' ones about such matters as the British constitution and the power of the Prime Minister. But if there are very few general answers, that does not mean that there are very few general questions. It seems to me that there are potentially quite a number of these, as I hope the following chapters will demonstrate. It seems to me too that there are *some* safe generalizations to be found, but these are (exclusively, I suspect) to do with mechanisms that are widely found.

In the chapters that follow, I draw on evidence from a variety of sources.

These include official documents, contemporary press reports and comment, and a number of book-length and chapter-length case studies of policy making, as well as various articles in academic and professional journals. The memoirs of Thatcher and several of her ministers contain a great deal of useful material, and I draw on them extensively. Although it is common to disparage memoirs as self-serving and self-justificatory, they are written from first-hand experience, they are invaluable in drawing up a chronology of events, different accounts of the same events can be compared, and self-justifying statements tell us what kinds of behaviour the author regards as justified. It is of course important to seek corroboration wherever possible, and to identify and treat with particular care hearsay evidence, such as accounts of meetings at which the author wasn't present, and descriptions of what was going on in someone else's mind. But where Margaret Thatcher is concerned to disparage and blame, we see something of the emotions and value judgements that she brought to policy making. Nigel Lawson's descriptions of policy making reveal both thoughtfulness and a susceptibility to embarrassment. The gaps in Norman Fowler's accounts appear to tell us where matters were taken out of his hands. We can learn more from their accounts than they think are telling us. Please remember, however, that all quotations are taken out of context (because that is the nature of quotations) and so cannot be a perfect substitute for the original sources.

In the case study chapters, the raw material is presented as such, with its source given in the text or in footnotes. My inferences and interpretations, if not clearly 'flagged' as such, can be recognized by the usual academic 'weasel words' and expressions and synonyms for 'I think': 'the evidence suggests', 'clearly', 'evidently', 'it seems/appears that', 'possibly', 'perhaps', and 'will have'. I use quotation marks both to signify actual quotations, in which case their source is footnoted, and to denote colloquialisms and metaphors.

I hope that by being explicit and 'up-front' about my methodology I will enable you, the reader, to use it – doubtless discarding some bits and adding others – to make sense of current events in the field of government and politics and social policy, to appreciate the significance of what you see and read in the media, and to keep your knowledge up to date. I hope too that it will enable you to make your own check on my reasoning and conclusions. I would like to stress that it is not absolutely vital that you agree with me on every point and come to conclusions that are the same as mine. As you may already know, writers in this field do not agree with each other on everything. And the status of my conclusions is that they are the best 'working model' that I can find for the time being in the light of the evidence available to me. New evidence might prompt me to reassess it: other observers with different perspectives might draw different conclusions from exactly the same evidence. So what I write should be read with a critical eye, not treated as 'gospel truth'. Indeed, I would like to encourage you to develop for yourself the habit and techniques of questioning and thinking critically about everything that you are told about government and politics and policy, whether by politicians or officials, or the media, or researchers, or the writers of textbooks. There is one respect in which I believe we are all equal: we all have the moral right to ask questions, and no one should be immune from being questioned.

Outline of the book

Before we go any further in our explorations, we need to have a picture of the policy-making machinery in the central government of the UK, placed in the context of the wider political system (embracing political parties, pressure groups etc.) and the UK's membership of the European Union. This is the subject of Chapter 2. It is also necessary to clear up some of the confusion that surrounds the terms 'policy' and 'social policy': I address this in Chapter 3. Chapter 4 – 'Approaches and methods' – is the 'methodology chapter'. It presents my analytical approaches, with the four conceptual frameworks and the sets of questions derived from them. Chapters 5–9 are the case study chapters. In each one I give an outline of the relevant events, and then apply in turn the analytical approaches set out in Chapter 4. In the final chapter, Chapter 10, I examine what we have learned from the case studies about the mechanisms of policy making.

Chapter
two

THE POLICY-MAKING
MACHINERY

Introduction

This chapter introduces the core institutions – bodies, organizations – of UK central government and the government of the European Union (formerly the European Community), concentrating on those which play a part in the policy-making processes that are the subject of the case studies presented in Chapters 5–9.[1] It concentrates on the formal structures, i.e. on the positions and formal relationships that exist irrespective of who the occupants of the positions are. So in reading it, please bear in mind the important distinction, often obscured, between positions (posts) and their occupants: for example, 'the Prime Minister' denotes a particular person in a particular position, and the combination – the person in the position – possesses a combination of her or his own personal attributes and the attributes of that position, such as the formal powers that go with it.

The Prime Minister and the Cabinet

A list of Cabinet posts and their occupants is published by the Cabinet Office's Machinery of Government Division after every general election and reshuffle, and reproduced (not always accurately) in the broadsheet newspapers. It can also be found in *Hansard*[2] and in *Dod's Parliamentary Companion*[3] (also known as *Dod*, published annually) and *Vacher's Parliamentary Companion*[4] (*Vacher's*, published quarterly). The Cabinet formed by Margaret Thatcher in September 1985 is shown in Box 2.1. All but two members were MPs, members of the House of Commons. The other two – the Lord Chancellor and the Leader of the House of

---

Box 2.1   The Cabinet, from September 1985

1	Prime Minister	Margaret Thatcher
2	Lord President of the Council and Leader of the House of Lords	Viscount Whitelaw
3	Lord Chancellor	Lord Hailsham
4	Secretary of State for Foreign and Commonwealth Affairs	Geoffrey Howe
5	Chancellor of the Exchequer	Nigel Lawson
6	Secretary of State for the Home Department (Home Secretary)	Douglas Hurd
7	Secretary of State for Education and Science	Sir Keith Joseph
8	Secretary of State for Energy	Peter Walker
9	Secretary of State for Defence	George Younger
10	Secretary of State for Wales	Nicholas Edwards
11	Lord Privy Seal and Leader of the House of Commons	John Biffen
12	Secretary of State for Social Services	Norman Fowler
13	Chancellor of the Duchy of Lancaster	Norman Tebbit
14	Secretary of State for Northern Ireland	Tom King
15	Minister of Agriculture, Fisheries and Food	Michael Jopling
16	Secretary of State for Transport	Nicholas Ridley
17	Secretary of State for Employment	Lord Young
18	Secretary of State for the Environment	Kenneth Baker
19	Paymaster General and Minister for Employment	Kenneth Clarke
20	Chief Secretary to the Treasury	John MacGregor
21	Secretary of State for Scotland	Malcolm Rifkind
22	Secretary of State for Trade and Industry and President of the Board of Trade	Paul Channon

---

Lords – were Peers, members of the House of Lords. The list of posts does not necessarily stay the same from year to year: new posts have been created and old ones abolished; existing posts have been combined and divided, and raised to or demoted from Cabinet rank; and the order of posts – the 'pecking order' – changes frequently.

The 'pecking order' is decided by the Prime Minister. The particular ranking of a post and its occupant reflects a combination of the perceived status of the post – the Foreign Secretary, the Chancellor of the Exchequer and the Home Secretary are always high in the order – and the perceived seniority of the individual who occupies it, as gauged by, for example, the length of time that he or she has been in the Cabinet. If we compare this list with previous ones, or watch what happens when a Cabinet reshuffle takes place, we see that a post rises in the list when it is given to a long-standing member of the Cabinet, and drops when it is given to a relative newcomer.

Certain Cabinet posts carry responsibility for particular social policy fields, such as education, housing (assigned to the Secretary of State for the Environment), and health, social work and social security: in September 1985 the Secretary of State for Social Services had responsibility for all of the latter group, but since 1988 there has been a Secretary of State for Health (including social work) and a Secretary of State for Social Security. Each of these ministers heads a government department (see below) that has the same title as the minister (with the confusing exception that prior to 1988 the Secretary of State for Social Services headed the Department of Health and Social Security). There are also three 'territorial' ministers – for Wales, Scotland and Northern Ireland – who are concerned with health, education and environment matters in their respective countries. Ministers in these two groups have usually been in the bottom half of the pecking order. (The placing of education at no. 7 in the September 1985 list is consistent with Sir Keith Joseph's long-standing membership of Conservative Cabinets, dating back to 1962.)

The Prime Minister occupies her or his position by virtue of being the leader of the largest party in the House of Commons. The Prime Minister offers posts in the Cabinet (as well as junior ministerial posts) to other members of the party, and – if they accept – appoints them: she or he also has the formal power to dismiss them. In practice this freedom of appointment and dismissal is not unlimited, especially if the Prime Minister is new to the post: she or he may feel, and be advised, that positions must be found for the most senior and experienced of their parliamentary colleagues; for those who, if relegated to the backbenches, might provide a focus for dissidence and disaffection; and for people from different wings of the party to provide a balance and help maintain the unity of the Parliamentary party. She or he might also want to have in the Cabinet a particular person who can be depended on to support her or him and their views, and a new Prime Minister may want to reward those who supported her or his leadership bid.

Few Cabinet Ministers have continued in the same post for more than three years, as can be seen from the potted biographies in *Dod* and *BBC-Vacher's Biographical Guide*,[5] also published annually. There have been numerous reshuffles, and social policy posts have often suffered a particularly rapid turnover. From past lists of ministers we see that there was a new Secretary of State for Education in 1979, 1981, 1986, 1989, 1990, 1992 and 1994 (seven in 16 years, despite one five-year stay); for the Environment in 1979, 1983 (twice), 1985, 1986, 1989, 1992 and 1993; and for Health and Social Security in 1979, 1981 and 1987, then – after the splitting of that Department – for Health in 1988, 1990 and 1992, and for Social Security in 1989 and 1992.

In addition to appointing Cabinet ministers, the Prime Minister also decides what Cabinet committees and sub-committees there shall be and who (mostly Cabinet ministers) shall be members of them. There are two types of Cabinet committee – standing committees and *ad hoc* committees. Both report to the full Cabinet. The list of standing Cabinet committees and their membership and terms of reference was made public for the first time by John Major, after the April 1992 general election.[6] (For the current list consult the most recent *Vacher's*.) Standing committees are assigned tasks that continue from one year to another. Some are given the task of keeping a particular field 'under review', or considering 'issues' which arise, or coordinating the Government's policies on it. Others have tasks that recur every session, such as examining draft bills. As of November 1995 the full quartet of social policy ministers mentioned above (the Secretaries of State for Education, Environment, Health and Social Security) is found on only two standing committees: the Committee on Home and Social Affairs (EDH), the terms of reference of which are 'to consider home and social policy issues'; and the Committee on Local Government (EDL), set up 'to consider issues affecting local government, including the annual allocation of resources'. Of those four ministers, only the Environment Secretary is on the leading Committee on Economic and Domestic Policy (EDP), chaired by the Prime Minister (unlike EDH and EDL), which considers 'strategic' policy issues. The Secretaries of State for Wales, Scotland and Northern Ireland, however, *are* members of this Committee. Other standing committees exist to prepare and submit to the Cabinet drafts of the Queen's speeches to Parliament and proposals for the Government's legislative programme each session; to examine all draft bills and consider how they and other Parliamentary business should be handled; and (EDX, a recent innovation) 'to consider the allocation of . . . public expenditure . . . and make recommendations to the Cabinet'. None of the four social policy ministers is a member of the committee on public expenditure: all are regarded as 'spending ministers'.

Ad hoc committees deal with particular issues. They are set up as the need arises, and disbanded when they have finished work. They have titles like 'MISC 11' and 'GEN 24'. Several such committees feature in the case studies in Chapters 5–9.

Parliament

Strictly speaking, Parliament comprises the House of Commons, the House of Lords, and the 'Queen (or King) in Parliament'.

The House of Commons. For the 1987 general election the UK was divided into 650 geographical constituencies, each returning a single member to the House of Commons, the winner being the candidate for that constituency who received the largest number of votes. In the general election of 1987, the Conservatives won 375 seats as against Labour's 229, the other parties and the then Speaker adding up to the remaining 46. The Conservatives thus had a majority of 101 over all other parties. (In 1992, there were 651 constituencies, of which the Conservatives won 336, Labour 271, and the other parties a total of 44, giving the Conservatives an overall majority of 21.)

Among the majority party, a large number occupy posts in the Government. Numbers have fluctuated, but at the beginning of 1990, 20 Conservative MPs were Cabinet ministers, two were law officers, 24 were non-Cabinet (middle-ranking) ministers and 24 were Parliamentary under-secretaries of state or equivalent (sometimes described as junior ministers). Nearly every Cabinet and non-Cabinet minister had a parliamentary private secretary (PPS), a 'back-bench' MP to assist with the minister's Parliamentary duties. (In effect, the ladder PPS to junior minister to middle-ranking minister to Cabinet minister to Prime Minister constitutes a 'career' structure for politicians who aspire to government office.) There were also 14 Government whips, headed by the Chief Whip, who has an office at 12 Downing Street: the best-known function of the whips is that of making sure that their side turn out and vote when necessary. Including PPSs, the 'payroll vote' amounted to some 130 MPs. Subtracting these from the 1987 Conservative total of 375 MPs, there remained approximately 245 Conservative MPs as backbenchers without government duties.

Much of the formal business of the House takes place in select committees and standing committees. The several different kinds of each are described succinctly but comprehensively in *Dod's Parliamentary Companion* and *Standing Orders of the House of Commons*.[7] The task of most select committees is to inquire into specified matters and report to the House. As of November 1995 they include 17 'departmental' select committees, whose brief – as set out in the House's Standing Orders – is to examine the expenditure, administration and policy of specified government departments and their associated public bodies. All but one have a maximum of 11 members, drawn from the parties in approximate proportion to their total numbers in the House. (The 17 chairs are similarly apportioned.) Members are appointed by the nine-member Committee of Selection, the members of which are themselves selected through the 'usual channels' (the whips' offices of the various parties). Since 1992 most of the Conservative members have been MPs first elected in 1992, and some of the independent-minded 'old hands' who were previously prominent have been dropped. Also of particular significance are the Committee of Public Accounts, which considers reports from the Comptroller and Auditor General (an officer of the House and head of the National Audit Office) on the accounts of government departments and certain public bodies, and the Select Committee on European Legislation, which sifts through European Union legislative proposals and other documents, picking out those which it recommends for further consideration.

Among standing committees, there are legislative standing committees, which scrutinize Government (public) Bills and Private Members' Bills; standing committees on statutory instruments, etc., which have limited powers to consider the merits of regulations, etc., that are in draft form or have already been made by the minister concerned; and two European standing committees, which examine European Union documents referred to them for further consideration by the Select Committee on European Legislation. Their members are appointed in the same way as those of select committees.

In addition to select and standing committees, which are part of the formal machinery of the House of Commons, there are unofficial 'all-party groups' of

MPs and Peers devoted to particular subjects or overseas countries. There are also backbench committees within each party, notably the 1922 Committee, composed of all backbench Conservative MPs, and the Labour equivalent, the Parliamentary Labour Party (PLP), as well as committees on particular subjects, such as the Conservative Education Committee and the Labour Environment Committee. Finally there are various organized groups of like-minded people among the MPs of the two main parties, such as, today, the No Turning Back Group of Conservative MPs, which is dedicated to maintaining the ethos and approach of Mrs Thatcher's governments.

There are thus many formal and informal positions to be filled by those majority-party MPs who do not hold government posts and are not PPSs. Some, of course, after a lengthy period of government by the same party, are former ministers or PPSs, or have spent years in the House of Commons without attaining any kind of government office, and now have no prospect of doing so.

The House of Lords. As of November 1995 there are nearly 1200 members of the House of Lords, of whom more than 750 are hereditary Peers, who have inherited their titles: only a small proportion of these attend regularly. Some 400 are Life Peers, appointed by the Queen on the recommendation of the Prime Minister of the day (some of these are usually passed-on recommendations from the leaders of the other parties in the Commons), and a higher proportion of these take an active part. Approximately 480 take the Conservative whip, 110 Labour and 50 Liberal Democrat, while nearly 300 sit as cross-benchers. The House of Lords does not make use of standing committees on the House of Commons model, and has fewer select committees: these include the Select Committee on the European Communities, which considers European Union legislative proposals and reports on those which seem to raise important questions. There is no equivalent to the departmental select committees of the House of Commons, although a select committee on a particular topic may be set up at any time.

Government departments[8]

The UK central government departments concerned with social policy can be divided into the following categories:

- 'Functional' departments, whose responsibilities are defined – like those of the Cabinet ministers who are their political heads – in terms of a particular field of policy. Examples from 1985 are the Department of Education and Science, the Department of the Environment and the Department of Health and Social Security: their counterparts in November 1995 are the Department for Education and Employment, the Department of the Environment, the Department of Health, and the Department of Social Security. They are sometimes referred to as 'spending' departments.
- Three departments – the Treasury, the Cabinet Office and the Prime Minister's Office – whose work ranges across all policy fields and is most easily

defined in terms of the *activities* they undertake, such as planning, coordination and briefing on issues.

- The three 'territorial' departments, the Northern Ireland, Scottish and Welsh Offices, all of which have a base in London as well as in their national capital.

The 'functional' departments. One of the long-established structural features of the functional departments is that the highest posts are shared among two distinct groups: politicians and officials. Politicians occupy ministerial posts: they are mostly MPs, but it is common for one middle-ranking or junior ministerial post in a department to be occupied by a Peer. Officials are 'career' civil servants – technically they are servants of the Crown – and unlike ministers do not lose their jobs when the party in power changes. The political head of each functional department is a secretary of state, who is a member of the Cabinet. He or she leads a ministerial team of middle-ranking and junior ministers, each of whom is usually given responsibility under the secretary of state for certain policy fields. Each secretary of state has his or her own Private Office and also one or two special advisers, often people who have previously worked for the party in some capacity.

Among officials, the senior person in each department is the Permanent Secretary, who is at the apex of a hierarchy of civil servants. He (it's usually a he) occupies a Grade 1 post in what is known as the 'open structure'. To him report a handful of deputy secretaries (Grade 2), each with a certain field of responsibility. In turn, reporting to each deputy secretary are a number of under secretaries (Grade 3), who again have their own, smaller, fields of responsibility. (Each of these fields is in most cases also overseen by a named middle-ranking or junior minister.) The current organizational structure can be found in *The Whitehall Companion*, while significant changes are likely to be mentioned in the annual reports of the various departments.[9]

The Treasury. The Treasury is known in Whitehall[10] as HM (for 'Her Majesty's') Treasury. Its terms of reference include the duty 'to plan public expenditure and see that it conforms to the approved plans' and 'to formulate and put into effect the Government's financial and economic policy'.[11] The Treasury too has a team of ministers, under the Chancellor of the Exchequer: a second Treasury minister – the Chief Secretary to the Treasury – is also a member of the Cabinet. On the official side, as well as the Permanent Secretary at Grade 1, the Treasury has two Second Permanent Secretaries and a Chief Economic Adviser to the Treasury, all at Grade 1A.

Like the functional departments, the Treasury is organized on hierarchical lines, and again – below the deputy secretaries and under secretaries – there are assistant secretaries with particular fields of responsibility. For example, in the Public Expenditure: Public Services Division, one has designated responsibility for social security benefits and National Insurance contributions; another for health and personal social services; another for local government finance; yet another for housing and environment. These necessarily bring Treasury officials into contact with the respective functional departments. In a sense, the business of the functional departments is education, housing etc.; the business of the Treasury is the functional departments and their expenditure.

The Cabinet Office.   The Cabinet Office contains the Cabinet Secretariat, which is headed by the Secretary of the Cabinet, who is also Head of the Home Civil Service (and occupies the only Grade 0 post in the Service): it is responsible for supporting ministers collectively in the conduct of Cabinet business. Within it are specialist secretariats, including the Economic Secretariat (covering economic policy and inner cities policy), the European Affairs Secretariat (EU business), and the Home and Social Affairs and Legislation Secretariat (social policy, education, housing, local government, and the planning of the Government's legislative programme). Each of them is headed by a deputy secretary or assistant secretary, who has usually spent his or her career in one of the functional departments prior to taking up their Cabinet Office post.

The Cabinet Office today also contains the Office of Public Service and Science, which itself contains the Citizen's Charter Unit, the Efficiency Unit, and the Office of the Civil Service Commissioner, which is responsible for – among other things – senior civil service appointments and recruitment to the 'fast stream'.

The Prime Minister's Office.   The Prime Minister's Office has four main components – the Private Office, the Political Office, the Press Office, and the Prime Minister's Policy Unit (also known as the No. 10 Policy Unit). The significance of all of them lies in their position in the Prime Minister's communications network. The Private Office handles virtually all official communications to or from the Prime Minister, written or verbal.[12] It is headed by the Prime Minister's Principal Private Secretary, and its work is divided into four categories: economic affairs, Parliamentary affairs, home affairs and the Prime Minister's diary.

The Political Office is a channel for political as opposed to official communications. It contains the Prime Minister's PPS, who is an important link between the Prime Minister and the Parliamentary party, and the Prime Minister's Political Secretary, who is not a civil servant: he handles party matters and is a link to the PM's constituency. The Press Office is headed by the Chief Press Secretary, who handles the PM's relationships with the media. The seven or so members of the No. 10 Policy Unit are appointed by the Prime Minister herself or himself: as well as giving advice in specific fields they have their own networks and can channel advice and ideas from other experts in their fields in to the Prime Minister.

The territorial departments.   Scotland, Wales and Northern Ireland are governed in different ways from England. Scotland has its own legislation, passed by the UK Parliament, in the fields of education, housing, health and social work (but not social security) and its own legal system. The Scottish Office in Edinburgh is like a mini-Whitehall: it is divided into six departments, including the Education, Environment, and Home and Health departments, each headed by a deputy secretary. Wales and England share the same legislation, but there is a

Welsh Office in Cardiff with functional departments. Northern Ireland has its own legislation, but since 1972 this has been enacted by the UK Parliament. There are six functional departments in Belfast.

European Union (Community) institutions[13]

By virtue of its membership of the European Union (formerly – prior to the ratification of the Maastricht Treaty – the European Community), the UK is obliged to respect the laws of the Union. As yet there has been little European legislation in the fields of education, housing, health and personal social services, but recent Directives and Council Recommendations have begun to have an impact on social security and employees' rights in the UK. The following EU institutions all play some part in the making or enforcing of Union legislation. The membership figures are for November 1995: they thus reflect the enlargement of the Union from 12 to 15 in January 1995 with the accession of Austria, Finland and Sweden.

The Council of Ministers. The Council of Ministers (officially the Council of the European Communities) is the chief legislating body of the EU. It consists of a minister from each of the 15 member states. Its members change according to the subject being considered: for example, environment matters are the province of what has become known as the Council of Environment Ministers. Preparation for the meetings is carried out by the Committee of Permanent Representatives (COREPER), which consists of the 15 'ambassadors' from the national governments to the EU: they and their staffs are permanently based in Brussels. The Council and COREPER are supported by the Council's General Secretariat, also based in Brussels.

The European Council. The European Council comprises the heads of state or government of the member states, including the Prime Minister of the UK. It meets twice a year in 'summit' meetings, where issues between the members are discussed, agreements reached and declarations of intention uttered. The presidency of the European Council rotates among the member states, each holding it for six months. During this period its representatives chair all meetings of the Council of Ministers and host the six-monthly summit. Hence we find references to 'the European Council of' Madrid, Strasbourg, etc.

The European Commission. The role of the Brussels-based European Commission is to initiate Union policy, to implement the decisions of the Council of Ministers, to act as the guardian of the European treaties, and to ensure that European legislation is implemented in the member states. It currently consists of a 'college' of 20 commissioners nominated by the various governments (the UK, like France, Germany, Italy and Spain, nominates two). On appointment, the commissioners pledge allegiance to the Union: they undertake not to act as representatives of the countries that they come from. There is a commissioner whose brief includes employment and social affairs and who, like his colleagues, is supported by a 'cabinet' of advisers; and there is a Directorate-General of Employment, Industrial Relations and Social Affairs, manned by the Commission's 'civil servants', the head of which is responsible to the commissioner in those fields where his policy responsibilities match the commissioner's brief. (There is another commissioner whose brief includes industrial affairs.)

The European Parliament.   There are now 626 Members of the European Parliament (MEPs), of whom 87 represent UK constituencies.[14] The EP does not have the same role in the enacting of EU legislation as the UK Parliament does in the enacting of UK legislation, since the EP is not 'sovereign' in the way that the UK Parliament is. However there are Parliamentary stages in the EU legislative and budgetary procedures. Parliamentary committees – such as those on women's rights and on social affairs and employment – scrutinize proposals from the Commission and also the work of the directorates-general. Full sessions of the Parliament are held in Strasbourg, the committees meet in Brussels, and the headquarters of the Parliament's secretariat are in Luxembourg.

The Economic and Social Committee.   This Committee, established under the treaties, now has 222 members, including 24 from the UK. Roughly one-third represent employers (industrial, public enterprises and commercial organizations), one-third workers (mostly members of national trade unions), and one-third various other groupings (including the professions, local authorities, consumer groups and environmental protection bodies). Members are formally nominated by national governments and appointed by the Council of Ministers. The committee's opinion is sought on legislative proposals and other matters.

The European Court of Justice.   The European Court of Justice (ECJ) consists of 15 judges, who are assisted by nine advocates-general. They are appointed by the governments of the member states acting together. Membership of the EU, enshrined by the acceptance of the Treaty of Rome, the Single European Act and the Maastricht Treaty on European Union, carries with it the obligation to accept the ECJ as the ultimate court of appeal on matters of EU law. Thus one of its functions is to resolve disputes between the Commission and the national governments. Courts in the UK and other countries also frequently ask it for its interpretation of EU legislation.

Although EU legislation is supranational in the sense that it applies throughout the Union and takes precedence over national legislation, the body which formally adopts it, the Council of Ministers, is like the European Council, essentially intergovernmental: its members are present as representatives of the governments of the member states. (They are not members of the European Parliament.) In contrast, the Commission and the ECJ are more appropriately thought of as supranational, since they do not share their membership with national governments.

'POLICY' AND 'SOCIAL POLICY'

Introduction

The terms 'policy' and 'social policy' are employed in different ways by different people. In particular, they mean different things to people *in* government – politicians and officials, the central participants in the making of policy – on the one hand, and to academic writers, people *outside* government, on the other. In this chapter I explore these different meanings, and ask how they relate to what people in government actually do.

What do politicians and officials mean by 'policy'?

A search through references to 'policy' by British politicians and officials reveals a variety of usages. But they can, I suggest, appropriately be grouped under the following four headings:

- 'Policy' as a stated intention
- 'Policy' as a current or past action
- 'Policy' as an organizational practice
- 'Policy' as an indicator of the formal or claimed status of a past, present or proposed course of action.

'Policy' as a stated intention

'Policy' as a stated intention – to take a particular action, or bring about a

Find - action

particular situation, in the future – is found in abundance in the manifestos published by political parties during general election campaigns:

> [The] policies in this manifesto . . .[1]

> The Conservative manifesto . . . is very much the party leader's own statement of policies.[2]

Of particular significance for subsequent events are the policies that were set out in the manifesto of the party that won the election, since the Government cannot – and its members may in any case not wish to – dissociate itself from what was written. In election manifestos we find very specific intentions:

> We will legislate in the first Session of the new Parliament to abolish the unfair domestic rating system and replace rates with a fairer Community Charge.[3]

> We will exempt war widows' pensions from tax . . .[4]

We find less specific ones:

> We will continue to improve the Health Service.[5]

> We will keep the present system of mortgage tax relief.[6]

And we find intentions expressed only indirectly, in terms of the outcome they are intended to bring about:

> We will continue to encourage the creation of nursery places.[7]

> We will take steps to ensure that individuals who need residential or nursing care continue to have a choice of homes, including independent homes.[8]

Policies in the sense of stated intentions can also be found in Government White Papers, which are often produced as the precursor to the tabling in Parliament of legislative proposals. An example is provided by the Conservative Government's 1987 White Paper, *Housing: The Government's Proposals:*

Increase rented housing + quality

> The Government has four principal aims. First, to reverse the decline of rented housing and to improve its quality; second, to give council tenants the right to transfer to other landlords if they choose to do so; third, to target money more accurately on the most acute problems; and fourth, to continue to encourage the growth of home ownership. Many of these policies require primary legislation.[9]

Specific intentions, less specific ones, and intentions expressed in terms of desired outcomes, are all present here.

Note the significance of *stating* the intention. We might well conclude that to all intents and purposes the Government – or sometimes, indeed, the Prime Minister alone – can make policy simply by announcing it. On this basis, policy is simply what the Government or Prime Minister says it is.

'Policy' as a current or past action

This usage of the term 'policy' can be as unspecific and all-embracing as the colloquial language of the following extracts suggests:

> The Government's policy is what the Government is doing, from day to day and week to week.[10]

> I asked [the Ministers] to come in and discuss with me the whole of our housing policy – both about where we stood on existing initiatives and where we should go from here.[11]

As an example of policy as something that has been done in the past, we have:

> There has been an extra squeeze on London hospitals because of the policy of redistributing resources to other regions which are held not to have been getting their fair share.[12]

Here not only is the word 'policy' being used synonymously with 'action': the implication is that the Government had deliberately adopted and then acted on the intention of redistributing resources.

'Policy' as an organizational practice

'Policy' is often used to denote the established practices of an organization: the rules and regulations, the ways in which things are customarily done, or attitudes that are customarily taken. For example,

> [It] was believed that the Child Support Agency had adopted a policy of giving priority to preparing maintenance payments for absent parents who were already paying an amount of child maintenance, either by agreement or by Court Order.[13]

> A Parliamentary Question. John Battle MP: To ask the Secretary of State for Social Security what is his policy with regard to the use of the word 'poverty' in official government reports? Peter Lloyd MP: It is our policy that, in reports prepared by the Department, the word 'poverty' should be used whenever it is the appropriate word.[14]

In these cases, it was 'policy' that would govern the organization's response to an issue or a situation that arose.

'Policy' as an indicator of the formal or claimed status of a past, present or proposed course of action

We frequently find a course of action described as 'policy' in a context where the term appears to denote a claim for status of some kind. In the statement attributed to Margaret Thatcher,

> The conclusions of the Cabinet Economic Committee laid down a clear policy . . .[15]

the implication is that those conclusions had the status of 'policy' by virtue of being the product of the deliberations of a Cabinet committee. Likewise, when we find in a departmental report,

> It is government policy that the executive functions of Departments should be carried out by agencies operating within a policy framework and using the resources set by the Secretary of State,[16]

the label 'government policy' seems to denote the *status* of this course of action: the Government is firmly wedded to it: it is not open to challenge. The same can be said of references to 'departmental policy' in official documents and elsewhere.[17]

If a policy can successfully be labelled 'government policy' – i.e. the appropriateness of the label is not contested – that policy will have a valid claim to priority over others not so labelled: in the allocation of money or other scarce resource, for example. This can be seen in the process of deciding public expenditure. In UK central government, part of the methodology used in determining the allocation of public expenditure for the year or years ahead is to project the costs of continuing current 'policies'. As the American academics Heclo and Wildavsky observed in the early 1970s, those concerned find themselves trying to discover what 'existing policy' is: one way in which they do this is by looking to see what has been agreed (formal status): another is by seeing what is currently being done (current action):

> What is existing policy? Surely everyone knows. [But] the fact is that there are continual battles in the bowels of the bureaucracy on this issue with, as one participant put it, 'the [spending] department trying to fiddle it up and the Treasury saying that ministers haven't agreed to this'. Is existing policy that which is agreed upon, or that which is done despite the fact that no one agreed? . . . 'Existing policy', concluded a finance officer, 'is one of those delightful phrases that one exploits as well as one can.' [What] is called existing policy [may appear] quite different, depending on who is doing the looking.[18]

Imagine that a certain policy – in the sense of intended action – is agreed upon on the basis of certain objectives and projections of costs. Subsequently, after the action is embarked upon, it is found that the objectives are not being achieved in full and that the actual costs are exceeding the cost projections because circumstances have changed. The Treasury, ever on the look-out for economies, might argue that in the changed circumstances that course of action no longer rightfully has the status of 'policy' and should accordingly be abandoned. But the department concerned might well argue that it is the Government's policy to achieve the stated objectives and consequently the higher spending is permitted. In such a case, 'policy' will effectively be *defined*, by whoever wins the argument over how 'policy' is to be ascertained, rather than discovered.

The attributes of 'policy'

The various ways in which politicians and officials use the term 'policy' seem to have some common elements. In particular, they use the term as a 'label', to denote certain attributes:

- 'Policy' denotes belongingness: a policy belongs to someone, or some body. It is the Government's policy, 'departmental policy', 'party policy', for example.
- 'Policy' denotes commitment. A policy 'carries' commitment on the part of those to whom the policy belongs. A stated intention, for example, is not merely a proposal: it is a proposal to which the Government (say) is committed. As Thatcher put it, when writing about the Conservative Party's 1983 election manifesto: '[The] party leader cannot dictate to senior colleagues: the rest of the government and parliamentary party need to feel committed to the manifesto's proposals.'[19] Note the reference to a *feeling*. Commitment implies a psychological stake in going ahead with the action specified in the description of the policy, and those involved are in a sense bound by their commitment, as when they are 'wedded' to the policy: there are psychological disincentives to backing down or making a U-turn: doing such a thing involves paying a penalty of some kind. Thus the stating of an intention or the taking of a decision to do X has the effect of creating or reinforcing feelings of commitment to doing X. In Heclo and Wildavsky's example, when civil servants were trying to establish what 'existing policy' was, they seem to have been trying to discover what it was that the Government was *committed* to – by looking for what was agreed upon, or what had tacit approval. Again, the existence of an organizational practice implies that those concerned feel a commitment to following that practice when the relevant circumstances arise.
- The description of a proposal or current course of action as 'policy' may also denote that it has, or is claimed to have, a certain status, possibly conferred upon it by a prior event of some kind – such as a Cabinet decision or public announcement – or by being acted on even though no agreement to that effect has been reached. (Commitment and status necessarily often go together – decisions and announcements create commitment too.) The assertion that a proposal (say) 'is policy' may constitute an attempt to get other people to accept it and to concede that it has a strong claim upon resources.
- A policy also possesses the attribute of 'specificity'. We have seen that some stated intentions are quite specific, where it is clear what action is intended: at the other extreme, it is sometimes very unclear what action would be involved. The less specific a policy, the more options it leaves open when it comes to translating the policy into action. Conversely, the more specific it is, the closer it is to being a single blueprint for action. A policy must have at least some degree of specificity for it to be distinguishable from other policies.

Policies and measures: what does the Government actually do?

In the case studies presented in this book we mostly find the word 'policy' used by politicians to denote a proposal or set of proposals carrying commitment to future action. So there are questions we need to ask about who takes those actions, and what form those actions take. In relation to central government in the United Kingdom, a simple but useful question to ask is:

What do ministers and senior officials in Westminster and Whitehall actually do?

It is important to bear in mind the self-evident truth that it is not ministers and officials who look after sick people, educate children, run homes for the elderly, and dispense social security benefits. Those tasks are organized and carried out by other people, in other organizations: in health authorities and trusts; hospitals, surgeries and clinics; local authority education, housing and social services departments; schools, colleges and universities; not-for-profit and commercial organizations; and executive agencies (like the Benefits Agency and the Child Support Agency). When the Government consciously adopts policies in these fields – when ministers commit themselves to getting these things done, and done in a certain way – it has to work through these various provider, purchaser and executive organizations. Ministers and senior officials spend a significant amount of time fashioning the instruments or 'measures' by which it does this. These measures include the following:

- Legislative measures: Acts of Parliament and delegated legislation
- Public expenditure: spending plans which allocate funds among departments and categories of expenditure, followed by the actual paying out of the money
- Organizational structuring: the creating, abolishing or modifying of organizational structures
- A variety of 'management activities', such as making appointments to positions, setting performance targets, prescribing organizational practices, and supervising the activities of provider, purchaser and executive organizations.

Legislative measures

One thing that the Government does is promote legislation in Parliament, introducing Bills and taking them through the prescribed formal stages, doing its best to ensure that they secure the necessary majorities when voted on in the various 'divisions', to the bestowing of the Royal Assent, at which point the Bill in its final form gets on to 'the Statute book': it becomes an Act of Parliament, a legislative measure. What does an Act of Parliament do?

- It confers, removes or modifies the *powers* – the legal entitlement to do certain things – that the occupants of certain positions possess. Where appropriate, it specifies the *domains* over which these powers may be exercised.
- It confers, removes or modifies *rights* and imposes, removes or modifies *duties*.

• It may set out *procedures* that must be followed when powers or rights are exercised, or duties performed.

For example, in the Housing Act 1985 we find that Section 1 defines local housing authorities (mostly district councils or London borough councils). Section 2 defines their domains ('districts'). Section 9 confers on them the power to provide housing, recognizable by the use of the word 'may': 'A local housing authority may provide housing accommodation' by building or acquiring houses or converting other buildings into houses. (Whether and to what extent a housing authority actually does this will depend on other factors, including the availability of resources, which the Act does not deal with.) Section 8 of the Act imposes on all local housing authorities the duty to 'consider housing conditions in their district' and the 'needs' of the district for additional housing. In Sections 118 to 188 we find set out 'the right to buy' and 'the right to a mortgage' conferred on most local authority tenants. The right to buy must imply a corresponding duty on local authorities to sell, and we find those corresponding duties imposed on the landlord authorities, recognizable by the words: 'The landlord shall . . . ' The Act also sets out the procedure that must be followed for the right to buy to be exercised.

An important power that many Acts of Parliament confer upon government ministers is the power to make 'delegated legislation' – rules and regulations, which have the force of law. Technically they are 'Statutory Instruments'. Particular use is made of them in the social security field. The Social Security Act 1986 specified the main kinds of benefit that would be available (e.g. Income Support and Family Credit) and the conditions that a claimant had to meet in order to be entitled to them. Numerous sets of Regulations were then published, specifying in detail how the conditions applied to claimants in particular circumstances. Since the mid-1980s, the Government has made increasing use of this approach, the resultant Acts of Parliament being described as 'framework' or 'skeleton' legislation.[20] The Child Support Act 1991 contains more than one hundred regulation-making powers.

Finally, also under the heading of 'legislation', there are European Union Regulations and Directives. Regulations have the force of law throughout the member states. Directives have to be given effect in the national legislation of the country concerned: in the UK they are translated into Acts of Parliament and delegated legislation.[21]

Public expenditure

Besides promoting legislation, the Government takes decisions about public expenditure – how the money for it should be raised and how it should be spent. These decisions are announced each year by the Chancellor of the Exchequer, nowadays in his combined Financial Statement and Budget Report in November.[22] Taxation decisions are incorporated in the annual Finance Bill and Act: expenditure decisions are set out in 'spending plans' which can be thought of as constituting measures in their own right, since they effectively entitle spending departments to use the funds for the specified programmes.

Most of the money raised is passed on to other bodies, for example in the form of grants – sometimes earmarked for special purposes, sometimes not. Some grants are designated as 'subsidies', when their purpose is to offset certain expenditures or an excess of expenditure over income (e.g. housing subsidies to local authorities). Some monies are allocated to an agency to be passed on in the form of social security cash benefits and (under the Social Fund) loans. Sometimes competitions are held, with local authorities bidding against one another for resources for certain purposes, such as housing investment or urban regeneration projects.

Organizational structuring

One important class of powers contained in Acts of Parliament comprises those conferred on Government ministers which empower them to set up organizations of one kind or another and appoint people to fill the positions thereby created. Sometimes the legislation actually makes this a duty as well. For example, the Education Reform Act 1988 required that 'there shall be established a body corporate known as the National Curriculum Council' which 'shall perform the functions' (i.e. duties) 'assigned to it by [this Act]' and 'shall consist of not less than ten or more than fifteen members appointed by the Secretary of State [for Education]'. The creating, abolishing or modifying of organizations involves assigning or reassigning powers, rights and duties to and from designated institutions and positions, and has the effect of linking institutions and positions with one another and sometimes with citizens and consumers. The institutions and positions comprise what can be thought of as an 'organizational structure'. The reforms of the National Health Service since 1972 under a succession of Acts of Parliament are examples of organizational structuring.

Management activities

The fourth answer to the question: 'What do ministers and senior officials actually do?' is that they undertake a variety of what can be labelled 'management activities'. Particularly important are the following:

- Making appointments. As we have already seen, under powers conferred by Acts of Parliament, secretaries of state appoint people to various positions in advisory and executive bodies and agencies.
- Setting targets and giving guidance. Examples are performance targets set by ministers for executive bodies and agencies and the standards promulgated in *The Patient's Charter*.[23] Guidance is contained in codes of practice and 'circulars' issued by central government departments to local authorities. These have no statutory force – they are not part of the law – but not to follow them could lead to a financial or other kind of penalty.
- Monitoring and inspection. Departments monitor performance and currently publish certain information, such as school 'league tables' and tables showing how hospitals have performed. The Audit Commission arranges for the

auditing of local authorities and health authorities, and carries out 'value for money' studies. The Department of Health Social Services Inspectorate carries out inspections of local units of services – such as residential homes – and Ofsted, the Office for Standards in Education, oversees the system of school inspection and has certain inspection responsibilities of its own.[24] Departments also commission 'policy evaluation' and other studies from universities and research institutes.

- Exercising 'default powers'. In certain circumstances, a secretary of state can exercise 'default powers' conferred on him or her by Act of Parliament. For example, if a local housing authority is defaulting on its duty to sell council houses by putting obstacles in the way of tenants who wish to exercise their right to buy, the Secretary of State for the Environment has the general power under the Housing Act 1985 to intervene and transfer the house to the tenant (this can be done by employing local solicitors), effectively overriding the local authority.

These, then, are the formal means available to the Government of the UK to move from intention to action in or upon society and the 'real world'. They are employed in conjunction with one another, especially when new machinery is being set up, as the example of the Child Support Agency (CSA) demonstrates. The sequence of events was as follows. In January 1990 Thatcher made a speech stating the Government's intention to find effective ways of ensuring that absent fathers contributed to the maintenance of their children.[25] In October 1990 a White Paper, spelling out in some detail the Government's intentions and commitment to securing legislation, was published.[26] The Child Support Bill was tabled in Parliament in February 1991 and became a legislative measure in July of that year. In July 1992 the first four sets of Regulations under the Act were made by the Secretary of State for Social Security. Another set followed in August, five more in October, another in December, and three more in March 1992, followed by another making miscellaneous amendments to the earlier ones. Meanwhile the necessary expenditure was earmarked in the Government's spending plans, and the CSA was set up (organizational structuring). On 1 April 1993 the Act came into force and the organization began running. It was set a target of saving the Exchequer £530 million in its first year of operation. In September 1993 a CSA internal memorandum was leaked to the press – 'The name of the game is maximizing the maintenance yield: don't waste a lot of time on non-profitable stuff'[27] – revealing how the organization's policies (in the sense of working practices) were being adapted to enable it to meet the target set for it.

Academic views of 'policy'

How do academics see 'policy'? Characteristic of the academic approach in the field of government and politics is that writers set out to *define* 'policy' rather than investigate how politicians and officials use the term. Ham and Hill summarize the debate:

But what is policy? Again this is a question that has attracted much interest but little agreement. Heclo notes that 'Policy is not . . . a self-evident term' and he suggests that 'A policy may usefully be considered as a course of action or inaction rather than specific decisions or actions'. As a variant on this, David Easton notes that 'a policy . . . consists of a web of decisions or actions that allocate . . . values'. A further definition is offered by Jenkins who sees policy as 'a set of interrelated decisions . . . concerning the selection of goals and the means of achieving them within a specified situation . . .' Other writers have suggested even vaguer definitions: Friend and his colleagues say 'policy is essentially a *stance* which, once articulated, contributes to the context within which a succession of future decisions will be made' . . . The definitional problems posed by the concept of policy suggest that it is difficult to treat it as a very specific and concrete phenomenon.[28]

The most striking thing about these definitions is how completely they fail to 'capture' the features of 'policy' that are salient to politicians and officials – their belongingness, commitment and formal 'status'. And how, as a consequence, they do not enable us to recognize a policy when we see it. (Imagine yourself going to hunt for an organization's 'policy' armed only with these definitions.) Although Heclo's equating of 'policy' with 'action' *is* sometimes encountered (see above), this is a very unhelpful definition because if we equate policy with action – i.e. measures – we are unable to explore the relationship *between* policy and action. (In contrast, the practical notion of 'commitment' *is*, as we shall see, invaluable for doing precisely this.) And unfortunately the very question 'What is policy?' leads one into the delusion that 'policy' is something that *is* – a 'concrete' phenomenon, to be identified by an academic explorer. In fact, as we have already observed, people in government use the word 'policy' as a label to denote the belongingness, commitment and status of a proposal. It is not helpful to ask what a label *is*. The appropriate question is: What do people who use the term 'policy' in their daily life mean by it?

Another example of an unhelpful definition is provided by Hall, Land, Parker and Webb:

> The growth of health centres [during the period 1946–71] provides us with an example of an evolutionary policy; a policy which emerged as a result of decisions made by a variety of groups, both central and local, administrative and professional.[29]

In referring to 'policy' in this way, the authors completely overlook the elements of belongingness and commitment to future action. This has the bizarre result that while they describe the slow growth in the number of health centres between 1951 and 1964 as the 'failure' of the health centre policy, that slow growth conformed precisely to the stated intention of the Conservative Government then in power that 'the health centre programme was to be restricted to the creation of a small number of units only'.[30] In other words, if we ascertain 'policy' by asking what the government of the day – to whom the policy belonged – was committed to, we find that 'policy' was implemented with complete success.

'Social policy'

There is no single, universally accepted definition of 'social policy'. The term is used primarily by academics in university departments of social policy or 'social administration', who do not agree among themselves on what they mean by it: each evidently feels free, when writing a book or learned paper, to invent a new definition or remodel an old one. Invariably they attempt to define it by producing an all-encompassing description. Marshall focused on means (i.e. instruments) and impact:

> In this book [social policy] is taken to refer to the policy of governments with regard to action having a direct impact on the welfare of the citizens, by providing them with services or income.[31]

Rodgers highlights means and purpose, and also equates policy with action, defining social policy as 'collective action for social welfare',[32] while Jones likewise seizes on 'purpose':

> Social policy represents an attempt to interfere in and, by some criteria, to 'improve' or correct a given social order.[33]

So do Kleinman and Piachaud:

> We define as 'social policy' government interventions that are designed to affect individual behaviour or command over resources or to influence the economic system in order to shape society in some way.[34]

These purpose-based definitions all equate policy with action and require us to discover the intentions of the government or the designer if we are to ascertain whether a policy is 'social' or not.

Other writers have sought to define the boundaries of social policy, or presupposed that such boundaries exist. Members of the Central Policy Review Staff concluded: 'The boundaries of social policy in its widest sense are not easy to define.'[35] But Walker, focusing on the judgements entailed, concluded:

> The [1988] Budget should have made it clear to everyone that the simplistic division between economic management and social policy is false: issues such as the distribution of taxation (not just how revenue is spent) and incentives (low wages for the poor and high wages for the rich) entail social and moral judgements as much as economic ones.[36]

Hill found that trying to define the scope of social policy by explaining what it is that distinguishes it from other kinds of policy is difficult. 'Perhaps it is best just to list the policy areas to be discussed [social security, the personal social services, the health service, education, employment services, housing].'[37] Here he comes close to Thatcher's approach, when she refers to 'all that goes under the heading of social policy – education, criminal justice, housing, the family and so on'.[38]

While the scope of social policy does appear to be most readily illustrated by reference to 'fields' – health, housing, education, social security and personal social services are the ones most commonly cited by British academics – it is worth noting that the 'Agreement on social policy' annexed to the Maastricht Treaty on European Union covers the health and safety of workers, conditions of employment, employers' duties to inform and consult workers, equality of men and women in the labour market and the workplace, and the widening of opportunities to work. So the meaning attached to 'social policy' in European Union institutions is one that includes the world of work as well as that of personal and social life. This usage seems to me to highlight the narrowness and ethnocentricity of British academic definitions: almost all British writers on social policy have ignored the world of work and workplace relationships in their writings, although Titmuss drew attention to 'occupational welfare', benefits provided by firms to their employees.[39] In this book, my standpoint is that I am writing about a *phenomenon*, the coming into being of policies and measures, which is part of a wider phenomenon, the interaction of government and society. From this standpoint, the definitions and boundaries which academics seek to assign to 'social policy' are irrelevant as well as arbitrary. It will be more helpful to be able to cover all the fields mentioned above and the full range of measures that play a part in that interaction.

It is interesting to compare my answers to the question, 'What do ministers and senior officials in Westminster and Whitehall actually do?' with perceptions found in the academic social policy literature. Banting identifies 'three major mechanisms' employed by 'modern governments . . . to alter existing social patterns'. They are

- Regulation. 'The state sets rules, backed by sanctions, which prescribe certain behaviour within a sector of the economy or society.'
- Income transfers. 'Each citizen or corporate body is involved in a set of direct cash transfers with the state. Taxes of various types are paid to the state and a variety of benefits, grants and subsidies are provided by the state.'
- Services. 'Modern states provide a range of services which either supplement or displace private provision.'[40]

Le Grand *et al.* specify three very similar 'general categories within which government policies fall': government regulation of the market system, which 'involves specifying, via law, what activities may, or may not, have to be undertaken'; the use of tax or subsidy policies to deter some activities and encourage others; and direct provision, replacing the market system.[41]

As can be seen, these classifications have some points of 'fit' with my description of what people in government actually do, but in some important respects they don't. By defining government in a monolithic way, as 'the state', they fail to 'capture' central government's reliance on local agencies for regulation and (especially) the provision of services, and so are of no help in analysing that aspect of the machinery. The use of legislative measures to create or abolish institutions is not captured, nor is their use to confer powers and rights and impose duties, which amounts to much more than prescribing or prohibiting certain activities or behaviour. And the *interaction* between subsidy and provision, as when central government subsidizes local bodies, and it is they who then make the actual provision, is also not captured. These classifications are thus of very limited use as analytical tools. They make abstract what it is that governments do, and thus mystify rather than clarify.

Conclusions

In this chapter I have looked at the ways in which politicians and officials – participants in the making of policy – think of and use the term 'policy', and found what seem to me to be serious discrepancies between their usages on the one hand and academic definitions in the fields of government and politics and social policy on the other. It is important, I have suggested, to pay attention to the former. If we are trying to understand policy making, it is bad science to ignore the language and perceptions of the participants, not only because they constitute a rich source of data but also because they reveal concepts – such as 'commitment' – that are then available to us to use in making sense of our observations. Many academic definitions impose the writer's conceptual framework and ignore those of the participants, and have limited or no value as analytical tools. Definitions that equate 'policy' with 'action', for example, are of no assistance in enquiring into the relationship between policy and action.

In making case studies such as those presented in this book, which deal with the coming into being of policies and measures, we need to be clear about the precise form that measures take – vague terms like 'state intervention' and 'regulation' will not do – and about those attributes of 'policy' that are seen by participants as highly significant. Policies belong to someone or some body; 'policy' denotes commitment to future measures; a 'policy' has, or is claimed to have, a certain status. It is this concept of 'policy' that underlies the remainder of this book.

Chapter
four

APPROACHES AND
METHODS

Introduction

This chapter begins by contrasting the 'thematic' approaches that are found in
the existing literature on policy making and allied subjects with the analytic
approaches which I try to adopt in this book. It goes on to set out four such
approaches and the questions that they generate, which will be put to use in
the following five case study chapters.

Argument: 'thematic' versus 'analytic' approaches

We saw in Chapter 3 that some academic writings on policy and social policy
fail signally to 'capture' what actually goes on in the world of government and
politics. Such writings – and the abstractions that they employ – seem to me to
tell us more about what goes on in the minds of their authors than about any
phenomenon. When academic writers use terms like 'social policy', 'social justice', 'poverty' and 'equity' – terms over the definition of which they do not
agree – they are writing about *themes*, not phenomena: they are imposing their
own concepts and paying scant heed to those used by the politicians, officials
and ordinary people who experience at first hand the phenomena concerned.

Hall *et al.* argue that case studies can be used for producing generalizations if,
among other things, the researchers search for regularities. Producing generalizations and finding regularities requires starting with a conceptual framework:
'Only in this way will sufficient order be imposed upon the mass of information
which case studies provide.' And they do mean 'imposed': 'We must reduce
a myriad variables to a small number which interact with each other in a

reasonably predictable and regular way.'[1] In equally cavalier fashion, Barr consolidates the 'objectives' of housing policy from two Conservative White Papers 16 years apart and an intervening Labour Green Paper: 'It is helpful for subsequent discussion if some order is imposed on these objectives.'[2]

Unfortunately this approach is profoundly unscientific. Scientists see their task as revealing order, not imposing it. If the phenomenon is one where many variables interact unpredictably and irregularly, this cannot be ignored: the challenge is to find a way of handling the variety. This is the aim of what I term the 'analytic' approach.

The goal of the thematic approach is to find generalizations. We see this in the explicit attempts by other authors of books of case studies – not only Hall *et al.* – to generalize from their particular findings. Donnison *et al.* do this linguistically, making extensive use of the words 'typically', usually', 'often' and 'tend'.[3] Greenaway *et al.* admit to 'the worry that our case studies are not typical, that they [give] a misleading picture of how decisions get made in Britain'.[4] Implicit in this statement is the assumption that there *is* an accurate picture or typical case study to be found, and that there *is* some 'standard' way of making decisions in Britain. They also write that 'it would be foolhardy to move from six [case studies] to general statements about the British political system', but then go on to write that the case studies do '*suggest* certain conclusions about British politics' (their italics) – i.e. they continue to aim at a very high level of generality.[5] Absent from their writings is any concept of discriminating between what it is and is not safe to generalize about.

In the natural and physical sciences, the key intellectual step is not generalization but unification. A good theory is one that is consistent with a wide range of observations: those observations will accordingly all be consistent with one another: they will fit together, form part of a unified whole. Such a theory provides a perspective from which all observations are themselves mutually consistent. *Unification* is the aim; *consistency* is the test. These again are characteristics of the analytic approach. In contrast, the thematic approach is characterized by the aim of generalization, and the test is *plausibility*, as we see from the literature.[6] This is a test that relies heavily on the intuition of the writer. If the reader is to accept it, he or she has no alternative but to accept the writer's authority. I reject this approach.

Thematic and analytic approaches contrast in many other ways, as shown in Box 4.1. Thus while the thematic approach offers definitions that are all-embracing, and hence abstract, the analytic approach offers definitions that enable you to recognize X when you see it. The dichotomy is repeated in the language used when discussing cause and effect. The thematic approach is characterized by a very non-rigorous terminology: we find terms like 'origins', 'shaped', 'led to', 'forced' and 'evolved'.[7] In contrast, an analytic explanation would refer to the *mechanisms* at work, the particular circumstances, and perhaps conjunctions of factors of different types.

The 'mode of discourse' too is different as between the two approaches. Thematic writings essentially take the form of argument and attempts to persuade: they employ metaphors and a vocabulary belonging to the writers rather

Box 4.1   Thematic and analytic approaches

	Thematic	*Analytic*
'Focus'	A theme	A phenomenon
Definitions	Abstract, all-encompassing	Concrete, to enable you to recognize X when you see it
Goal	Generalization	Unification
Use of conceptual framework	To impose order. Likely that only one conceptual framework is used	To reveal order. Likely that several conceptual frameworks are used in conjunction
Attitude to explanation	Theories explain	Mechanisms and circumstances explain
Mode of discourse	Argument, commentary, attempt to persuade	Report: non-judgemental description of findings, analysis and conclusions
Material	Views, metaphors	Evidence (even 'anecdotal')
Test of validity	Plausibility (appeal to intuition)	Consistency
Terminology of causation	'Led to', 'shaped', 'forced', 'origins', 'evolved' . . .	References to circumstances, mechanisms, conjunctions of factors of different types
Mode of learning	'You read for a degree.' Writer and teacher are interposed (as interpreter/ authority) between student and raw material.	Acquisition of methods of enquiry – how to observe, marshal relevant evidence and draw reasoned conclusions from it. Students are exposed directly to the phenomenon.

than the participants: they support their arguments by adducing the views of other writers: they are essentially commentary, 'contributions to the debate'. Analytic writings, on the other hand, are essentially reports of inquiries and findings: they present evidence, assess its validity and draw reasoned conclusions from it; they pay attention to the vocabulary and metaphors employed by those whom they are studying; they give the reader the opportunity to draw his or her own conclusions from the evidence presented. In effect, thematic writers (and teachers) interpose themselves between the reader and the raw material; analytic writers try to bring reader and raw material together.

In writing this book, I have not been able to avoid using the thematic approach – there are places where I have had to 'sketch' and interpret what has taken place, necessarily using my own metaphors and hoping that they will 'ring bells' with you – but I have tried to use the analytic approach where I can. In particular, I have followed what I take to be the *modus operandi* of the person described by Newton-Smith as 'the good experimenter . . . sadly ignored by philosophers of science in favour of the great theoretician'.[8] The good experimenter does not approach every phenomenon by setting up hypotheses and trying to test or invalidate them, although this may come later: the first step is to *explore* the phenomenon, and to do so by applying a variety of different techniques. If you want to know how heating changes a piece of metal, and what the mechanisms are by which it does so, you weigh it, look at it through an optical microscope and an electron microscope, bounce a beam of electrons off the surface and examine the resulting diffraction patterns, and so on, and then heat it up by stages, repeating your observations each time.[9] It is extremely important to use a range of techniques. If you use only one, you risk drawing conclusions which prove invalid when tested using others.[10]

In studying government and policy making, the equivalent of this approach is to use techniques that take the form of 'heuristics' – sets of questions that we can use for 'interrogating' the phenomenon that we are studying. Each set of questions will be 'rooted' in a particular conceptual framework and the 'perspective' that that conceptual framework provides. This is the method of working that I have employed.

Recognizing policies and measures

To uncover the mechanisms at work in the production of policies and measures, we must be able to recognize these policies and measures. Recognizing measures is a relatively straightforward matter. An Act of Parliament, for example, cannot easily be overlooked or mistaken for a hat. Recognizing 'policy' can be more difficult. In the conceptual framework common to politicians and officials, policy has certain attributes: belongingness, commitment and claimed or formal status. It is commitment in particular that distinguishes policy from a mere proposal. So the crucial question in looking for 'policy' seems to be the one which politicians and officials would ask:

What action is the Government committed to taking?

Or, in the case of a retrospective case study, what action was the Government committed, at successive points in time, to taking?

Conceptual frameworks

Anyone who sets out to study a phenomenon will necessarily do so with a 'conceptual framework' of some kind: expectations, taken-for-granteds, a 'mental set'. Without such a framework nothing would 'register' with us or 'make sense' – or not make sense, i.e. constitute a puzzle. We can get some idea of a writer's conceptual framework by seeing what questions he or she asks. For example, when Parker writes:

> Despite . . . evidence that periods of acute and killing smoke pollution were a recurrent risk, no British government had shown any marked concern for the air pollution problem. Two questions, therefore, arise. First, why should this issue have secured so little priority, and second, why, during the mid-1950s was there a change which led to firmer and more effective regulation?[11]

he is (I suggest) revealing a conceptual framework which makes use of comparison, implicitly regards inconsistencies as needing to be explained, assumes that British governments prioritize issues, and incorporates the expectation that a British government would respond to evidence of a recurring health hazard.

In the social policy literature we find many examples of policies and measures 'characterized' in certain ways. For example, they may be viewed as a response to 'social problems', as a victory for a particular pressure group, as conditioned by economic constraints, as the culmination of a historical process and so on.[12] But some conceptual frameworks seem more useful than others for uncovering mechanisms, and with this criterion in mind I have chosen to use the following four, which involve viewing a policy or measure as, respectively,

- the product of a rationale
- a selective response to interests
- the outcome of a process
- a reflection of the 'power structure'.

These terms are thematic, being no more than loosely descriptive of the mechanisms entailed. But the perspectives complement one another. The 'rationale' and 'interests' perspectives provide ways of examining policies and measures themselves: we thus learn something about mechanisms from seeing what they produce. The 'process' perspective gives us a more direct view of the mechanisms at work, because it highlights the dynamics of the forming and processing of issues. The 'power structure' perspective allows us to examine the effect that the structure of the machinery of government and the wider political system have on the mechanisms of policy making.

Policies and measures as products of a rationale

Viewed as the product of a rationale, a policy or measure is calculated to achieve certain aims, goals or objectives. It is the means adopted to bring about certain ends. This perspective is widespread in the academic literature, as witness such book titles as *The Goals of Social Policy*[13] and *The State and*

Social Welfare: The Objectives of Policy.[14] It also dominates the work of social economists, who take it for granted that social policy and 'the welfare state' have objectives. For example, Hills writes: 'The welfare state has much wider aims than just the relief of poverty.'[15] Barr compiles his single list of 'objectives of housing policy'[16] from Conservative Governments' White Papers[17] and a Labour Government's Green Paper,[18] while Le Grand *et al.* claim to discern 'society's objectives', most of which – they say – can be grouped under the headings of 'efficiency' and 'equity'.[19] (This also implies a conceptual framework in which society is seen as monolithic and in which 'substantive' objectives – e.g. 'an objective of the National Health Service is to make sick people better' – are taken for granted.[20])

In all these examples, the conceptual framework is one of perceived 'means and ends', logically connected and hence mutually consistent. Implicit in this conceptual framework is the notion that the answer to the question, 'Why did this policy take the form that it did?' is to be found by describing ends and available means. Implicit too is a 'rational actor' mechanism, in which objectives are formulated, alternative courses of action are set out and the likely consequences of each identified, and that course of action chosen which is seen as having the set of likely consequences that best fits the objectives.[21] March and Simon's model of 'satisficing', a variant on this model, allows for the objectives to be 'raised' when alternatives that would meet them are easy to discover, and 'lowered' when they are difficult to discover: in effect this is a procedure for arriving at a chosen alternative and objectives that are mutually consistent.[22] Although in the rational actor model it is the *mechanism* that is supposedly rational, the *policy chosen* should also be rational in the sense of being consistent with the objectives adopted.

The style and language of means and ends are frequently employed by governments in official documents and by politicians in their writings. Margaret Thatcher does this in the section of her memoirs that deals with her approach to education reform.[23] We can distinguish in her description of her thinking an 'ends dimension' and a 'means dimension'. In the ends dimension we find: *desired outcomes*, such as 'better education', 'parental choice and educational variety' and a situation in which 'parents, teachers and others know what [is] going right and wrong and [are able] to take remedial action if necessary'; and *outcomes to be avoided*, such as the existing situation in which children who moved to a school in another area were liable to encounter 'a course of work different in almost all respects from that to which they had become accustomed'. In the means dimension we find: *proposals and possibilities*, both those that were adopted, such as open enrolment and giving more powers and responsibility to individual schools, and those that were rejected, such as maintaining the existing system and bringing in a 'straightforward education voucher scheme'; and *constraints on action*, such as unacceptability in Britain, which, she said, ruled out emulating the French centralized education system. We also find *reasoning that links means and ends*, sometimes directly – open enrolment and per capita funding were seen as leading to the rewarding of successful schools – but mostly via means–ends 'chains': more powers and responsibility for individual schools (means) would result in decisions being taken at local level (intermediate end); decisions being taken at local level (means) would in turn make for better education (ultimate end). In this example, the intermediate end is also a means to a further end.

It is this 'picture', or 'calculus', constructed around perceptions of ends and means, the desirable and the feasible, that exists in someone's mind at the point when they choose one means – one course of action – in preference to another, to which I give the label 'rationale'. Note that I am using it to mean something more than the justification for a choice.

Applying this conceptual framework, there are three kinds of analysis that we can undertake. We can carry out a 'means–ends analysis'; we can examine the part played by 'considerations' of various kinds; and we can examine the 'ingredients' of the rationale.

Means and ends

Carrying out a means–ends analysis involves probing the logic behind a proposal or policy. It requires that we don't take the presented rationale at face value – that we don't accept without question that the stated objectives were indeed the ones that were held at the time, or that the mechanism was one of choosing policies in order to attain objectives. Instead we try to dig below the surface, looking for signs of other – 'real' – reasons or for clues that policies were being arrived at by other-than-rational mechanisms. We begin by asking what information we have about the policy makers' rationale or rationales, distinguishing between what we know 'for certain' and what we have to treat as merely claimed by the participants or speculatively guessed at by academics, reporters or other observers. We then ask:

Were alternative proposals considered? How were the rejected ones ruled out?

The answers to these questions will give us information about the criteria and constraints that were applied, and reveal whether the same ones were applied to all alternatives. If they weren't, or if alternatives to the proposal eventually adopted weren't seriously considered, then an other-than-rational process has been taking place.

Did the policies (adopted proposals) follow logically from stated objectives and constraints?

If the answer is 'no', proposals may have followed from unstated objectives and constraints, or they may have been treated as good in their own right – worth implementing for the sake of it – or possibly the outcome was less important than that the Government be seen to be doing *something*.

With what detail (specificity) were proposals and objectives expressed?

To describe proposals and objectives in vague terms may indicate that they have not been formulated clearly, but it may also conceal 'true' ones or a lack of agreement as to what they should be. Detail may be withheld intentionally to obscure inconsistency or lack of agreement.

Was there consistency among proposals and among objectives?

Seeming inconsistencies are always worth exploring. On the face of it, it was inconsistent of Thatcher to support both centralizing and decentralizing proposals for education reform. But if we inspect her stated rationale for mutually consistent elements, we find that both sets of proposals would have been consistent with an objective of removing powers from local education authorities, i.e. if that had been her underlying objective, there would have been no inconsistency.

In justifying a proposal, was there selective use of evidence, reliance on extreme cases, citing of single-cause explanations, or use of blaming or disparaging language?

These too may lead us to suspect that a policy was seen as good or bad in its own right, or arrived at with objectives in mind other than those stated. Thatcher's justification of education reforms contains examples of all of these, local authorities in particular coming in for disparaging comment, as we shall see in Chapter 5.

Were there omissions and unaddressed consequences ('loose ends')?

As an example of an observable omission, we have the 1971 Conservative White Paper, *Fair Deal for Housing*,[24] which listed three objectives: a decent home for every family at a price within their means; a fairer choice between owning a home and renting one; and fairness between one citizen and another in giving and receiving help towards housing costs. Its proposals were primarily to do with raising council house rents, introducing a statutory rent rebate scheme and considerably reducing Exchequer subsidies to local authorities. What they did not address was the matter of tax relief on mortgage interest for home-owners: this system, whereby people on the highest incomes and with the largest mortgages got most tax relief, was left alone. We may, I suggest, reasonably suspect that cutting Exchequer subsidies was also a prime objective – if not *the* prime objective – and that the White Paper was based on one particular interpretation of 'fairness'. Objectives stated in Government White Papers should not necessarily be taken at face value.[25]

'Considerations'

The second way of analysing a rationale is to search it for 'considerations' of various kinds as they existed in the minds of ministers or officials. It is important to be alert to the classification used by the writer or speaker rather than to impose our own, although it is sometimes convenient to use our own labels. Thatcher refers to the arguments against education vouchers as being more political than practical; and the term 'financial considerations' is in common usage. Former senior civil servant Leo Pliatzky refers to the 'real world' in the sense in which I use the term;[26] he also distinguishes between 'the force of ideas and the force of circumstances'. Possible categories, then, are:

√ • *Real-world considerations*, to do with what goes on in the 'real world'. The perception that children were leaving school without the education required by prospective employers, and the perceived need to raise school standards, were real-world considerations that entered into Thatcher's education rationale.

√ • *Political considerations* may include the giving of priority to the winning of elections and maintaining party unity – i.e. 'Party' political considerations – and political-with-a-small-'p' considerations, such as the objective of reducing the powers of local authorities and the need to gain the support of people whose opposition or neutrality could frustrate proposals. Members of the Central Policy Review Staff (the 'think tank') which advised the Cabinet from 1971 to 1983 saw it as necessary to have 'either the Treasury or the spending departments on your side. With both opposed, the prospects of proposals for change being accepted were greatly reduced'.[27]

• *Presentational considerations*, to do with the presentation of proposals, reports etc. in a way that gains credit and places blame elsewhere, or avoids embarrassment. Edwards and Batley found 'presentational' to be a commonly used Civil Service word implying a concern with the appearance or 'image' of a public statement.[28] Presentational considerations can be recognized by expressions like 'we can't be seen to . . . ' in accounts of behind-the-scenes deliberations and sometimes by descriptions of proposals and decisions as 'fair', 'balanced' or 'reasonable' – terms that are unquantifiable but may be thought to appeal to British readers and listeners.

√ • *Practical considerations* arise where the real world and the world of government and politics meet: they are to do with the feasibility and mechanics of implementing reforms, and the day-to-day delivery of services and operation of systems once they are 'up and running'.

√ • *Financial considerations* are mostly to do with existing and projected costs and charges of different kinds, and who – or what body – bears them. The large and increasing cost of state maintenance for one-parent families as at January 1990 was a financial consideration in ministers' minds when they launched what became the Child Support Act 1991.[29] The cost of implementing a proposal is of course a financial consideration.

√ • *Legal considerations* would include the possibility of a Government action being successfully challenged in the courts.

√ • *Ideological considerations* would include a belief in the free market and competition as the best way of distributing goods and services, or aspirations such as 'rolling back the frontiers of the state'.

• *Ethical considerations* would enter into questions of whether it was right or wrong – permissible or impermissible on ethical grounds – to do certain things.

So the main question here is:

What part was played by considerations of different kinds?

And this can be broken down into finer questions:

Was the adopted policy the product of considerations of one kind rather than another: for example, of political or financial considerations as opposed to real-world ones? Was the test of a good policy whether it would be 'good for the people', or whether it would be easy to get through Parliament, or would diminish the powers of local authorities?

Did the presented and/or underlying rationale cover the whole range of considerations? If some – financial, say, or ethical – were excluded, what is the significance of that? Is there a mechanism at work that gives priority to political considerations?

Finally, as far as considerations are concerned, there is the 'Whose views?' question:

Did any significant considerations enter into the rationale at the behest of any particular individual or group of people?

'Ingredients'

The third way of analysing a rationale is to look for the 'ingredients' of the policy or measure and, by implication, of the rationale as well. I find it helpful to distinguish four kinds of ingredient: perceptions, theories, ideas and value judgements. (This is my categorization, i.e. an 'observer' categorization rather than one taken from participants.) They all enter into statements of means and ends, and into considerations of the kinds listed above.

Perceptions. Every rationale incorporates at least some perceptions of a present or past situation. They are often presented as incontrovertible – as 'facts' or 'realities'. Over some there will indeed be no dispute, but others will be subjective, in the sense that different people looking at the same situation will register different things. For example, where one person registers that expenditure on state education has been increasing, another might register that it has been increasing less rapidly than the number of children in state schools.

Theories. Everyone involved in policy making relies on theories of some kind. Sometimes they are expressed as theories, sometimes as hypotheses, conjectures or assumptions; often they appear in the form of assertions. They are frequently matters of belief rather than established as incontrovertible. People make use of theories in identifying the causes of an existing situation, in projecting what would happen if an existing situation were allowed to continue (i.e. nothing were done) and – by using theories that logically connect means and ends – in calculating what requires to be done to achieve a given end, or what the effect would be of taking a particular action. Because this involves looking into the future, assumptions always have to be made: for example, about how people would behave if a particular measure were adopted. Making such assumptions always involves taking the risk that they might prove to be wrong.

Ideas. Many policies, and all innovative ones, are based on ideas about what might be done, what action might be taken. Their novelty usually makes them easy to recognize. The 'education voucher' is an example of an idea.

Value judgements. 'Value judgements' supply the normative, or 'ought', statements in any rationale. They are in a different category from perceptions and theories, which are all to do with what is or, projected into the future, what could be. To recognize them is usually straightforward: they contain words like 'ought' and 'should', or cite principles of some kind, or imply by their language that certain situations or courses of action are good and others bad. ('I knew . . . that too many people left school without a basic knowledge of reading, writing and arithmetic.'[30]) We find them not only in explicit statements of objectives, but also in the diagnosis of existing problems, especially those that attribute blame or imply that some people are 'deserving' and that others are not.

There are many questions that we can ask about these ingredients of a rationale. For example:

> *Did any particular perceptions, theories, ideas or value judgements dominate the rationale? Did they correspond to the views of any particular person or group?*

> *To what extent did perceptions and theories conform to what we might call 'reality' – the situation in the 'real world' (social, demographic, economic etc.) as ascertained by research findings or independent observations? Were there any significant omissions: was relevant information (or what seems in hindsight to be relevant information) not taken into account? Did some ingredients have the status merely of assumptions about reality?*

> *What part was played by individual judgement and interpretation in determining what 'ingredients' were admitted to the rationale?*

Policies and measures as selective responses to interests

When we view a policy or measure as the product of a rationale, as calculated to achieve certain objectives, we are treating it purely as the product of an intellectual, problem-solving mechanism. We are taking the objectives as given, and not asking why they were regarded as good ones, what their attraction was to those who subscribed to them. Even if we identify political considerations that played a part in the conscious thinking of the politicians and officials involved, we may learn little about what motivated or 'drove' them at a deeper level – to put it colloquially, about 'what was in it for them' and for their friends and others whom they regarded as deserving. Likewise an ideological attachment, to the free market, say, or to 'equality', may conceal an underlying sympathy towards those who would gain from it and antipathy towards those who would lose. (There may of course also be potential gainers and losers of whom the policy makers are not aware.)

The concept of 'interest' helps us to bring out into the open these underlying factors in policy making. Those who stand to gain, to benefit, from a proposed policy or measure have, we may say, an 'interest' in the proposal being adopted. Underlying that interest is a deeper one, an interest in having the benefits that are seen as following from the implementation of the measure. What we wish to discover is what those envisaged benefits are.

The word 'interest' is well established in the vocabulary of people in the world of government and politics. It is used mainly in one of two senses. One is the sense in which I use it above, i.e. in relation to a proposal or to an eventuality of some other kind. For example, Sarah Hogg, former head of John Major's No. 10 Policy Unit, tells us that once a Bill has been tabled in Parliament, 'government does have a strong interest of its own . . . in avoiding the embarrassment of revision and repeal'.[31] In the other sense, 'interest' is used to denote an organized group of people in a position of privilege, as in references to 'vested interests'; or in a given position in society or the economy, as in references to 'sectional interests'; or in government, as in references to 'departmental interests'; and as in statements like: 'All relevant interests have been consulted.' The implication here is that these interests exist by virtue of the position of those concerned within a *structure* of some kind. (Indeed, structures may *give rise* to interests, as when the division of an organization into departments has the effect of generating 'departmental interests'.) Which usage is being employed is usually self-evident from the context. The expression 'interest in' always denotes the first usage.

I also find it helpful to make a distinction between 'political/institutional interests' and 'consumer interests'. By 'political/institutional interests' I mean the interests of politicians, officials, advisers, pressure group leaders and members of policy 'think-tanks' – people who stand to gain or lose in terms of their position in the world of government and politics (as gauged by their reputation and place on the career ladder, for example) and in terms of how far their personal 'drives' and 'missions' are satisfied and accomplished. By 'consumer interests' I mean the interests of people who are on the 'receiving end' of legislative and other measures in the 'social policy' fields and/or who stand to gain or lose from new ones – for example, in terms of the amount of Housing Benefit or tax relief on mortgage interest that they receive, the length of time they wait for hospital treatment, or the extent to which they might benefit from parental choice of school. Politicians, officials, advisers and pressure group leaders act in varying degrees as advocates of consumer interests. And there may be an 'alignment' between consumer interests and political/institutional interests, as when a pressure group campaign will, if successful, both materially benefit consumers and enhance the reputation of the group's leaders.

When a new proposal is put forward in the social policy field, there is always public debate about the interests of consumers in the proposal, about how various groups of consumers would gain or lose. In the culture of government and politics in the UK, there is rarely the same openness about political/institutional interests, about who would gain or lose in the world of government and politics. Proposals are claimed publicly by their advocates to be in the national interest or the public interest: we have to look behind these claims, dig beneath the expressed policy preferences, to discover the underlying private motives. The questions suggested in this section are designed to elicit these.

On another point of language, I find it helpful to think of interests as 'making their mark' on policy, or failing to do so. This is especially useful where there is a sequence of proposals. While the (adjudged) interests of people who stood to gain from all of them can be said to have made their mark on policy – the proposal finally adopted – so too can the interests of those who stood to lose more from the earlier proposals than from the adopted one.

The concept of 'interest' features in the political science and social philosophy literatures. I find none of the argument helpful in analysing policy making. We find Connolly arguing that there are such things as 'real interests', and supporting his argument by citing extreme cases – those of slavery and choosing to become addicted to debilitating drugs – as being contrary to real interests. Five pages later, however, we find that in an example taken from industrial relations, 'real interests' are matters of 'judgement' and 'assessment': evidently they are not capable of being objectively ascertained, in which case, I suggest, we must doubt that their existence has been demonstrated.[32] Saunders puts forward 'a definition of interests which . . . rests on the assumption that real interests refer to the achievement of benefits and the avoidance of costs in any particular situation'.[33] This assumption does no more than *define* 'real interests' in terms of benefits and costs: it doesn't reveal their fundamental properties. He goes on to argue that 'costs and benefits do exist objectively and may be analysed empirically in any specified context of action'. I would contest the 'exist objectively' – in the context of issues, when policy is not yet 'made', costs and benefits are necessarily *anticipated* rather than having an objective existence, and judgement necessarily enters into the anticipation. Allied to this debate is another over whether an individual is the best judge of his or her own interests: I deal with this by accepting that the individual's judgements and those of other would-be judges may well be different and do not find it necessary to address the (in my view unanswerable) question of who is the best judge. All that we need to do is note that whenever we refer to something as being in someone's interests, we need to add the qualifier: 'in X's judgement'.

'Interests' also feature in the literature on 'public choice theory', where we find assertions to the effect that bureaucrats have personal interests in power, salary, reputation etc., and that these may get in the way of serving 'the public interest'. Unfortunately this literature offers us no guidance on how to inspect a governmental body and identify such interests on the part of its members.[34]

When we view a policy or measure as a selective response to interests, we inspect the policy or measure itself; what was said or written about it by way of description, justification or commentary; and the behaviour of those involved. The general questions about interests are:

> *Whose interests (as judged by whom?) made a mark on this policy or measure, in the sense that they stood to gain from it, or to lose less than they would have done under earlier proposals? Whose interests made no mark, in the sense that they stood to lose throughout?*

More incisively, to identify relevant consumer interests we can ask the following questions:

> *Did the proposed policy or measure specify groups or categories of 'consumers' who plainly would – or were plainly intended to – gain or lose? Does the documentation suggest that an attempt was made to identify potential gainers and losers?*

With which people were sympathies expressed, as by manifest advocacy or the use of language denoting merit or deservingness?

Whose point of view appears to have been particularly well appreciated? (Even if sympathies are not expressed overtly, close familiarity with, say, the 'problems' experienced by a particular group may denote sympathy with that group's interests.)

To identify relevant political/institutional interests, whether derived from the structure or evoked by a proposal, from whatever source, we can ask:

Who stood to gain or lose from it, in terms of their personal position (reputation, position on the career ladder, self-esteem) or their powers, domain, autonomy, control over resources or other people's dependence on them being enhanced or diminished?

What did participants support or defend? Is there evidence in their behaviour or writings that they were motivated by the expectation that they themselves would gain or lose from a particular proposal going ahead?

Are there references to a group or groups whom 'we can't afford to alienate' or 'we have to carry with us'?

Did the participants evince strong personal antagonism to anyone or any group?

Are there indications that the promoters of a proposal identified themselves personally with a particular goal or objective? Do they describe attaining it as a personal 'mission' of some kind? Does their behaviour indicate a strong personal stake in attaining it?

Are there indications that any participants were strongly motivated to avoid certain situations or eventualities, which might denote an interest in, for example, avoiding embarrassment or damage to reputation?

Were there instances of claiming credit for achieving outcome X or of placing elsewhere blame for outcome Y? (This may indicate an interest in achieving X (and avoiding Y) that had not previously been revealed, as well as an interest for its own sake in claiming credit and avoiding blame.)

What was the Government (or any other body) prepared to spend money on? In some sense or other, it will often be found that money is being spent on furthering someone's interests.

Policies and measures as outcomes of a process

Viewing a policy or measure as the outcome of a process directs our attention to the events and activities that took place in the course of its 'adoption', and to the mechanisms by which belongingness, commitment, status and specificity appear and subsequently change over time as the process runs its course. So this perspective should enable us to 'capture' the dynamics of making policy and translating it into measures.

Issues: perceptions and imperatives

Books and articles on a particular social policy commonly have a section on tracing its 'origins': it is usually found that a number of 'strands' have 'come together'. My approach is that for the purposes of analysis it is helpful to look for the point at which a person or group of people within government first felt that they were faced with an 'issue'. We have already seen that the terms of reference of many Cabinet committees require them to consider issues. Politicians and officials appear to 'register' or apprehend issues as the conjunction of two sets of elements: perceptions of a particular situation (in the real world and/or the world of government and politics); and an imperative to act, a *feeling* that they *ought* to take action, to *do* something. As Kenneth Baker writes, 'By the time that I became Minister for Local Government in September 1984 it was clear that something had to be done [about the rating system] . . . One of the first issues I had to deal with . . .'[35] (Note that the word 'issue' is not being used here in the sense merely of a subject of dispute, or of contention between political parties or other protagonists, although the issues examined in the following chapters did indeed become subjects of dispute.)

Academic writers sometimes refer to 'issues' as if they existed in their own right – as when an issue is said to 'get on to the agenda' – rather than existing by virtue of being experienced by someone or some body, as a conjunction of perceptions and imperatives. It would be more consistent with the language of participants to talk of a matter having got on to a *minister's* agenda, for example, at the point when he or she registers it as an issue.

We may find out about issues from contemporary or after-the-event writings. In some cases the existence of an issue may be marked at the time by agitated behaviour, meetings held at short notice, contradictory responses to media enquiries, discrepancies between public and private statements, the setting up of working parties, rushed decision taking, including the rapid allocation of funds, and the stating of intentions (including the intention to do nothing) that are reversed within a short time. So we ask:

What was 'the issue', and for whom was it an issue?

What statements of the form 'We must do something about X' were made?

What behavioural signs of participants being faced with an issue were there?

Imperatives, like motivations, arise in a variety of circumstances. Examples are: (a) imperatives supplied by the political calendar – to have a manifesto on which to fight a general election, to draw up a legislative programme to be announced in the Queen's speech, to make applause-winning announcements at annual party conferences; (b) the imperative to fulfil pledges in the general election manifesto on which the Government was elected to power, unless an excuse such as an unforeseeable change of circumstances can be found; (c) the imperative to respond to challenges to the Government's standing or 'credibility' or the authority of the Prime Minister, as when it appears that the Government has lost the initiative on a particular subject, or that local authorities or other agencies are not doing what the Government wants, or politically sensitive targets are not being met; (d) the imperative to mitigate bad publicity, as when a succession of 'scandals' has occurred (e.g. in residential homes for children or the elderly, or when people have been discharged from institutions into the community), especially where the Government is being blamed in the media; (e) the imperative to respond to events in the real world, even those which occur independently of government (such as the AIDS epidemic, and instances of children being attacked by dogs), especially when ministers sense that there is a 'public expectation' that they will do so; (f) the imperative to respond to pressures exerted by groups of various kinds, felt by ministers when they are susceptible to pressures from that particular source.

Note that in each of these cases there is an underlying interest – in staying in power, in maintaining the Government's credibility, in having 'a good press', for example. But whereas when viewing policy as a selective response to interests we were asking 'Why did the policy take the form that it did?', when we are asking about imperatives the leading questions are

Why did the policy change at all?

Why did the policy change when it did?

Who experienced the imperative? What circumstances and what interests of theirs underlay it?

We also need to ask about the perceptions that accompanied the imperative:

What were the significant perceptions in their minds? Were these new perceptions of an existing situation, or perceptions of a new or changed situation?

It is important not to fall into the trap of assuming that there is a single issue which is present at the outset and continues to be 'the issue' throughout the process. We need to be alert to the fact that an issue may be part of a 'bundle' of interrelated issues (as when what is done in response to one affects what can be done in response to another), and that new issues may arise in the course of the process. So we must ask:

What other, related, issues were registered at the time?

Chronology: events

During the period between the registering of an issue and the adopting of a policy and coming into effect of a measure, there always take place numerous events, such as meetings, decisions, announcements, the publication of documents and the steps in any formal procedure. These punctuate the process; they provide us with 'landmarks'. In getting acquainted with a process, it is always helpful to begin by drawing up a chronology that shows these landmark events. (It is particularly helpful to read political memoirs with the questions 'What actually happened?' and 'How would the author know?' in mind; the answers may assist us to distinguish fact from supposition and commentary.) So we ask the straightforward question:

What were the main landmark events in the process?

Essentially this involves drawing up a chronology of dates and events. Later we may wish to make our own judgement of what was relevant, using whatever evidence comes to hand. In practice it is rare to draw up a chronology and not find that it needs amending later as our knowledge and appreciation of events and their significance develop. A chronology also needs to include significant, or possibly significant, contextual events, such as general elections, party conferences and appointments to Cabinet posts.

The initial responses to an issue may take the form of decisions about organizational structure and procedure. (If these decisions are taken in private, we may not know about them until they are put into effect.) A structure-creating response may be to set up a Cabinet committee, a working party or an inquiry team or task force of some kind, and to appoint particular individuals to positions on it. The accompanying procedural response will be to give the group terms of reference and instructions about submitting its recommendations: a Cabinet committee will be required to submit its recommendations to the full Cabinet, for example. So we need to ask:

What organizational structures were set up, and what procedures were embarked on and followed?

In tracing the formation of responses to an issue and piecing together the sequence of events, those events that involve the submitting or publishing of proposals – e.g. in the form of a consultative document, Green Paper, White Paper, Parliamentary Bill – and the formal adopting of proposals as 'policy' will be found to be of particular importance. So we have two more questions:

What proposals (including drafts) were published, what proposals were formally adopted, and when?

What changes took place between one proposal and the next one in the sequence? (These changes may tell us a good deal about the activities that took place between successive proposals.)

Commitment, pre-empting and 'mandate'

The dynamic nature of government policy making is revealed in the metaphors used by politicians and officials to describe the process. Lord Bridges, former Cabinet Secretary, refers to 'hardening':

The experience of anyone who has worked in Whitehall is that there is an early stage in any project when things are fluid; when, if you are in touch with those concerned and get hold of the facts, it is fairly easy to influence decisions. But after a scheme has been worked on for weeks and months, and has hardened into a particular shape, and come up for formal decisions, then it is often very difficult to do anything except either approve it or throw it overboard.[36]

And it won't be thrown overboard if *something* must be done. A different metaphor is employed by Nigel Lawson, who refers to the poll tax proposal as possessing 'momentum' when it had become difficult to halt ('The steamroller rolls').[37]

There are, I suggest, three mechanisms through which certain events and activities in the course of a policy-making process have significance for what happens subsequently: (a) they create commitment to the current proposal, on the part of its promoters and those who endorse it; (b) they pre-empt certain alternatives, ruling them out or putting an obstacle in the way of adopting them, purely as a consequence of the procedure adopted; (c) they are regarded as creating a 'mandate' or permission for going ahead with certain proposals, thus making it easier to go ahead with those proposals rather than others. All three mechanisms have the effect of reducing the scope for later events and activities to make a mark on the eventual policy and measure.

Of the three mechanisms, the most commonly encountered is the creation of commitment. As we saw in Chapter 3, commitment is a state of mind on the part of those to whom the policy or proposal 'belongs'. In the course of a policy-making process, they become increasingly committed to going ahead with – or proposing, supporting or resisting – certain courses of action. Commitment can be created in a number of ways.

Putting a case.   Policy making within a network of institutions frequently involves making a case: to the Treasury for money, to the Cabinet Committee on Future Legislation and the Queen's Speech for Parliamentary time for a Bill, for example. In putting such a case, in putting forward a justification, those concerned are always staking their judgement – 'putting their reputations on the line' – on the proposition that the resources requested will be well spent. They are thus committing themselves to going ahead with the proposal if the money and Parliamentary time are forthcoming.

Reaching an agreement.   Policy making within a network of institutions seems always to involve some negotiating, bargaining and exerting of pressure. The outcome may be that a compromise is reached between different proposals, or that a 'deal' of some kind is done (as when support is gained from A over this issue in return for giving support *to* A over another), or that some way is found of 'squaring' or 'buying off' other people who have interests at stake and who are in a position to obstruct the proposal. When a compromise, deal or 'squaring' is agreed, the person or body whose support is recruited acquires an interest in the proposal going ahead. And the agreement literally commits the parties to honouring it and fulfilling their side of the bargain.

Taking a decision.   It is characteristic of policy-making processes that at various points certain central participants take what they regard as a 'decision'. Some are 'substantive' decisions, e.g. to adopt a particular proposal as 'policy'; others are 'procedural', such as a decision to commission research, hold public consultations, authorize further work on a particular proposal. Substantive decisions self-evidently create commitment, on the part of those involved, to proceeding with the proposal, while procedural decisions create commitment to whatever intermediate steps are decided on. But procedural decisions may also have a pre-empting effect: see below.

Making an announcement.   Decisions and agreements may be announced publicly or merely made known within a restricted circle. In either case, as we have already seen when 'policy' takes the form of a statement of intention, the announcement both proclaims the existence of commitment and adds to it: announcing it publicly or to one's peer group makes it more difficult to retreat from. When making an announcement also involves justifying and defending a decision or compromise, those concerned are also staking their judgement: this can only have the effect of strengthening their commitment even further.

Putting a case, reaching an agreement, taking a decision and making an announcement have the effect of binding the promoters of the proposal to going ahead with it: they acquire a very strong disincentive to going back on it. Commitments act as 'shackles': they inhibit policy makers from changing their minds. For most people, to abandon a commitment without good reason creates an inconsistency between recent and present behaviour that is psychologically uncomfortable and disturbing.[38] As Eckstein put it, 'Decision makers who are fully and publicly accountable acquire political and psychological stakes in their own decisions and develop a justificatory rather than a critical attitude towards them.'[39] Three kinds of penalty can be distinguished: damage to self-esteem; damage to the image that one presents ('loss of face'); and damage to relationships with others.[40] These penalties will grow as the process goes on. We should note, though, that commitment does not *guarantee* that a proposal won't be changed: it constitutes an obstacle to changing it, but sometimes the price of surmounting it is considered worth paying.

Given the nature of commitment, there are several questions we can ask to identify it:

To what extent did events such as putting a case, reaching an agreement, taking a decision and making an announcement (a) create commitment, or (b) keep options open?

After each such event, what penalty was attached to going back and reopening the issue? Was the proposal seen as 'unstoppable' and the outcome as 'a foregone conclusion'?

Did any 'U-turns' take place? What made it possible for the existing commitment to be overcome?

What can we learn about the strength of commitment from unsuccessful attempts to bring about a 'U-turn'?

Pre-empting may involve the ruling out of courses of action because they are never considered or because events occur during the process that 'tip the scales' heavily against them. Pre-empting may come about in a number of ways.

Scarce resources have been used up.   If scarce resources (manpower and money) have been used in developing a proposal, and there is reluctance to make more available to repeat the exercise, this is an obstacle to developing an alternative.

Time has been used up. Likewise, if time has been used up and a deadline is approaching, leaving no time to develop an alternative proposal, there is no option but to go ahead with the one already developed. The end of the financial year, when unspent money may have to be returned to the Treasury, and the end of the Parliamentary session, when any Bills which have not received the Royal Assent are automatically lost, are two major institutional deadlines. Similarly, informing ministers about a proposal the night before the Cabinet meeting at which it is to be discussed gives them no time to consult with other people about drawing up an alternative. Using up time also has the effect that to embark on drawing up an alternative would delay the benefits of the measure. This is particularly the case where a procedure has to be followed – because it is dictated by convention or laid down in legislation – which permits only a single proposal to be dealt with at a time.

Earlier decisions and events have effectively removed or 'tilted the scales' against certain options. For example, a decision on whether to close or to modernize a hospital may be found to have been pre-empted by an earlier decision to build a new one in the locality, so that modernization is not worthwhile or not affordable, or by professional bodies withdrawing their recognition of it for training purposes, with the consequence that it has been effectively 'blighted'.[41]

As with commitment, pre-empting may be employed as a deliberate strategy – obeying the precept that 'the first law of politics is *fait accompli'*[42] – and may on occasion rule out many potential alternatives in the early stages.

In relation to pre-empting, then, we have the following questions:

Which events or activities had the effect of pre-empting alternatives, by using up scarce resources or time, or by effectively removing or 'tilting the scales' against certain options?

What points were 'deadlines', and what opportunities elapsed with them?

Were there events or activities after which the eventual outcome was a 'foregone conclusion' by virtue of factors other than commitment?

At first sight, giving a mandate – to a minister or committee to produce proposals, to officials to carry out a study – does not involve commitment or pre-empting. But the giving of the mandate implies that those who gave it accepted the case for it, and if the proposals are not surprising – i.e. they are what might have been expected – those who gave the mandate may find it difficult to resist accepting them. In other words, on giving the mandate they acquired a 'contingent commitment'. The question then is:

What mandates, if any, were given? Did any of them amount to contingent commitments?

Access and the scope for making an impact

When we view policies and measures as products of a rationale and as selective responses to interests, we take no account of the point in the process at which particular ingredients of the rationale were 'fed in' and at which particular interests were brought to bear. But timing can be crucial, because how much scope there is for perceptions etc. from 'outside' sources, and for the interests of outsiders, to make an impact on policy will depend heavily on how much commitment to a particular option already exists at that point, and on how much pre-empting of other options has already taken place. Consider the two extremes. If the growth of commitment has been restrained – minds are relatively open – and no pre-empting has yet taken place, a relatively wide range of options will be genuinely available, and there will correspondingly be significant scope for perceptions etc. and interests to make a mark on the policy. On the other hand, if the early stages of the process are confined to a small group of policy makers, who soon become strongly committed to a particular proposal and manage to pre-empt the 'working up' of alternatives, those alternatives will thereby have been closed off, and accordingly there will be little scope for responding subsequently to outsiders who attempt to contribute their perceptions etc. and press their interests: by the time they come on the scene, it will be 'too late'. (Note that for there to be genuine access and scope for influencing the outcome, outsiders must know that policy making is actually going on. And note that we can't generalize about *all* outsiders: there may be people outside the central participants who have 'privileged' access.)

There are thus some important questions to be asked about access:

What opportunities were there, at what points in the process, for considerations to be 'fed in' to the process and interests brought to bear?

At those points in the process, what commitment and pre-empting had taken place? What scope was there for newly-contributed considerations and interests to make a mark on the policy?

For whom were such opportunities available? How well informed were people outside government about what proposals (including alternatives) were currently being considered?

Did considerations and interests which had privileged, early access actually make a greater mark on the policy than those which did not?

The effects of procedures

The availability of access to outsiders relative to the coming about of commitment, pre-empting and mandate will depend on procedural decisions – possibly amounting to a consciously-adopted 'strategy' or 'game plan' – and on any formal procedures that have to be followed, such as the Parliamentary procedure for enacting legislation. Such procedures may require the early growth of commitment (as when a single proposal has to be put forward and publicly justified); some may require principles to be decided before it is known what the consequences will be; some may simply exclude outsiders until a late stage; and so on. So we need to ask:

To what extent was the availability of access to outsiders relative to the coming about of commitment, pre-empting and mandate determined by procedural decisions or by prescribed formal procedures?

Box 4.2   Stages and phases in the policy-making process

Jones *et al.*(3)

- Initiation
- Formulation
- Implementation

'For our purposes . . . the three familiar stages will suffice' (Jones *et al.*).

Banting(5)

- Awareness
- Salience
- Definition of the problem
- Specification of alternatives
- Choice

'These different phases of judgement seldom occur in such a neat chronological sequence, but they are all essential and can be distinguished for analytical purposes' (Banting).

Forman(5)

- Policy germination
- Policy formulation
- Decision making
- Policy execution
- Policy fulfilment

This division is 'somewhat artificial' (Forman).

Hogwood and Gunn(9)

- Deciding to decide (issue search or agenda-setting)
- Deciding how to decide (or issue filtration)
- Issue definition
- Forecasting
- Setting objectives and priorities
- Options analysis
- Policy implementation, monitoring, and control
- Evaluation and review
- Policy maintenance, succession, or termination

'Viewing the policy process in terms of stages may seem to suggest that any policy episode is more or less self-contained and comprises a neat cycle of initial, intermediate and culminating events. In practice, of course, policy is often a seamless web involving a bewildering mesh of interactions and ramifications' (Hogwood and Gunn).

Sources: B. Jones *et al.* (1994) *Politics UK*, 2nd edn, p. 537. Hemel Hempstead: Harvester Wheatsheaf; K. G. Banting (1979) *Poverty, Politics and Policy*, p. 10. London: Macmillan; F. N. Forman (1991) *Mastering British Politics*, 2nd edn, p. 226. Basingstoke: Macmillan; B. W. Hogwood and L. A. Gunn (1984) *Policy Analysis for the Real World*, pp. 4, 24. Oxford: Oxford University Press.

Did the procedural decisions amount to a deliberate strategy, e.g. for creating commitment early or keeping options open?

Academic models: stages and phases in the process

A number of academic writers have attempted to depict the policy-making process in terms of stages or phases.[43] Some examples are shown in Box 4.2. All the models, especially those of Banting and of Hogwood and Gunn, rely heavily on logic – definition of the problem must logically precede choice, and so on, although Hogwood and Gunn, like Jones *et al.*, don't actually incorporate choice in their models – and in that sense all the models are redolent of the 'rational actor' model. Moreover, it is clear from the language employed that the conceptual frameworks are being imposed by the writers rather than elicited from the subject matter. Thus, we know that politicians and officials think very much in terms of issues and imperatives, and are very sensitive to progressions over time – 'hardening' and the growth of 'momentum' – but no writer mentions these. Hogwood and Gunn's 'issue search' and 'issue filtration' are concepts of their own, and while Banting comes closest to imperatives with 'salience', in other respects his model, like the others, is based on a perception of the process primarily as one of problem solving. Consequently these models do *not* lend themselves to making case studies: indeed Banting sets out his phases and then largely ignores them in recounting and discussing his case histories.

When we draw up a chronology we immediately see the importance of *events*, as opposed to stages or phases. Events provide punctuation marks in a process, and have meaning for the participants in it. They provide perfectly satisfactory markers of the beginnings and ends of segments of the process.

For discussion purposes, a convenient formulation is

formulation → *adoption* → implementation

where the adoption event divides the sequence of actions and activities into those that precede it (formulation) and those that follow it (implementation). ('Adoption', incidentally, isn't my invention: in the European Union, Regulations and Directives are 'adopted'.) This allows us to accommodate the fact that in every real-life process there is a succession of adoptions of measures as well as intentions/proposals. In the case of the Child Support Act, mentioned in Chapter 3, there was Thatcher's announcement of the Government's intentions, the decision to promote legislation, the publication of the White Paper and then the Bill, the passing of the Act, the earmarking of expenditure in spending plans, the organizational structuring of the Child Support Agency, the making of statutory Regulations, the setting of organizational targets, and the establishing of organizational working practices. Each successive adoption had its own formulation-adoption-implementation sequence. *Each successive adoption fell within the implementation phase of all previous ones.* It is important not to treat the process as though there were only one formulation, adoption and implementation. Writings in the genre of 'implementation theory' should be read with this in mind.[44] Some concentrate on asking whether the implementation complies with the policy makers' intentions. In practice, original intentions frequently change and/or become clarified and supplemented as each successive adoption, frequently involving different participants, is approached. To ask whether 'the intentions' were fulfilled – implicitly treating intentions as though they were clear, shared by all participants, and 'set in concrete' at a particular point in time – may not be fruitful.

Policies and measures as reflections of the 'power structure'

When we view policies and measures as reflections of the 'power structure', our attention is directed to: (a) the formal, permanent structure – the institutions and the formal positions that are found in the machinery of government and the wider political system (the electorate, party organization, sectional interest groups etc.), and the formal relationships among them; (b) the temporary *ad hoc* structures that are set up to handle a particular issue and then disbanded; and (c) social structures, made up of the *people* who occupy those institutions and positions, and the relationships of all kinds among those people, including sympathies, loyalties and financial connections.

The term 'power structure' reminds us that the institutions and positions carry with them certain 'powers' which their 'inhabitants' are able to exercise, and that the linkages among those institutions and positions, and among their inhabitants, bind them into a recognizable 'structure'. The term 'structure' is often used to denote the way in which central government as a whole, individual departments or a body such as the National Health Service are organized, and illustrated by block diagrams (organizational charts).[45]

Successive reorganizations of the NHS since 1970 have been specifically aimed at improving the service. Implicit in these has been the notion: 'Get the structure right, and better policies and measures and services to patients will result.' The following two extracts from the social policy case study literature both make a connection between structure and policy. Banting concluded from his case study of poverty policy in the 1960s:

> The administrative structures . . . have profound policy consequences . . . With regard to the social policies of the 1960s . . . divisions of administrative responsibility compartmentalized social policy. A functional division of responsibility takes the situation of a single social group such as the poor and divides it up between a number of departments and agencies. Social security, wages and employment, education and housing are all dealt with by separate departments, and the assumption of responsibility for a problem by one department effectively determines the range of policy responses considered. The fact that the Ministry of Social Security took up the family poverty issue ensured an income-transfer approach: regulation of the wage structure through a minimum wage or a social service approach such as community action fell outside the department's jurisdiction and were not even considered. No co-ordinated discussion of the best approach to poverty ever occurred, simply because the relevant administrative structures did not facilitate it.[46]

Hencke concluded from his case study of the closure and amalgamation of teacher-training colleges in the 1970s:

> However weak and contradictory national policy became, it was still implemented effectively outside Whitehall and on institutions which the Department [of Education and Science] did not even own. The main reason for the effectiveness of the decisions the Department and ministers took is the centralization of power in this country. For outside the small political circle in central government and the top level of civil servants, other bodies have little major influence. All three groups, the local authorities and voluntary bodies, which between them owned all the colleges [and employed all the staff], and the unions, which represented all the lecturers, were powerless to impose alternative solutions to central government decisions . . . [The] Department's control over two crucial areas – finance and information – ensured that it always had the upper hand. Local authorities were in no position to defy the Government because they had no money to do so and little means of raising the necessary funds. Over 60% of their revenue came from central government grants . . . Voluntary bodies . . . were in a worse position . . . The second area of control was more subtle. Information is an essential commodity when a group wants to understand the policy process. The lack of information available to local authorities and voluntary bodies was a major factor in keeping central government control.[47]

What's the reasoning here? In the first example, the perceptions etc. of officials in the Ministry of Social Security dominated the policy adopted: this *correlated* with their position in a ministry that existed, like other functional departments, in a 'compartment' of its own, divided off from its fellows. The *mechanism* comprised that ministry first taking up the issue, and then developing policy without contact with other functional departments. In the second example, there was a *correlation* between the positions of the three groups outside government and their lack of impact on the outcome; implied too is the absence of an information-disseminating *mechanism* which would, among other things, have enabled the three groups to get together to oppose the Department's plans. In the absence of such a mechanism, colleges could only argue that their neighbours rather than themselves should be closed or amalgamated.

Evidently there are some questions that we can ask for ourselves:

> *Is there a correlation between the extent to which a policy or measure was based on the views of, or was a response to the interests of, a particular person or group, and that person's or group's position in the power structure? For example, did the strong mark on a policy made by the Prime Minister's views reflect her central position in the power structure? Did the strong mark made by the interests of one particular pressure group reflect its privileged access to ministers, and the weak mark made by those of another group reflect that group's lack of such access?*

> *What mechanisms can we discover by which the position or access was actually made use of? (These should be visible in the behaviours that made up the process.)*

Did people's positions in the power structure give rise to certain interests – for example, by giving them a domain or territory to defend – and/or to the possession of knowledge and expertise which enabled their views to make a distinctive contribution to the rationale?

We should note that the connection between power structure and process is a 'can happen' one, in contrast to the deterministic connection between process and policy. A particular power structure may facilitate or encourage certain events or activities to take place as part of the process, but will rarely *dictate* that they do. Likewise it may inhibit or discourage others, but will rarely prevent them absolutely. The departmental structure of central government in the UK may make coordinated discussion among departments difficult but does not (as Banting implies) prohibit it.

Visualizing the power structure

One of the ways in which we think about power structures is that we construct mental diagrams, or 'maps', of them. We may visualize a centralized structure as having a strong central 'blob', with strong linkages radiating from it to lesser blobs on the periphery, and linkages among those lesser blobs to one another being weak or non-existent. An organizational hierarchy, whether it has many tiers or few, will look like an upside-down tree, with the branches of the tree representing branches of the organization. A collegiate organizational structure, in which everyone is on predominantly equal terms with everyone else, will look like a network rather than a hierarchy: in contrast to centralized and hierarchical structures there will be a number of different 'routes' from one point to another.

It is important to look not only for linkages but also for the *absence* of linkages, for 'cleavages'. In a highly departmentalized structure, like the central government of the UK, with many hierarchical, up-and-down connections within each department but relatively few across from one department to another, the cleavages between departments are particularly prominent. The structure is not only departmentalized but compartmentalized. Another highly important cleavage in British central government is that between ministers and officials.

'Power' and powers

Politicians tend to use the term 'power' colloquially and loosely. Nicholas Ridley, a Cabinet minister under Margaret Thatcher from 1983 to 1990, refers to his dislike of 'trade union power'.[48] It is the political party 'in power' that forms the Government. Cabinet ministers are said to have 'power bases' on the backbenches in the House of Commons if they have supporters among other MPs. There is a substantial literature on 'the power of the Prime Minister'. Among academics who have gone into politics, Bernard Donoughue, who was Senior Policy Adviser to two Labour Prime Ministers during 1974–9, refers to the limitations upon 'the Prime Minister's nominally great power to influence policy'.[49] John P. Mackintosh, Professor of Politics turned Labour MP, in his book *The British Cabinet*, writing about the Cabinet in the mid-nineteenth century, comments: 'Most obviously, the Cabinet was the centre of political power; it was the body which determined policy.'[50] G. W. Jones, in his paper 'The Prime Minister's power',[51] equates 'power' with 'predominance', but also refers to specific powers, such as the Prime Minister's 'power to obtain a dissolution of Parliament' and 'power to choose his colleagues' and 'the power . . . to decide policy'. He concludes: 'A Prime Minister who can carry his colleagues with him can be in a very powerful position, but he is only as strong as they let him be.'

Numerous definitions of 'power' are to be found in the academic literature. Among the writers of textbooks, Jones *et al.* define 'power in politics' in one place as 'the ability to get others to act in a particular way', but later present a different usage, referring to the Prime Minister's 'power of appointment to ministerial positions' and 'power to set the agenda for Cabinet'.[52] Among other academics, Lukes, in his book *Power: A Radical View*, discusses several different 'views of power' and goes on to write: 'I have defined the concept of power by saying that A exercises power over B when A affects B in a manner contrary to B's interests.'[53] D. H. Wrong, in his book *Power: Its Forms, Bases and Uses*, adopts the definition: 'Power is the capacity of some persons to produce intended and foreseen effects on others.' However, later on he writes: 'I . . . define power . . . as simply the capacity to produce intended effects.'[54] Hadley and Forster use 'power' to denote the ability of a person or group 'to gain the compliance or obedience of others to his/her/their will'.[55]

What are we to make of this assortment of usages and definitions? If we look for common elements, we find that power is mostly regarded as a *capacity*, or ability. But 'power', in that sense of a 'capacity', may be seen as denoting one of three different things:

- *Power to do*, to take an action oneself (without depending on others), e.g. the power of the Prime Minister to appoint the other Cabinet ministers (see G. W. Jones, Jones *et al.*).
- *Power over*, e.g. the power of A over B (Lukes gives us the clearest example, but Wrong's first definition also appears to fall into this category).
- *Power to achieve*, to realize one's will – to determine that a policy and/or measure will incorporate at least some characteristics desired by the power-holder (see Donoughue, Mackintosh and G. W. Jones) or to secure the compliance of other people, to get them to do certain things (see Jones *et al.*, p. 6, and Hadley and Forster).

What do we find when we test these usages and definitions against real life, and try to use them for analytical purposes?

Power to do

As we saw in Chapter 3, we can identify some 'powers to do' in a very straightforward way, by looking at what Acts of Parliament say. In the Housing Act

1985 we find sections explicitly headed 'Secretary of State's general power to intervene' (s. 164) and 'General powers of local housing authority' (s. 243). And the common form of words 'A local authority may provide . . .' implies the *power* to make that provision. Likewise the imposition of a statutory duty on a local authority carries the implication that it will possess the 'powers to do' that are necessary to enable it to fulfil that duty.

The Prime Minister's 'power' to choose individuals to offer Cabinet posts to is an example of his or her 'power to do' – literally, something that he or she is actually able to do – although it is not an unfettered power: the Prime Minister does not have an entirely free choice of whom to offer Cabinet posts to. Prime Ministers can do many other things too: make speeches, call for reports, issue instructions to officials, give full or uninformative answers to Parliamentary Questions, invite people to dinner at No. 10 Downing Street and so on. To an extent they can also create organizational structures, in that if the Prime Minister says there will be a Cabinet committee or working party on X, one there will be.

We can apply this technique, of inferring the existence of 'powers to do' from what is actually done (i.e. the *exercise* of the power) to anyone. If we observe a doctor, say, exercising autonomy (or 'clinical freedom') in making judgements and choices, we are observing the exercise of a 'power to do'. If we find evidence that an official decided not to pass on a piece of information to the minister, again we have uncovered the existence of a 'power to do'.

A person's possession of a 'power to do' will explain his or her deeds insofar as it *enables* them to perform them. It won't, however, explain why they are *motivated* to perform them.

There is, however, one special case of 'power to do' which we must be aware of. Sometimes individuals – especially the Prime Minister, though other ministers may do this too – can *create a commitment* to a policy or measure simply by exercising a 'power to do'. If the Prime Minister exercises the power to make a public announcement, and says: 'the Government will do X', he or she is creating (or strengthening) a commitment to doing X. Importantly, this commitment usually extends to the Cabinet as a whole, via the obligation which ministers customarily feel to preserve Cabinet unity or, more formally, to conform to the convention of collective Cabinet responsibility.

Power over

Unlike 'power to do', 'power over' specifically embraces a relationship between the power-wielder A and 'under-dog' B. Theorists Lukes and Wrong set down definitions rather than offer us meanings or usages. What is their relevance to real life? On examination, the essence of 'A's power over B' proves to be that A can exercise 'powers to do' in a way that will be contrary to B's interests (presumably as identified by B). So 'A's power over B' is a complex (a function) of three other factors: A's 'power to do', B's interests and B's dependence on A for the satisfying of those interests. Since B's interests may vary according to who he or she is, and vary too from issue to issue, 'A's power over B' is not a fixed attribute of a formal or informal structure. It is accordingly *not* a helpful concept for analytical purposes.

Power to achieve

By 'power to achieve', I mean the capacity to bring about a desired state of affairs: for example, to determine policy or to get someone else to do what you want, i.e. secure their compliance. Dependences are crucial to 'power to achieve'. Even during the Thatcher era the desires and preferences of the Prime Minister did not always override everyone else's. As G. W. Jones points out, the Prime Minister cannot decide policy single-handed. He or she depends on others, just as the Government depends on its backbenchers to secure the passing of legislation. In general, A's power to secure the compliance of B is (as with 'power over') a function of A's 'power to do', B's interests, and B's resultant dependence on A for the protecting or furthering of his or her interests. (If B has an interest in promotion, say, and A has the power to confer or withhold it, then B is dependent on A. If B has no interest in promotion, there is no such dependence.) Once again, since B's interests may vary according to who he or she is, and vary too from issue to issue, 'A's power to secure the compliance of B' is not a fixed attribute of their respective and relative positions in the power structure.

Moreover, it is common to find in real life that there is a reciprocal dependence: A depends on B for something too. So A's power to secure the compliance of B will also depend on A's interests, B's 'power to do', and A's dependence on B for the furthering of A's own interests.

There is yet another complexity. A and B do not exist in isolation from the rest of the system. Typically the interests of C, D, E, F and G are affected, and they want B to do something different. If 'A's power to secure the compliance of B' depends also on the interests of C, D, E, F and G and on B's relationships with them, it depends on far too many variables (even more if C *et al.* may form coalitions), including issues and the personal characteristics of individuals, to serve as an analytical tool. This seems true of all forms of 'power to achieve'. One consequence is that we can only identify *after the event* where 'power to achieve' lay in a particular case – effectively by seeing who 'won'. And it is a tautology, not a description of a mechanism, to say that A secured the compliance of B because A had the power to secure the compliance of B, or that the Prime Minister determined the policy by virtue of having the power to determine the policy.

The capacity to exert pressure

Notwithstanding all this, it is a commonplace of life in the world of government and politics that people come 'under pressure' from others. There is a colloquial term, 'clout', which seems to translate as 'the capacity to exert pressure'. Ministers write about coming under pressure from the Prime Minister and from the whips, backbench MPs, vested interests, and pressure groups of various kinds. And they may cite it to explain their actions: Nigel Lawson explains his introduction in the 1989 budget of tax relief for contributions to private health insurance schemes by or on behalf of the over-sixties by citing the 'heavy pressure' he was under from Margaret Thatcher.[56]

For A to exert pressure on B may, at its simplest, involve threatening B's interests in a situation where B is dependent on A for the satisfying of those interests. Essentially the dependence provides A with a 'lever' that can be used to exert pressure on B. (A lever is literally 'a means of exerting pressure'.[57]) But when people describe coming under pressure, they often also give indications that they were experiencing a feeling of discomfort, distress or confusion, which it was open to them to mitigate by doing what the exerter of the pressure wanted. This feeling evidently derived from A's exercise of a 'power to do', i.e. to behave in a certain way, in conjunction with B's susceptibility to that behaviour. Given that B has an interest in not feeling discomfort etc. he or she is dependent on A for satisfying that interest. By virtue of this dependence, A has a further lever that he or she can use to exert pressure on B.

Not every attempt to exert pressure is actually experienced as pressurizing. B may not regard his or her interests as genuinely threatened, or may simply not feel discomfort, distress or confusion when A attempts to induce it. And even if B does indeed experience pressure, it may fail to yield the desired result because he or she is prepared to tolerate the discomfort etc. or is under pressure from other people (like C *et al.*), to do different, incompatible things, or to do nothing.

The mechanisms by which policy is made and measures come about evidently involve the exercise of 'powers to do' and the use of linkages to affect the perceptions and feelings of other people. As observers of these phenomena, we need ways of identifying these powers and linkages.

Identifying powers

We have already seen that to identify the powers that were relevant in the production of a policy or measure (from now on I shall use the simple terms 'power' and 'powers' instead of the rather clumsy 'power to do'), we can ask:

What formal powers, e.g. as set down in legislation, did the various participants have?

What powers can we infer from what particular participants actually did in the course of the process? What choices did they make, and from what ranges of alternatives (i.e. within what domains and subject to what constraints)?

What did other bodies or individuals in similar situations do? (The answer may give us further indications of the participants' scope for action.)

What did particular participants do or say that amounted to the exercise of a power, e.g. in terms of creating a commitment or exerting pressure?

What powers were exercised in the setting up of organizational and other structures?

Linkages

Mapping a power structure involves linkages as well as powers. There are, I suggest, two particular kinds of linkages that we need to look out for: (a) levers, especially obligations and dependences, by which pressure can be exerted; and (b) communication channels. Communication channels are simply the medium by which views are communicated from one individual or body to another. Frequently, of course, the two kinds of linkage coincide: a group that is exerting pressure on policy makers will simultaneously be communicating its views (although the converse will not necessarily be true). Again, we need to be alert to the absence of linkages as well as to their presence.

Identifying obligations and dependences

We can identify obligations and dependences in three ways: by seeing what is laid down in statutes, constitutional conventions, contracts, agreements etc.; by inferring their existence from the array of interests and powers; and by inferring their existence from behaviour. Particularly relevant behaviours for this purpose are the exerting of pressure, which implies the existence of a 'lever' through which the pressure was exerted, and the seeking of support, which implies dependence on the support for attaining an objective. Often the exerting of pressure – and even more so the anticipation of pressure, as in 'We must avoid alienating A' – takes place 'behind the scenes' and is not readily apparent to the outside observer. So we have to look for behavioural clues, or mentions in memoirs or other accounts of policy making. Questions we might ask are:

What evidence have we that pressure was exerted and experienced? What levers were used?

Direct evidence would include personal accounts of the exerting of threats. Indirect evidence, from which we might infer that pressure had been exerted, would include: U-turns or other deviations from stated intentions; half-hearted or embarrassed support for a proposal from people who would normally be expected to oppose it; and the sudden dropping of opposition to a proposal, although this may also happen as a response to the offer of an inducement of some kind.

What evidence have we of support being sought? Why was it sought? What was the nature of the dependence on it?

Again, direct evidence would include personal accounts of support being sought. Evidence from which we might infer that support had been sought would include deals, concessions in exchange for support, evident care to avoid alienating a person or group, and the abandoning of opposition by others.

When we have evidence of such behaviour, what kinds of levers – obligations and dependences – might be being employed? Examples are:

- The dependence of one person on another for the satisfying of his or her interests, e.g. in personal advancement or, in certain circumstances not being subjected to behaviour that induces discomfort etc. A Cabinet minister's dependence on the Prime Minister in these respects is an example of the former, if not the latter. It puts the Prime Minister in a position to exert pressure on the minister (but bear in mind that some ministers will be less susceptible to pressure than others).

- The dependence of one person or body on another for the performance of a task. The Prime Minister depends on Cabinet ministers to do the job assigned to them. Central government depends on local authorities and other bodies for the implementation of its policy in certain fields, such as community care and education. The bodies concerned may make use of this dependence to press ministers and officials to take account of their wishes when deciding policy, if necessary hinting at or using the threat to withhold their cooperation.

- The obligations imposed by constitutional conventions. Collective Cabinet responsibility obliges ministers not to voice dissent publicly if they disagree with a decision that has been taken. Individual ministerial responsibility obliges ministers to account to Parliament for their actions and those of their departments. Another convention obliges a minister who wishes to table a Government Bill entailing public expenditure first to have it initialled by the Financial Secretary to the Treasury (a middle-ranking Treasury minister): unless he or she has signified their assent, the House of Commons clerks will refuse to accept it. And when a minister wishes to circulate to the Cabinet or a Cabinet committee a memorandum which proposes new or additional expenditure, he or she is obliged by 'a long-standing rule laid down by successive Prime Ministers' to discuss it first with the Treasury.[58]

- The obligations of membership of the Parliamentary party in power. Acceptance of the 'party whip' requires backbench MPs to support the Government over major issues, such discipline being enforced by the whips, who are able to exert pressure on recalcitrant MPs by threatening a variety of social sanctions ('arm-twisting') as well as the sanction of withdrawing the whip. At the same time, ministers are anxious to carry their backbenchers with them, and to head off any threat of a backbench rebellion or demonstration of a lack of confidence in the leadership: this need for support enables backbenchers to exert pressure on *them*.

- Dependence for re-election: the electoral sanction. An MP who wishes to be re-elected at the next general election may, to avoid the discomfort of finding himself or herself under pressure from their constituency – whether from sectional interest groups, campaigning groups or the officers and members of the constituency party – be careful to take their interests into account when deciding how to vote in Parliament or which causes to take up or support.

- The dependence of one body on another for funds. The spending departments of central government depend heavily on the Treasury for approval of their spending plans. The Treasury can use this dependence to exert pressure on the spending departments by threatening to obstruct applications for funding if they don't conform to its judgements. Likewise, local authorities depend on central government for permission to borrow money for certain purposes: central government can use this dependence to exert pressure on them to conform to its wishes by reducing their borrowing power if they don't do so.

- Obligations arising out of statutory rights and duties. Rights and duties are counterparts of one another. For example, the counterpart of a local authority tenant's 'right to buy' his or her house or flat is the local authority's duty to sell, at a discount on market value, and to make mortgage finance available. The right can be exercised – the duty invoked – whenever the tenant wishes. These rights are conferred by legislation, and can if necessary be enforced by the courts. Sometimes an institution will acknowledge itself to be under a 'moral obligation' and respond to pressure for that reason.

- Informal dependence for – and obligations to render – loyalty and support. These may stem from social connections, such as friendship and family ties, and from membership of an organization, especially one that members are 'socialized' into, such as the higher Civil Service, or a professional body, or an 'old boy network' of some kind. Members may use such links to press others for favours (which entitles them to receive them in return) and support. To fail to respond is to be disloyal and forfeit the benefits of membership. Government ministers often develop a loyalty to their departments through a socialization process of this kind, and go on to 'fight their corner' in the share-out of public expenditure among departments.[59]

- Contractual obligations. An employee who occupies a junior position in a traditional organization is under an obligation by virtue of his or her contract to obey when their superior gives an order. Failure to do so may lead to a sanction such as reprimand, demotion or dismissal. The contractual connection and the employee's interest in avoiding such a sanction together constitute a lever through which the superior can exert pressure. Organizations which depend on government bodies for contracts – e.g. 'providers' which have contracts with 'purchasers' – and wish to keep those contracts are similarly open and susceptible to pressure being exerted upon them.

- Obligations arising out of financial connections. Those who support the party in power financially, or sponsor MPs, or pay retainers to MPs to act as consultants, may have expectations of some return for this support: leading members of the party may feel under an obligation, even if not actively pressed, to heed their concerns and give assistance when it is asked for, e.g. when an issue arises that affects their concerns.

- Obligations arising out of feelings of sympathy or altruism. Ministers and officials within government may feel sympathy with certain groups of people outside in the 'real world', whether as a result of appreciating the difficulties faced by their department's 'clients', or out of 'social conscience' or feelings of duty. As a result, they may feel under an obligation to 'do something' on their behalf when the opportunity or perceived need arises, and act as advocates of their interests.

- The dependence of one person or body on another for political support, in the sense that if that support is not given, the proposal, say, will not be allowed to proceed. In the Thatcher Cabinets, it seems to have been the norm that for a minister's proposal to go forward the support of the Prime Minister was necessary.

Identifying communication channels

We can identify communication channels chiefly by seeing what arrangements there are for conveying information, views, proposals etc.: we can also infer their existence from behaviour, i.e. from actual communicating we can infer that there existed communication channels which permitted it. Again, many communications take place 'behind the scenes' and are not readily observable by the outsider, and we have to look for behavioural clues or mentions in memoirs or other accounts. We get some help from the fact that exerting pressure always involves communicating too: those who are exerting it must necessarily communicate to those being pressed what it is that they are pressing for. Likewise communicating may involuntarily involve exerting pressure, as in some instances when the recipients are given information they cannot ignore. Some of the questions that we can ask are the same as in the case of obligations and dependences, but there are some others, such as:

What evidence have we of communicating taking place? Who talked to whom? For indirect communicating, what channel or channels were used?

Was anyone in the position of 'gatekeeper', able to control the dissemination of views and information, or to choose whether to pass them on or not?

Did anyone have privileged access to the central participants, such as ministers and officials?

Direct evidence would include accounts of meetings, discussions etc. Evidence that there might have been communication would include: a seemingly disproportionate amount of attention given in published documents to the position of a particular group or groups; new views and considerations entering into a rationale some time into the process (although communication can take place without such an outcome being achieved); complaints that certain information or considerations have been ignored; accounts of 'gatekeeping behaviour', such as the forwarding or non-forwarding of views to ministers; and claims of having had privileged access to policy makers.

When we find such evidence, what kinds of communication channel might be being employed? Examples are:

- Arrangements for meetings of all kinds, including those of the Cabinet and Cabinet committees.
- Interdepartmental working parties in central government, which act as a mechanism for bringing together information from the different departments represented and for sending back to those departments the views of others and whatever agreed 'view' emerges.
- Arrangements for ministers to receive briefings from their officials and advice from political advisers, members of policy units etc.
- Arrangements for MPs to submit Parliamentary Questions to ministers, and for the latter to reply: the convention of individual ministerial responsibility stipulates that ministers are accountable to Parliament for the actions of their departments.
- Proceedings of Parliamentary select committees, when witnesses are interrogated etc.
- Consultation procedures; public inquiries conducted by a review body or tribunal of some kind.

- Publication of official documents: consultation documents, Green Papers, White Papers, statutes, Statutory Instruments, ministerial directions, Codes of Guidance, law reports.
- Promulgation of ministers' views in the media: interviews, speeches, party political broadcasts.
- Newspaper reports of 'leaks', briefings to lobby correspondents, reporters' investigations, surveys, public opinion polls.
- Regular face-to-face meetings in the course of work, e.g. for carrying out a task or for consultation, liaison, reporting.
- Facilities for pressure groups to lobby MPs and present their case to ministers or officials.
- Party conferences.
- Intermediaries, e.g. principal finance officers in government departments, whose job it is to liaise with the Treasury; delegates sent by local branches of a political party to national conferences; professional lobbyists.
- Machinery for monitoring, coordination and consultation in the NHS.
- Letters: from constituents to their MPs; from MPs to ministers; from central departments to local authorities requesting them to supply certain statistics; and replies.
- Political, professional and business networks: the 'education establishment'.
- Social networks: networks of friends, membership of the same clubs, habits of dining together, 'old boy' networks, people on 'the grapevine'. Membership of the same social stratum, having the same concerns, possessing a common language and sharing understandings and political perspectives are highly conducive to communication: they make it easier, for example, to pick up the phone and ask a favour of someone you've never met.

Note that these communication channels are 'structural', like the obligations and dependences described above. They are an integral part of the power structure, be it the formal, permanent structure, the temporary *ad hoc* structure, or the social structure. The latter would change in a major way if and when the Labour Party, say, replaced the Conservatives in power, but it may also change when the occupants of particular posts change. For example, the channels and ease of communication between the Secretary of State for Education and members of the education professions have been known to depend heavily on who occupied the former position.

A note on the psychology of policy making

In this chapter I have not discussed policy explicitly in terms of the characteristics of the *people* involved. However, each of the four perspectives that I am using introduces aspects of human psychology.

When we view policy as the product of a rationale we are implicitly relying on a model of the human being as a 'rational actor', who formulates – and seeks to attain – goals and objectives, with which their envisaged policies must be logically consistent. We are intellectual beings; we have *reasons* for what we do.

When we view policy as a selective response to interests, we see the participants as beings with other attributes besides intellectual ones. Desires for power, material gain and psychological gratification may have been 'programmed' into them: put them in a policy-making situation and their programme takes over. A politician, official, adviser or campaigner who is motivated by sympathy for the plight of elderly people on low incomes – or perhaps antipathy towards certain providers – may likewise have been programmed or sensitized by past experiences, perhaps to the extent that feelings of guilt, say, are aroused when he or she encounters elderly people or feelings of satisfaction are aroused by working on their behalf. Evidently the psychological mechanism here is quite different from that of the rational actor.

When we view policy as the outcome of a process, we are focusing on individual and interpersonal behaviour, including the performing of roles, the creating of commitment and the exerting of pressure. Here there seem to be a number of other psychological mechanisms at work. Someone's response to an imperative may take the form of a programmed response to a threat or to a competitive situation. Possibly a stimulus–response mechanism is at work: the situation provides the stimulus and a built-in response machinery automatically goes into operation. People choose a policy that allows them to claim 'victory'. Or doing something, taking the initiative rather than reacting to others, may be satisfying in its own right. Commitment appears to be bound up with self-esteem (as when we identify with a policy), fear of losing 'face', and fear of damaging relationships with others. The successful exerting of pressure seems sometimes to involve the psychology of bullying and the inducing of feelings of discomfort, distress or confusion in the victim, sometimes even resulting in the victim identifying with the oppressor.

When we view policy as a reflection of the power structure, we encounter the propensities of some people to see the world of government and politics primarily in terms of territories – 'empires', fiefdoms, fields of responsibility – and to seek to establish and hold territories of their own (defending both their boundaries and their autonomy within those boundaries). Some other people, however, seem more predisposed to see this world in terms of networks – linkages and connections; obligations, dependences and communication channels. Are there significant psychological differences here? 'Behaviour within a governmental and political structure' seems to call for a psychology all its own.

Where does this lead us to? In the writings of participants and academic and other observers we frequently find certain policies and measures attributed to a particular person with a distinctive 'personality'. Does this mean that to identify the mechanisms of policy making we need to be able to psychoanalyse every politician, official and other participant in the processes we are studying?

Greenstein and others attempt to use the concept of 'personality' in their work.[60] This is another word used by different people in different ways: a book published as long ago as 1937 listed no fewer than fifty *types* of definition.[61] 'Personality' is a monolithic concept: the majority of us are supposed to have only one. Greenstein and his colleagues seek to identify someone's personality from observing 'regularities of behaviour'. Their method thus depends on identifying *consistency* among observations and establishing consistency between observations and mental constructs. But his own observation of 'luxuriant irrationality' in politics suggests a *lack* of consistency: evidently behaviour frequently *does not* correspond to what one would expect from the 'unitary personality' model.

What happens if we free ourselves from the monolithic concept of personality and try out instead the idea that each of us has a number of 'subpersonalities', as Rowan suggests?[62] The basic observation is that we behave differently in different kinds of situation. The theory is that each situation evokes a particular subpersonality, and that subpersonalities may be very different from one another, which would allow for seemingly inconsistent behaviour patterns – e.g. bullying towards one's subordinates, kind and thoughtful in away-from-work situations. Subpersonalities are said to be formed by life experiences, from infancy onwards (traumas, socialization etc.) and by our psychological reactions to them. In effect, the situation evokes in us the infant, the child at school, the adolescent, the new recruit or whoever, at the formative time or moment, complete with the associated feelings (anxiety, worthlessness, frustration, excitement, superiority and so on), attitudes (acquiescent, rebellious etc.), deep-down memories of what are the right and what are the wrong things to do, and conditioned behaviour patterns, instilled so firmly that we perform them automatically and unthinkingly.

My conclusion is that in studying government policy making, we should be alert to inconsistencies in an individual's behaviour, and 'accept' them, rather than force them into a single conceptual 'mould', as the academic conditioning to generalize and the notion of monolithic personality encourage us to do.

I suggested above that each of my four perspectives on policy making introduces different aspects of human psychology. Possibly these can be associated with different subpersonalities. Conceivably there is a 'bit' of each of us that is a rational actor; another that fights for the interests of ourselves and others; another that forms commitments and seeks them from others; and another that strives for a particular kind of place within a particular kind of power structure. Different people may have these 'bits' in different measure, and find them evoked differently by the same situation. For my present purposes it is not necessary to take this conjecturing any further. But it cautions us, when observing policy making, to pay attention to 'the individual in the situation' and the possibility that the individual's behaviour has been evoked by the conjunction of his or her situation and a particular subpersonality.

Looking for mechanisms

I think of mechanisms in the context of government and politics as comprising both individual psychological routines and interactive 'procedures within structures' which offer participants ways of securing that their views and interests 'make their mark' on policies and measures. Mechanisms, then, are ways of doing things. A procedure may be formally prescribed (e.g. the Parliamentary stages in the legislative process) or an informal one chosen by participants as a strategy for gaining their ends.

The four approaches set out above – in which a policy or measure is viewed as, respectively, the product of a rationale, a selective response to interests, the outcome of a process, and a reflection of the power structure – 'highlight' mechanisms of different kinds. The mechanisms encountered when we view them as the product of a rationale are essentially intellectual ones, to do with ways of thinking and reasoning. Those encountered when we view them as a selective response to interests are essentially to do with *feeling* as opposed to reasoning. The policy maker is implicitly seen as an 'emotional actor' rather than a 'rational actor', and the interests of different individuals and groups make their mark on policies and measures via 'personal' mechanisms, such as empathizing or making moral judgements. These often occur in the course of interactions among participants, as when pressure is exerted. Such interactions are highlighted when we view a policy or measure as the outcome of a process, a perspective which also reveals mechanisms such as commitment, pre-empting and mandate. Finally, viewing a policy or measure as a reflection of the power structure makes explicit the structural features like powers and linkages of various kinds which facilitate or inhibit the use of these mechanisms by the occupants of particular positions to make the mark on policy that they desire.

Identifying factors.   In searching for the mechanisms that operated in a particular case, we are in a sense asking why a policy or measure came into being and why it possessed the characteristics that it did. The risk in posing questions in this simple form is that they invite answers that merely *describe* elements of the rationale, interests, process and/or power structure, and that implicitly assume that these *determined* the characteristics of the policy or measure.

It is almost always more helpful to think in terms of 'factors' of different kinds and the interplay between them. (This, I suggest, is what the 'good experimenter' would do.) For example, we can distinguish

• motivational factors: political considerations, pressures and interests, and the imperatives and motivations to which they give rise;
• opportunity factors: the availability of procedures and structural linkages (levers and communication channels); susceptibility to pressure;
• resource factors: the availability of powers that enable opportunities to be taken advantage of.

This approach will be utilized in the case study chapters that follow. As can be seen, it brings together all four of the conceptual frameworks set out above.

Chapter five

FORMULATING INTENTIONS: HOUSING AND EDUCATION IN THE CONSERVATIVE 1987 ELECTION MANIFESTO

Introduction

The main political parties in Britain all publish an election manifesto at the beginning of their general election campaigns. A party's election manifesto does a number of things: it presents a vision of the future and the party's competence to bring it about, it disparages rivals, and – if the party is currently in power – it presents its claim to credit for the Government's achievements. Most important, perhaps, the manifesto also sets out the party's programme – what it pledges to do if it wins. It thus contains 'policy' in the form of statements of intention.

Election manifestos deserve serious study. In the opinion of the senior civil servants' trade union, the Association of First Division Civil Servants, given in 1992: 'Commitments in the governing party's manifesto [are a main source of] proposals for major substantive legislation.'[1] Sir Ian Bancroft, then Head of the Home Civil Service, said in a television interview in 1981 that manifestos 'written in indelible ink . . . are studied with great consuming care by the civil service during an election campaign. Various briefs are written' and these are submitted to the incoming ministers.[2] Leo Pliatzky tells us that negotiations on public expenditure between Treasury ministers and spending ministers take place in the context of, among other things, the Government's 'manifesto commitments'.[3] Margaret Thatcher took the manifesto sufficiently seriously to regard it as her 'main responsibility'.[4] In taking policy decisions, ministers feel considerably constrained by commitments contained in the manifesto on which they were elected: ' "Benefits covered by manifesto commitments will have to be for the next Parliament" [i.e. cannot be altered in the present one], said a ministerial source.'[5] The contents of the election manifesto on which it was elected are also sometimes said to provide a 'mandate' for carrying out its programme. And conversely, as de Smith and Brazier put it, 'One may accept that there exists a loose convention [to the effect] that the Government must not "exceed its electoral mandate" by introducing major constitutional changes which have not been "foreshadowed" by its election manifesto', although this is qualified: for example, it does happen that unforeseen contingencies arise during the life of a Parliament.[6]

The post-1987 Conservative Government was elected on a manifesto, *The Next Moves Forward*,[7] drawn up in the hope and anticipation of a third term of office for the Thatcher Government. It presented a number of reforms – including reforms in housing and education – described by Thatcher as 'the third stage of a rolling Thatcherite programme'.[8] And indeed it ushered in an era of intense government activity in the social policy field, with wide-ranging legislation and considerable expenditure. In the autumn of 1986 there had already taken place what the political writer Hugo Young describes as 'a sudden shift in the element of policy to which the Government had been most firmly attached, maintaining a curb on public spending. More than £5,000 million was made available above the previously allotted sums for 1987–88, with the largest share going to education, health and housing.'[9] The 1987 Conservative election manifesto is therefore worth exploring in some detail. In this chapter I concentrate on the housing and education proposals in particular, since both foreshadowed major legislation.

Because the manifesto was that of the party already in power, its preparation involved ministers and was superimposed on the work that they were doing in the course of the annual cycle of government: preparing legislation, negotiating public expenditure etc. So studying the manifesto sheds light on this work too. Many of the ministerial participants have since published their memoirs: this chapter draws primarily on those of the Prime Minister, Margaret Thatcher, and her then Chancellor of the Exchequer, Nigel Lawson; Secretary of State for the Environment, Nicholas Ridley; and Secretary of State for Education and Science, Kenneth Baker.

The next section of this chapter presents 'the story' of the drawing up of the manifesto, and briefly outlines the legislative processes that followed. The following section asks what the policy was, what future action the manifesto committed the Government to taking – how precisely specified and how strongly committed. This is followed by sections on housing and education, each divided into four sub-sections in which the manifesto is examined in turn from the four different perspectives set out in Chapter 4 – viewing a policy or measure respectively as the product of a rationale, a selective response to interests, the outcome of a process, and a reflection of the power structure – using the set of questions associated with each. A concluding section draws the findings together.

The story

A chronology of the main 'landmarks' in the process – those, that is, which we know about and which seem relevant to the outcome – is shown in Box 5.1. We

---

Box 5.1   Chronology: the Conservative 1987 election manifesto

1986

May	Cabinet reshuffle: Baker to Education, Ridley to Environment.
June/July	Strategy group ('A-team') and 11 party policy groups (chaired by the relevant Cabinet ministers) set up.
10 October	Conservative Party conference. Speeches by Thatcher and Baker.
December	Policy groups submit reports; read by Thatcher over Christmas.

1987

1 February	Meeting at Chequers to discuss proposals for manifesto.
February	Thatcher asks Cabinet ministers to bring forward proposals for legislation in the next Parliament.
	Thatcher sets up Manifesto Committee reporting directly to her.
	Cabinet committees on housing and education reforms set up.
3 April	First draft of the manifesto completed.
13 April	First draft considered by 'a manifesto committee'.
16 April	Second draft completed.
21 April	Meeting at Chequers to go through the whole text. Thatcher 'in a mood' for a June election.
	Manifesto rewritten by O'Sullivan and Sir Ronald Millar (a speech writer for Mrs Thatcher).
28 April	Strategy Group meeting.
End April/ early May	'The rush at the end was horrendous and a small group of us had some hard work to do to put the proposals into manifesto form' (Tebbit).
5 May	'A final manifesto meeting . . . the Prime Minister had redrafted the whole section on employment and jobs . . . the evening before' (Young).
12 May	Today 'the manifesto was largely settled' (Fowler).
19 May	Manifesto published.
11 June	Election held.

can take up the story in the spring of 1986, when in her May reshuffle Thatcher appointed Kenneth Baker to be Education Secretary – 'I felt that a first-class communicator like Ken Baker was now needed at Education' – and Nicholas Ridley to be Environment Secretary – 'Housing was certainly one area which required the application of a penetrating intellect.'[10] The last general election had been held in May 1983: the next would have to be held not later than May 1988, but by May 1987 'we would have served the four years that I felt a government should', as Thatcher put it.[11]

During the summer of 1986 Thatcher held her usual meeting to discuss themes for her speech to the Conservative Party conference in October. Speech contributions were commissioned from ministers, advisers, friendly journalists and academics. In June or July she set up an election strategy group, which came to be known as 'the A-team', and 11 party policy groups, each chaired by the relevant Cabinet minister.[12]

At the party conference in October 1986, Thatcher's speech 'looked ahead to the manifesto reforms of education and housing designed to give ordinary people more choice in public services'.[13] Baker also made a speech to the conference, announcing the launch of City Technology Colleges, despite, he says, the adamant opposition of his officials. 'I received huge cheers from the Conference.'[14]

Over Christmas 1986, Thatcher read reports submitted to her by the party policy groups. She judged that their conclusions 'bore an unremarkable similarity to the suggestions for policy initiatives advanced by departments'.[15]

At a meeting at Chequers on Sunday, 1 February 1987, attended by Lawson, Ridley and Tebbit, the proposals from ministers and policy groups were discussed. Thatcher tells us that it was at this meeting that the main shape of the manifesto proposals became clear.[16] She was already clear what the education proposals should be, 'largely as a result of work done by Brian Griffiths', head of the Prime Minister's Policy Unit. On housing, there were papers from Ridley 'which were yet to be properly discussed'. As for health, however, 'not enough work had yet been done' and there were 'so many questions still unanswered that I eventually ruled out any substantial new proposals on Health for the manifesto'.[17]

Following this meeting, Thatcher established a Manifesto Committee, reporting to her, to 'knock [the various] submissions into a coherent whole'. It was chaired by a Cabinet minister, John MacGregor (Chief Secretary to the Treasury): other members were Brian Griffiths, Stephen Sherbourne (her Political Secretary) and Robin Harris (Director of the Conservative Research Department).[18] In March the committee was joined by John O'Sullivan, a journalist, who was assigned the task of drafting the document.[19]

After the 1 February meeting, Thatcher also 'wrote to Cabinet ministers asking them to bring forward any proposals which required policy approval for implementation in the next Parliament'.[20] This approval has to be obtained from the Cabinet Committee on the Queen's Speeches and Future Legislation. Evidently some approvals were given, because we next hear of the setting up of a Cabinet committee on Education Reform, chaired by the Prime Minister and including Lawson, Ridley and Baker.[21] Lawson tells us that its proceedings were unlike those of any other on which he had served. They would begin by Margaret putting forward various ideas . . . and there would be a general discussion . . . At the end of it, Margaret would sum up and give Kenneth [Baker] his marching orders. He would then return to the next meeting with a worked out proposal which bore little resemblance to what everyone else recalled as having been agreed at the previous meeting, and owed rather more to his officials at the DES. After receiving a metaphorical handbagging for his pains, he would then come back with something that corresponded more closely to her ideas, but as often as not without any attempt by his Department to work them out properly . . . This procedure was repeated on most of the aspects of the reform. Kenneth remained in unruffled good humour throughout this process.[22]

Ridley also describes these meetings:

Kenneth Baker took a lot of 'driving' – he was hesitant about the plan throughout. There were some magnificent scenes as she dragged him inch-by-inch in the direction we all wanted to go. He was pulled back by the officials in the DES when he got back there; many times his papers were rejected. The meetings were all conducted in good humour. I think even Kenneth enjoyed them, although it was he who received the rough end of her tongue.[23]

Baker himself comments: 'This intense round of meetings with Number 10, and the preparation of policy papers by DES officials, allowed us to set out a full programme of major education reforms' in the manifesto.[24] Elsewhere he puts the meetings in a rather different light, recalling a meeting where he 'won agreement' on two issues,[25] and another where there was 'a series of quite furious exchanges . . . I stuck to my position . . . and I was asked to bring back the policy again in a slightly different form. I would often respond with such lengthy and detailed papers that the close attention of my colleagues could not be guaranteed.'[26]

We do know that, as regards the national curriculum, what went into the manifesto reflected the fact that agreement was not reached in these meetings: commitment to introduce 'a National Core Curriculum' covering 'a basic range of subjects' left open the 'central issue' of whether the curriculum should concentrate on the three subjects of English, maths and science, as the Prime Minister wanted, or should be a 'balanced curriculum of ten subjects, including history, technology and foreign languages', as Baker wanted.[27]

Successive drafts of the manifesto were considered in April 1987, and Thatcher relates holding a meeting at Chequers on Tuesday, 21 April, to go through the text. 'Then the redrafting and checking began.'[28] By then she was 'in a mood' for a June election.[29] However, the meetings of the Cabinet sub-committees on the education and housing proposals appear to have gone on well past 21 April. As Ridley describes it, both the housing and the education reforms were hammered out in a remarkably short period of time – no more than a month. The Prime Minister 'drove the Education and Housing groups to complete the outlines of both policies in time for the Manifesto. We sat on into May, beyond the Dissolution of Parliament.'[30] Norman Tebbit corroborates this: 'The rush at the end was horrendous and a small group of us had some hard work to do to put the proposals into manifesto form.'[31]

On 28 April 1987 there was a meeting of the Strategy Group (also attended by Lord Young, John MacGregor, Kenneth Baker and Norman Fowler). A week later, on 5 May, there was, as Young describes,

A final manifesto meeting, and the Prime Minister was in pugnacious form – criticising the work that had been done so far . . . Out of the blue, they suddenly produced a brand new paper . . . it quickly transpired that the Prime Minister had redrafted the whole section on employment and jobs – she had done it at a session they'd had the evening before.[32]

On Saturday, 9 May, Thatcher went through the final text with Lawson and Tebbit. After consulting 'senior colleagues' at Chequers on Sunday, 10 May, she saw the Queen on Monday, 11 May to seek the dissolution of Parliament for an election on 11 June.[33] On Tuesday, 12 May, 'the manifesto was largely settled',[34] and within a day or two it went to press. On Tuesday, 19 May, it was unveiled at Conservative Central Office, Thatcher highlighting three 'flagships', the proposals to reform education, housing and local government finance.[35]

Subsequently, however, at a press conference on 22 May, Thatcher contradicted or seemed to contradict the agreed but unpublished line that opted out schools would not be able to charge fees or change their character and become selective. Amid considerable embarrassment on the part of Baker and others, the authoritative version was hastily publicized and the Party firmly committed to it.[36]

The sequel. Although this case study ends at this point, a brief survey of subsequent events adds something to the story. A White Paper on housing was published in September 1987, followed by a series of consultative documents on particular aspects of the proposals. The Housing Act 1988 reached the statute book in November 1988 after a Parliamentary process that was greatly extended while the Government prepared and introduced many amendments of its own. Financial matters were left to the Local Government and Housing Act 1989. Six consultation papers on the education reforms were published in June and July 1987. The widespread criticism expressed in the responses made very little mark on the Education Reform Bill tabled in the Commons in November 1987. Its 147 clauses and 11 schedules had grown to 238 clauses and 13 schedules in the Act that received Royal Assent in July 1988, most of the additional clauses having been tabled by the Government itself.[37] The experience of putting it into effect has been turbulent. Its provisions have been extended and in some cases repealed by subsequent legislation – the Education (Schools) Act 1992 and the Education Act 1993. The National Curriculum and assessment have been particularly affected. An early wave of opting out, encouraged by preferential treatment in the allocation of grants for capital expenditure, has not been the precursor to a large-scale movement of schools out of local authority control.

Box 5.2   Extracts from the Conservative 1987 election manifesto: housing

BETTER HOUSING FOR ALL

Home Ownership

Buying their own home is the first step most people take towards building up capital to hand down to their children and grandchildren. It gives people a stake in society – something to conserve. It is the foundation stone of a capital-owning democracy.

Home-ownership has been the great success story of housing policy in the last eight years. One million council tenants have become home-owners and another one and a half million more families have become home-owners for the first time.

Two out of every three homes are now owned by the people who live in them. This is a very high proportion, one of the largest in the world. We are determined to make it larger still.

We will keep the present system of mortgage tax relief.

We will target improvement grants to where they are most needed – to the least well-off. To meet the special needs of old people, we will ensure that all local authorities have powers to give improvement grants, where necessary, for properties where elderly people move in with relatives. We will extend the 30 per cent housing association grant to help schemes for old people.

A Right to Rent

Most problems in housing now arise in the rented sector. Controls, although well-meant, have dramatically reduced the private rented accommodation to a mere 8 per cent of the housing market.

This restricts housing choice and hinders the economy. People looking for work cannot easily move to a different area to do so. Those who find work may not be able to find rented accommodation nearby. Those who would prefer to rent rather than buy are forced to become reluctant owner-occupiers or to swell the queue for council houses. Some may even become temporarily homeless . . . [And] the economy as a whole is damaged when workers cannot move to fill jobs because there are no homes to rent in the neighbourhood.

This must be remedied . . . The next Conservative Government . . . will increase practical opportunities to rent.

We must attract new private investment into rented housing – both from large institutions such as building societies and housing associations. To do this we intend, in particular, to build on two initiatives we have already taken.

First, to encourage more investment by institutions, we will extend the system of *assured tenancies*. This will permit new lettings in which rents and the period of lease will be freely agreed between tenants and landlords. The tenant will have security of tenure and will renegotiate the rent at the end of the lease, with provision for arbitration if necessary.

Second, to encourage new lettings by smaller landlords, we will develop the system of *shorthold*. The rents of landlords will be limited to a reasonable rate of return, and the tenant's security of tenure will be limited to the term of the lease, which would be not less than 6 months. This will bring back into use many of the

550,000 private dwellings which now stand empty because of controls, as well as making the provision of new rented housing a more attractive investment.

And we will revise the *housing benefit* system to ensure that it prevents landlords from increasing rents to unreasonable levels at the taxpayer's expense.

Rights for Council Tenants

Many council estates built in the sixties and seventies are badly designed, vulnerable to crime and vandalism and in bad repair. In many areas, rent arrears are high. In all, over 110,000 council dwellings stand empty. Yet it is often difficult for tenants to move. If they are ever to enjoy the prospect of independence, municipal monopoly must be replaced by choice in renting.

We will give groups of tenants the right to form tenant co-operatives, owning and running their management and budget for themselves. They will also have the right to ask other institutions to take over their housing. Tenants who wish to remain with the local authority will be able to do so.

We will give each council house tenant individually the right to transfer the ownership of his or her house to a housing association or other independent, approved landlord.

In some areas more may be necessary . . . We will take powers to create Housing Action Trusts – initially as pilot schemes – to take over [poor] housing, renovate it, and pass it on to different tenures and ownerships including housing associations, tenant co-operatives, owner-occupiers or approved private landlords.

We will reform the structure of local authority housing accounts so that public funds are directed at the problems of repair and renovation; maintenance and management are improved; resources are directed to the areas where the problems are greatest; rent arrears are reduced; and fewer houses are left empty.

The policies and measures

Extracts from the manifesto, covering housing and education, are shown in Boxes 5.2 and 5.3. In one sense, it is clear what the policies were: they were what the manifesto said they were. But we need to ask the question that civil servants ask when they scrutinize manifestos: What exactly would the Government, if returned to power, be committed to?

A manifesto, by its nature, contains statements of intention. Look first for references to legislating, and to changing powers, rights and duties, all of which also necessarily involve legislation. In the fields of housing and education, we find, among other examples: 'We will take powers to create Housing Action Trusts'; 'We will give groups of [council] tenants the right to form co-operatives'; 'We will establish a National Core Curriculum'; 'Governing bodies and head teachers . . . will be given control over their own budgets'; 'Schools will be required to enrol children up to the school's agreed physical capacity.'

Box 5.3   Extracts from the Conservative 1987 election manifesto: education

RAISING STANDARDS IN EDUCATION

Parents want schools to provide their children with the knowledge, training and character that will fit them for today's world. They want them to be taught basic educational skills. They want schools that will encourage moral values: honesty, hard work and responsibility. And they should have the right to choose those schools which do these things for their children.

Raising Standards in Schools

How can all this be done? . . . [Money] alone is not enough. Increased resources have not produced uniformly higher standards. Parents and employers are rightly concerned that not enough children master the basic skills, that some of what is taught seems irrelevant to a good education and that standards of personal discipline and aspirations are too low. In certain cases education is used for political indoctrination and sexual propaganda. The time has now come for school reform.

First, we will establish a National Core Curriculum. It is vital to ensure that all pupils between the ages of 5 to 16 study a basic range of subjects – including maths, English and science. In each of these basic subjects syllabuses will be published and attainment levels set so that the progress of pupils can be assessed at around ages 7, 11 and 14, and in preparation for the GCSE at 16. Parents, teachers and pupils will then know how well each child is doing. We will consult widely among those concerned in establishing the curriculum.

Second, within five years governing bodies and head teachers of all secondary schools and many primary schools will be given control over their own budgets. They know best the needs of their school. With this independence they will manage their resources and decide their priorities, covering the cost of books, equipment, maintenance and staff. Several pilot schemes . . . have already proved their worth . . .

Third, we will increase parental choice. To achieve this: We will ensure that Local Education Authorities (LEAs) set school budgets in line with the number of pupils who will be attending each school. Schools will be required to enrol children up to the school's agreed physical capacity instead of artificially restricting pupil numbers, as can happen today. Popular schools, which have earned parental support by offering good education, will then be able to expand beyond present pupil numbers.

These steps will compel schools to respond to the views of parents. But there must also be variety of educational provision so that parents can better compare one school with another. We will therefore support the co-existence of a variety of schools – comprehensive, grammar, secondary modern, voluntary controlled and aided, independent, sixth form and tertiary colleges – as well as the reasonable rights of schools to retain their sixth forms, all of which will give parents greater choice and lead to higher standards.

We will establish a pilot network of City Technology Colleges. Already two have been announced and support for two more has been pledged by industrial sponsors. We will expand the Assisted Places Scheme to 35,000. This highly successful scheme has enabled 25,000 talented children from less-well-off backgrounds to gain places at the 230 independent schools currently in the scheme. We will continue to defend the right to independent education as part of a free society. It is under threat from all the other parties.

Fourth, we will allow state schools to opt out of LEA control. If, in a particular school, parents and governing bodies wish to become independent of the LEA, they will be given the choice to do so. Those schools which opt out of LEA control will receive a full grant direct from the Department of Education and Science. They would become independent charitable trusts. In the area covered by the Inner London Education Authority, where entire borough councils wish to become independent of the LEA, they will be able to submit proposals to the Secretary of State requesting permission to take over the provision of education within their boundaries.

Village Schools

We recognise the important contribution made by small rural primary schools to education and to the community life of our villages. We will ensure, therefore, that the future of these schools is judged by wider factors than merely the number of pupils attending them.

Pre-School Education

Eighty per cent of all three- and four-year-olds in this country attend nursery classes, reception classes or playgroups. Formal nursery education is not necessarily the most appropriate experience for children. Diversity of provision is desirable. LEAs should look to support the voluntary sector alongside their own provision.

These references to powers, rights, duties and control denote an intention to legislate, to bring Bills before Parliament and use the Government's majority to secure their passing into law.

How strongly committed was the Government to doing these things? The definite 'We will . . . ' denotes a strong commitment to act, although the powers, rights etc. are set out only in general terms. Other intentions are stated in more detail: for example, the proposals to assess the progress of school pupils at the ages of 7, 11 and 14, and prior to the GCSE at 16. From that degree of specificity, and the use of the term 'we will', without attaching any conditions, we might conclude that the Government had a strong commitment to taking the legislative action described. But this must be a tentative conclusion, to be checked when we look at the manifesto from other perspectives.

Other housing proposals involve offering money or forgoing tax: 'We will keep the present system of mortgage tax relief' (whereby people with earned income didn't pay tax on that part of it which went to pay interest on up to £30,000-worth of mortgage on the house or flat they lived in); 'We will target improvement grants to where they are most needed'. The usage 'We will . . . '

again suggests strong commitment. But how specific are the intentions? Again look for the detail. Was it clear to people who would be on the receiving end precisely how they would be affected? In the case of tax relief on mortgage interest, people on the receiving end can't be clear how much they will benefit because there is no mention of the rate of tax relief or of an upper limit. In effect, there is a high commitment only to the principle of not abolishing the tax relief, and no commitment at all to keeping it at its current level. The pledges on improvement grants are similarly unspecific. The Government was literally not committing itself to anything in particular.

HOUSING

Rationale

Means and ends. The manifesto commitment to keep 'the present system of mortgage tax relief' is notably unspecific, lacking any detail on levels of tax relief, or limits to the amount that can be claimed. Nor is it supported by reference to a rationale, although it does appear (in a separate paragraph) immediately after the commitment to increase the proportion of homes that are owned by the people who live in them beyond its already 'very high' level – more than two-thirds of all householders. Thatcher believed that tax relief, by reducing the cost of mortgages to home-buyers, encouraged them to buy.[38] (A contrary argument is that the bulk of tax relief merely goes into bidding up prices, so would-be purchasers do not gain from it.) Home ownership is said in the manifesto to give people 'a stake in society' – one of those aspirations or higher goals to which no right-minded person could possibly object – and also to be 'the foundation stone of a capital-owning democracy': Thatcher describes it as 'socially desirable'.[39] Evidently increasing home ownership was valued 'in its own right' – a component of a vision rather than a means to an end. There is no evidence that the policy was arrived at by its authors sitting down and asking, 'What is the best way of giving people a stake in society?', or, 'What are the implications of a capital-owning democracy?', which might have led them to consider the citizenship rights of those who didn't own capital.

In the memoirs of Ridley and Thatcher, we find some other reasons for increasing home ownership. Ridley tells us that housing was the area where Margaret Thatcher thought it was easiest to start to dismantle the dependency culture. 'Many council tenants were quite well off, and so an obvious way of making them into home owners was to allow them to buy their council houses. In addition, it was made attractive by allowing large discounts [up to 55 per cent] to compensate tenants for rents already paid.'[40]

Thatcher herself does not refer to the 'dependency culture' as such when discussing housing policy. For her, 'The state in the form of local authorities had frequently proved an insensitive, incompetent and corrupt landlord . . .

The philosophical starting point for the housing reforms . . . was that the state should be withdrawn from . . . building, ownership, management and regulation [of housing] just as far and as fast as possible.'[41] So reducing the number of local authority tenancies was a goal in its own right as well as a means to the end of more home ownership. And the reforms were not rooted in a diagnosis of current problems but derived from the political goal – 'philosophical' tenet – that local authorities should lose their housing powers.

Thatcher also envisaged that central government would play a role, through the Housing Action Trusts (HATs) proposed in the manifesto, in 'redeveloping badly run down council estates and passing them on to other forms of ownership and management'.[42] This would meet both the goal of improving the housing stock and the goal of removing housing from the local authority sector. From her comments on the subsequent low take-up of HAT proposals – 'One would never have guessed that we were offering huge sums of taxpayers' money'[43] – it appears that she may have already anticipated massive public expenditure on these. Although, according to her, the Department of the Environment envisaged renovation programmes being carried out through local authorities, she did not believe that local authorities should be the main agents for improvement.[44] This belief evidently constituted a constraint on action.

Proposals for new forms of private tenancies – assured tenancies and shortholds[45] – are justified in the manifesto by the goal of increasing the amount of housing available to rent; by the implied deservingness of people who find work in a 'different area' but are 'forced' to become owner-occupiers or swell the queue for council houses, or may even become temporarily homeless; by the importance of not damaging the economy, through local shortages of housing for people coming to work in an area; and by the theory that existing 'controls' were the cause of 550,000 private dwellings standing empty. Statutory controls are cited by both Ridley and Thatcher as the cause of the decline of the private rented sector. Ridley refers to 'the Rent Acts which had been in existence since 1919 and had had the dubiously successful result of reducing private rented properties from 7 million to 2.3 million'.[46] Thatcher concurs: 'State intervention to control rents and give tenants security of tenure in the private rented sector had been disastrous in reducing the supply of rented properties.'[47] They are thus both putting forward the same single-cause theory as an explanation of the decline. However, it is and was well known that much of the growth of owner-occupation since 1919 had come about through the purchase of houses that were formerly privately rented, *and that this had been encouraged by the Government's own policy of giving tax relief on mortgage interest* (so that if you were looking for somewhere to live, you got more for your money by buying than by renting).[48] The decline, then, had come about not through rent control and security of tenure alone but through a combination of those controls and the Government's own tax-relief policy on mortgages, if not other factors too.[49] There is evidence that Ridley was well aware of this: Nigel Lawson relates that in 1987 Ridley asked him to give rented accommodation the same degree of tax relief as owner-occupiers enjoyed, in order to boost the private rented sector (Lawson refused).[50] However, the manifesto blames only the controls, and conceals the part known to be played by the Government's tax-relief policy.

Giving council tenants the right to form tenant cooperatives or transfer the ownership of their homes to other landlords is presented both as a goal in its own right and as a means of attaining the further goal of ending municipal monopoly, said to be associated with bad design, crime, vandalism, bad repair, high rent arrears, large numbers of vacancies and the spending of public funds on purposes other than repair and renovation. The reader is invited to accept the theory that there is a causal connection between local authority ownership and management and these undesirable manifestations. As to the council housing that remained, the manifesto proposal to 'reform the structure of local authority housing accounts' would meet the goals of directing public funds at the problems of repair and renovation, improving maintenance and management, directing resources to the areas where the problems were greatest, reducing rent arrears and reducing the number of houses left empty. What does 'reforming the structure of local authority housing accounts' actually *mean?*

Let's consult Ridley. He writes that when he became Secretary of State for the Environment in 1986, he anticipated that within a short time all council tenants who wanted to buy their homes would have done so. Consequently, he was faced with the problem of 'how best to provide for those who will remain tenants', whether because they were too poor to buy, because their homes were unattractive (e.g. in tower blocks) or because they just preferred to rent. He describes his solution and the rationale behind it:

> I was determined to weaken the almost incestuous relationship between some councils and their tenants. Absurdly low rents, and a monopoly position in providing rented housing, allowed some councils to make their tenants entirely dependent upon them. They received a rotten service – repairs and maintenance and improvements were minimal – yet the tenants were trapped in their houses by the lack of availability of alternative accommodation to rent, and by such cheap rents that no other landlord could match them, even if he had a house to offer them. The tenants felt beholden to the Council, and most paid the price expected of them by giving their political support to them . . . The rate payers in many areas were being milked to subsidize the council tenants, rich and poor alike, for political reasons . . . I saw the solution as being to provide housing benefit on a sufficiently generous scale to enable all tenants to be in a position to pay their rents, and at the same time to bring rents up towards market levels. This would put all three classes of landlord . . . into the same competitive position, giving tenants a choice, and putting the councils into a position where they had to improve their standard of service if they were to retain their tenants. In addition, I suggested giving tenants the right to form a cooperative to manage their own properties . . . I hoped through time to provide a diversity of provision for rented accommodation, a large reduction in the costs to the State of providing public housing, and a

choice of landlords for tenants, while ensuring that everyone could afford a decent home.[51]

In her memoirs, Thatcher comments:

The most difficult aspect of [Ridley's] package seemed likely to be the higher council rents, which would also mean much higher state spending on housing benefit. More people on housing benefit means more welfare dependency; on the other hand, it seemed better to provide help with housing costs through benefit than through subsidizing the rents of local authority tenants indiscriminately. Moreover, the higher rents paid by those not on benefit would provide an added incentive for them to buy their homes and escape from the net altogether.[52]

We see, then, that 'We will reform the structure of local authority housing accounts . . .' means, among other things, 'We will raise council rents towards market levels and thereby shift to tenants, especially the minority not receiving housing benefit, a large portion of the council housing costs currently borne by the taxpayer.' Note that the language effectively concealed from council tenants the fact that rent rises were in prospect.

Interestingly, while Ridley describes the restructuring as a means of preventing local authorities from charging 'absurdly low' and 'cheap' rents, Thatcher describes it as a means of stopping local authorities from using the income from rents to subsidize the general rate fund.[53] Evidently some local authorities were making a profit on their housing, which suggests that at least some rents were *not* absurdly low. Thus they were using the extremes of local authority behaviour to make their respective cases. They shared, however, the political goal, not stated in the manifesto, of preventing local authorities from claiming credit for themselves at the expense (literally) of the Exchequer or taxpayer.

There does appear to be an inconsistency between the objective of reducing 'welfare dependency' and the policy of forcing local authorities to charge higher rents and thus forcing more tenants to be dependent on Housing Benefit. There is also an unacknowledged inconsistency between viewing it as a cultural phenomenon – the 'dependency culture' – and Thatcher's realization that reducing housing subsidy would increase it, i.e. that falling into 'welfare dependency' can be a consequence of government action. And there is no addressing of the possible social consequences if the majority of those tenants who were not on benefit *did* buy their homes and 'escape from the net altogether', leaving behind in the council sector a population largely dependent on Housing Benefit and possibly with the majority of adults out of work. (Because Housing Benefit is means-tested and withdrawn at a steep rate – 65p for every extra pound of income in 1990 – there is a strong disincentive to seek employment.)

Another apparent inconsistency is between the Government's professed desire to reduce public expenditure and its preparedness to spend taxpayers' money or forgo tax revenue – which in practice amounts to the same thing – on increasing home ownership (mortgage tax relief) and reducing the local authority housing sector ('huge sums of taxpayers' money' for HATs, and discounts for those exercising the right to buy). This and the inconsistency over 'welfare dependency' are explicable only in terms of their common factor: that they would have the effect of shrinking the domains of the local housing authorities. Evidently Thatcher and her colleagues considered that the Government was justified in spending taxpayers' money or forgoing tax revenue to achieve this end: financial constraints could be disregarded when the Government chose.

Considerations. What part was played in the rationale by considerations of different kinds? It is noticeable that the only explicit real-world consideration was the goal of making it easier for people to find rented accommodation, to be attained by attracting new private investment into private renting – a solution which recognized the ideological desirability of freeing the market. The only policy adopted for dealing with run-down council estates was the as yet untried one of creating HATs, which fitted in with the political objective of shrinking the local authority sector. Ideological and/or political desirability appear to have been tests which any policy proposal was required to pass.

A major political consideration was evidently the importance of winning the election, with which the 'camouflaging' of prospective rent rises for council tenants was consistent. Practical (feasibility) considerations appear to have played little part in the thinking behind the manifesto proposals, other than those concerning the private rented sector. Because there were no proposals to improve housing estates that remained in council ownership, or to address housing shortage, or to safeguard the security of tenure of new owner-occupiers on low incomes, no practical problems would be encountered.

Thatcher makes it clear that presentational considerations were also present (not surprising, perhaps, in the run-up to a general election). She writes that she saw it as important to dispel

> any idea that we were stale and running out of ideas. We therefore had to advance a number of clear, specific, new and well-worked-out reforms. At the same time we had to protect ourselves against the jibe: if these ideas are so good, why haven't you introduced them before? We did so by presenting our reforms as the third stage of a rolling Thatcherite programme. In our first term, we revived the economy and reformed trade union law. In our second, we extended wealth and capital ownership more widely than ever before. In our third, we would give ordinary people the kind of choice and quality in public services that the rich already enjoyed.[54]

'Ingredients'.   We have seen something of the ingredients of the housing policy rationale – the perceptions, theories, ideas and value judgements – in ministers' descriptions of what was in their minds. Of particular interest is the value judgement associated with the word 'market': charging 'market rents' to council tenants who can afford them is by definition a good thing. This usage

deserves closer inspection. First of all, buying a home of your own, although it involves participating in the housing market, *is actually a way of removing yourself from the market*. Once you have bought, although your mortgage payments may rise and fall with interest rates, they do not reflect changes in the capital value of your home. The exactly similar house next door may change hands at ten times the amount that you paid for yours, but your payments to the building society or bank will not be affected. In contrast, if you are a council tenant paying a 'market rent', the amount of rent that you pay *will* be affected by the value of the owner-occupied house next door, and will rise as that house's value rises, because the value of your house will be taken to be the same. (However, it may not be wise to count on your rent falling if there is a fall in house prices locally!) The consequence is that the rents charged to council tenants reflect the amounts that people who purchase their homes can afford, boosted by tax relief on mortgage interest (if not the right-to-buy discount as well, together with any wealth already accumulated by trading up through the housing market). In other words, charging 'market rents' is a method of 'gearing' tenants' rents to the generally higher incomes, enhanced by tax relief etc. of recent house-purchasers.

Other significant value judgements are revealed in the language used by Thatcher and Ridley about local authorities. Thatcher: 'The state in the form of local authorities had frequently proved an insensitive, incompetent and corrupt landlord.'[55] Ridley refers to 'the almost incestuous relationship between some councils and their tenants' and to ratepayers being 'milked' by councils to subsidize tenants for political reasons.[56]

The one prominent idea in the housing proposals is that of HATs. Ridley disclaims authorship of the HAT idea: it 'was added' to his own proposed reforms.[57] It evidently reached Thatcher from another source.

Interests

Consumer interests. Which groups among the population, out in the real world, were targeted by the manifesto's housing proposals? The offer of the prospect of an improvement grant 'where necessary' to elderly people who were considering whether to move in with relatives in houses that were in need of improvement indicates that the interest of this group in being better housed and cared for did make some mark on policy. The fact that this group was carefully singled out and demarcated seems at first sight to indicate a clear commitment to helping them – the concession was manifestly intended – but the qualifications attached (the pledge was merely to give local authorities a permissive power to give grants, and subject to a 'where necessary' that might rule out all but a few applicants) highlight the fact that no *right* to a grant was promised. In that sense the interests of this group made only a relatively superficial mark on policy. The proposed additional help for housing association schemes for old people similarly seems to suggest that the interests of 'old people', an all-embracing rather than special category, made a mark on policy, but the commitment is to so unspecific a proposal that it again appears to be a very superficial mark. We do not find in Thatcher's or Ridley's memoirs any indication of a personal commitment to giving special help to old people with their housing, from which we might conclude that such help would not necessarily take priority, or might have onerous conditions attached, when it came to deciding what resources should be allocated to it.

The manifesto also contained a proposed measure which can be seen as a response to the interests of prospective tenants of private landlords: under the shorthold proposals, the rents charged would be limited to 'a reasonable rate of return'. Here we see a very general category of beneficiaries, embracing people who prefer to rent and those who have no option, and at first sight a clear commitment to safeguarding them against unreasonable rents. But there is no knowing how in practice the word 'reasonable' will be interpreted, and we should note that it applies not to rents but to the 'return' on, presumably, the capital value of the property, which could reflect the incomes of home-owners appreciably wealthier than themselves. So once more, we find that what appears to be an unambiguous and clear commitment is to a very unspecific proposal: the interests of this group thus made a very superficial mark on policy. For existing and prospective landlords, however, there is the specific assurance, unambiguously in their interests, that shorthold tenants' security of tenure would not exceed the term of the lease. Here, then, *is* a significant mark on policy. We may conclude that it was genuinely intentional, rather than presentational, from the sympathy for private landlords expressed by Ridley: he was determined to end 'stupid and spiteful legislation, which had caused so much hardship to so many poor landlords'.[58]

The manifesto set out, in a certain amount of detail, proposed 'rights' for council tenants in general, i.e. not for any specific groups among them, apart from potential exercisers of the rights conferred. The authors of the manifesto were at the very least presenting the conferring of rights, and the concomitant scope for choice, as being in the interests of tenants generally. It is difficult to say how far this was genuinely intended for the benefit of the tenants themselves, but given that Thatcher describes the 'philosophical starting point' of the proposed housing reforms as being that the state should be withdrawn from the ownership, management etc. of housing 'as far and as fast as possible', and Ridley's package of proposals as having been devised in response to this, it appears that giving rights to tenants was seen as incidental rather than central. Insofar as the interest of tenants *did* make a mark on this policy – and it remained to be seen what the costs to them of exercising the rights (e.g. in higher rents) would be – it was not as a result of sympathy with the entire category of tenants. (A tenant's right to choose another landlord would be contingent on another landlord choosing to make an offer for the property. This element of 'landlord's choice' was not spelled out in the manifesto.)

As we have seen, the manifesto said nothing specific about rent rises, containing only the 'coded' message, 'We will reform the structure of local authority housing accounts', but the Thatcher and Ridley memoirs make it clear that the Government's commitment was to force councils to raise rents. In itself, this would clearly not be in the interest of those tenants who wouldn't qualify for Housing Benefit; but it could be argued that the extra rent income would finance repairs, which *would* be in those tenants' interests, and that the higher rents would force them out of the 'dependency culture', which in Thatcher's opinion would be good for them – and hence in their interest – even if they didn't like it.

Although the assurance that 'we will keep the present system of mortgage tax relief' appears at first sight to have been a response to the interest of existing and would-be home-owners in getting help with their housing costs – a casual reader might well have inferred that his or her tax relief was 'safe' – the assurance was so unspecific that it wouldn't protect them against future cuts in the amount of tax relief, and in that sense their interest made only a superficial mark on the policy.

Which groups did not get mentioned in the manifesto's housing proposals? One noticeable omission is that of homeless people (other than those who find work in a 'different area'). While it could be argued that measures to encourage the private rented sector and bring into use dwellings currently standing empty would assist people without homes of their own, the manifesto did not deploy this argument. Thatcher and Ridley both make the point that people counted by local authorities as homeless were in fact rehoused.[59] Thatcher writes that in the DoE's view 'there was a "housing shortage" which required the public sector to provide more new low-cost homes': in her view, however, 'insofar as there were shortages in specific categories of housing, these were in the private rented sector'.[60]

Political/institutional interests. To what extent did political/institutional interests make a mark on the housing proposals? Thatcher's and the Government's evident political interest in being re-elected, and consequential interests in demonstrating freshness and in protecting themselves against jibes, have already been noted as political and presentational considerations. They made their mark on policy in that they contributed to the Government's committing itself – in publishing the manifesto – to 'far-reaching proposals [for] reform'.[61] The appearance in the manifesto of general and unspecific pledges to help the elderly and people with mortgages, which are so unspecific as to cast doubt on whether the Government was genuinely committed to action on their behalf, is nevertheless consistent with an interest on the Government's part in winning the votes of those groups and in protecting itself against the accusation that it was ignoring their interests. The absence of a commitment to *increase* tax relief on mortgage interest can be interpreted as a response to the personal interest of the Chancellor of the Exchequer, Nigel Lawson. Having identified himself strongly with the opinion that tax concessions should not be used as a policy instrument, it was in his interest not to incur the embarrassment of announcing that he was extending an existing concession.[62]

Once the manifesto proposals had been published, who would gain from their being translated into measures if the Conservatives won the election? Clearly Thatcher, having identified herself so strongly with her 'flagship' reforms in particular, would have a stake in this happening: her 'credibility' would suffer if she backed away from them. Ridley too was strongly identified with the housing and education reforms. From their writings, Thatcher and Ridley appear also to have had a personal stake in seeing the domains and autonomy of local authorities diminished. Insofar as the members and officers of local authorities had an interest in defending their domains and autonomy, these interests failed to make a mark on the housing proposals: the authorities would lose housing stock; and within what remained of their domains, they would lose management powers to tenant cooperatives, and be 'hemmed in' by central government rules when it came to setting rents etc.

Process

Issues.   In general terms, the imperative here was supplied by the electoral calendar. The prime issues for the Government, on Thatcher's account, were how to find 'clear, specific, new and well-worked-out reforms' to put into the manifesto, and how to present them in a way that was proof against the jibe: if these ideas are so good, why haven't you introduced them before? More specifically, given 'the philosophical starting point for the housing reforms', the issue was how to withdraw the state from the building, ownership, management and regulation of housing 'as far and as fast as possible'.[63]

Commitment.   There is much that we don't know about the detail of the process by which the housing proposals were formulated. But Thatcher tells us that at the meeting at Chequers on Sunday, 1 February 1987, which was attended by Lawson, Ridley and Tebbit, the proposals from ministers and policy groups were discussed. She writes:

> I regarded the manifesto as my main responsibility . . . It was as important at this stage to rule out as to rule in different proposals: I like a manifesto which contains a limited number of radical and striking measures, rather than irritating little clutches of minor ones. It was at this meeting that the main shape of the manifesto proposals became clear.[64]

The references to 'ruling in' and 'ruling out' evidently signify commitment, and on her account it was the Prime Minister's commitment that was crucial. This is corroborated by Lawson, whose preference for a 'bland' manifesto and for fighting the election on what he considered to be 'the most favourable territory for the Tories . . . defence, central government taxation and the economy in general' was evidently ignored or overruled.[65]

Successive drafts of the manifesto were considered in April 1987, and Thatcher relates holding a meeting at Chequers on Tuesday, 21 April, to go through the whole text. However, the meetings of the Cabinet committee on the housing proposals, which met almost daily,[66] apparently went on into May. The confining of decision making first to Ridley and his officials or advisers (he doesn't mention either) and then to the committee, and the short life of the latter, make it difficult and possibly redundant to attempt an analysis of the growth of commitment. We do know that in the course of the process the HAT proposals were added – by Thatcher and not Ridley, to judge by her enthusiasm for them and his dismissiveness of them.[67] The new financial discipline for local authority housing was evidently discussed, but it appears that it was not possible to do more than arrive at a form of words for the manifesto: proposals for this did not form part of the Bill that became the Housing Act 1988, but were the subject of consultation papers published in the summer of 1988.

Events in the course of the process, involving Thatcher and Lawson, give us some insight into why the manifesto commitment 'to keep the present system of mortgage tax relief' was so unspecific. According to Thatcher, 'We had some differences – not least about mortgage tax relief which he would probably have liked to abolish and whose threshold I would certainly have liked to raise.'[68] According to Lawson, prior to the March 1987 budget,

> Margaret pressed me to raise the £30,000 mortgage interest relief ceiling – she had successfully induced Geoffrey [Howe] to raise it from £25,000 in the pre-election Budget of 1983, and had wanted to go considerably higher – but when I made it clear that I was prepared to do so only as part of a package in which the relief was restricted to the basic rate, she quickly desisted.[69]

The relatively unspecific commitment to retain the system of tax relief on mortgage interest thus appears to have been an agreed compromise between what Thatcher wanted and what Lawson wanted. The compromise 'kept the door open' both for an increase and for a decrease in mortgage tax relief. For both Thatcher and Lawson it was a second-best option forced on them by disagreement with a determined colleague. It did *not* derive from a single, unified rationale. However, if we view it in terms of considerations, we can see it as a trade-off between electoral considerations, uppermost in Thatcher's mind, and two financial/ideological considerations uppermost in Lawson's: that the tax system ought not be used for social purposes, however 'virtuous', and that the amount of tax forgone by the Exchequer should be lessened.

Power structure

The participants in the process were linked in relation to the manifesto issue by their membership of an *ad hoc* network created by Thatcher, in the exercise of her powers as both Prime Minister and party leader. This network was a radial one, like spokes radiating from a hub – a wheel without a rim – with herself at the centre. From her memoirs and others we know that the election Strategy Group (the 'A-team') was appointed by her and chaired by her; the party policy group on housing was set up by her and she was the first to receive its report; she set up and chaired the Cabinet committee on the housing reforms; the Manifesto committee which included the head of her Policy Unit, her Political Secretary, and the Director of the Conservative Research Department, was appointed by her and reported directly to her. This network was itself at the core of a more extensive network with the Prime Minister at the centre, receiving from all quarters policy suggestions and ideas for speeches and the manifesto. Sherbourne, through whom much of this inflow was channelled, also occupied a central position, acting as a 'gatekeeper'.

But as the process continued, the party policy groups and to an extent the Strategy Group were marginalized, to judge by Thatcher's description of their 'real value' as being to make the Party, the Cabinet and Government respectively 'feel fully involved in what was happening' and Lawson's description of them as 'a waste of time'.[70] The active part of the structure shrank to manifesto drafting meetings chaired by Thatcher and meetings of the Cabinet committee on the housing reforms, also chaired by her. Within that committee the other main figure was Ridley, Environment Secretary and her like-minded ally. We know very little about the interpersonal structure that developed in this committee, although over the housing proposals she depended on Ridley, whom she clearly trusted, to do much of the necessary work. He was evidently loyal to her, and regarded himself as having obligations to her as her servant: 'Cabinet ministers have no status or independent positions: they are there to help the Prime Minister.'[71] Unfortunately, Ridley says very little about his own links, so we don't know who if anyone besides his departmental officials helped him to draw up his proposals. Although, according to Thatcher, DoE officials did have their own concerns about the Government's housing policy,[72] Ridley – unlike Baker at the DES – seems not to have acted as a channel for them.

Structure and policies.   Did the impact on the policies in the manifesto of certain views and interests reflect the positions in the power structure of the people whose views and interests they were? We have seen that the policies strongly reflected the views of both Thatcher and Ridley as to goals and the choice of means to achieve them. This is of course consistent with her central position throughout and with Ridley's position too. Because he and Thatcher were, so far as we can ascertain, in agreement on most matters, there was no conflict between them and therefore no test of who was the 'stronger' when it came to getting ideas taken up. The exception was the HAT policy, which seems to have been adopted at Thatcher's insistence and despite Ridley's scepticism: his giving way would be consistent with regarding himself as her servant.

Other linkages were those of advocacy and electoral dependence. Ridley expressed sympathy for 'many poor landlords', who had been caused so much hardship by 'stupid and spiteful legislation'. Although there were probably not electorally significant numbers of such people, if his sentiments were genuine – and there is no reason to think they were not – they denote a link of 'felt obligation' towards those consumers of policy, which gave them a connection into the heart of the power structure.

In the case of the beneficiaries of mortgage tax relief, the undertaking to keep the present system, especially now that two-thirds of all households owned their own homes, can be seen as an acknowledgement of the size of the 'home-owner vote' and of the Government's dependence on it for re-election.

However, the fact that the commitment was so unspecific may reflect the perception that people with mortgages were unlikely to feel that their tax relief would be safer under Labour. In other words, although the Government would depend on that vote, it would have to exert itself less to win it.

No obligation was apparently felt towards the various categories of homeless people, who were viewed by Thatcher as an issue and a problem rather than as people with a valid claim where housing policy was concerned.[73] While they are only a small proportion of the population, this lack of felt obligation towards them is of course not inconsistent with the fact that people who have been without a fixed abode for some time don't have votes, for the simple reason that they don't have an address in any constituency.

Structure and process. In some respects the pattern of the power structure and the form of the process were closely related. The initial radial pattern allowed Thatcher at the centre to exercise 'gatekeeper' powers and her power to create commitment by endorsing proposals of which she approved and by reaching agreement with the Chancellor over mortgage tax relief. The formal and interpersonal structure of the Cabinet committee dealing with the housing proposals appears to have allowed her to dominate decision making in that context too.

EDUCATION

Rationale

Means and ends. The manifesto policies for primary and secondary education comprised a bundle of four proposals, all entailing legislation: a national core curriculum, local management of schools, 'per capita funding' with no 'artificial' restrictions on pupil numbers, and allowing state schools to opt out of LEA control.

Establishing a national core curriculum, with prescribed syllabuses and attainment levels, is justified by the goals of more children mastering the basic skills, removing irrelevant or objectionable material from what is taught, and parents, teachers and pupils knowing how well each child is doing. What do we find in ministerial memoirs?

Thatcher herself writes:

> I did come to the conclusion that there had to be some consistency in the curriculum, at least in the core subjects. The state could not just ignore what children learned: they were, after all, its future citizens and we had a duty to them. Moreover, it was disruptive if children who moved from a school in one area to a school elsewhere found themselves confronted with a course of work different in almost all respects from that to which they had become accustomed. [And] a nationally recognized and reliably monitored system of testing at various stages of the child's school career . . . would allow parents, teachers, local authorities and central

government to know what was going right and wrong and take remedial action if necessary.[74]

Note the language here. Thatcher's view that 'the state could not just ignore what children learned', with its implication that this is what 'the state' *had* been doing, is an 'ought' statement, based on a value judgement, and she does not cite evidence that existing low standards were the result, even in part, of the current diversity of school curricula, or evidence that existing arrangements for inspecting schools were an inadequate means of monitoring them. (However, she may have shared Baker's view that reports on schools by Her Majesty's Inspectors of Education 'were written with an opaque quality which defied any reader to judge whether the school being inspected was any good or not'.[75]) A national core curriculum as such would not necessarily eliminate so-called 'political indoctrination and sexual propaganda'[76] in the remainder of the school timetable. And supporting the proposals with the extreme case of a child moving school and encountering a new course of work *different in almost all respects* from his or her old one gives the impression of a lack of a stronger argument.

Were, then, the national core curriculum proposals an end in themselves or a means to other ends besides national uniformity and better education? Imposing the curriculum would reduce the freedom – the autonomy – of teachers in deciding what they taught, and some of Thatcher's comments on teachers are consistent with this having been, if not a primary goal, at least a welcome by-product. There is some inconsistency in her writings. On the one hand, she believed that 'too many teachers were less competent and more ideological than their predecessors'. Moreover 'propaganda was coming not only from left-wing local authorities and pressure groups but from teachers too'.[77] But on the other hand she evidently wanted the curriculum to comprise only a basic syllabus for English, mathematics and science, opining that there ought to be 'plenty of scope . . . for the individual teacher to concentrate with children on the particular aspects of the subject in which he or she felt a special enthusiasm or interest',[78] from which we might conclude that she was perfectly prepared to leave teachers with significant autonomy.

Baker shows more concern with the content of the syllabus. He was particularly concerned about the teaching of English, which as he saw it

> had fallen victim to the ludicrous political fashion that language was an instrument of class. As a way of breaking down class and ethnic barriers there was therefore to be no 'correct' form of language . . . Formal grammar and correct spelling and punctuation were dismissed by some teachers as irrelevant or at best secondary to the need for 'children's rich imagination, and creative expression'. That this meant a generation of children for whom the construction of a written letter, or completed application form, was beyond them mattered not one jot to the ideologues who had captured much of the education world.[79]

Baker also wanted a ten-subject curriculum, taking up 85–90 per cent of teaching time. This would leave teachers with much less autonomy than Thatcher's core curriculum would do. In the light of his language, such a reduction in their autonomy may for him have been a primary goal, not merely a welcome by-product.

Baker found himself in dispute with Thatcher over what he calls 'the National Curriculum' (not *core* curriculum). In contrast to the 'balanced curriculum of ten subjects' which he sought, 'she wanted to concentrate on the core subjects of English, maths and science'.[80] In choosing the wording of the manifesto, both alternatives were rejected, in favour of a commitment to 'a basic range of subjects, including maths, English and science'. This left the door open for both.

'Local management of schools', with governing bodies and headteachers having control over their own budgets, is justified in the manifesto on the basis that 'the needs of their school' will be better met than by leaving such powers with the LEA. Thatcher adds that 'the very fact of having all the important decisions taken at the level closest to parents and teachers, not by a distant and insensitive bureaucracy, would make for a better education'.[81] ('Distant and insensitive bureaucracy' evidently refers to the local authority, not to the Department of Education.) Meeting the needs of the school, like achieving 'better education', is a very unspecific goal. No evidence is supplied that decisions by LEAs were causing problems. The reference to 'the needs of the school', incidentally, draws our attention to the lack of any mention of the needs of *people living in the area*, such as the existence of minorities of children with special needs. We find, too, the seeming inconsistency that, on the one hand, headteachers and governors of schools evidently cannot be trusted to implement a national core curriculum: compulsion, in the shape of a statutory duty, is called for. But on the other hand, they *can* evidently be trusted with their own budgets, to manage their own resources and decide their own priorities.

Is this seeming inconsistency, taken together with the very unspecific goals, a clue that the means adopted, the modifying of the power structure, may have been an end in its own right? Baker tells us:

> Hitherto most thought on education reform had centred upon increasing the powers of the Department and reducing the powers of the LEAs. I was deeply suspicious of such a change, which merely reflected competition between bureaucracies. I wanted to empower local schools . . . and thereby give real influence to parents and children . . . I was impressed with the success of pioneer schemes of delegated budgets in schools [in certain areas]. They were welcomed by the teachers, the governors and the parents, all of whom liked the extra responsibility and greater freedom that a delegated budget gave them. [But] some LEAs and their Directors [of Education] were hostile to any reduction of the control that they had over their schools. So the local management of schools became one of the pillars of our reforms.[82]

Achieving a structure in which powers rest not with LEAs or the DES but with governors, teachers and parents – giving them greater responsibility and autonomy – appears to have been, if not Baker's prime goal, welcome for its own sake.

Setting school budgets in line with the number of pupils ('per capita funding'), abolishing LEA-imposed artificial restrictions on pupil numbers and supporting the coexistence of several different types of school – including grammar schools and secondary moderns – are justified by the goals of widening parental choice and allowing popular schools to expand. The proposals appear to have been developed out of the idea of providing 'vouchers' for education, as Nicholas Ridley describes:

> Far more difficult was the question of how to get more choice, more parental control, and higher standards into schools. There was a strong body of opinion in favour of some sort of voucher scheme. The basic idea was that a voucher could be issued for each child . . . and parents could encash it at the school of their choice. On the surface, it seemed an ideal solution . . . But it had difficulties. One problem was how far away from their home parents might choose to send their children, and who would pay for the travel costs. Another, more serious one, was what would happen if a certain school became fashionable, and another one un-fashionable: would the first school be allowed to expand, and the second one to contract or even close? Wouldn't this result in a very wasteful use of school buildings? Or would a school close its doors once it was fully enrolled, in which case there was very little difference between the voucher system and the existing system . . . These and other difficulties had persuaded the education establishment and the Education Depart-ment to oppose the voucher system. Successive education secretaries were asked by Margaret Thatcher to study it again; they all came to the conclu-sion that it was undesirable.[83]

Thatcher writes that she had always been attracted by the education voucher, which she saw as enabling parents to 'shop around' in the public and private sectors for the school which was best for their children. Although for her the arguments against vouchers were 'more political than practical', she accepted that it was not possible to bring in a straightforward education voucher scheme. But she saw the measures proposed in the manifesto as 'moving some way towards this objective' (bringing in a voucher scheme) without mention-ing the word 'voucher'. Indeed, the combination of open enrolment and per capita funding, which meant that 'state money followed the child', amounted to giving vouchers directly to the (state) school in proportion to the number of pupils it attracted, rather than giving them to the parents to pass on to the school. 'In effect we had gone as far as we could towards a "public sector voucher".' And opting out and local management would give schools some freedom to seek ways of attracting 'money-bearing' pupils.[84]

Allowing state schools to opt out of LEA control is also presented in the mani-festo as a goal in its own right: no 'ulterior' justification is offered. Thatcher writes that this was very much in line with her instinctive preference for smaller schools rooted in real local communities, and would add to the range of choice for parents. And as with local management of the schools that remained in the LEA sector, having decisions taken close to parents would make for 'better education'.[85]

Considerations. We have seen that educational considerations mainly took the form of high aspirations: raising standards, better education, meeting the needs of the school, parental choice. No mention was made of practical or financial considerations. But it was taken as axiomatic that the educational aspirations would be realized if two objectives, at the same time ideological and political, were first attained: that of creating a form of market, instituting pressure-carrying 'horizontal' linkages of competitive rivalry between schools in place of the (by comparison) supportive 'vertical' linkages between schools and their parent LEAs; and that of reducing the domains and powers of LEAs. The one sense in which the centralizing national curriculum and the de-centralizing local management of schools were consistent was that both would have that diminishing effect on the LEAs. That appears to have been what was intended.

'Ingredients'. The political objectives were underpinned by value judgements expressed in language strongly hostile to LEAs. No discrimination was made between members and officers, little between Conservative and Labour-controlled LEAs: they were all part of the 'education establishment'. As for ideas, Thatcher writes that it was Brian Griffiths (Head of her Policy Unit) who devised the 'extremely successful model' of the grant-maintained (GM) schools, which would be entirely free from LEA control and directly funded from the DES.[86] Ridley also claims authorship of the opt-out proposal: 'I put forward the plan that was eventually adopted, which was to allow all schools eventually to opt out of local authority control and be run by their governors.'[87] Chitty points out that variants of the ideas which found their way into the Education Reform Bill can be found in pamphlets published by two right-wing think-tanks, the Institute for Economic Affairs and the Hillgate Group, during the winter of 1986–7.[88]

Interests

Consumer interests. In the education section of the manifesto, the unequivocal pledge to establish a national core curriculum was presented as a response to the interests of 'parents and employers', implicitly treating them as monolithic, homogeneous groups. If the curriculum was in the interests of parents, it would presumably be in the interests of children too. No distinction is made among children, except for the 'talented children from less-well-off back-grounds' making use of the Assisted Places Scheme. No reference is made to children with special needs or those living in poor inner-city areas.

It is 'parents' upon whom choice in the educational market place is to be conferred. In effect, it is suggested that it would be in the interests of all parents to be able to choose among competing schools for their children. No distinction is made between those with their own transport and those without, who will have less genuine choice of school for their children. However, the interests of the inhabitants of villages in rural areas in retaining their small primary schools is acknowledged, albeit with no more specific commitment than to judge their future by wider factors than pupil numbers. And while reference is made to the 'needs' of schools (which governing bodies and head-teachers 'know best'), nothing is said about meeting the needs *of the area*, at the time the responsibility of LEAs but potentially more difficult for an LEA to fulfil if some or all of the schools in its area have opted out. In other words, the interests of 'need' groups and of the inhabitants of geographical areas other than villages did not make a mark on the policy.

Political/institutional interests.   We have already noted the interest of Thatcher and her colleagues in advancing innovative reforms, to show they had not run out of ideas. As in the case of housing, Thatcher, having identified herself so strongly with the reforms, stood to gain from their implementation: her cred-ibility would suffer if she backed away from them. Baker, too, was strongly identified with the education reforms. Again, Thatcher and Baker appear also to have had a personal stake in seeing the domains and autonomy of local authorities diminished. Thatcher envisaged the opting out of LEA control of schools 'which wanted to escape from the clutches of some left-wing local authority keen to impose its own ideological priorities',[89] and demonstrates her opposition to 'vested interests' in education and the 'educational establish-ment'.[90] Kenneth Baker, who seems not to have been quite so antagonistic towards LEAs, writes that at a meeting in February 1987 she wanted to quicken the pace on devolution, 'which would have spelt the end of LEAs in a matter of months'.[91]

Some 'vested interests' made a superficial mark on policy. The interests of the teaching profession, HM Inspectorate, and others who would be involved in establishing the national core curriculum and carrying out the assessments – of whom Thatcher herself appears to have accepted that 'it was necessary to take as many as possible . . . with us in the reforms we were making'[92] – were acknowledged by the manifesto undertaking to 'consult widely among those concerned'. But subsequent experience showed, consultation would not guar-antee that views and interests would be taken into account.

Insofar as local authority members and officers had an interest in defending their domains and autonomy, these interests failed to make a mark on the education proposals, since local authorities stood to lose schools. Within what remained of their domains, LEAs would lose powers to budget-controlling governing bodies and headteachers of schools. But where they stood to lose, school governing bodies and headteachers stood, at least superficially, to gain, either through parents and governing bodies choosing to opt out of LEA con-trol, or through gaining autonomy in the shape of control over their own budgets. Whether there would be a price to pay, in terms of extra work, or forfeiting local authority support services, or incurring blame for inflicting cuts (would the freedom to spend the school budget as they chose prove to be nothing more than the freedom to decide which teacher to sack?), was not apparent. Thatcher's professed view that all the important decisions should be taken 'at the level closest to parents and teachers'[93] is at first sight inconsistent with the proposal to remove to the centre decisions over the curriculum and the total budget for each opted out school. But both are entirely consistent with Thatcher's personal 'mission' to deprive LEAs and teachers of their domains and autonomy, and we may infer that it was this interest of hers, rather than the interests of parents and teachers in escaping their LEA's 'clutches', that 'drove' the policy.

We must not overlook the interests of Baker himself. A man of some education, and an author, he was said to have been appointed for his skills as a communicator to head a department in which he had never been a junior minister. One would expect him to have a strong interest in demonstrating that he was something more than a mouthpiece, and his involvement in the national curriculum is consistent with this. The severity of Thatcher's metaphorical 'handbagging' of him would be consistent with some exasperation on her part that he was exceeding the brief she had given him.

Officials in the Department of Education and Science (DES) stood to gain in terms of an extension of their domain by virtue of acquiring responsibility for the national curriculum, and Baker tells us that the Department 'was glad to be given the green light to develop proposals for a National Curriculum, a policy for which they had a great deal of sympathy'.[94] It appears, then, that the officials may have felt that it was in the interests not only of children at state schools but also themselves: they were being given what they evidently felt was a worthwhile job to do, and being given it was a sign of the Government's dependence on them and an acknowledgment of their expertise. Having a large and innovative piece of legislation to prepare and see through Parliament would also be a major challenge and responsibility. Baker also gives us a glimpse of another interest of officials: the Department's adamant opposition to his announcing the city technology college proposals at the Conservative Party conference in 1986, on the grounds that it would so politicize the policy as to guarantee future opposition from the Labour and Liberal parties, is consistent with officials having an interest in continuity and consensus.

Process

Issues. The imperative of the electoral calendar and the general issues for the Government have been discussed above in connection with the housing proposals. In relation to education, Thatcher tells us that the starting point for the education reforms outlined in the manifesto was a deep dissatisfaction, which she fully shared, with Britain's standard of education.[95]

Commitment. As we have seen, in her speech to the party conference in October 1986 Thatcher announced that reforms of education were on the way. Baker, in his speech at that conference, announced the city technology colleges programme. Both statements of intention registered and added to commitment on the part of the Government. Thatcher tells us that Brian Griffiths had been working on reforms, and by the Chequers meeting on 1 February 1987, 'I was already clear what these should be'.[96] Work was also going on in the DES.

The Cabinet committee on education reform, set up after the meeting at Chequers on Tuesday, 21 April 1987, was chaired by Thatcher and included Lawson, Ridley and Baker.[97] The accounts of the meetings make it clear that Thatcher attempted to use them to exert pressure on Baker to accept her ideas and work them up into more detailed proposals. He appears frequently to have responded with lengthy papers that did not correspond to what she had in mind. But evidently the committee eventually agreed a set of proposals for the manifesto, the commitment thus created extending to the Government as a whole. We do know, however, that as regards the national curriculum, what went into the manifesto reflected the fact that on at least one matter agreement was not reached – commitment not created – in these meetings. The agreed form of words left to be resolved later the 'central issue' of whether the curriculum should concentrate on the core subjects of English, maths and science, as the Prime Minister wanted, or should be a 'balanced curriculum of ten subjects, including history, technology and foreign languages', as Baker wanted.[98]

Access. Chitty notes that during the period when the manifesto proposals were being formulated, three right-wing think-tanks had access to Thatcher and Baker. They were the Institute for Economic Affairs, with a recently established Education Unit headed by Stuart Sexton, a former adviser to the Conservative Party and then the Government; the Centre for Policy Studies (CPS: Thatcher had been one of its founders in 1974); and the Hillgate Group, campaigning for a return to traditional educational values.[99] Chitty refers to Baker meeting with the Education Study Group of the CPS in the spring of 1987, and to a series of educational planning meetings held at No. 10 Downing Street in 1986 and 1987 to which members of the groups were invited. It would be consistent with this that their publications containing ideas for the reform of the education system had already found their way to Thatcher via Stephen Sherbourne. Evidently these groups had 'privileged' access to Thatcher and to Baker before Thatcher and the Government had committed themselves to any particular proposals.

Power structure

The power structure in relation to the education reforms was initially very similar to that for housing, with the addition of linkages to the three right-wing think-tanks. Within that structure, Thatcher's relationship with Baker is of particular interest. They were of course bound together by the convention of collective Cabinet responsibility. And insofar as he had an interest in promotion, he depended on her for satisfying it. However, he does not appear to have shared his colleagues' vulnerability to being discomforted by her aggressive behaviour when directed towards him. At the same time, however, Thatcher depended upon him: the 'levers' were two-way. She could not sack him so soon after appointing him in May 1986 without casting doubt on her judgement in making the appointment. She would necessarily rely on Baker and his officials in the DES for judgements of the feasibility of proposals and help in formulating tactics for coping with the 'education establishment' – matters in which Griffiths would have been able to give only limited help.

As in the case of the housing reforms, the party policy groups and to an extent the Strategy Group became marginalized: the decision making was restricted to manifesto drafting meetings chaired by Thatcher and meetings of the Cabinet committee, also chaired by her. But Baker, with whom she came into conflict, built up his own network, making contact with Griffiths in the No. 10 Policy Unit and evidently establishing an informal link with him: 'We were to work closely together over the coming years, during which Brian helped me in brokering various settlements with Number 10.'[100] Baker and Thatcher had their own links to the think-tanks, as mentioned above. And Baker had his day-to-day links with the officials in his department: DES officials and members of HM Inspectorate had links to the LEAs, the teachers' unions, individual schools etc.

Structure and policies.   Did the impact on the policies in the manifesto of certain views and interests reflect the position in the power structure of the people whose views and interests they were? We have seen that the policies strongly reflected Thatcher's views as to goals, the diagnosis of problems and the choice of means of solving them. This is of course consistent with the powers that she possessed and with her position at the centre of the 'manifesto structure' in the early stages. Her powers and position enabled her to 'fend off' the policy groups' reports: if these had received wider circulation or had been discussed at a party conference there would have been the possibility of her coming under pressure to defend her rejection of them. And where the education proposals were concerned, if she had not received briefings and papers from Griffiths and had discussions with think-tank members, she would have been wholly dependent on the DES for proposals and advice about what was and was not feasible: she would have found it much more difficult – if not impossible – to query and resist the advice that Baker did give and relay to her from the DES. Her central position and the use she made of it considerably strengthened her capacity to impose some of her own views on the policy. But the fact that Baker's views were to some extent reflected in the manifesto, contrary to Thatcher's wishes – e.g. in keeping open the option of a 'broad' national curriculum – is consistent with the nature of her relationship with Baker, discussed above, and with Baker himself having some 'clout', by virtue of being Education Secretary, with the resources of his department behind him, and a member of the Cabinet committee on the education reforms.

Did the other interests that made a mark on the manifesto policies reflect their positions in, or connections to, the power structure? The consumer interests of parents and pupils were 'imparted' via the judgements of Thatcher and

Baker as to where those interests lay. As for vested interests, the minimal undertaking to 'consult widely among those concerned', making no mention of *when* they would be consulted or of the time that would be allowed, was consistent with their exclusion from the 'manifesto structure'. Lawson gives us his view that Thatcher was initially attracted to a proposal of his to remove education from local authorities, 'but on further reflection she decided that it was too radical and that she was not prepared to take on the local authorities, who would greatly resent the loss of their responsibility for the schools'.[101] If he is correct, the power of the LEAs to be obstructive had the effect that their interest in retaining their responsibilities made a significant mark on policy, for the time being. The opt-out proposals did make a start in the direction of removing education from them.

Structure and process. As in the case of housing, the radial structure that Thatcher set up allowed her to dominate the creating of commitments in the early stages. But when she found herself in the formal machinery of the Cabinet committee on the education proposals, faced with a minister who did not give way, the structure determined that she could not conclusively decide policy as she wished. Baker demonstrated the power of a Cabinet minister and his department to withhold agreement and submit lengthy papers, and thereby keep a complex issue partially open.

We can see that in some respects the pattern of the power structure and the form of the process were closely related. In terms of activity, the power structure changed from a highly radial pattern to a combination of radial and committee-based, and this was mirrored in a shift away from the creation of commitments largely (it would seem) by Thatcher's unilateral endorsement to the creation of at least some commitments by agreement over compromise proposals.

* * *

Conclusions

Most of the manifesto proposals were presented as 'means' to the achieving of certain 'ends': goals or objectives expressed in terms of the benefits they would bring to people in the 'real world' (as opposed to the world of government and politics). So the proposals were at least presented as the products of a rationale. Some of these goals were quite specific, like the housing goal of making more private rented accommodation available: it would be possible to tell within two years or five years whether and how much progress had been made towards attaining them. Other goals took the form of vaguely expressed aspirations, like 'raising standards in schools': without further details of how standards would be gauged, it would be purely a matter of individual judgement two or five years later whether this had been achieved. Where proposals were very unspecific, leaving options open as to how they would be translated into practice, commitment was held back, as in the case of proposals for mortgage tax relief.

The reasoning presented involves 'chains' of means and ends, of proposed measures and goals. In education, for example, the Government's immediate goal was to get legislation on to the statute book. The legislation was a means to achieve the goal of giving more powers and responsibility to school governors and headteachers. That goal was a means to achieve the further goal of having all the important decisions taken at the level closest to parents and teachers. And the taking of decisions at that level was a means to achieve the goal of 'better education'.[102] As is characteristic of goals that are expressed only vaguely, the last link in the chain is heavily conditioned by personal value judgement: the proposal does not follow from the goal as stated; no reasoning or testable theory is advanced to connect them; the relationship is taken as axiomatic. Other people would have conceived of 'better education' differently, and seen it as calling for different measures.

Proposed measures that were not derived by reasoning from goals appear to have been regarded as good in their own right. We have found that what these measures had in common was that they would shrink the domains of local authorities and reduce the powers that they could exercise within such domain as remained. Other possible measures were regarded by Thatcher as bad in their own right, notably measures involving local authorities in improving their own council estates.

'Regarding' takes place in the minds of individuals. The central participants in this case all appear to have had their own rationales. Some of the less specific measures proposed were ones where ministers could not agree on a more specific proposal (mortgage tax relief, the national curriculum). And when ministers collectively committed themselves to such unspecific proposals, they personally had in mind somewhat different goals, wishing to see different powers, rights and duties set out in the legislation, for example, and having different mental pictures of how the system to be set up would work in practice.

The fact that a number of the more innovative proposed measures were regarded as good in their own right, rather than derived from goals, is consistent with a rationale that was focused on taking action – on the 'radical and striking measures' which Thatcher liked – rather than on achieving certain clearly defined goals. Especially where education was concerned, the aim was to set a revolution in train. It is in the nature of revolutions that their precise outcome cannot be foreseen. What Thatcher and her colleagues were aiming to do was to move *in a direction* – in the direction of removing local authorities from state education and from the building, ownership, management and regulation of housing. The lack of attention to the possible incidental consequences and side-effects of implementing the proposals – e.g. those for per capita funding of schools, abolishing artificial restrictions on pupil numbers and supporting the coexistence of several different types of school – is consistent with such an approach having been adopted. Note that it is not an approach which corresponds to the 'rational actor' model of decision making.

Contradictions in government statements are always interesting. They may tell us something about 'real' priorities, the ordering of considerations of different kinds that underlie the rationale. In this case, some of the manifesto proposals contradicted the Government's professed commitment to reducing public expenditure. It was prepared to spend taxpayers' money, or forgo tax revenue (which in practice amounts to the same thing), on increasing home ownership (mortgage tax relief), reducing the local authority housing sector ('huge sums of taxpayers' money' for HATs, giving discounts to those exercising the right to buy) and removing schools from local education authorities (grants for opting out schools). The common element here is the diminution that would result in the domains and powers of local authorities: the desirability of bringing this about appears to have been so important to the Government that it took priority over the desirability of reducing public expenditure. Again, despite the Government's professed desire to maximize personal choice, its policies were directed towards removing the local authority as a feasible option for people looking for somewhere to live. Shrinking the local authority sector took priority.

Another example of contradiction is revealed by Thatcher's and Ridley's references to 'welfare dependency'. On the one hand, they were committed to eliminating 'welfare dependency'; on the other, the Government was committed, at the instigation of Thatcher and Ridley, to compelling local authorities to charge so-called market rents for council housing. This would have the effect, as Thatcher says, of *increasing* the number of 'welfare dependants', defined as people who qualified for and claimed a state benefit (Housing Benefit in this case). Behind this contradiction lies another. Where Thatcher and Ridley refer to their aim of eliminating 'welfare dependency', they write about it as if it is a cultural phenomenon. Yet in the context of increasing rents, they appreciated that higher numbers would be a consequence of government action.

This example also exhibits what may be a common feature of government policy making, namely that policy makers face dilemmas. In this case the dilemma was whether to reduce subsidies to local authorities' housing revenue accounts, necessitating rent rises towards 'market levels' and thus higher expenditure on Housing Benefit, or to retain those subsidies and hold expenditure on Housing Benefit down. The choice was between two 'evils'.

The dominant considerations appear to have been political, ideological and presentational. Political considerations underlay the attack on the powers and domains of local authorities; ideological ones underlay the moves in the direction of free markets in private rented housing and schooling; presentational ones underlay the concealing of the intention to force up council rents and the fact that the Government's own taxation regime had been encouraging the decline of private renting (and would continue to do so). Political and ideological came into conflict over mortgage tax relief, where Thatcher (who saw it as attracting votes) and Lawson (who saw it as an interference with the free market) agreed a form of words that concealed the difference between them. It is noticeable that, taking housing and education together, the only 'down-to-earth' real-world goal was that of making it easier for people to find rented accommodation, an objective with which the ideological desirability of stimulating the private market coincided. Likewise, the only policy for dealing with run-down council estates, the as yet untried one of creating HATs, accorded with the political desirability of shrinking the local authority sector.

What *does* go on in ministers' minds? Ridley's references to 'the almost incestuous relationship' between councils and tenants, ratepayers being 'milked', and 'weaning people out of council housing',[103] and Thatcher's citing of extreme cases to justify measures – e.g. the case of the child moving school and encountering a new course *different in almost all respects* from his or her old one, used to justify introducing a national curriculum – are perhaps indications of how their imaginations can enter into their calculations.

As for interests, some groups of consumers of policy were explicitly referred to and targeted in the manifesto, but, with the exception of private landlords, their interests – acknowledged as 'needs' – made only a superficial positive mark on policy. The most strongly affirmed commitments in the manifesto were to make changes to 'the system', as in education, not to meet 'needs' or satisfy the interests of recognized categories of consumers. Parents who were able to drive their children to school might have seen themselves as standing to gain from 'parental choice'; so too might parents who wished to choose a single-sex school for their child or one which was not in an area where many people of minority ethnic groups lived. Such parents might have been correct in their interpretation of the words used (we have no conclusive evidence on this point) but there was no overt commitment to this effect. Conceivably, a policy based on a principle such as parental choice or local management of schools can be formulated without making any calculation as to who would gain and who would lose. But it would be inconsistent with the sensitivity of politicians to the electoral implications of possible policies for such calculations not to have been made, especially in the run-up to a general election.

We have seen that the interests of council tenants in general failed to make a mark on the manifesto proposals. They would incur costs, not benefits. Rents would rise, and run-down estates would not be improved unless tenants accepted removal from the local authority sector via HATs. Tenants who were compelled by the rent rises to have recourse to Housing Benefit would be regarded by Thatcher as 'welfare dependants'.

As to political/institutional interests, it is very apparent that some political interests did make a very significant mark on policy, not least the interest of Thatcher and her colleagues in staying in power. The presentational considerations remarked on above reveal one way in which that interest was manifested. Thatcher in particular makes no secret of her interest in *presenting* the reforms in a way that did not leave the Conservatives open to jibes and accusations; and her and Ridley's personal stake in reducing the domains and autonomy of local authorities and in stimulating provision through markets of some kind – both of which were given expression in the objectives within the Government's rationale – is very apparent.

In her two-fold capacity of party leader and Prime Minister, Thatcher first set up the radial 'manifesto structure', herself determining who would have privileged access to her in the early stages of the process. Her central position gave her the seemingly unchallenged power to 'rule in' some proposals and 'rule out' others. When it came to developing proposals more fully, she followed the machinery-of-government precedent by setting up Cabinet committees. She was thus able to draw on the resources of the departments concerned and the Cabinet Office for this party political process. In the committee setting, her capacity to influence the outcome was a function of the particular 'levers' at her disposal, and of those at the disposal of other ministers. They varied according to who those ministers were. She had very different interpersonal relationships with Baker and Ridley, whose own interests were very different. Her capacity to exert pressure successfully on Baker proved unusually limited, to judge by the reports that we have. And her dependence on the cooperation of Baker and his department, despite being able to draw on the resources of her Policy Unit and the advice of right-wing think-tanks, in effect gave him a lever that he was able to use to exert pressure on her. That the outcome over the national curriculum was a compromise reflects the 'balance of power' between the two of them.

As well as exercising her powers, as Prime Minister and party leader, to create *ad hoc* structures, Thatcher also made use of her power to create commitment, by publicly declaring policy in televised speeches, like that to the annual party conference, and by personally taking charge of the policy drafting process, including making last-minute alterations, as well as using her central position to pre-empt proposals of which she disapproved by unilaterally 'ruling them out'. None of these are formal 'powers of the Prime Minister', but she asserted her claim to them and this claim was not challenged by her ministers. The powers available to her were not unfettered, however: dissenting views from the Chancellor of the Exchequer could not be ignored, and Baker demonstrated the capacity of a determined Cabinet minister with the backing of his department to keep a complex issue open.

Think-tanks are in a special position. They have no means of exerting pressure on ministers. Indeed, rather than ministers being dependent on them, they are dependent on ministers – to listen to them and accept their proposals, on which their reputation depends. But the imperative on the Government to produce an election manifesto, because Thatcher was looking for radical, striking measures, provided them with an opportunity to make a significant mark on policy. For a brief period, the Prime Minister did depend on them.

Whether the views and interests of the consumers of social policy made a mark on the policies adopted appears to have depended on a number of factors, including how dependent on their votes ministers felt, and whether they had a well-placed advocate within the power structure. It may also have depended on the 'scope' for decision left after political/institutional interests and ideas about revolutionary restructurings have had an impact. The weak mark made by the interests of consumers on housing and education policy is consistent with there having been little scope once the main principles of the reform proposals had been adopted.

An important observation is that 'structure enables but does not determine'. Being in a certain position in the network, and having available the powers and levers that go with that position, does not determine that those powers and levers will be used in a particular way, or at all. Whether and how they are used will depend on the individuals who occupy that and other positions. Thus whether the views and interests of someone in the power structure make a mark on the policies adopted may depend not only on what powers and levers are available to them but also on what use they make of them. We have seen that many of the manifesto proposals strongly reflected those of Thatcher, who was at the centre of the manifesto network in the early stages. But Baker's views were to some extent reflected in the manifesto, contrary to Thatcher's wishes: evidently his position allowed him to wield some 'clout'.

Chapter six

THE DEPENDENCE OF THE PRIME MINISTER: THE 'POLL TAX' SAGA

Introduction

The 'poll tax' – or 'Community Charge', as it was officially known – was the local tax levied by English and Welsh local authorities from April 1990 (and by those in Scotland from April 1989) until its abolition in April 1993, on each individual adult living in domestic accommodation (houses, flats etc.) in their areas. Everyone living in the same local authority area was liable for the same amount, irrespective of income, although a means-tested benefit was available for the poorest. The poll tax replaced the domestic 'rates', a tax levied on each *property*, which only the 'householder' was required to pay. After the changeover, some households – especially those occupying larger houses and those with only a single adult – found themselves paying less than under the rates system, but others found themselves paying more, in some cases much more. Householders' spouses and adult children living at home found themselves personally liable to pay a local tax for the first time.

The introduction of the poll tax was preceded by a number of investigations and studies, which considered several other forms of local taxation. Thatcher herself proceeded with some caution, taking advice from several sources before committing herself to it. But the events that followed its introduction, culminating in her resignation, were evidently not what she anticipated. The poll tax saga is thus a case study in the *limitations* on the power of the Prime Minister and her dependence on others for advice and support.

There are four valuable ministerial sources for this case study: the memoirs of Prime Minister Margaret Thatcher,[1] Chancellor of the Exchequer Nigel Lawson[2] and two successive Secretaries of State for the Environment, Kenneth Baker[3] and Nicholas Ridley.[4] Another very useful source, drawing on documentary evidence and interviews with central participants, is *Failure in British Gov-*

ernment: the Politics of the Poll Tax, by Butler, Adonis and Travers.[5] An article entitled 'Mrs Thatcher's greatest blunder' by Crick and Van Klaveren, in the journal *Contemporary Record*,[6] also draws on interviews, as did a Channel Four TV programme *A Tax Too Far*, broadcast in March 1993, in which a number of ex-ministers took part.

The remainder of this chapter is organized as follows. I first tell the story – necessarily selectively but as factually as I can. I then examine (a) the legislative proposals, and (b) the financial decisions and measures that followed, from the four different perspectives already applied in Chapter 5.

The story

Margaret Thatcher first became involved with the issue of local government finance in 1974. In the run-up to the October 1974 general election, as shadow Environment Secretary, she had drawn up a package of proposals including abolition of the rates. Although she writes that 'this was a last-minute pledge insisted upon by Ted Heath [then Conservative Party leader] about which I had considerable doubts for we had not properly thought through what to put in their place', she adds: '[But] I had witnessed the anger and distress caused by the 1973 rate revaluation and believed strongly that something new must replace the existing discredited system.'[7]

Events and activities following the Conservatives' return to power under Thatcher in 1979 are outlined in the chronology in Box 6.1. Officials in the Department of the Environment (DoE), under Secretary of State Michael Heseltine, made a study of local government finance, and the results were published on 16 December 1981 as a Green Paper, *Alternatives to Domestic Rates*.[8] It suggested three alternatives to the rates, including a poll tax, but did not support any of them, concluding that a poll tax of £120 per head 'would almost certainly not be a practical proposition'. Two months after the June 1983 general election, which returned the Conservatives to power on a manifesto which promised to limit the rate increases of some or all local authorities but did not mention abolishing the rates, the Government published a White Paper, *Rates*,[9] which anticipated that the rating system would remain for the foreseeable future. The possibility of a poll tax was briefly mentioned, but rejected, and the Rates Act 1984 gave the Government powers to cap the rates of some or all local authorities. In July 1984 the Government announced its intention to use those powers.

Thatcher tells us that in the summer of 1984 'popular discontent with the rates surfaced strongly' in the motions submitted for the forthcoming Conservative Party conference in October. 'Conservatives in local government were unhappy at the apparatus of central controls.' And within the DoE 'there was concern that these controls gave rise to so many anomalies and political difficulties that they could not be sustained for many more years'.[10] On 2 September 1984, Patrick Jenkin, who had replaced Heseltine as Environment Secretary, met Thatcher at Chequers and sought her agreement to announce to the conference a major review of local government finance.[11] According to Thatcher, she was very wary of raising expectations that could not be met:

Box 6.1   Chronology: the poll tax

May 1979	General election. Conservative Government, Thatcher Prime Minister. Manifesto gives cutting income tax priority over abolishing rates.
16 December 1981	Heseltine's Green Paper on local government finance, *Alternatives to Domestic Rates*, published. Suggests three alternatives, including a poll tax, does not support any of them. Concludes that £120 per head 'would almost certainly not be a practical proposition'.
June 1983	General election: Conservatives stay in power. No mention of abolition of the rates. Jenkin appointed Environment Secretary.
August 1983	White paper *Rates*. Rates will remain for the foreseeable future. Poll tax briefly mentioned, but rejected.
June 1984	Rates Act gives ministers power to 'rate-cap' local authorities.
Summer 1984	Motions on rates for Conservative Party conference.
2 September 1984	Meeting at Chequers: Jenkin asks Thatcher to allow a new inquiry into local government finance. Agreed he will submit a paper to Cabinet.
27 September 1984	Meeting at No. 10: Jenkin presents his case for a review of local government finance: agreed.
October 1984	Conservative Party conference. Several motions call for rates to be abolished. Jenkin promises 'study', not review.
	Baker put in charge of review, delegates task to Waldegrave, who sets up studies team and recruits outsiders.
February 1985	Rate levels in Scotland for 1985–6 announced, to take effect on 1 April: domestic rates to rise sharply following revaluation.
	Scottish Conservative Party Chairman tells Thatcher of fury over new rateable values.
March 1985	Whitelaw heckled on visit to Scottish Conservatives.
31 March 1985	Seminar at Chequers on alternatives to rates. Lawson absent.
20 May 1985	First meeting of Cabinet sub-committee E(LF).
August 1985	Lawson memo to E(LF) on modified property tax.
September 1985	Baker appointed Environment Secretary.
23 September 1985	E(LF) meets, confirms that the local domestic tax should be a combination of a residents' charge and a property charge.
12 December 1985	E(LF) approves Baker's Green Paper *Paying for Local Government*.

End 1985	Baker takes proposal to Cabinet.
31 December 1985	Baker discusses Green Paper with Thatcher at Chequers.
9 January 1986	Heseltine walks out of Cabinet. Poll tax discussed by full Cabinet for the first time. Ten-year phasing-in recommended.
28 January 1986	Green Paper published. Announced by Baker in Commons.
21 May 1986	Ridley replaces Baker as Environment Secretary.
October 1986	Scottish Bill introduced into Parliament.
31 October 1986	Green Paper consultation period ends.
February 1987	Cabinet decides to introduce poll tax in Scotland from 1 April 1989.
15 May 1987	Abolition of Domestic Rates Etc. (Scotland) Bill receives Royal Assent.
19 May 1987	Conservative election manifesto published: 'We will legislate . . .'
11 June 1987	Conservative victory in general election.
July 1987	Cabinet agrees 4-year dual running in England and Wales. Local Government Finance Bill tabled in Parliament.
October 1987	Conservative Party conference. Succession of speakers from floor call for single-step introduction of Community Charge.
17 November 1987	E(LF) agrees single-step introduction of Community Charge for majority of councils.
April 1988	Committee stage: Government fights off Mates amendment.
June 1988	Cabinet abandons dual running entirely.
29 July 1988	Local Government Finance Bill receives Royal Assent.
May 1989	Ridley, Lawson and Major begin discussions on level of local authority grant settlement for 1990–1.
22 June 1989	Crucial meeting on level of local government settlement for 1990–1.
July 1989	Chris Patten replaces Ridley as Environment Secretary.
12 July 1989	Cabinet meeting on public expenditure. No more money for Community Charge relief.
September 1989	Chris Patten begins review of poll tax.
October 1989	Conservative Party conference: £1.2 billion over 3 years for transitional relief scheme/safety net announced.
22 March 1990	Mid-Staffordshire by-election. Conservatives lose hitherto 'safe' seat.
1 April 1990	Community Charge comes into effect in England and Wales.

November 1990 Major replaces Thatcher as Prime Minister.

19 March 1991 Lamont's Budget speech: VAT to be raised by 2½ per cent to 17 per cent, allowing individual poll tax bills to be cut by £140.

6 March 1992 Local Government Finance Bill receives Royal Assent.

1 April 1993 Council Tax replaces Community Charge.

[We] must be absolutely clear that we had a workable alternative to put in place of the present system. I authorized Patrick to say no more than that we would undertake studies of the most serious inequities and deficiencies of the present system. There would be no publicly announced 'review' and no hint that we might go as far as abolishing the rates.[12]

After the party conference, at which Jenkin did promise a study of local government finance,[13] there was a 'small meeting' at Chequers on the subject, at the end of which Thatcher was 'more convinced than ever of the fundamental absurdities of the present system'.[14] Afterwards she discussed the proposed studies with William Waldegrave (Parliamentary Under-Secretary of State in the DoE) and suggested that Lord Rothschild (a banker and former head of the Central Policy Review Staff) should be involved.[15]

In November 1984 a 'studies team' of officials was set up in the DoE. Waldegrave was the junior minister in charge and is said to have worked closely with them.[16] Nominally the official leader of the team was Terence Heiser, Deputy Secretary with responsibility for local government, but in practice the work was led by Anthony Mayer, an Assistant Secretary. The team included two DoE economists with expertise in local government finance and two officials on secondment from other departments, one from the Treasury and one from the Department of Health and Social Security.

Waldegrave also organized the group of outside advisers: in addition to Lord Rothschild this comprised a lawyer, Leonard Hoffman QC; Tom Wilson, a retired Glasgow University economics professor; and Christopher Foster, a director of the accountancy firm Coopers and Lybrand, former professor of economics at the LSE, one-time adviser to Labour ministers and assessor to the Roskill commission on the third London airport, and joint author of *Local Government Finance in a Unitary State*, published in 1980, in which the idea of funding local government with a poll tax was put forward.[17]

While the studies were progressing, concern was being expressed about the consequences of the rating revaluation (reassessment of every property's liability for tax) that had just been carried out in Scotland, where under Scottish law a revaluation was obligatory every five years. Thatcher was visited in mid-February 1985 by the Scottish Conservative Party Chairman, who described the 'fury' which had broken out when the new rateable values became known. Scottish local authorities had a high level of spending, and the revaluation had led to a large shift in the rates burden from industry to domestic ratepayers. By the end of the month, 'Scottish ministers, businessmen and Tory supporters began with one voice to call for an immediate end to the rating system'.[18] Although there was no legal requirement for a revaluation at set intervals in England and Wales, the last – very unpopular – one had been in 1973. For Thatcher the unrest was 'powerful evidence' of what would happen if another were carried out.[19] Towards the end of March 1985, Lord Whitelaw, Deputy Prime Minister, to whose shrewd advice and steadfast support Thatcher pays tribute in her memoirs, visited a marginal constituency in Scotland, where he was reportedly heckled by Conservative supporters: 'The reception I received indicated that revaluation was not tolerable.'[20]

On Sunday, 31 March 1985, a 'seminar' was held at Chequers. Among ministers reportedly present were Thatcher, Whitelaw, Jenkin, George Younger (Scottish Secretary), Nicholas Edwards (Welsh Secretary), Baker, Waldegrave and Peter Rees (Chief Secretary to the Treasury). Nigel Lawson was not present, although invited:

> I never liked giving up a Sunday in this way; and having been assured that this was simply a preliminary discussion at which no decisions would be taken, I foolishly decided not to go and to send Peter Rees . . . in my place . . . I briefed him to register my firm opposition to a poll tax, and gave him the arguments to use.[21]

Also present were Rothschild, Heiser and Mayer.[22]

At the seminar, Waldegrave presented on behalf of the studies team a 'package' of proposals: that the whole cost of a council's spending above a set level should be borne by local taxpayers, not the Exchequer; that rates on business and other non-domestic property should be set by central government, collected in and apportioned among councils by a formula; and that domestic rates should be replaced by a combination of a modified property tax and a poll tax, with the poll tax taking a gradually increasing share over the years.[23] Baker writes that Waldegrave concluded with the words: 'And so, Prime Minister, you will have fulfilled your promise to abolish rates.'[24]

According to Thatcher, there was tough questioning but general support for what she called 'the DoE approach':

> It was at the Chequers meeting that the community charge was born. They convinced me that we should abolish domestic rates and replace them with a community charge levied at a flat rate on all resident adults . . . [Everyone] should contribute something, and therefore have something to lose from electing a spendthrift council. This principle of accountability underlay the whole reform.[25]

Baker adds that the meeting was told that for a poll tax to replace domestic rates entirely (i.e. to match the full amount that they raised) an average charge of £140 would be necessary. He adds: 'If we had known that in 1990, the first year, the average level . . . was to be £363 then I am sure we would have suspended work immediately.'[26]

In that spring of 1985 Younger was seeking more funds from the Exchequer to cushion the effect of the Scottish rates revaluation, and there were 'heated and increasingly public' exchanges between him and Lawson.[27] At the Scottish Conservative Party conference in the second week of May, Thatcher and Younger committed themselves to producing proposals for rectifying the 'anomalies and unfairness' of the present system of local government finance.[28]

On 20 May 1985 there took place the first meeting of a Cabinet committee known as E(LF) – LF stands for 'Local Finance' – to consider 'future policy relating to local government finance'. It was chaired by Thatcher. According to Lawson, it 'comprised two-thirds of the entire Cabinet': Baker tells us that 'most senior Cabinet ministers were members', but also describes the committee as 'consisting of ten Cabinet ministers' at the meeting on 20 May.[29] He and Waldegrave presented their key proposal for a flat-rate residents' charge with a rebate for the less well-off. Lawson had prepared a Cabinet memorandum strongly condemning a poll tax as 'completely unworkable and politically catastrophic',[30] but very few of his colleagues supported him. Baker and Waldegrave were given the task of 'working up a more detailed proposal for the community charge'.[31] E(LF) continued to meet. In August Lawson tried again with a paper suggesting a 'modified property tax', but it won no support from ministers outside the Treasury.[32]

On 2 September 1985, Thatcher promoted Baker to Environment Secretary, replacing Jenkin. At a meeting of E(LF) on 23 September 1985, Lawson again voiced his misgivings, but (according to Baker) the meeting confirmed that the local domestic tax should be a combination of a residents' charge and a property charge.[33] (Lawson writes that 'the meeting was inconclusive', and a further meeting was held on 3 October to clarify what Baker could tell the Party Conference the following week.[34]) On 12 December 1985, E(LF) approved a draft Green Paper, *Paying for Local Government*.[35] It was briefly discussed by the Cabinet and approved on 9 January 1986. This was the first time the full Cabinet had discussed the poll tax, although at least half its members had discussed it in committee. Earlier in that same meeting Michael Heseltine had walked out and resigned from the Cabinet in connection with what became known as the Westland affair.

Baker presented the Green Paper to the House of Commons on 28 January 1986. It was published over the signatures of the Scottish and Welsh Secretaries in addition to his own. It invited comments to be submitted by 31 July 1986. In summary, the main proposals were:

- Rates on non-domestic properties (businesses etc.) should be set by central government, at a nationally uniform rate, the proceeds being pooled and redistributed to local authorities in proportion to the number of adults living in their area.
- Domestic rates should be phased out over a period of up to ten years and replaced by a 'flat rate community charge', which each authority would set and which would be payable by each adult resident.

- The system of central grants to local authorities should be radically simplified. It would consist of 'needs grant', which would compensate for differences in what authorities needed to spend to provide a comparable standard of service, and 'standard grant', which would be paid to all authorities as a common amount (the same to every authority) per adult.
- Distributional changes resulting from the introduction of the new system would be offset by 'a system of self-financing adjustments', under which authorities which gained financially from the changes would temporarily forgo some of their gains to compensate authorities which lost.

On 21 May 1986, Baker was replaced as Environment Secretary by Nicholas Ridley. (Baker became Education Secretary.) On 26 November 1986, the Bill to implement the Community Charge in Scotland was tabled in Parliament. During its passage Malcolm Rifkind, Secretary of State for Scotland (since January 1986) and an enthusiastic supporter of the poll tax, which he is thought to have seen as essential to holding his marginal seat in Edinburgh, persuaded his Cabinet colleagues to accept a backbench amendment to introduce it in a single step on 1 April 1989.[36] Otherwise the Bill went through the Parliamentary stages of the legislative process with little difficulty. A few English Conservative MPs who had reservations were apparently told by Scottish ministers that it was 'utterly vital' in electoral terms.[37] The Abolition of Domestic Rates Etc. (Scotland) Act 1987 received its Royal Assent on 15 May 1987.

On 18 May 1987, Parliament was dissolved, and the following day the Conservatives published their manifesto for the general election. Extracts are shown in Box 6.2. It contained a firm commitment to abolishing the domestic rates and putting a 'fairer' Community Charge in their place. During the election campaign, the Labour Party did not use the issue to attack the Conservatives. After the Conservatives were returned to power there were further discussions in July 1987 in E(LF) and Cabinet. The whips had estimated that while more than 150 Conservative backbenchers were clear supporters, there were nearly 100 'doubters', with 24 outright opponents.[38] To the issue of how to win over the doubters, part of Ridley's 'characteristically robust' response was to propose abandoning dual running. (He also proposed drastically cutting down the safety net.) Lawson and Major opposed this: four years was the compromise figure on which agreement was reached.[39]

At the October 1987 Conservative Party Conference, the Community Charge/poll tax was received with acclaim, but a succession of speakers from the floor called for its introduction in a single step instead of dual running. Ridley writes that Thatcher whispered in his ear: 'We shall have to have a look at this again, Nick.'[40] Thatcher tells us that backbench opinion too was very strongly opposed. At a meeting of E(LF) on 17 November 1987, Ridley again proposed abandoning dual running, Lawson opposed once more, but the majority, including Thatcher, was for abandonment, except in certain London authorities.[41]

On 4 December 1987, the Local Government Finance Bill, containing provisions for the introduction of the Community Charge in England and Wales, was tabled in Parliament. Its passage was marked by strenuous attempts by

---

Box 6.2   Extracts from the Conservative 1987 election manifesto, on local government

The Conservative view of local government is that local people should look after the interests of the local community which they were elected to serve, maintaining and improving essential services at a price people can afford. That is an honourable tradition of public service, still upheld by councillors in most local authorities. But the abuses of left-wing Labour councils have shocked the nation. The Labour Party leadership pretends that this is a problem in only a few London boroughs. The truth is that the far Left control town halls in many of our cities. The extremists have gained power in these areas partly because too few ratepayers have an interest in voting for responsible councillors pursuing sensible policies. Many people benefit from local services yet make little or no contribution towards them: this throws too heavy a burden on too few shoulders . . . There is much else wrong with the present system of domestic rates. They seem unfair and arbitrary. And companies are left with little protection against huge rate rises levied by councils controlled by Labour, Liberals and Social Democrats . . .

We will now tackle the roots of the problem. We will reform local government finance to strengthen local democracy and accountability. Local electors must be able to decide the level of service they want and how much they are prepared to pay for it. We will legislate . . . to abolish the unfair domestic rating system and replace rates with a fairer Community Charge. This will be a fixed rate charge for local services paid by those over the age of 18, except the mentally ill and elderly people living in homes and hospitals. The less-well-off and students will not have to pay the full charge – but everyone will be aware of the costs as well as the benefits of local services. This should encourage people to take a greater interest in the policies of their local council and in getting value for money. Business ratepayers will pay a Unified Business Rate at a standard rate pegged to inflation.

---

some Conservative backbenchers to amend it. Michael Mates, a senior Conservative backbencher (a former Army officer, he had recently become Secretary of the Conservative 1922 Committee), tabled an amendment at the Report Stage[42] to 'band' the poll tax according to income. People paying income tax at the standard rate would pay a 'standard' level of poll tax: people who did not pay income tax would be liable for only half the standard level: people who paid income tax at the higher rate would be liable for one and a half times the standard level.

The Mates amendment was strongly resisted by the Government. Butler *et al.* describe how severe pressure was brought on Mates, both through his constituency ('though the whips backed off after one fruitless approach to one member of my East Hampshire executive') and in a face-to-face interview with the Chief Whip, David Waddington, who claimed ('as whips always do') that the Government was set for defeat on his amendment, which would be likely to undermine the Prime Minister.[43] Similar pressure was brought to bear on potential supporters of Mates's amendment: at least two newly elected MPs are said to have gone to Mates 'in tears, or pretty close to it' after interviews with Waddington.[44] And when Mates made his speech proposing his amendment in the Report Stage debate on 18 April 1988, he was heckled and interrupted throughout, 'and a string of loyal backbenchers proceeded to denounce him'.[45] The Government had a majority of 25 in the vote at the end of the debate: 38 Conservative MPs voted against the Government and 13 abstained.

In June 1988, while the Bill was still going through Parliament, the Cabinet abandoned dual running for the remaining London authorities, after the Government had decided to abolish the Inner London Education Authority, a late amendment to the Bill giving effect to the decision. On 29 July 1988, the Bill received its Royal Assent. Apart from the abandonment of dual running, its provisions conformed to the Green Paper proposals described above (pp. 108–9).

In May 1989, Ridley, Lawson and John Major (Chief Secretary to the Treasury) began discussions on how much Revenue Support Grant English local authorities should receive from the Treasury for 1990–1, the first year of the poll tax in England. The local authorities had made bids totalling £35 billion.[46] At some point in May or June there was a meeting between Ridley and Lawson: Baker recounts being told by Ridley afterwards that he had been forced to agree to £32.8 billion, against his better judgement. At a subsequent 'crucial' meeting at No. 10, chaired by Thatcher on 22 June 1989, Baker argued – with, he says, Ridley's encouragement – that the figure should be £34.4 billion. He writes:

At the Number 10 meeting I predicted that . . . local authorities were going to spend close to the figures that I proposed, and a lower figure would in no way influence their spending decisions. It would be sensible, therefore, to base their grants on the higher figure, or else the Government would be blamed for the ensuing high community charge. Unfortunately the Prime Minister supported Nick's official line. I began to sense a stitch-up by the Treasury when John Moore and Norman Fowler [did the same], as did Ken Clarke, who vented his usual spleen on local authorities because he knew that if they got an increase in the summer then there would be less for his Health budget in the autumn . . . The Prime Minister was convinced that unless we had a tough settlement, local government expenditure would go through the roof . . . On 12 July, at the Cabinet meeting to discuss public expenditure, I argued for more money to cushion the effect of the first year of the community charge, but again I lost.[47]

(Baker's description of what was in Thatcher's and Clarke's minds can only be based on his impressions, but the references to Thatcher are consistent with her own account.)

The amount that each authority received from the Exchequer by way of Revenue Support Grant was based on its 'Standard Spending Assessment' (SSA): the amount that the Environment Secretary (advised by his officials) considered that the authority *ought* to be spending in order to provide a level of services that was standard – the same everywhere in the country. The formula that was used took into account indicators of the need for services, like numbers of schoolchildren and of potential elderly domiciliary clients of personal social services: the greater those numbers, the higher the SSA would be. But the formula also took into account the total funds made available by central government: the 'needs elements' were scaled down to fit the total Revenue Support Grant that the Government would make available. *Essentially, it was a formula for sharing out the Grant, not for ensuring that 'needs' were met.* The effect was that all English authorities whose spending in the year ahead was expected to match exactly their respective SSAs, calculated in this way, would charge exactly the same poll tax (and similarly for Scotland and Wales). For them, poll tax would be funding about one-quarter of the authority's expenditure on services. But if its actual expenditure was above the SSA amount, *all* of the extra costs, instead of only one-quarter, would have to be met from the poll tax.[48]

The sequel. Later in July 1989, Thatcher appointed Chris Patten to be Environment Secretary, replacing Ridley, and early in September 1989, with Thatcher's approval, he began a review of the operation of the poll tax.[49] At the party conference in October 1989, David Hunt, Minister for Local Government in the DoE, announced a transitional relief scheme costing £1.2 billion over three years. He said the effect should be that in 1990–1 no household of one or two adults would pay in Community Charge more than £3 per week above their rates bill in 1989–90.[50]

In November 1989, the DoE published a list showing an assumed Community Charge figure – presented in the press as the 'likely' figure – for each English district and London borough council. It was based on the assumption that the authority (or both authorities, county and district, in the two-tier 'shire' counties) would hit its standard spending target, which reflected, because of the scaling down to match the total funds made available, the 3.8 per cent growth limit.[51] Most local authorities' own calculations were showing that they would be spending much more, and that the charge would accordingly be considerably higher, and over the next three months anxiety was increasingly voiced by Conservative and other local councillors.[52]

In the event, poll tax charges in England proved to be considerably higher than had been projected, averaging £363: £85 higher than the figure announced by Patten in November 1989 and more than two and a half times the £140 mentioned at the Chequers seminar in March 1985.[53] Some local authorities announced poll tax bills up to £159 above the 'likely' figures the Government had published. Some households would be paying £7 per week more than they had in rates, not £3 as Hunt had forecast. It is estimated that some 27 million people lived in households that lost from the change, with higher bills to pay than under the rates, while eight million lived in households that gained. The heaviest losers were people living in small, older properties with modest incomes and/or savings just high enough to disqualify them from receiving a new means-tested social security benefit – Community Charge Benefit.[54] For people receiving Income Support, this benefit defrayed 80 per cent of their poll tax bill, i.e. they had to pay the other 20 per cent. While national rates of Income Support ostensibly included an allowance for this (they had been uprated when liability to pay 20 per cent of the rates bill had been introduced in 1988),[55] that allowance was based on the *national average* poll tax bill. Thus, where their bill was above the national average, they had to find the difference out of their benefit. Young people living in their parental homes who were unemployed or earned very little, yet were now liable to pay 20 per cent of the poll tax, comprised another significant category of 'losers'.

Ridley has acknowledged that the Government underprovided for inflation and underestimated the start-up costs of the new tax. It had also set the Revenue Support Grant below the figure that Ridley and Baker thought was realistic. But the local authorities had also contributed to the high bills, having increased their spending by about 13 per cent in cash,[56] and they would have to set the poll tax high enough to cover non-payment by a proportion of those liable. Under the domestic rates system, 99 per cent of the amounts due were collected: in inner-city areas up to 20 per cent of poll tax revenues went uncollected.[57]

In February and March 1990, there were demonstrations against the poll tax at council meetings around England. Many 'ordinary, middle-class people' took part.[58] On 1 March, 18 West Oxfordshire district councillors resigned from the Conservative group and a delegation of backbench Conservative MPs unsuccessfully lobbied Thatcher to seek extra financial help for local authorities.[59] On 22 March, the Conservatives lost a hitherto 'safe' seat in the Mid-Staffordshire by-election. On 31 March, an anti-poll tax march and demonstration in London turned into 'a full-scale and bloody riot'.[60] In the local elections in May, Baker's strategy – in July 1989 he had become Party Chairman – was 'to throw the blame for high community charges on high-spending Labour local authorities',[61] but the Conservatives suffered heavy losses throughout Britain. However, they increased their majorities in two Conservative 'flagship' authorities, the London Boroughs of Wandsworth and Westminster, which had been able to set their poll tax low – an outcome presented by Baker as a victory for the principle of the poll tax.

On 18 October, another 'safe' Parliamentary seat, in Eastbourne, was lost in a by-election. Later that month, Thatcher's leadership of the Conservative Party was challenged by Michael Heseltine, who promised that if he replaced her as leader and Prime Minister he would immediately review the poll tax. Thatcher received the highest number of votes in the first leadership ballot, but not enough to win outright, and she resigned. In the second ballot, Heseltine was joined by John Major and by Douglas Hurd: they too undertook to review the poll tax if they won. Major, the successful contender, fulfilled his undertaking, and set a review in train. In March 1991, while it was in progress, the new Chancellor, Norman Lamont, announced in his Budget speech that the Exchequer would provide £3 billion to reduce each chargepayer's bill for 1991–2 by £140. The money would be found by increasing Value Added Tax by 2.5 per cent. Baker writes that in 1991 he received no letters of complaint from his constituents about the charge.[62]

In 1992, a new Local Government Finance Act reached the statute book. It provided for the replacing of the Community Charge by a new property-based 'Council Tax', based on market values (grouped into six bands) and incorporating a discount where only one adult lived in the property.

The policies and measures

To what proposals were Thatcher and her colleagues committed? We need to examine commitment at successive points in the process. Thatcher makes clear that at the conclusion of the Chequers seminar she was 'convinced' that domestic rates should be abolished and replaced by a poll tax. But how strong a commitment on the Government's part was there to the proposals published in the Green Paper? This is not an easy question to answer. Although the convention is, as Lawson puts it, that a Green Paper is a discussion document which sets out the Government's provisional conclusions on an issue, and which may or may not be a prelude to action,[63] this one stated: 'The Government is committed to a system of local government finance' which was going to be very different from the existing one. Its main proposals lay 'at the heart of the Government's reforms'.[64] No alternative forms of local tax were suggested, and none had been developed in the way that the poll tax had. I conclude that Thatcher and the Cabinet were indeed strongly committed to the proposals, although the proposal to phase the replacement of the rates by the poll tax over a period 'up to ten years' seems to indicate some tentativeness about the duration of that 'dual running' period. Otherwise, in its central respects the document was in effect a *White* Paper, expressing a definite intention, in all but its formal designation: we can think of it as a White Paper with green edges and a green cover.

The next sets of proposals to be published were the Scottish and the English and Welsh Bills, each registering the Government's firm intention – and thus carrying strong commitment on its part – to securing their enactment. The final legislative proposals to carry commitment were the Bills in their final forms, modified during the Parliamentary legislative stages, prior to receiving Royal Assent.

For the sake of conciseness, I have chosen to apply the four perspectives to the legislative proposals in their final forms, rather than to the policy at each separate stage of its formulation. Accordingly, the following sections deal first with the legislation – especially the Local Government Finance Act 1988 – and some of its main elements, such as the flat-rate poll tax and the single-step introduction of the tax. I then go on to examine the financial measures that followed the legislation.

THE LEGISLATION

Rationale

Insofar as there was a unified rationale underlying the Bill as finally enacted, it was 'assembled' over the period from the Chequers seminar to the final Reading of the Bill. Elements of it are presented in the Green Paper and various ministerial statements, as well as in Thatcher's and other memoirs.

Means and ends. Both the Green Paper and Thatcher describe the poll tax policy as deriving from an analysis of how the rates system worked. But their descriptions are significantly different. The Green Paper uses the terms 'shortcomings', 'problems' and 'flaws':

> The Government's concern to restrain local authority expenditure and taxation has revealed that the existing financial framework has serious shortcomings which significantly weaken local accountability. These problems have not been *caused* by what has happened since 1979. The flaws have been inherent in successive systems over many years . . . Shortcomings arise as a result of problems in three main areas – the extent to which local authorities' marginal spending is funded by non-domestic ratepayers; the mismatch between those who are entitled to vote in local elections, those who benefit from local authority services, and those who pay domestic rates; [and] the operation of the grant system.[65]

In a section headed 'The direction of reform', the Green Paper identified three main possibilities for reform: changing the structure of local government, rejected as likely to cause enormous disruption while failing to deal with the underlying financial problems; imposing much greater control over local authorities, rejected as throwing too much responsibility on central government for local matters and requiring more civil servants, whether it took the form of detailed rate-capping or the full or partial central funding of a major service such as education; and financial reform designed to improve local accountability. The third option was the preferable way forward. From the problems and shortcomings listed above, three main elements required in a new finance system were directly inferred:

> better arrangements for the taxation of non-domestic ratepayers, so that the payments they make towards local services do not conceal from local voters the true costs of increased spending; a more direct and fairer link between voting and paying, with more local voters contributing towards the cost of providing local authority services; [and] clearer grant arrangements, so that the consequences of increases or reductions in spending are felt directly and straightforwardly by local domestic ratepayers.[66]

As we can see, these three 'main elements' correspond directly to the first three of the Green Paper's proposals: non-domestic rates to be set and the proceeds to be collected by central Government; domestic rates to be phased out and replaced by a 'flat rate community charge' payable by each adult resident; and the system of central grants to local authorities to be radically simplified.

As presented in Chapter 1 of the Green Paper, the procedure followed had been to 'consider the shortcomings of the existing arrangements and set out possible alternatives'.[67] The intellectual activity appears to have consisted of 'juggling' with alternatives to achieve a desired effect, the alternatives being identified 'by inspection'. The language is not that of 'objectives', and the criteria referred to are not explicitly spelled out. However, in later chapters (perhaps written by different hands?), we find a more thoughtful and reasoned exposition. Chapter 3 considers the tests that a local tax should satisfy – Is it technically adequate? Is it fair? Does it encourage local democratic account-ability? – and briefly examines a different set of alternatives – property taxes, sales taxes, income taxes and residence taxes – before settling on the last of these.[68] It continues:

> The search for the best local tax has been an attempt to reconcile conflict-ing objectives – the 'redistributive principle' [under which you pay accord-ing to what you can afford] and the 'beneficial principle' [under which you pay according to the benefit you receive]. It is clear that *no* tax could satisfy both aims simultaneously.[69]

Essentially, then, the author or authors of Chapter 3 saw the formulation of proposals as requiring the resolving of a dilemma.

This seems not to have been Thatcher's perception. She presents the pro-posed new system as being calculated to attain four main objectives. All were derived from her perceptions of what was wrong with the existing system. They coincided in part but not entirely with those revealed in the Green Paper.

First, the new system had to afford central government an effective means of holding down local spending, which was growing inexorably, year after year.[70] 'Rate-capping', although effective, stretched the capacity of the DoE and risked being challenged in the Courts.[71]

Second, it had to provide accountability, by way of giving electors 'an incen-tive to think twice before re-electing high-spending councils'.[72] It was lack of accountability which lay behind the continued overspending:[73]

> Of the 35 million local electors in England, 17 million were not themselves liable for rates, and of the 18 million liable, 3 million paid less than full rates and 3 million paid nothing at all. Though some of those not liable contributed to the rates paid by others (for example, spouses and working children living at home), many people had no direct reason to be con-cerned about their council's overspending, because somebody else picked up all or most of the bill. Worse still, people lacked the information they needed to hold their local authority to account . . . many councillors felt free to pursue policies which no properly operating democratic discipline would have permitted.[74]

Third, it had to ensure 'fair' treatment of local businesses by councils:

> In the summer of 1985 . . . some 60 per cent of the rate income of local authorities was coming from business rates. In some areas, though, it was a far higher percentage. For example, in the Labour-controlled London borough of Camden it reached 75 per cent. Socialist councils were thus able to squeeze local businesses dry.[75]

Fourth, it had to meet the goal of ensuring fairness between households of different types:

In my constituency and in letters received from people all over the country I witnessed a chorus of complaints from people living alone – widows for example – who consumed far less of local authority services than the large family next door with several working sons, but who were expected to pay the same rates bills, regardless of their income.[76]

Another objective, of course, was that of allaying the dissatisfaction with levels of rates expressed by party activists in Scotland and elsewhere.

Thatcher also had objections to rates for what they were – a tax on property. 'Any property tax is essentially a tax on improving one's own home. It was manifestly unfair and un-Conservative.' Rates had made sense, perhaps, when the bulk of local authority services were supplied to property – roads, water and drains, and so on – but local authorities had increasingly become providers of services for *people*, such as education, libraries and personal social services. The only serious argument for the rates was that they were relatively easy to collect.[77] Her views evidently amounted to a strong constraint against adopting a new form of property tax. Such a tax was bad in its own right: she ruled it out more for what it was than for what its consequences would be.

Other ministers too had views about possible proposals. Most wanted if possible to avoid further centralization, as by central government taking over responsibility for education or teachers' pay: this was evidently undesirable in its own right. A local income tax would have undermined the Government's efforts to lower national income tax. (As Baker put it, it would have been a way of establishing a Labour Chancellor of the Exchequer in town halls.[78]) A local sales tax would have resulted in high-spending authorities driving shoppers to low-spending neighbours 'only minutes away'.[79]

Thatcher was, she says, also concerned about two sets of consequential outcomes. One was the amount of the charge. The Chequers seminar had been told that for a poll tax to replace domestic rates entirely (i.e. to match the full amount that they raised), an average charge of £140 would be necessary.[80] This was evidently acceptable to her. Her other concern was the number of gainers and losers and the impact upon different households. She wanted more work done on this.[81]

What did the Green Paper have to say about poll tax levels and about gainers and losers? Interestingly, no figure for the average charge was given. In the body of the Green Paper was a diagram purporting to show that – ignoring the rate rebates from which people on lower incomes benefited – the shift to poll tax would result in lower payments for the poorest households (net weekly household income of £0–75 at 1984–5 prices) and higher payments for households with middle and higher incomes (£100–400): tiny numbers in the highest income group (£500+) would also gain.[82] In an annex at the end of the volume was a diagram showing the effect of the change after means-tested rebates had been taken into account, but grouping households by '*equivalent*' net weekly income' – a statistical technique that 'adjusts' actual income to take differences in household composition into account. (Thus a single adult with the same net income as a couple would have an equivalent net income nearly double that of the couple.) *This* diagram showed higher payments only for the 'adjusted' households with an 'equivalent net weekly income' of £75–150: all others would pay less under the poll tax system.[83]

There are two highly significant points to make about these diagrams and the accompanying tables. First, they were based on the assumption that the poll tax would raise no more money than the domestic rates had done. (Net rates and net poll tax would both average 3 per cent of equivalent net income.) Second, they did not distinguish between single-adult and multi-adult households: all were 'lumped together' in their income brackets. This presentation thus concealed the fact that in the not-quite-poor income groups, whose income was just above the level where they would have qualified for rebates, single-adult households would predominantly gain, as Thatcher specifically intended, while multi-adult households would lose. Multi-adult households living in low-rated properties – especially small houses built before 1914 for working-class people – would be particularly hard hit. Although some or all of the authors of the Green Paper possessed the data that demonstrated how multi-adult households would lose from the changeover (without those data they could not have adjusted their figures for household size), they evidently chose not to present it. *They chose not to point out that not-quite-poor multi-adult households would be badly hit by the change from rates to poll tax, even on the optimistic assumption that the poll tax would be required to raise no more money than the domestic rates had done.*

Moreover, the lumping together of single-adult gainer households and multi-adult losers concealed electoral implications, because multi-adult households have two or more votes, whereas single-adult households have only one. In the £150–200 'equivalent net weekly income' bracket, where on average households would pay the same poll tax as they had rates – i.e. overall gains and losses balanced out – there would thus be appreciably more losing voters than gainers. So this fact too was concealed by the Green Paper's authors.

The rationale underlying the Green Paper and the legislation also did not incorporate Lawson's conclusion, expressed in his Cabinet memorandum of May 1985, that a consequence of going ahead with a flat-rate poll tax would be that 'a pensioner couple in inner London could find themselves paying 22 per cent of their income in poll tax, whereas a better off couple in the suburbs would pay only 1 per cent',[84] although his calculation was based, he said, on the DoE's own projections of gainers and losers. Nor had attention been paid to his further conclusion that the political consequences would be 'catastrophic'. These conclusions were evidently inconsistent with the rationale that came to be set out in the Green Paper, and could not comfortably be accommodated within it.

Considerations.   We can see in the Green Paper and Thatcher's memoirs, and in the behaviour of the participants, signs of a number of political considerations. For Thatcher, the 'political arguments' against dual running came to be powerful: among other things, having two local taxes instead of one, albeit temporarily, would have been 'a gift to our opponents'.[85] Another important political consideration was evidently the desirability of retaining the support of English and Welsh Conservative MPs – especially when the Mates amendment offered them an opportunity to cast their votes against the flat-rate poll tax – and the support of the activists present at the 1987 party conference.

We find frequent references to 'fairness' in the Green Paper, ministerial memoirs and public statements, such as the 1987 election manifesto and ministers' speeches. (In July 1987, Michael Howard, who had been appointed Minister for Local Government after the general election, said on BBC Radio: 'We told a lot of people during the election, those who suffer from the present system, single pensioners and single parent families who pay the same rates as large families next door, that we would . . . remedy these injustices.'[86]) But there is a striking inconsistency between such public statements and the ignoring of the effect on not-quite-poor multi-adult households: we can, I suggest, infer from this that the Government merely wished to give the impression of 'fairness', that this was a label attached for presentational purposes. Its resistance to the 'Mates amendment', which would have 'banded' the poll tax according to income tax thresholds, is consistent with this.

If references to 'fairness' were essentially presentational, what was the Government's 'real' objective?

We have seen that Thatcher was strongly attracted by the poll tax proposals. There would be a new accountability of local authorities to local taxpayers, because the whole cost of a council's spending above a set level would be borne by the latter. Poor people would receive rebates but would not be shielded from these marginal costs. But what did 'accountability' *mean* to Thatcher and her colleagues? What did she understand to be involved in not shielding poor people from marginal costs? She gives us a clue:

> When the community charge system had been developed, we had assumed that if authorities persisted with high levels of spending, the blame for the resultant high community charges would fall on them rather than the Government.[87]

For Thatcher, then, a system designed around 'accountability' was one that would place blame for high poll tax charges with the body closest to the chargepayer. Central government might hold down the Revenue Support Grant to local authorities: if the latter in consequence put up the poll tax rather than cut back services, the blame should be placed on them. Put another way, if local authorities were anxious to avoid blame, they would be under pressure to comply with the Government's wishes. In short, what Thatcher was doing was promoting a system – a mechanism – for bringing pressure to bear on local authorities. *It was integral – fundamental – to this mechanism that poor and not-quite-poor people should not be shielded from councils' marginal costs. It was their potential hardship if poll tax levels were set high that would provide the lever by which that pressure would be exerted.*

The impact of 'administrative' – or practical – considerations, allied with political ones, is evident in the changing rationale to do with the introduction of the poll tax and associated measures. While the poll tax had been conceived of by the studies team first as a supplement to the rates and then as a tax to defray the cost of additional spending above what the Government deemed necessary, Thatcher had become convinced at Chequers that the rates should be abolished and replaced by it. Within the Green Paper's rationale, a period of 'dual running' would accustom people gradually to the new tax, and, as Baker put it, would lessen 'the risk of asking too much too quickly and [bringing] the whole system down'.[88] For Lawson, it would also have the desirable outcome that if the poll tax did prove to be a political liability the rates system would not have been discarded: the option of continuing to use it would not have been pre-empted.[89] Butler *et al.* have discovered that even before the 1987 general election, DoE officials were urging the abandonment of dual running, anticipating that its 'administrative consequences' would be complex, controversial and unpredictable.[90] This would be consistent with the view expressed by local authorities and their associations in response to the Green Paper, that the poll tax even on its own would be expensive and difficult to collect and operate.[91] In July 1987, the view held by Ridley – who had replaced Baker as Environment Secretary in May 1986 – that the bureaucracy and expense consequent upon dual running would be too great, made its mark in the decision to reduce the transitional period to four years. Thatcher too had come to appreciate the expense and difficulty of administering the poll tax.[92] Moreover, she seriously doubted, at the point when the last remnants of dual running were abandoned, whether the authorities concerned 'were administratively competent to do the job'.[93] Single-step introduction would present a lower administrative burden and costs, and would bring forward what the proponents of the poll tax perceived as its political benefits.

In the sequence of decisions that culminated in the single-step introduction of the poll tax, a smaller and smaller part was played by considerations of the impact of the changeover on individuals and households, and the electoral consideration that the impact of such a change should be felt only gradually. Such considerations had been 'pushed into the background' by the time the legislation was finalized.

Ingredients of the rationale. Many of the perceptions, theories, ideas and value judgements that entered into Thatcher's rationale at the Chequers seminar were manifested in the four objectives that formed part of her rationale. Baker has argued that a crucial ingredient of the rationale at that point – crucial in the sense that if it had not been present the outcome might well have been different – was the perception or estimate of the average level of poll tax that would be demanded by local authorities: the estimate supplied by officials proved to be well under half the actual figure. However, if it was indeed the case that to Thatcher the real goal was to set up a system for putting pressure on local authorities, any projections of future charges were incidental: the system would automatically deter high charges.

With regard to value judgements, Thatcher also makes clear that she subscribed to the Victorian distinction between the 'undeserving poor' and the 'deserving'.[94] By compelling everyone to pay at least something towards the poll tax, a 'whole class of people – an "underclass" if you will – had been dragged back into the ranks of responsible society and asked to become not just dependants but citizens'. Her attitude towards people who had been receiving 100 per cent rate rebates seems to have been that they were 'undeserving' and irresponsible, and required to be *dragged* back into society. To her, such people were taking advantage of the 'conscientious middle' who paid their way, just as 'spendthrift' local authorities were taking advantage of the lack of existing adequate accountability mechanisms. Set alongside her propensity for seeing accountability in terms of blame, a common element – an underlying consideration in her rationale – seems to have been the value judgement that the appropriate treatment for those whom she saw as undeserving and taking advantage was a punitive and pressurizing one.

Interests

Consumer interests. We have seen something of these in the above discussion of prospective gainers and losers. Broadly, in terms of financial benefits and costs, the interests of people in single-adult households and those living in modern, high-rated houses – especially the wealthiest – did make a mark on the proposals, while those of people living in multi-adult households and older, low-rated houses did not. For Thatcher, the gainers and losers were personalized, in the shape of widows (the deserving) on the one hand and those who benefited from services without paying for them (the undeserving) on the other.[95] By April 1990, however, consumer interests seem to have become indistinguishable from political interests in her mind, as when she registered the impact of the poll tax on 'our own people', 'people who had always looked to me for protection from exploitation by the socialist state . . . who were by no means well off and who had scrimped and saved to buy their homes', and people in middle income groups, the 'conscientious middle'.[96]

Regionally, the inhabitants of areas like the older industrial towns would suffer from the removal of the equalization schemes that had existed under the rates system to compensate for the generally low rateable values of their property. But the Green Paper did pay some attention to this 'distributional' effect, and its proposal to offset them by a system of 'self-financing adjustments' or 'safety nets' was given effect in the Act. These would have the effect that 'gaining' authorities, mainly in the South-East, would forgo part of their gains to compensate 'losing' authorities in the Midlands and North.[97] The damage to the interests of the latter's inhabitants would thus be limited, although the benefits would be spread among all the inhabitants of those authorities, by keeping the level of poll tax down, and not concentrated on the individual households who were suffering most from the changeover.

Political/institutional interests. Thatcher's actions, once she had taken on the mission of controlling local authority spending and committed herself emotionally to the defeat of socialist councils, are consistent with her having acquired a strong personal interest (stake) in achieving these ends. She had 'seen – and did not intend to forget – the perversity, incompetence and often straightforward malice of many local councils'.[98] Baker and Ridley clearly had a similar personal interest: they expressed strong antagonism to Labour-controlled local authorities. Both they and Thatcher also seem to have had a self-interest in having the popularity and electoral success and acclaim of their party, inside and outside Parliament, which they thought a poll tax would bring them. In addition, it appears that Thatcher may have had a 'latent' self-interest in fulfilling her 1974 pledge to abolish the rates – latent in the sense that she did not allow it to be re-awakened until she was reminded of it, and offered a means of fulfilling it, at the Chequers seminar. As she wrote, she 'had always disliked the rates intensely'.[99]

An interest that may have affected Thatcher's espousing of the poll tax at the Chequers seminar was that of William Waldegrave, who is said to have been its most enthusiastic supporter. Butler *et al.* conclude from their interviews with those present that 'what clearly appealed to Waldegrave' was that it afforded 'a theoretically elegant way of ensuring that every adult made a direct contribution towards the cost of each marginal pound of council spending'.[100] Evidently Waldegrave had a personal and (as a minister) institutional stake in finding an elegant solution to a problem set.

Lawson's interest in defending his autonomy – in the form of his freedom to make future income tax cuts – did not make a mark on the proposals. He felt that Thatcher had an interest in 'seeing him off',[101] and that he commanded little support from his senior colleagues, who 'tended to view the matter very much from a departmental perspective rather than a political one'.[102] Evidently they did not see themselves as having an interest in supporting him.

We must not overlook the interests of the DoE officials who contributed to the adoption of the poll tax. According to Crick and Van Klaveren, among DoE officials 'there was a feeling that previously the DoE had let Mrs Thatcher down: this time they had to succeed'.[103] They apparently had a self-interest in providing her with a solution to the rates problem that would appeal to her, and raise them in her esteem, as well as in escaping from the intractable problems of administering the cumbersome system of targets and penalties that now existed. Butler *et al.* describe Terry Heiser, Deputy Secretary, then (from February 1985) Permanent Secretary, at the DoE, as having an 'activist', 'can-do' mentality. Once it was clear that Patrick Jenkin wanted to reopen the question of local taxation, Heiser took on a personal interest in finding an alternative to the rates, setting up a special team composed of his most able officials. Working very closely with Waldegrave, sometimes until late at night, they appear to have become 'infected with their masters' zeal'.[104] Their self-seclusion, denying the exchange of ideas and comment with officials in other departments – even the Treasury and the Scottish and Welsh Offices – and with local government, is perhaps also indicative of how an interest in defending their own autonomy affected procedure and thereby the substance of the proposals that emerged.

Similar zeal may have infected Letwin and Redwood, in the Prime Minister's Policy Unit, who are said to have given advice to the studies team after the Chequers meeting and 'acted as go-betweens with the Waldegrave team and the Prime Minister'.[105] Any interest they might have had in critically examining the Green Paper seems to have been outweighed by an interest in promoting the poll tax.

Finally, Conservative MPs in different parts of the country had a vested interest in the Government having a policy that commanded support from the electorate, and of course in holding on to their own seats. Butler *et al.* quote one studies team member as saying: 'All the time we talked about the differential impact on shires and cities – which was code for Tory and Labour voters.'[106] It may also have been code for 'Tory and Labour MPs'. Conservative MPs also had an interest in not laying themselves open to pressure from the whips, and for some this played a part in their voting against the Mates amendment. Party activists shared their interest in the party's success, but many also appear to have had a personal interest in the introduction of the poll tax. Butler *et al.* comment that constituency party executive committees were disproportionately composed of pensioners,

> particularly *single* pensioners, who never ceased to complain about their rates bills. When Tory MPs said they were subject to 'strong constituency pressure' to 'do something about the rates', further questioning usually ascertained that the pressure came most strongly from their constituency parties, particularly at social and other events involving the older members.[107] (Italics in the original.)

Thatcher clearly had an interest in carrying her backbenchers with her (notably in not being defeated over the 'Mates amendment'), especially after it became clear to her that many Conservative backbenchers in the new Parliament 'had got the jitters',[108] and this made a mark in the shape of limited concessions during the Parliamentary stages of the legislative process. She also had an interest in being seen to respond positively to the wishes of party activists, manifested in her preparedness to reopen the issue of dual running after the 1987 party conference.

Examining consumer and political/institutional interests together, it appears that consumer interests made a mark (a) where it was clear how those consumers would be affected, and (b) where they were 'aligned' with political/institutional ones, i.e. where ministers, officials, MPs and party activists saw it as being in their interests for those consumers to be favoured. The interests of not-quite-poor multi-adult households did not make a mark on the legislation: it was not made clear how those households would be affected, and few within the governmental/political system saw it as being in their own interests to protect them.

Process

Issues.   An important imperative at the time of the Chequers seminar was still the discontent with the rates that had 'surfaced strongly' in the motions for the 1984 Conservative Party conference, which were seen as requiring a response from the Government. What that response should be had been the immediate issue, and we have seen that it was resolved for the time being by giving Jenkin a mandate to carry out fresh studies. An associated long-standing imperative for ministers and officials was that generated by their frustration at their inability to find a satisfactory means of controlling local authority spending. Much more recently, the unrest among Scottish Conservatives and their supporters over the rates revaluation, and the treatment administered to Whitelaw on his visit to Scotland, had now provided another political imperative: 'something had to be done' to address their discontent.

Decisions about structure and procedure.   It was evidently Thatcher who, exercising her powers as Prime Minister, decided that the Chequers seminar should be held, and then that a studies team and a group of outside advisers should be set up. The studies team worked in secret – there were no consultations with local government associations or professional bodies – and Cabinet committee E(LF) met a number of times prior to the Green Paper being approved by the Cabinet. It was evidently decided to publish the proposals as approved by the Cabinet as a Green Paper, and later to proceed with legislation for Scotland in advance of England. Possibly a conscious decision was taken not to publish a White Paper before any legislation was tabled.

Commitment.   At the Chequers seminar the enthusiasm with which Waldegrave presented the studies team's package of reforms, and the fact that no alternative packages were presented (local income tax etc. appear to have been mentioned only to be dismissed), suggest that he was strongly committed to getting the proposal accepted. The long hours which he and the DoE team had invested in the project may well have reinforced their commitment. Prior to the seminar Thatcher appears to have been wary of letting it appear that there was any commitment on her part to abolishing the rates, evidently desiring not to have to retreat from such a commitment. At Chequers, however, she became 'convinced' – her word – that domestic rates should be replaced with a flat-rate poll tax.[109] She became, in other words, personally and strongly committed to that course of action. This is consistent with her failure to await information on the likely numbers of gainers and losers, and with Lawson's experience when trying to change her mind. He and others formed the impression that the poll tax had acquired considerable 'momentum' and become 'unstoppable' by September 1985:[110] 'the steamroller rolls', as Lawson put it.[111] The endorsement of the poll tax by E(LF) and then the Cabinet (on 3 October 1985) strengthened that commitment, as did Baker's warmly received announcement to the party conference a few days later.

We can also infer commitment on the part of the studies team from the fact that projections of the impact of the changeover on multi-adult households were deliberately withheld from the Green Paper. This is consistent with the team being so committed that, rather than reconsider the poll tax proposal, or provide ammunition for opponents, they preferred to ignore the projections.

As noted above, there are contradictory indications of how committed the Government was to the Green Paper's proposals. Although calling a document a *Green* (as opposed to White) Paper conventionally denotes that its proposals are tentative, this one stated that the Government was *committed* to a system of local government finance which was different from the existing one. Its main proposals lay 'at the heart of the Government's reforms'. No alternatives were put forward, and no work on developing alternatives had been done. I conclude that the Government was indeed strongly committed to them, despite the colour of the document's cover, although the proposal for a phased changeover over a period of 'up to ten years' leaves open the precise duration of that 'dual running' period.

As we have seen, there was a sequence of decisions to do with dual running. The Green Paper proposed up to ten years of dual running. The Scottish Bill as tabled provided for three years, but dual running was abandoned at the Report stage in the Commons. For England and Wales, the Cabinet decision of July 1987 reduced the ten years to four;[112] another in November 1987 eliminated dual running everywhere except in some London authorities; finally, in June 1988, while the English and Welsh Bill was going through Parliament, those exceptions too were abandoned. There is an interesting inconsistency here between Thatcher's unwavering commitment after Chequers to the principle of the poll tax and the overturning of one decision after another over the question of dual running.

Access.   No papers were circulated in advance to the participants at the Chequers seminar (despite which Lawson had evidently anticipated the poll tax proposal and briefed his Chief Secretary with arguments to use against it). Nor were they offered Hoffman's critique. Apart from the Scottish Secretary, they had thus not been stimulated to inform themselves about the issue. Thatcher's commitment was generated without their having an opportunity to reflect or consult their officials. Although a number of departments other than the DoE were involved, there was no interdepartmental committee of officials making preparations, as there would have been with a properly constituted Cabinet committee.

Butler *et al.* make the point that people from local government were not invited to the Chequers seminar. Nor were they consulted during the preparation of the Green Paper. This is perfectly consistent with Thatcher's 'real' aim – and that of the studies team – being to design a system to exert pressure on local authorities. As one of the insiders told them, 'After all, they were the problem.'[113]

The meetings of E(LF) in May and September 1985 might have provided an opportunity for testing the rationale. Thatcher comments that 'few pieces of legislation have ever received such a thorough and scrupulous examination by ministers and officials in the relevant Cabinet committees'.[114] But this examination began only *after* the Chequers seminar, *after* (as we have seen) she had become committed to going ahead with the poll tax. Lawson's May 1986 memorandum was effectively ignored. And if he was the only one prepared to challenge her commitment, with the attendant risk of 'handbagging', the examination was perhaps not as 'thorough and scrupulous' as it might otherwise have been. Indeed, Thatcher's worry and hurt on discovering that the people who were suffering most 'were the people who were just above the level at which community charge benefit stopped'[115] might have been avoided had she or Letwin or Redwood scrupulously digested the Green Paper's warning: 'The greatest burden of local taxation . . . is borne by households whose income is a little above the level where they qualify for housing benefit.'[116]

The banding provisions of the 'Mates amendment' rejected by the Commons might also have provided an opportunity for testing the rationale, but its proposals for a 'fairer' charge, reflecting – albeit crudely – individual adults' ability to pay, were countered by pointing to the 'earnings trap' that would be created for those whose income rose by an amount that took them into a higher band: their extra earnings would effectively suffer an extra income tax. The point was also made that the system would be cumbersome to administer and would require extra data – on people's incomes – to be collected. What part the arguments played in the thinking of individual Conservative MPs we do not know. We do know that the whips exerted considerable pressure on backbenchers who were inclined to support the amendment; others, including ministers, may have regarded the Government's case as good enough to allow them to follow the whips' instructions without giving the matter any special thought, as Foreign Secretary Geoffrey Howe did.[117]

As for the sequence of decisions on dual running, Scottish ministers, MPs and activists gained direct and indirect (via Whitelaw) private access to Thatcher to urge a single-step changeover in Scotland, and after the June 1987 general election the whips' sounding-out of backbench opinion was 'fed in' to the July 1987 Cabinet decision to compromise on a four-year dual-running period in England and Wales. The 1987 party conference offered party activists access to Thatcher in public to urge a single-step changeover in those countries.

In this sequence of events, we see, first, a succession of fresh political imperatives for the Cabinet, created by: pressure from Rifkind; Thatcher herself when she felt the necessity to elicit support from her backbenchers; pressure from speakers at the party conference. Second, Thatcher was far less strongly committed to the ten-year dual running period than she was to the principle of the poll tax. This provided the scope – the opportunity – for pressures to be effective in changing her mind: her interest in carrying backbenchers and activists with her provided the motivation for her to do so. Third, the successive decisions did not so much generate commitment as provide an expedient for resolving the immediate political situation: that a four-year transitional period had been decided in July seems to have been no obstacle to the reopening of the issue in November. That there was a 'long and hard' argument[118] rather than a terse laying down of policy may also be an indication that Thatcher did not feel strongly committed. Fourth, in such a situation the issue was, in each case, 'What do we do now?' and not 'How do we deal with the considerations that led us to adopt dual running in the first place?' The likely impact on households was not considered. Fifth, senior DoE officials were now advising a 'clean break', and Baker, who had been insistent on dual running, had been replaced by Ridley, who was not.

Evidently the 'dual running issue' was significantly transformed once the responses to the Green Paper had been received. During the drafting of the Green Paper, the issue was how to render the poll tax as acceptable as possible, and how to establish the Government's commitment to ending the rates. (Baker had at one point wanted to leave open the question of whether the rates would ever be abolished.[119]) Once the poll tax had been generally accepted – by the Conservative Party, at least – that issue had been resolved. How long dual running should last, and indeed whether there should be any at all, was treated as a subsidiary issue, and Thatcher seems to have had no particular personal stake in how it was resolved.

Power structure

The development of a strong commitment on the part of the Government to the statutory creation of a poll tax and the realizing of that commitment in legislative measures, as Thatcher wished, can be seen as reflecting her central position in, and dominance of, the power structure – the governmental and political network. A map of the power structure at the time of the Chequers seminar would show a strong link between Thatcher and Waldegrave, insofar as her interest in finding an alternative to the rates and his expertise made her dependent upon his advice and the work that he had done. For his part, Waldegrave evidently depended on her to bestow on him the favour and acceptance that he sought. The officials in the DoE team, given their interest in not letting Thatcher down, evidently felt some obligation and/or loyalty towards her. Waldegrave had forged strong links with them, to the extent that they had become a social unit as well as a work unit, transcending the formal divide between ministers and officials. Butler *et al.* describe this as 'politicization' of the officials,[120] but it might be more accurately described as making a technician of Waldegrave, in the sense that he appears, as noted above, to have been preoccupied with finding an elegant solution to the problem set, and a solution that would meet the requirement of gaining Thatcher's support, to the point of failing to pay attention to wider political considerations. The self-casting of Heiser and other senior DoE officials in the role of technicians was apparent too, notably in what appears as their disregard of the classic civil service axiom: 'At all costs, my boy, keep the minister out of trouble.'[121]

Interestingly, while the studies team was at work, it appears to have been effectively sealed off from the outside world: no outsiders other than the assessors were kept in touch with progress.[122] There was no contact with or input from right-wing think-tanks. (The Adam Smith Institute published a pamphlet on the subject in April 1985, after the Chequers seminar.[123]) Secrecy was maintained until the publication of the Green Paper in January 1986.

The 'microstructure' of the Chequers seminar deserves some thought. The seminar didn't have the formal status of a Cabinet committee: there was no expectation that its conclusions would go to the full Cabinet to be cursorily discussed and then ratified, rubber-stamped. (None of the participants has suggested that the convention of collective Cabinet responsibility was invoked.) But the occasion was a collective one, not a presentation to Thatcher alone: other ministers participated in and witnessed Thatcher making up her mind at Chequers, and in most cases silently or vocally acquiesced in what was taking place. Through their shared participation and witness a bond of some kind seems to have formed between them. (Lawson, who 'foolishly' did not attend, may have had some sense of exclusion from that circle: this would be consistent with him determinedly following his own path – being his own man – subsequently.) Moreover, there was an 'authoritative' outcome in that the studies team was given a mandate to continue its work, and at the end of the day Thatcher had acquired a commitment to bringing about the poll tax. One of the powers of the Prime Minister is to create a commitment which extends to her Cabinet. If other ministers did not share that commitment, and made this known, the onus would be on them to resign.

The officials in the studies team evidently continued to operate after the Chequers seminar as a tightly knit group, working in secret and without establishing links to local government, which is reflected in the Green Paper doing no more than outlining how the new system would operate, and leaving open the practical question of the length of any period of dual running. And communications from the team to ministers appear to have been tightly controlled by the officials. Baker complains:

> One of the difficulties that I had, as did all those later concerned with the subject, was that we were never able to get from the DoE exemplifications of the precise impact which the community charge would have . . . [we wanted] a house-by-house comparison with the rates paid by householders in several streets in a sample area . . . but the Department resisted it.[124]

Instead officials provided theoretical community charge figures for whole local authorities.

The setting up of E(LF) demarcated its members from ministers who were not members. Geoffrey Howe describes how, as Foreign Secretary, he had not been at all involved in the poll tax – he was 'not on any of the relevant economic committees' – and when he became Deputy Prime Minister in July 1989, he found that the committee 'had long since acquired a jargon-laden life of its own. It was much too late for me to be admitted to the club'.[125] In effect the activities of the group had 'fashioned' a deeper structure – internally cohesive, with most members acquiring what Norman Fowler describes in another case as a 'collective loyalty to the proposals made',[126] and, perhaps, an interest in maintaining the exclusivity of the club. A 'cleavage' was formed between insiders and outsiders. Howe evidently felt inhibited from attempting to contribute. (Such an attempt might have exposed him to the charge that he was upset at having been excluded.) Even those who were members might have felt inhibited: Fowler, a member of E(LF), makes no comment whatever on the process in his memoirs, from which we may perhaps infer that he did not play a significant part in its proceedings.

Lawson was evidently not party to any 'bonding' that took place among members of E(LF): he found he had no allies among the other senior members of E(LF), and, he says, came to view the poll tax issue as being outside his domain, outside his 'own range of ministerial responsibilities'.[127] As we have seen, Lawson's observations on the political consequences of switching from the rates to a poll tax failed to make a mark on the Green Paper. This failure is mirrored by what appears to have been something of a cleavage between Thatcher and Lawson – an absence of shared interests and commitment, and of linkages of mutual obligation and dependence. Lawson writes that at this time she boasted to journalists about how she had 'seen him off',[128] and he appears to have been affronted by the ignoring of his advice that the poll tax was likely to be a disaster. Subsequently his personal interest appears to have been in dissociating himself from it. (He makes the point in his memoirs that when the Local Government Finance Bill was tabled in the House of Commons his name was not on it as one of its 'backers' – supporters – as would normally have been the case for a major financial Bill.)

After the publishing of the Green Paper, we see Thatcher at the centre of a wider radial network, with linkages to Cabinet colleagues, backbench MPs and party activists (in the setting of the party conference). Over dual running, the linkages were used to exert pressure on *her*, rather than being used by her to exert pressure on others, and E(LF) appears to have operated over this issue in a much more collegiate fashion, less dominated by her, than have other such committees. A number of factors, singly or in conjunction, may have operated here: her seeming lack of a strong commitment to a particular course of action; her knowledge that she had an ally in Ridley at the head of the DoE; possibly a felt dependence on her Cabinet colleagues, as on her backbench MPs; anticipation that she would need to call on allies for a much more difficult battle, over the issue of tailoring the poll tax to ability to pay. Other relevant links connected Thatcher to people in the wider political system with whom she had sympathies: widows and other people living alone, and shopkeepers, whom she felt had been 'squeezed dry' by 'socialist councils'.

Over the Mates amendment, however, we see the conventional structure of the governing party in Parliament mobilized to inhibit dissent. The interest of many backbench MPs in advancement, in staying on good terms with the officers of their constituency party and with their fellow MPs and in not being labelled disloyal and held responsible for any Parliamentary disaster, rendered them highly dependent on the Prime Minister and the whips, who were in a position to frustrate these interests of theirs. Newly elected MPs could be expected to be particularly vulnerable.

THE FINANCIAL MEASURES

the financial measures with which I am concerned here are:

- the 1989 public expenditure allocation of funds to Revenue Support Grant for English local authorities for 1990–1;
- schemes for alleviating the short-term impact of the poll tax – money for preparation costs, transitional relief etc. and exemptions for particular categories of people;
- the Department of the Environment's calculations of Standard Spending Assessments for individual local authorities.

Public expenditure allocations

Rationale

In deciding the amount of the English Revenue Support Grant (RSG), a judgement had to be made. Ministers appear to have had three main related objectives: to hold down the total of local authority spending, to keep poll tax charges down, and to ensure that local authorities did not take advantage of the changeover to put up their spending and blame the Government. The decision appears to have been reached largely on the basis of the first and third of these. Baker writes that his colleagues were preoccupied with the objective of controlling public expenditure,[129] but Thatcher makes it clear that the third objective too was a major one for her.[130] As for the second, it wasn't possible to calculate reliably the implications for poll tax charges of allocating different amounts to the RSG, because too many unknowns were involved. As a result, those implications appear to have been ignored: the figure arrived at by the Cabinet at the meeting in July 1989 was not derived from them. This in turn had the result that real-world considerations, to do with the impact of the changeover on individual payers and households, played little part in ministers' rationale.

Interests

The decision on the 1989 public expenditure allocation to the RSG was taken on the basis of a very 'aggregated' view of the consumer interests involved. In a sense it balanced the interests of the taxpayer against those of the recipient of and payer for local services, but there was no registering of the interests of particular groups within those all-encompassing categories. Instead it appears to have been dominated by Thatcher's and Lawson's personal interests – which here coincided – in holding down local authority spending and in preventing local authorities from taking advantage of the changeover, and by Lawson's interest in preserving his freedom to make future cuts in income tax. Their interests overrode Baker's interest as a 'midwife' of the poll tax in seeing it introduced smoothly and being accepted: the extra money that he saw as being necessary to achieve that outcome was not made available. The interests of other 'spending ministers' in defending their departmental budgets coincided with the interests of Thatcher and Lawson. These political/institutional interests evidently took priority over the interests of those poll-tax payers who would lose by the changeover.

Process

A significant step in the process of reaching the decision was evidently a meeting or series of meetings between Ridley, Lawson and Thatcher, at which, according to Baker, Ridley was 'talked out of' asking for more money and 'forced to agree to the lower figure'. It is perhaps conceivable that Ridley might have put up more resistance, and achieved a better result for poll-tax payers, if he had had the support of other ministers in this confrontation. As a consequence of the preliminary 'bilateral' meeting, it was left to Baker to ask for more at the 'crucial' meeting at Number 10 on 22 June 1989 and again at the Cabinet meeting on 12 July.

Structure

The figure finally decided reflects the centrality and dominance of Prime Minister and Chancellor where public expenditure decisions are concerned. Not only was it difficult for other ministers to challenge their judgement, lacking as they did the means of exerting pressure upon the two of them: the others had their own interests – arising out of the departmental structure of central government – in minimizing the share of the public expenditure 'cake' that went to local government. Moreover, Thatcher and Lawson also had the power to decide the sequence of decisions and, as it transpired, thereby to prevent the formation of an effective coalition between Ridley and Baker.

Alleviation schemes

Two schemes for alleviating the impact of the poll tax are of particular interest. One, announced on 19 July 1989 at the same time as the RSG settlement, involved modifying the safety-net arrangements, so that authorities which gained under the Act (from the formula for distributing RSG and the product of the national non-domestic rate) would not then have those gains reduced so much – via the 'self-financing adjustments' mentioned in the Green Paper – to compensate authorities which lost. Instead those which lost most heavily would receive a new 'extra protection grant', at a total cost to the Exchequer of £100 million.[131]

The second alleviation scheme, pressed for by Patten, reluctantly agreed to by Lawson (the cost was a further £345 million) at a Cabinet committee meeting in late September, and announced by David Hunt to the Conservative Party Conference on 11 October 1989, was for 'transitional relief' to compensate households (as opposed to authorities) that would lose from the changeover. The effect would be, he said, that no household of one or two adults would pay more than £3 per week above its rates bill for 1989–90. The relief would be phased out over three years.[132] It later transpired that the £3 figure was based on the Government's *assumed* poll tax figures, which were appreciably less than those anticipated by the local authorities, and that the difference would have to be met by the poll-tax payers. In November 1989 councils were anticipating that the gap would average £1 per week for every payer, so a two-adult household could be paying £5 per week more. For higher-spending authorities, the increase could be much more.[133]

Rationale and interests

The rationale behind modifying the safety net was overtly political: it was designed to reduce the extent to which Conservative-controlled authorities received less than what would be their due under the new RSG formula, while some Labour-controlled authorities received more. Such a change would in turn reduce opposition to the poll tax from Conservative MPs and local councillors and voters. It was thus in the interests of the Government, the MPs and other prospective beneficiaries. That change would deprive low-rated (and Labour-controlled) authorities in the North of England, and the award to them of 'extra protection grant' recognized this.

The 'transitional relief' scheme directed relief to individual households rather than to local authorities. According to Butler *et al.*, it was the product of the work of a group chaired by a senior Cabinet Office official, which was convinced that 'the problem of losing *households* was far more important than the political hue-and-cry created by Conservative authorities which were having to finance the safety net. Ironically, one of the worst-affected groups was pensioners living in low-rated properties'.[134] Whether it was viewed as a matter of justice or of not alienating support for the Government, it is clear that the scheme was seen as being in the interests of losing groups. (Interestingly, four years earlier Lawson had cited the example of a pensioner couple in Inner London paying 22 per cent of their net income in poll tax in his memorandum of 16 May 1985 as a 'horrifying' instance of the impact of the new tax.[135])

It is apparent, however, that with the party conference due to be held shortly, presentational considerations were to the forefront of ministers' minds. We do not know whether or not Hunt and other ministers genuinely believed that the transitional relief scheme *would* keep the extra costs to households of one or two adults down to £3 per week, but it is clear that Hunt's claim that it would do so was a misrepresentation of the inevitable outcome.

Process

The modifications to the safety net were clearly a response to pressures: they followed on pressures from backbench Conservative MPs for precisely those changes. The 'transitional relief' scheme, however, appears to have been developed by officials[136] in anticipation that the impact of the poll tax on low-income households who had previously been paying low rates would become a major issue for the Government.

We saw earlier in this chapter that Thatcher's 'real' aim appeared to be to design a structure of local finance whereby local authorities would be blamed for spending above the 'target' set by the Government. Thatcher had assumed, when the poll tax was being developed, that if local authorities persisted with high levels of spending, the blame for the resultant high community charges would fall on them rather than the Government. (She was not pleased in April 1990 when 'that was not in fact happening. The public were blaming us.'[137]) In this context, Hunt's announcement of the 'transitional relief' scheme is consistent with an attempt to place blame for poll tax bills that would be more than £3 per week above rates bills (for a household of one or two adults) upon local authorities rather than the Government. It can be seen, then, as a move in a game of 'place the blame'. At the very least, the onus would be upon the local authorities rather than the Government to explain the higher charge.

Power structure

The modifications to the safety net in response to pressures from Conservative MPs and others can be seen as reflecting the dependence of ministers upon their supporters inside and outside Parliament. They can also be seen as reflecting the position of MPs as intermediaries between constituency parties and local councillors on the one hand and ministers on the other, and dependent on the support of the former (as well as on the electorate) for retaining their seat in Parliament. Their interest in remaining MPs, in addition to any genuine concern for the welfare of their constituents, thus gave them an interest in being – and in being seen as – effective advocates of local interests.

We also have a glimpse of the position of the Cabinet Office, creating a cross-departmental team led by one of its own officials to address an issue facing the Government, in contrast to the team wholly within the DoE which invented and developed the poll tax.

Standard Spending Assessments

Under the new legislation, a Standard Spending Assessment (SSA) was to be calculated annually for each English authority using a formula established by the Environment Secretary. An SSA represents the Secretary of State's view of what a local authority needs to spend to provide a standard level of service *consistent with a given spending total for all authorities.* (So it is essentially a means of sharing out the total Revenue Support Grant.) It takes account of the social, demographic and geographical characteristics of the authority's area and the functions for which it is responsible.[138] The formula for calculating an SSA was used to put authorities with different needs on the same footing: 'needs equalization'. (Needs were gauged by numbers of school-age children, elderly people etc., and measures of special circumstances, such as 'social and economic disadvantage' and a population distributed over a large area.) So the theory was that if each local authority spent its SSA amount they would all be delivering the same level of service. In that (hypothetical) situation, to raise funds for that spending, they would receive their population-related share of the National Non-Domestic Rate, and the Government would give each one enough RSG to allow all of them, across the country, to charge the same level of poll tax. (The RSG was thus a means of 'resource equalization'.) Consequently the national poll tax level would also be set by the Government. It was anticipated that an authority's income from the poll tax would meet about one-quarter of its expenditure on services. If its actual expenditure exceeded its SSA amount, all of the excess would have to be met from the poll tax: 100 per cent instead of 25 per cent.

Rationale and interests

How was the SSA formula arrived at? When the DoE published the list of SSAs, there were numerous complaints that these were insensitive to local circumstances, were out of date, and did not allow for the 'true' drivers of local costs: in other words, the perceptions on which they were based did not correspond accurately with reality. These and other 'problems' were discussed in a study by the Audit Commission, published in 1993, which drew attention to the part played in the calculations by the ingredient of value judgements and the way in which this was concealed by the formulae:

> Some in local government allege political bias by ministers. One example cited is the decision in 1991 to allow the weighting for visitor nights to be doubled. It is alleged that this decision was made in order to favour a particular local authority and provided evidence of bias in the use of SSAs by ministers. However, such allegations are not easy to demonstrate convincingly.[139]

However, such an allegation is consistent with behind-the-scenes lobbying of the then Environment Secretary by the leaders of Westminster City Council, the authority concerned, that took place prior to the decision: it is also consistent with the complex setting of the capping formula in 1990–1 in such a way that no Conservative-controlled authority was affected.[140] The criterion was that councils whose spending was both 12½ per cent *and* £75 per head above their SSA amount would be capped: some Conservative councils met one criterion and others the other, but none met both.

The Audit Commission report continued:

> The use of formulae offers some safeguard against capricious ministerial behaviour but does not extinguish its possibility. Indeed, formulae, because they are little understood, can draw a disguising veil across the values which lie behind them. No formulation is value free, but formulae can disguise

what those values are. For example, SSAs for councils in Wales are calcu-lated on different formulae from SSAs for English councils. The two methods give different results.[141]

The Audit Commission showed that if SSAs for Welsh districts had been calcu-lated using the method used in England, five districts would have been assigned an SSA that was between 20 and 40 per cent less than that actually assigned to them, while for another five the assigned SSA would have been between 15 and 30 per cent higher. It follows that Environment ministers were in a position to choose the formula that produced the results that they wished, generally favour-ing Conservative councils which were cutting and contracting out services, while in terms of presentation giving the impression that the formula was an impartial one. The formula was evidently derived from other, political, objectives besides that of enabling local authorities to meet the needs of their areas. The disguised 'values' referred to by the Audit Commission were thus political ones.

Process and structure

The Audit Commission tells us:

Much work went into the initial creation of SSAs. The Needs Assessment Subgroup (NASG) met over 40 times in 1989 and considered over 140 papers written by various groups including DoE, other government depart-ments, local authority associations and university researchers. The NASG report was submitted to the Consultative Council on Local Government Finance (CCLGF) in July 1989 and the resulting Distribution Report, which set out details of the assessments to be used for 1990/91, was approved by Parliament in January 1990.[142]

Since then, there has existed an SSA Subgroup which submits a report to the CCLGF in September each year. It consists of representatives of the local auth-ority associations, the DoE and other government departments. The bulk of the research effort is provided by the DoE. 'The process is effectively controlled by DoE, which sets the agenda and chairs the meetings.'[143] But there was evidently considerably more 'input' from local government once the 1988 Act was on the statute book than there had been previously.

* * *

Conclusions

This case study has dealt with one policy, the legislative and other measures to which it gave rise, and the consequences when they took effect. It is a single and in some ways unique instance of policy making. But it sheds some light on what *can* happen in the course of policy making, especially 'behind the scenes'. The poll tax was presented in the Green Paper as the product of a rational selection between alternatives. The identifying and appraising of alternatives conforms in principle to the classic rational-actor model of decision making. But in this case each alternative, when envisaged in operation, elicited its own special criteria, and was assessed on those criteria too. The rejection of the possibility of a local income tax on the grounds that (in Baker's words) 'we can't have Labour Chancellors in town halls' did not come about through first thinking of the criterion 'there are not to be Labour Chancellors in town halls' and then applying it to all alternatives. And this criterion was a 'threshold' one, a constraint, not a scale on which a proposal could score high or low. Effectively, this and other constraints became apparent only in the process of imagining how proposed measures would work in practice.

Within her own frame of reference, Thatcher, at the Chequers seminar, made a rational choice, in the sense of selecting the option most consistent with her objectives and constraints once they had been identified. (As March and Simon argue, it is 'safest . . . to speak of rationality only relative to some specified frame of reference'.[144]) Her choice was based on what proved to be a considerable underestimate of what Community Charge levels would be in practice, but that does not detract from its rationality in this sense. (Whether the process of making that choice can appropriately be described as 'satisficing' is a matter of debate – certainly the element of seeking consistency was present – but it was certainly a 'process of elimination', to use a colloquial expression.)

But in the Green Paper the point is also made that the search for the best local tax had been an attempt to reconcile conflicting objectives: the 'redistributive principle' and the 'beneficial principle'. No tax could satisfy both aims simultaneously.[145] Formulating proposals thus entailed resolving a dilemma. This is a different matter from 'satisficing' or achieving the highest benefit on a single criterion.

The poll tax proposal was presented in the Conservatives' 1987 election manifesto as 'fairer' than the rates, and in the Green Paper as a measure for strengthening the democratic accountability of local authorities. But in the Green Paper, data on likely gainers and losers were deliberately presented in such a way – 'lumping together' single-adult and multi-adult households, and applying statistical 'adjustments' – as to make it impossible for householders and politicians alike to gauge its likely impact and make their own judgement of the 'fairness' of the proposals. Evidently presentational considerations – in this case concealing the impact on not-quite-poor multi-adult households – took priority over the accurate conveying of information in a document ostensibly intended to elicit public comment. In ministers' public statements, the unfairness of the rates system was highlighted by citing the injustice done to widows, single pensioners and single parent families, i.e. by comparing households on the basis of the number of adults, not their income.

What were the 'real' objectives of Thatcher and her ministers? We have seen that for Thatcher the poll tax was a means by which central government could hold down local spending, which had been growing inexorably, year after year. The Act did this by creating a new structure, a new set of relationships between central government, local authorities and electors. It allowed central government to prescribe how much an authority ought to spend, and effectively required any spending on services above that level to be financed entirely by the poll tax. Thatcher herself writes that 'we had assumed that if authorities persisted with high levels of spending, the blame for the resultant high community charges would fall on them rather than the Government'.[146] In effect, ministers and officials had constructed a mechanism (a) to exert pressure on local authorities to keep their spending within the prescribed limits, and (b) to blame them if they didn't. The lever for exerting pressure was that the authority, when it came to deciding the level of poll tax, would be responsible for inflicting hardship on people with low and modest incomes if it were to set a high poll tax. If it nevertheless did set a high poll tax, it – rather than the Government which had prescribed the limits – would take the blame. (People with high incomes would be paying a smaller proportion of their income in poll tax and so would be less sensitive to its level.)

This mechanism appears to have been well understood by Thatcher, Lawson and Baker, all three of whom refer to 'blame' in their writings. For each of them it appears to have raised different considerations. For Thatcher, it raised presentational considerations, which were dealt with by stressing 'accountability' and 'fairness'. For Lawson, it raised practical and political considerations: a poll tax would be 'completely unworkable and politically catastrophic'. For Baker, it was the transition to a poll tax that raised political considerations: a single-step changeover would have 'acute political consequences' and risk 'asking too much too quickly and [bringing] the whole system down'.[147] For none of them does the nature of the mechanism – its use of the inflicting of hardship – appear to have raised ethical considerations. Indeed, for Thatcher the compulsory 20 per cent contribution denoted that a 'whole class of people – an "underclass" if you will – had been dragged back into . . . responsible society and asked to become not just dependants but citizens'.[148] That they had to purchase their 'citizenship' out of low and modest incomes appears not to have been a relevant factor for her.

Unfortunately for the Government, and for Thatcher in particular, while the 'blame mechanism' might conceivably have worked as intended once the system was well established, in the short term electors were aware not only of high poll tax charges but also of the unequal impact of the changeover. People with high incomes were not only paying a smaller proportion of their income in poll tax: if they lived in high-rated homes they would have gained, perhaps greatly, from the changeover. Blame for this situation was placed by many electors on the Government that created the system: 'The public were blaming us.'[149] Two sets of levers, the dependence of Thatcher on the support of her fellow Conservative MPs and the dependence of those MPs on the support of electors, provided a mechanism by which, taking advantage of the opportunity afforded by the leadership contest, pressure was ultimately successfully exerted on Thatcher to resign.

On the face of it, Thatcher and her ministers and officials saw 'consumers' in socio-economic terms: household type and size, and income. Behind the scenes, however, officials were concerned with the impact on people living in different regions and in 'shires and cities' – which was code for 'Tory and Labour voters'.[150] And Thatcher reveals a completely different categorization when writing about the events of April 1990: now she was distinguishing groups according to whether they supported the Conservatives, referring to 'our own people', 'people who had always looked to me for protection from exploitation by the socialist state . . . who were by no means well off and who had scrimped and saved to buy their homes', and people in middle income groups, the 'conscientious middle'.[151]

We have also seen something of the political/institutional interests of ministers and officials: of Thatcher, Baker and Ridley in bringing about the conclusive defeat of socialist councils and winning the acclaim of their supporters; of Lawson's interest in defending his autonomy as Chancellor; of Waldegrave's personal interests in winning Thatcher's favour and in finding a 'theoretically elegant' way of solving the problem set him; of the DoE officials in the studies team in assisting him to find such a solution and in doing it on their own, shutting out other departments; and of the interests of individual MPs in holding on to their seats and of party activists in belonging to the winning party.

As in the manifesto case study, we have seen something of the power of the Prime Minister to set up *ad hoc* meetings – the Chequers seminar – and of the commitment on her part and the mandate given to officials that resulted. The Baker–Waldegrave case for a poll tax had a monopoly of access to the decision-making 'arena'. In an atmosphere of 'something must be done', Thatcher became committed to the poll tax, on the basis of an estimate of the average poll tax level which would later prove to be a very poor guide to what the actual level would be in 1990–1, and in the absence of information about its likely impact in terms of gainers and losers. The DoE officials too, it appears, became strongly committed to the poll tax in the course of their work: their concealment of the likely politically explosive repercussions of the poll tax is consistent with this.

Another important observation is that the Government's strong commitment to the central proposals in the Green Paper belied its labelling as 'Green', conventionally taken to denote that the proposals put forward are tentative ones. The scope for modifying them it appears to have been correspondingly small, and representations from local government had very little effect on the legislative proposals that were tabled in Parliament. And because of the misleading presentation of the impact in terms of gainers and losers, it was very difficult for outsiders to gauge its likely consequences and mobilize a campaign against it.

Over dual running, however, there was less commitment (the Green Paper proposed phasing out the rates 'over a period up to ten years') and correspondingly more scope for influencing the policy. We have seen that its ultimate abandonment came about through the exerting of pressure from outside the Government in conjunction with lack of commitment and fresh doubts about its wisdom inside: the latter evidently enabled (provided an opportunity for) the pressure to make a mark.

The passing of the legislation, still with very little information about gainers and losers, presupposed that the necessary funds for a smooth changeover would be available and implied a commitment to making them available. But when ministers came to take a decision on the RSG, that decision was effectively taken by Thatcher and Lawson on the basis not of ensuring a smooth changeover but of giving priority to holding the RSG down and preventing local authorities from taking advantage of the changeover, to the extent even of under-providing for inflation. Realistic estimates of the likely impact on households of different kinds, of different incomes or on Income Support, and living in properties of high or low rateable value, in different local authority areas, appear to have played little or no part in the decision.

Chapter seven

CONSULTATION AND PRESSURE: REFORMING SOCIAL SECURITY IN THE MID-1980s

Introduction

The Social Security Act 1986 brought considerable changes to the social security system in the UK. While some low-paid wage-earners with children gained from them, many people on low pay or pensions, or without paid work, found the cash support they received from the state reduced or removed. Someone facing an emergency with no means of support no longer had an entitlement to receive help: only a discretionary loan was on offer, from the new 'Social Fund', and only to those who were judged able to repay it. And the State Earnings-Related Pension Scheme, which supplemented the basic state pension, was sharply curtailed.

This is an interesting case study, for several reasons. As with the poll tax, a 'triangle' of ministers was involved, and again the Prime Minister (Thatcher) and Chancellor of the Exchequer (Lawson) were in disagreement over what should be done, but this time the dispute was resolved much sooner. The Secretary of State for Social Services, Norman Fowler, whose responsibility social security was, was low in the Cabinet 'pecking order', and social security spending was under attack from the Chancellor. But he pursued, both publicly and in private, strategies which enabled him to gain a certain amount of what he wanted. Both his successes and his failures are worthy of study.

Two valuable ministerial sources for this case study are Fowler's memoirs, *Ministers Decide*,[1] and those of Lawson.[2] A critical analysis of the reforms – both substance and process – is contained in *Punishing the Poor: Poverty under Thatcher*, by Kay Andrews and John Jacobs.[3] Andrews had worked in the House of Commons as a senior researcher in education and social policies, and then became a policy adviser to the opposition Labour leader, Neil Kinnock; Jacobs was a lecturer at Sussex University and a member of a social security appeals tribunal. Although their book uses polemical language in describing ministerial statements and behaviour, it clearly draws on detailed knowledge of the workings of the social security system and contains a great deal of useful factual material (supported by a model 'notes and sources' section) on the content of the policy and Act and the consequences of the latter. The judgemental words and expressions – 'totally', 'blatant', 'swindle', 'ludicrously', 'sheer hypocrisy' and so on – are easily enough recognized and treated with caution. There is also a single-chapter case study by Michael Adler of Edinburgh University,[4] which is particularly useful on the consultations and the Government's response to them, but having been written from the outside and before the ministerial memoirs were published, it perforce treats 'the Government' as a monolithic whole, which Fowler and Lawson reveal to have been far from the case. Unfortunately his approach is thematic rather than analytical (he begins 'It is the burden of this chapter to show . . .'), but he makes good use of government and political publications, studies by academics and campaigning groups, and contemporary press reports.

On the 1986 Act itself, the authoritative work is a law text, not a social policy one: the third edition of Ogus and Barendt's *The Law of Social Security.*[5] It contains all the necessary detail yet is very clearly written. It also relates the provisions of the Act to the pre-existing situation and to the relevant proposals in the Green and White Papers that preceded the act.

The next section of this chapter contains an outline history of the 'Fowler reforms'. After a section on the policy and measures, there follow four sections examining them – as in the previous case study chapters – from each of the four perspectives. A concluding section highlights the main findings.

The story

The salient features of the social security system as it existed in 1983 are shown in bare outline in Box 7.1. Some of them were 'inherited' from the 1974–9 Labour Government, notably Child Benefit and the State Earnings-Related Pension Scheme (SERPS). SERPS pensions supplemented the basic state pension, and both were financed mainly on a 'pay-as-you-go' basis by the taxes and National Insurance contributions being paid by people in work at the time, rather than from a fund built up by contributions paid in advance during the pensioner's working life. A range of income-related (i.e. 'means-tested') benefits were provided under the Supplementary Benefits scheme, which had been restructured by the Conservatives' own Social Security Act 1980. Among other things, this Act had changed the basis for deciding the amounts of single ('one-off') payments and regular weekly additions awarded to claimants in particular circumstances. Instead of officials in local offices of the Department of Health and Social Security (DHSS) exercising their discretion, guided by a set of internal instructions, as had previously been the case, there were detailed rules of entitlement, set down in published volumes of Regulations which – as Statutory Instruments – had the force of law. This change had been prompted by the rapid rise during the 1970s in the number of discretionary additions, both

Box 7.1   The social security system and proposals for change

	The Social Security system prior to 1986	The 'Wilton Park' proposals
Pensions for people above retirement age	State pension, comprising a basic flat-rate component (the same for everybody) and an additional component related to earnings prior to retirement, under the State Earnings-Related Pension Scheme (SERPS).	SERPS to be abolished. 'The second pension should come from a variety of new options in the private sector which we would make available.'
Weekly payments to people not in work	Supplementary Benefit, means-tested: basic rates plus weekly additions for a claimant's special needs.	Supplementary Benefit to be replaced by Income Support.
'One-off' payments to people not in work to meet immediate needs	Single payments under the Supplementary Benefit system.	The 'much-abused system of single payment' under the Supplementary Benefit system to be replaced by 'a Social Fund'.
Weekly payments to people in low-paid work who have respon-sibilities for children	Family Income Supplement, means-tested, paid to mother (book of cashable orders).	Family Income Supplement to be replaced by Family Credit 'so that people could no longer be worse off in work than on the dole'.
Weekly payments in respect of children	Child Benefit, for all children, irrespective of family income, paid to mother (order book).	Child Benefit to stay.
Weekly payments towards housing costs	Housing Benefit, means-tested.	Housing Benefit to be reformed so that it did not discriminate against the low-paid in work.

reen Paper	The White Paper and Social Security Bill	The Social Security Act 1986
►S to be abolished. ›ulsory for all earners to ‐ribe to an occupational k) or private pension scheme: ‹quirement for these to be ‹on-proofed.	SERPS to be retained but in a less advantageous form. Financial and other inducements to companies to set up their own schemes and to individuals to acquire personal pensions: element of compulsion withdrawn.	No significant change from the Bill.
‐ne Support to replace ‹ementary Benefit: standard ‹nal allowances (but lower ‹or people under 25) plus a ‹um depending on the ‹ant's 'client group'; weekly ‹ons for special needs ended.	Income Support proposals to go ahead with some amendments (e.g. lower personal allowances for people under 25 to apply to single persons only).	No significant change from the Bill.
‹able loans and (in certain ‹ grants from a 'Social Fund' ‹lace Supplementary Benefit ‹ payments: amount to be ‹nined by judgements of ‹list officers working within a ‹budget: no provision for ‹endent review of decisions.	Social Fund proposals to go ahead, but with provision for internal review of decisions by Social Fund Inspectors.	No major change from the Bill, but the right to have decisions reviewed was marginally strengthened.
‹y Credit to replace Family ‹e Supplement: to be paid by ‹yer (who would be ‹ursed) in the wage packet, ‹ting income tax and National ‹nce contributions; higher than Family Income ‹ement.	Family Credit proposals to go ahead, with some modifications.	One major change from the Bill: Family Credit to be paid not via the pay packet but direct to the mother (as with its precursor, Family Income Supplement).
‹Benefit to continue; no ‹itment to index link.	Child Benefit: no modification.	No legislative change to Child Benefit.
‹ng Benefit to be aligned with ‹e Support (similar ‹ment rules, assessment to ‹ed on income after tax, not ‹); students to be excluded ‹laiming; the same 'taper' for ‹ng the rent and rates ‹nents of Housing Benefit as ‹e rose above 'needs' level; ‹ne on Income Support and ‹ Credit to pay at least 20 per ‹ their rates.	Housing Benefit proposals to go ahead, except that rent and rates tapers would be different.	No significant change from the Bill.

weekly and 'one-off', paid to claimants of Supplementary Benefit over and abovethe normal weekly rates: the point had been reached where the scheme was expensive to administer and frequently produced different awards for people in similar circumstances, especially if they lived in different parts of the country.[6]

Also in existence was the Housing Benefit scheme for helping people on low incomes with their housing costs. It was set up by the Conservative Government under the Social Security and Housing Benefit Act 1982. Administered by local housing authorities, it was intended to integrate the housing element of Supplementary Benefit and local authorities' own rent and rate rebate schemes. However, its implementation is widely acknowledged to have brought 'widespread chaos and administrative difficulties'.[7]

In Box 7.2 is shown a chronology of 'landmark' events from Fowler's appointment in September 1981 as Secretary of State for Social Services, at the head of the DHSS, to May 1988, just after the coming into effect of the Act. Fowler appears to have done little work on social security prior to the 1983 general election – the Conservative manifesto said virtually nothing about social security – but, having been reappointed to his post, he soon became more active. In September 1983, he called a conference on pensions at the DHSS headquarters, to which he invited 'the pensions establishment' and others, and two months after that, in November 1983, he announced the setting up of an Inquiry into Provision for Retirement, which he personally would chair. A Review of Housing Benefit was announced in February 1984 and began work two months later: it comprised a three-person 'review team' chaired by the chairman of a new town development corporation, who was also Deputy Chairman of the Abbey National Building Society. It was followed in April 1984 by two more reviews – the Review of Benefits for Children and Young People, and the Review of Supplementary Benefit – both chaired by ministers. The full membership of the teams and their terms of reference are shown in Box 7.3.[8] All four review teams were to 'aim to identify the needs which should be provided for and consider how, within the resource constraints we face, those needs can most sensibly be met'.[9] Each team produced a summary of what it saw as the main issues in its area, and this was made available to organizations and individuals who requested it. All the teams received a great deal of written evidence and also held public sessions at which they heard oral evidence from invited witnesses, to whom they also put questions.[10]

The consultations were concluded by the end of July 1984. Six months later, in January 1985, Fowler held a conference with all the review teams and his special advisers and civil servants at Wilton Park, in Sussex, and then embarked on the drafting of what became the Green Paper. There then ensued, spread over the three months February to April 1985, a series of meetings of an *ad hoc* Cabinet committee – MISC 111 – chaired by Margaret Thatcher and comprising 'half the Cabinet':[11] it would be 'going through the proposals almost line by line'.[12] This committee's deliberations took place against the background of the early stages of the current public spending round, and pressure from the Chancellor and the Chief Secretary to the Treasury, who in late February 1985 were

Box 7.2 Chronology: the review and reform of social security 1983–1988

September 1981 — Fowler appointed Secretary of State for Social Services.

9 June 1983 — General election. Conservatives stay in power. Their manifesto contains no proposals for legislation on social security.

September 1983 — Fowler holds a conference on pensions at the DHSS headquarters.

End November 1983 — Fowler sets up and announces inquiry into occupational pensions (Inquiry into Provision for Retirement), chaired by himself. It would consider written submissions and take oral evidence at public sessions.

February 1984 — Fowler announces setting-up of Housing Benefit Review.

2 April 1984 — Fowler announces setting-up of Review of Benefits for Children and Young People and Supplementary Benefit Review.

April–December 1984 — Review teams take evidence and write reports.

January 1985 — Wilton Park seminar attended by review teams (including social security ministers), advisers and officials: 'outline of the report decided'.

6 February 1985 — First meeting of *ad hoc* Cabinet committee (MISC 111) on proposed social security reforms, chaired by the Prime Minister.

13 February 1985 — Second meeting of MISC 111.

14 February 1985 — Pre-Budget meeting of Cabinet. Lawson warns public spending 'still too high'.

22 February 1985 — Minute from Chancellor and Chief Secretary to the Prime Minister: The Government should aim to save £2 billion from the social security review by 1987–8.

Early April 1985 — 'Final' meeting of MISC 111.

2 and 9 May 1985 — Cabinet agrees proposals.

3 June 1985 — Green Paper (*Reform of Social Security*) published; Fowler makes announcement to House of Commons. Report of the Housing Benefit Review Team also published.

16 September 1985 — Consultation period on Green Paper ends.

15 October 1985 — MISC 111 meets again, agrees to drop the proposal for compulsory private pensions for all.

Just before Christmas 1985 — White Paper (*Reform of Social Security: Programme for Action*), setting out the Government's proposals for legislation, published.

17 January 1986 — Social Security Bill tabled in the House of Commons.

28 January 1986	Bill receives its Second Reading in the Commons.
22 May 1986	Bill goes to House of Lords.
21 July 1986	Bill returned to House of Commons, with Lords amendments.
23 July 1986	Commons accepts one Lords amendment, deletes others, adds new amendments. Bill returned to House of Lords.
24 July 1986	House of Lords considers Commons amendments, does not resist them.
25 July 1986	Social Security Bill receives Royal Assent.
March 1987	Draft Social Fund Manual published.
May 1987	Fowler gives undertaking to compensate Income Support claimants for their 20 per cent rates payments.
11 June 1987	General election. Conservatives stay in power. Fowler subsequently replaced by Moore at DHSS.
October 1987	'Impact tables' published.
11 April 1988	Main provisions of Social Security Act 1986 come into force.
April–May 1988	Outcry over Housing Benefit rules: eligibility qualifications relaxed.

Box 7.3   Social security review teams and terms of reference

INQUIRY INTO PROVISION FOR RETIREMENT

To study the future development, adequacy and costs of state, occupational and private provision for retirement in the United Kingdom including the portability of pension rights, and to consider possible changes in those arrangements taking account of the recommendations of the Select Committee on Social Services in their report on retirement age.

N. Fowler, Secretary of State for Social Services
R. Boyson, Minister of State for Social Security (to Sept. 1984)
T. Newton, Minister of State for Social Security (from Sept. 1984)
R. Whitney, B. Hayhoe, Minister of State, Treasury
P. Morrison, Minister of State, Dept of Employment
A. Fletcher, Parliamentary Under-Secretary of State, Dept of Trade and Industry
S. Lyon, General Manager (Finance) of Legal and General Assurance and President of the Institute of Actuaries
M. Field, General Manager and Actuary of Phoenix Assurance and Chairman of the Life Offices' Association and of the Occupational Pensions Schemes Joint Working Group
A. Peacock, Vice-Chancellor, University of Buckingham
M. Weinberg, Chairman of Hambro Life (sub-group on personal pensions only).

HOUSING BENEFIT REVIEW

To examine the structure and scope of the housing benefit scheme to ensure it is as simple as possible, and that help is concentrated on those most in need; and to improve its administration by local authorities.

J. Rowe, Chairman of Peterborough Development Corporation and Deputy Chairman, Abbey National Building Society
A. Blakemore, formerly Chief Executive, London Borough of Croydon
Rhea Martin, Lecturer in Law at Hatfield Polytechnic and a Vice-Chair of the National Association of Citizens' Advice Bureaux.

REVIEW OF BENEFITS FOR CHILDREN AND YOUNG PEOPLE

To review the present social security arrangements for giving financial help to families with children, and young people above school-leaving age.

R. Boyson, Minister of State for Social Security (to Sept. 1984)
N. Fowler, Secretary of State for Social Services (from Sept. 1984)
Barbara Shenfield, associated with the Women's Royal Voluntary Service
T. G. Parry Rogers, Director, Personnel and Europe, Plessey Company.

SUPPLEMENTARY BENEFIT REVIEW

To review the scope of the scheme and consider the scope for easing its administration.

T. Newton, Minister for the Disabled and Parliamentary Under-Secretary of State for Social Security (to Sept. 1984), Minister of State for Social Security (from Sept. 1984)
R. Wendt, Chief Executive, Cheshire County Council, and member of the Social Security Advisory Committee
B. Collins, Chairman, Nabisco Brands Ltd.

Source: Cmnd 9519 (1985) *Reform of Social Security: Background Papers*, p. 131. London: HMSO.

asking for a cut of £2 billion in social security spending by 1987–8. Fowler writes that with the Prime Minister's support he was able to fend off this demand. By April 'we had certainly made some fully justified cuts in Housing Benefit, but these were a very long way' from £2 billion.[13]

The Green Paper *Reform of Social Security*,[14] with its contents agreed by the Cabinet, was published on 3 June 1985. It set out 'the Government's proposals for a new and better structure for our social security system', including the abolition of SERPS. In its place employers and employees would be required to contribute to an occupational or personal pension. Published independently at the same time was the report of the Housing Benefit Review Team.[15] (The reports of the other review teams were not published.) The main proposals are shown in Box 7.1.

Immediately after the publication of the Green Paper, the House of Commons Select Committee on Social Services held an inquiry into the proposals.

In its report, published on 17 July 1985, it gave its own estimates of the likely gainers and losers from the proposed measures. It concluded that people who were young, single and unemployed were likely to lose most from the Income Support reforms, and elderly home-owners to lose most from the changes to Housing Benefit. The report expressed reservations about many of the proposals but also commended some aspects of them.[16]

The Green Paper invited responses, to be submitted by 16 September 1985. In total, more than 7,000 were received.[17] There was strong opposition to the proposals from a wide range of organizations.[18]

Three months after the closing date for responses to the Green Paper, just before Christmas 1985, a White Paper was published. It too bore the title *Reform of Social Security*, but was subtitled *Programme for Action*.[19] It was a definitive statement of intention. 'This White Paper sets out in detail the Government's decisions, and will form the basis of legislation which will be introduced soon.'[20] Its main proposals are also shown in Box 7.1. They mostly followed those of the Green Paper, with the significant exception that instead of SERPS being abolished, it was to be retained, but its cost was reduced – by lowering the payouts. Occupational pensions would not be compulsory, but, as Fowler put it, it would be easier for companies to set up their own schemes and everyone would have the right to a personal pension of their own. Unit trusts, building societies and banks would be able to provide personal pensions and Lawson agreed that as an incentive to join such a scheme those who opted out of SERPS and did so would be entitled to pay a reduced National Insurance contribution.[21] (In his March 1987 budget Lawson extended tax relief to payments into personal pension schemes.[22])

On 17 January 1986 the Social Security Bill was tabled in the House of Commons. In the Commons all attempts to amend the Bill were resisted and, with the use of the Government's majority, defeated. However, the Government suffered three significant defeats in the House of Lords. During the Lords stages the Social Security Consortium, an umbrella organization set up by 'poverty lobby' groups and other campaigning, voluntary, professional and local authority associations,[23] lobbied Peers and supplied them with briefs for use in debates. Its campaign against the Bill focused mainly on specific provisions, such as the abolition of free school meals, the 20 per cent domestic rates contribution, and the payment of Family Credit via the pay packet: the only general structural provision to be opposed was the setting up of the Social Fund. The Lords amended the Bill: (a) to provide for the payment of Family Credit to the mother rather than through the pay packet; (b) to provide for the right of appeal to an independent tribunal against the refusal of a Social Fund application; and (c) to remove the obligation on benefit recipients and others on low incomes to pay at least 20 per cent of their domestic rates bill. When the Bill came back to the Commons, the Government accepted the first of these amendments, used its majority to delete the second (but made a small concession), and used its majority again to delete the third but gave an undertaking to 'take into account the impact of [the 20 per cent compulsory rates payment] on the most vulnerable groups' when it came to set the levels for Income Support.[24]

After the Bill had received Royal Assent, and become an Act, in July 1986, the Secretary of State began to bring Regulations to Parliament setting out the more detailed provisions of the new schemes.[25] The Child Poverty Action Group summarized what happened in its evidence to the Hansard Society Commission on the legislative process in 1992:

> The Income Support (General) Regulations 1987, which contained all the main provisions concerning the operation of the Income Support scheme . . . came into force in April 1988. Meanwhile, the first amending Regulations came out on 31st March 1988 and between then and November 1988 there were eight sets of amending Regulations. During 1989, there were five sets of amending Regulations, three during 1990 and six during 1991 . . . The detail of the Family Credit scheme . . . is also contained in Regulations, and that scheme also saw five sets of amending Regulations during 1988.[26]

In March 1987 the DHSS published a draft Social Fund Manual, containing the directions and guidance under which it was proposed to operate the Fund. It laid down as an overriding principle that the total cost of payments made by a local office in any financial year must not exceed its allocated budget for that year. It also specified needs which it was appropriate to meet, conditions of eligibility, and criteria for determining priorities between applicants and needs. The draft manual was widely criticized. The Government-appointed Social Security Advisory Committee, set up under the Social Security Act 1980 to advise the Secretary of State, made it clear that the decision to proceed with the Social Fund substantially as planned 'is without our support'.[27]

In October 1987 – after the general election – the Government published 'impact tables'[28] showing: (a) the immediate effect of the impending benefit changes on existing claimants, who would receive some protection from 'transitional arrangements'; and (b) the effect on new claimants. The former tables showed that in certain categories (e.g. pensioners, lone parents, couples with children, and sick and disabled people) the great majority would not be worse off compared with what they were already receiving. (A comparison was not made with those figures uprated to take account of inflation: exceptionally, no such uprating took place in 1987.) The existing claimants would have their benefit frozen, if their circumstances stayed the same, until the benefits for new claimants had, with inflation, caught up with them. The tables for new claimants showed that overall the number of losers would exceed the number of gainers.

When the reforms took effect on 11 April 1988, claimants discovered for themselves how they would be affected by the changes. As Andrews and Jacobs relate, for many families with a parent in work the immediate cuts in Housing Benefit and the loss of free school meals more than offset the increases brought by the new Family Credit scheme.[29] Some 78 per cent of people transferring from Supplementary Benefit to Income Support, even with transitional protection, found themselves worse off because of the requirement to pay water rates and 20 per cent of their domestic rates bill. Pensioners too were hard hit by the cuts in Housing Benefit. Following protests, some concessions on eligibility for Housing Benefit were made in the following month, May 1988.

Other important decisions taken subsequent to the passing of the Act were to do with the Social Fund. In November 1987, John Moore, who had succeeded Fowler after the June general election as Secretary of State for Social Services, announced an allocation of £203 million for 1988–9 to the Fund, of which £140 million was for discretionary loans and £60 million for discretionary community care grants. These figures can be compared with the £346 million spent on single payments (grants) in 1985–6.[30] The total budget was allocated among DHSS local offices. The criteria by which this was done were not made explicit. It transpired that for 1988–9 some offices received only about 13 per cent of the amounts that they had paid out in single payments in 1986–7; others received 30, 40 or (in one case) 50 per cent.[31] Industrial cities in the North suffered most, retirement areas least.[32]

The policies and measures

Can the Green Paper be regarded as 'policy'? How committed was the Government to the reforms it outlined? In Fowler's preface and throughout the document they are described merely as 'proposals', but in other respects the language is more definite, the word 'will' being used extensively: 'All these changes *will* be carried through'[33] (my italics). And no alternatives were put forward, except to be summarily dismissed. It embodied the results of negotiations among Fowler, Thatcher and Lawson, and MISC 111, under Thatcher's chairmanship, had invested five months of meetings in going through Fowler's draft 'almost line by line'. There had already been one round of consultation, in the form of the reviews, and there was no obvious reason why ministers should want another. And the period allowed for responses covered the holiday season, which would make it difficult for some organizations to respond, and was timed to end in mid-September, by which time the drafting of the Bill would have to be well under way if it was to be introduced and complete its passage during the 1985–6 Parliamentary session. (The legislative programme for the next Parliamentary session would already have been decided.) So it appears that – as with the poll tax Green Paper – the Government was more strongly committed to the proposals than their Green Paper status, conventionally denoting tentativeness, would indicate.

Why, then, was the document not published as a White Paper? Seemingly a conscious choice was made to publish it in a green cover, and label it 'Green', rather than publish a White Paper straight away. Possibly this was intended to 'signal' that in some respects at least there was some room for modification (and so in itself constituted a withholding of commitment). If ministers anticipated that the pensions industry and employers would refuse to cooperate over the proposal to abolish SERPS, and/or that some provisions might fail to win enough backbench support to gain Parliamentary approval, publication as a Green Paper would give the Government the opportunity to make changes before the Bill was tabled in Parliament: to do so *after* that point would be more embarrassing and portrayed as a humiliating climb-down and a sign of weakness. Possibly the Cabinet was split – we know that Lawson was opposed to the proposal to abolish SERPS and make occupational pensions compulsory, as Thatcher was insisting – and publication as a Green rather than White Paper offered a way forward. For Lawson it would offer an 'escape route', for Thatcher and Fowler it would offer an opportunity to continue mobilizing support and accustoming everyone who would be affected to the inevitability of changes.

The subsequent White Paper was of course unmistakably a statement of definite intention, the Government being firmly committed to introducing legislation on its lines: in that sense it was manifestly 'policy'. And the Act and subsequent statutory Regulations constituted legislative measures, while spending allocations (including the one setting the total Social Fund budget) and the non-statutory directions issued by the Secretary of State (prescribing the working practices of those who administered the Social Fund) also fall within the definitions of 'policy' discussed in Chapter 3. Regulations, directions and budgetary constraints would also provide the context for 'local level policy', in the sense of the practices adopted by officials in DHSS local offices in exercising the discretion that they were allowed, especially in dispensing Social Fund monies.

The Green Paper, White Paper, Bill and Act dealt with the *structure* of the pension system and other parts of the social security system.[34] A stated purpose of their provisions was to 'bring the social security system firmly back under control.'[35] But it was the ensuing measures and policies that largely determined how the system operated in practice, and what cash help claimants would receive.

Rationale

Means and ends. We are dealing here with a succession of sets of proposals. All the proposals were justified in terms of objectives, although those that Fowler took to Wilton Park and those in the Green Paper were presented primarily as matters of principle, and/or to do with the system as a whole, while the objectives set out in the White Paper were expressed in terms of remedying the defects of the existing social security system. In all cases, however, the proposals focused on particular 'client groups' or kinds of benefit.

Fowler writes that he approached the Wilton Park conference with five 'objectives': (a) to achieve a social security system based on individual contributions as well as State provision; (b) to remove 'barriers – like National Insurance and pensions – which stand in the way of new employment and job mobility'; (c) to tackle 'real need' (it was low-income families with children – the families of the unemployed and low-wage earners – who were worst off); (d) to eliminate some of the complexity in the system; and (e) to achieve a better delivery system, with more cooperation with the tax system and better management. These would have to be achieved without spending more money: a 'cost-neutral' reform.[36]

Some of these objectives, albeit in rather different form, recurred in the Green Paper, which claimed to offer a new approach, that of 'a partnership between the individual and the state'. As Sir William Beveridge had argued in his report in 1942, state provision had an important role in supporting and sustaining the individual, but it should not discourage self-reliance or stand in the way of individual provision and responsibility. The Green Paper highlighted three main objectives:

First, the social security system must be capable of meeting genuine need . . . No individual should be left in a position where through no fault of his own he is unable to sustain himself or his family . . .

Second, the social security system must be consistent with the Government's overall objectives for the economy . . . Social security is already by far the largest government programme . . . It is responsible for a major share of the current heavy tax burden on individuals and companies . . . [Continued] growth of this burden could severely damage the prospects for economic growth. [The] social security system . . . is self-defeating if it creates barriers to the creation of jobs, to job mobility or to people rejoining the labour force. Clearly such obstacles exist if people believe themselves better off out of work than in work; or if employers regard the burden of national insurance as a substantial discouragement to providing new jobs. Equally restrictions in areas like pensions can discourage people from changing jobs. If we wish to encourage individuals to provide for themselves then the social security system – public and private – must not stand in their way.

Third, the social security system must be simpler to understand and easier to administer . . . [Today] the supplementary benefit system alone requires some 38,000 staff to administer it. The rules of entitlement are so complex that the manual of guidance to staff runs to two volumes and 16,000 paragraphs . . . All the main income-related benefits – supplementary benefit, housing benefit and family income supplement – use different measures of income and capital.[37]

(The claimed associations with Beveridge appear to have been Fowler's personal handiwork: in his statement to the House of Commons on 2 April 1984 announcing the social security reviews, he personally had inserted a sentence claiming that the reviews and studies amounted to 'the most substantial examination of the social security system since the Beveridge report forty years ago'.)

The presentation of objectives in the White Paper was very different from that in the Green Paper. It began not by enunciating principles but by stating the 'clear and fundamental . . . defects' of the social security system as it then was. Although the 'defects' were 'headlined' in general terms, specific instances were described too. In short:

1 Social security was too complex, requiring almost 40,000 staff to administer it, and mistakes were made, leaving the public dissatisfied if not bewildered.

2 It failed to give effective support to many of those in greatest need, especially low-income families with children.

3 It could leave too many people trapped in unemployment (because they were worse off in work than unemployed) or poverty (a pay rise at work can be largely offset – or more than offset – by the combined effect of increased deductions for tax and national insurance and reduced entitlement to benefits).

4 The rules prevented people from arranging their own personal pension which they can take from one job to another, and impeded the development of new occupational pension schemes.

5 The present system of state pensions was building up a very substantial financial debt to future pensioners, which – because 'tomorrow's contributors will pay for all of tomorrow's benefits' – it will fall to 'our children' to pay.[38]

Following this description of perceived 'defects', the White Paper set out principles for action that the Government would follow:

> The Government believe that the financial issues of pensions policy should be faced now, leaving future generations with the freedom to decide how best *they* want to allocate the resources which are then available. We believe that resources must be directed more effectively to areas of greatest need, notably low-income families with children. We want a system that is simpler to understand and better managed. We want sensible co-operation between the social security and tax systems. And we want a system which is consistent with the Government's overall objectives for the economy . . . Social security must not hinder [sustained economic] growth . . . [It] accounts for one third of all public spending. It cannot be ring fenced from the requirements of sensible management of the economy as a whole.[39]

(Incidentally, the style and language of the White Paper – the emphasis on 'defects' and 'facing issues', and expressions of personal commitment like 'we believe' – are noticeably different from those of the Green Paper, and Fowler does not claim authorship of the White Paper as he does of the Green Paper. It may be that the rewriting was undertaken by someone close to Thatcher and/or acting on her instructions – a member of the No. 10 Policy Unit, perhaps. Only the Prime Minister would have been able to authorize a White Paper commitment to cooperation between the social security and tax systems, with its implied curtailing of the Chancellor's prerogative over the latter.)

Did the policies and measures follow logically from the objectives, both concrete and abstract, which were set out? With regard to helping *families with children*, from the Wilton Park proposals to the Act it was consistently held that Child Benefit would stay and that there would be a new benefit, Family Credit, for families with children supported by someone on a low income. Fowler's Wilton Park objectives had included tackling 'real need', the Green Paper specified the objective of meeting 'genuine need', and the White Paper that of directing resources more effectively to areas of 'greatest need, notably low-income families with children',[40] but Child Benefit was – and would continue to be – available to *every* family with children, including families who were well able to meet the costs of bringing up their children. This is plainly inconsistent with the stated and restated objective of targeting families in 'need'. Keeping Child Benefit in its untargeted form was justified in the Green Paper as recognizing 'the additional costs all parents bear'.[41] The possibility of increasing it but means-testing or taxing it was rejected as likely to 'result in an unacceptable degree of "churning" (where the same people receive money through the benefit system and pay it back through the tax system) and means-testing'.[42] The White Paper added that increasing Child Benefit but taxing it 'would mean that many wage and salary earners would experience a sharp drop in their take home pay'.[43] Thatcher in her memoirs makes the further point that Child Benefit, which was paid tax free to 'many families whose incomes were such that they did not really need it, and was very expensive', had been introduced 'partly as an equivalent of the (now abolished) child tax allowances, so there was an argument on grounds of fairness that its real value should be sustained'.[44] (And paying Child Benefit to mothers and 'clawing it back' from fathers by taxing the latter's earnings would amount to a 'child tax' on fathers rather than a child tax allowance.)

The new Family Credit would provide extra support for the families of people on low wages (compared with Family Income Supplement (FIS), which it would replace), and was designed so that families would no longer be worse off when the adult(s) were in work than out of it, while if they earned more by greater effort they would not forfeit most of it through losing benefit and paying more in tax and national insurance. The White Paper particularly stressed the improved incentives to work that would result. The Green Paper, the White Paper and the Bill all proposed that it would be paid by employers through the pay packet, in the form of reduced deductions for national insurance and income tax. (FIS was normally paid to the mother, like Child Benefit.) This would 'make employees aware of the full extent of the help they are receiving',[45] and would be 'a sensible improvement in co-ordination between the benefit and tax systems'.[46] This aspect was widely criticized in responses to the Green Paper, but reaffirmed by the Government in the White Paper: '[We] do not accept . . . that, uniquely among the people of this country, those in full-time work on low earnings cannot be trusted to allocate their other resources responsibly within the family and must have the state do it for them.'[47] However, in the course of the Bill's passage through Parliament the Government did accept an amendment to pay Family Credit direct to the mother. This was self-evidently inconsistent with the Government's objectives and reasoning.

With regard to *provision for retirement*, it was a conclusion of the Wilton Park conference that 'SERPS should be abolished and that the second pension should come from a variety of new options in the private sector which we would make available'.[48] The Green Paper proposed that it would continue as at present for people within 15 years of retirement, while for those in younger age groups it would be phased out and replaced by a personal or occupational pension. However, the provisions of the White Paper, Bill and Act represented a withdrawal from the Green Paper's proposals and the objective of cutting drastically the future debt burden and compelling all earners to take out private pensions. Within the rationale, the objective of abolishing SERPS was replaced by the objective of cutting as much as was considered feasible and making the scheme less generous, which would provide 'realistic encouragement to extend occupational and personal pension coverage'.[49]

With regard to *weekly and 'one-off' benefits for people not in work*, the replacement of weekly Supplementary Benefit payments by the much simpler Income Support system was consistent with the objective of simplification, but it was not consistent with directing resources to people in 'real', 'genuine' or 'greatest' need, since by virtue of its simplicity the scheme did not make any but crude distinctions according to need. And there was nothing in either Paper's objectives that dictated or implied that people under 25 should receive a lower rate. Nor was there an objective which dictated that reducing the burden of social security costs should be achieved by making loans rather than grants from the 'Social Fund' to some of the poorest people in the country, i.e. those with the least capacity of anyone to repay loans.

As for *Housing Benefit*, the modified scheme would indeed meet the practical objective of simplification. It would also be consistent with 'the Government's overall objectives for the economy', in that the new structure of the scheme would allow, as the Government anticipated, expenditure on Housing Benefit 'to be significantly reduced' by around £450 million, roughly 15 per cent[50] (in contrast to Fowler's post-Wilton Park note that there were 'some comparatively small reductions to the Housing Benefit budget'[51]). And it would meet two other objectives not included among the general ones: there would be equity in the amount of help received as between people in work and people out of work, reducing the 'unemployment trap'; and help with domestic rates would be lowered, to 'strengthen local accountability by ensuring that everyone pays something towards their rates'.[52] This last objective was not part of a social security-based rationale (it was not one of Fowler's Wilton Park objectives): like the analogous poll tax provision, it was designed to create a link of dependence and accountability between local authorities and poorer people among their electorates.

To sum up, it appears that with regard to helping families with children, provision for retirement, and weekly and 'one-off' benefits for people not in work, not all of the policies and measures ultimately adopted followed logically from the objectives set out by Fowler for the Wilton Park conference, especially those to do with targeting help on those in 'need'. As a first step to discovering what they *did* follow from, we need to ask what considerations entered into those policies and measures.

Considerations. Real-world considerations evidently entered into such objectives as meeting the 'needs' of identified groups within the population, strengthening the 'work incentive', and enabling employees to acquire rights in personal pensions which they could take with them when they changed job. In translating those objectives into policies and measures, however, political considerations seem to have played a major part, as can be seen particularly from the two striking 'U-turns' that took place. Thus the Government's acceptance of an amendment to pay Family Credit direct to the mother, which was self-evidently inconsistent with the objectives and reasoning it had earlier put forward, appears to have come about as a result of the perception that it would not have sufficient support in the House of Commons to resist that amendment if it came to a vote. Likewise the U-turn over the abolition of SERPS is attributed by Fowler to the political consideration that a 'substantial body of opinion' favoured modifying SERPS rather than abolishing it.[53] Fowler tells us more about this political consideration:

> [The] big question remained pensions. I was becoming dangerously isolated. I had against me virtually the whole of the pensions industry. They were petrified that private pensions for all would mean a return to the years of political uncertainty. Over the previous eighteen months the pensions industry had had enough change thrust on them to last a lifetime. They regarded compulsory occupational pensions as several bridges too far and it was clear that they would continue to campaign against my proposals. Yet it was the industry I necessarily had to rely on to deliver the goods. Even more ominously, both the CBI [Confederation of British Industry] and the influential Engineering Employers' Federation had moved against me. They were concerned at the added costs they feared industry would have to bear. Yet even at this stage I would have proceeded had I been sure of my political support.
>
> Margaret Thatcher remained totally stalwart in her support throughout, but not everybody took the same view. In particular, the events of the last six months had revealed the intractable opposition of the Treasury. Nigel Lawson had made no secret of the fact that he saw the proposals as financially prohibitive. The successful introduction of a national occupational pension scheme was by any standards a massive undertaking. There were bound to be administrative problems and questions to be ironed out. To embark on this course without the support of the providers of the pensions, of the companies who were going to help finance them or of the Treasury itself was an extremely doubtful venture. I could be tripped up at any stage.[54]

Presentational considerations, demonstrating concern with the appearance or 'image' of the proposals, seem to me to be apparent in Fowler's attempt to associate the proposals with the tradition of Beveridge, effectively claiming that they be treated as seriously as the 1944 Beveridge report. References to 'sensible' cooperation and management in the White Paper are making use of the fact that no one could possibly (in British political discourse) oppose sensible measures, so they are presentational too. And the concern for the burden of pensions upon future generations, while on the face of it appearing responsible and statesman-like, also appears presentational: it is strikingly inconsistent with the unfailing preoccupation of British governments with here-and-now issues, and it is based on an analysis of the 'pensions burden' that focused almost entirely on demographic projections and the 'dependency ratio' of pensioners to the population of working age, while ignoring the impact of employment (and unemployment) patterns and paying little attention to the possibility of raising the age of retirement for women to 65 (which ten years later is indeed in the process of coming about).

Practical considerations are of course evident in the desire to simplify the benefits system, but it is financial considerations that appear most pervasive: to say in the White Paper 'we want' a system 'which is consistent with the Government's overall objectives for the economy', does not hinder sustained economic growth and is not 'ring fenced from the requirements of sensible management of the economy as a whole' was to say in three different ways 'we want a system in which costs are held down to the bare minimum'. Financial considerations also appear to have entered strongly into the Regulations made under the Act and into the setting of the total Social Fund budget and the directions that prescribed how the Social Fund was to be administered, since the aim appeared to be that the amount of money expended should be minimized.

Finally, an ideological consideration is present in the objective of encouraging self-reliance, but the emphasis in what was written was that individuals should provide for themselves: the implications of this in terms of creating dependence on the private market were left unstated. The ideology of 'fairness' – as difficult to oppose as 'sensible' measures – is cited by Thatcher as grounds for sustaining the 'real value' of Child Benefit for *all* parents.

Ingredients. Although the proposed reforms would address a field of policy in which the state was already deeply enmeshed, with provisions of different kinds affecting very large numbers of people, it is striking how great a part in the Government's rationale was played by subjective perceptions, belief-based theories, and value judgements. Although the White Paper showed, in its list of the defects of the present system, some awareness of how that system was working in practice, little attempt appears to have been made to calculate how the *new* system would operate once it was set up. Strikingly, too, as Adler points out, although one of the review teams had been given the task of examining benefits for children and young people, 'there was complete silence on benefits for the 16–19 age group'.[55] And the content of the Green Paper and White Paper bore little mark of the views submitted to the review teams or in response to the Green Paper respectively. There therefore seems to have been some deliberate exclusion from the rationale of the perceptions of consumers of policy who had little or no political 'clout'.

Interests

Consumer interests. It is not a straightforward matter to ascertain which consumer interests made a mark on the Act, partly because we do not know how clearly the Government envisaged, prior to the Bill receiving Royal Assent, the consequences for different categories of consumers. Certainly actual outcomes for consumers would depend not only on the *structure* for which the Act provided but also on the Regulations and directions yet to be made, and on future funding decisions. Although figures for weekly benefits were published in the 'impact tables' – these showed that among pensioners losers would outnumber gainers, while the reverse would be true for families with children and for people who were sick or disabled: among single people under 25 gainers and losers would approximately balance – subsequent research into actual outcomes (cited by Andrews and Jacobs) showed that while pensioners did on average lose, single people under 25 were heavy losers, and families with children transferring from Supplementary Benefit to Income Support also became predominantly losers since they had been the prime users of the now-abolished single payments.[56] As mentioned above, another study found that four out of five claimants transferring to Income Support were worse off, even with the protection in some cases of transitional arrangements, because of the requirement to pay water rates and 20 per cent of their domestic rates bill. ('The great majority' had to pay at least £1 above the £1.30 allowed as compensation for their domestic rates contribution, and almost all had to pay another £1 a week in water rates; 43 per cent had to pay between £2 and £4.)[57] Accordingly, large numbers lost as a result of the Act and the Regulations, directions and decisions that followed it: their interests failed to make a mark on these measures and decisions.

It is also the case that there were gainers and losers from the introduction of the new occupational and personal pensions. Prominent among the losers were mid-career employees in the public sector who were persuaded to withdraw from an occupational scheme conferring an index-linked pension and change to a non-index-linked personal pension plan. (The companies concerned, and their sales staff, who received a commission for each pension plan sold, were among the gainers.) Also a loser, it now transpires, was the taxpayer, by virtue of the tax and National Insurance concessions – the latter later admitted by Lawson to be 'quite unnecessarily costly'[58] – and the likely future dependence on the state of people who put into their personal pension only the amount they have saved by contracting out of the new SERPS.

From the changes in the proposals between successive stages of the process, and from various unsuccessful attempts to influence proposals, we can infer that there were other consumer interests which made a mark. Within families, substituting the payment of Family Credit by cashable orders to the mother for payment through the pay packet (as the White Paper had stipulated) can be interpreted as a mark made by the interests of the mother and children rather than of the father. And Child Benefit, the preservation of which was evidently in the interests of all families with children except those receiving Income Support and/or Housing Benefit (for whom Child Benefit was treated as income and their other benefits reduced accordingly), was not made subject to taxation or 'better targeting' despite, it appears, the desire of some ministers to bring this about.[59] So the interests of better-off families with children, who would have suffered a reduction or loss of benefit through taxation or targeting, made a mark on the Act. Moreover, the retention (albeit in less attractive form) of SERPS – in contrast to the Green Paper's proposal to abolish it – was seen as being in the interest of 'poor risks' whom pension companies would be reluctant to ensure. But retaining a form of SERPS was essentially ancillary to the abandoning of compulsory occupational and personal pensions, which – as Fowler's description of political considerations shows – was seen by pension companies and employers as very much in *their* interests.

There is more to consumer interests than gaining or losing in material terms. Whether a measure is in someone's interests is a matter of judgement: for example, there is scope for disagreement as to whether it is in someone's interests to receive special help as of right rather than at the discretion of a local official, or to be helped through a simpler, more understandable scheme at the cost of lower benefits. In the case of the social security reforms there was scope for ministers to exercise their judgement as to what was in people's best interests: in doing so they were able to give effect to their feelings about people whom they saw as 'taking advantage' of the system. As the Green Paper put it: 'Help may [be going] to those with the best knowledge who are not necessarily those who need extra help most.'[60]

Political/institutional interests.   The Act can be seen as a response to the interest of the Chancellor, Chief Secretary and Treasury officials, as well as the Government collectively, in establishing a mechanism for controlling and rationing social security spending. It can also be seen as a compromise between their interest in gaining credit for performing well as advocates of the taxpayer's interest and Fowler's interest in doing the same as an advocate of the interests of families with children. He also had a personal political interest in preventing 'indefensible' cuts: 'Nobody is going to thank you if you end up making changes which either cause real hardship or bring the political roof in – or manage to do both.'[61] And he seems to have had a similar ambition-based interest in being seen as 'a new Beveridge', demonstrated by the comparison that he makes between Sir William Beveridge (author of *Social Insurance and Allied Services*, the 1942 Beveridge report[62]) and himself. ('I had, however, one advantage that was denied to Beveridge . . . the opportunity as a politician of implementing the changes.'[63])

Fowler was moved from the DHSS after the general election in June 1987, and was therefore unable to promote his interest in defending the social security budget against pressure from the Treasury. His successor, John Moore, seems to have had an interest in identifying himself publicly with the changes, even as they were being put into effect: he was reported in *The Guardian* as being 'very, very proud to be able to participate in putting them into practice'.[64] Moore had formerly been a junior minister under Lawson at the Treasury, and Lawson writes that on his appointment to the DHSS Moore 'was determined to be more Thatcherite than his predecessor'.[65]

Fowler's interest in claiming credit for the social security reforms is illustrated by his memoirs:

And what has been the effect of the reforms? Family Credit now provides double the spending power for low-income families [that] its predecessor scheme [provided] and more help is provided for children through the Income Support system. The Social Fund has been successfully introduced without all the problems nervously predicted by some of the experts. The unemployment trap has been substantially eased and the simplification of social security has had major effects. The whole system is now operating more efficiently. The time taken to process claims has been reduced; the error rate is down; and claimants are spending less time waiting. Social security is no longer a jungle of files and paper where only the skilled claimant triumphs.[66]

(In describing the introduction of the Social Fund as 'successful', Fowler perhaps has in mind the absence of political repercussions: the problems faced by those who would formerly have had recourse to one-off payments are well attested to by organizations which are in close touch with claimants. And note that Fowler does not mention Housing Benefit, and the amendments to it within two weeks of its introduction. After the Wilton Park conference he had been working on the basis that there would be only 'some comparatively small reductions to the Housing Benefit budget'.)[67]

In relation to SERPS, we can again see the personal identification of participants with the point of view they are advocating. Fowler had a personal stake in the abolition of SERPS and Lawson seems to have had a personal stake in controlling the growth of public expenditure in the short term (rather than the long) and accordingly in resisting the abolition of SERPS. The provisions of the Act can be seen as a compromise between these two personal interests, and thus as a partial response to both of them. Conflicting interests were also revealed when, in April 1985, Fowler suggested to Lawson the setting-up of a joint Treasury–DHSS study group on the links between the taxation and social security systems. Lawson refused. As Fowler saw it, although tax policy could have a profound effect on those on low incomes, 'constitutionally any changes are a matter for the Chancellor [and] Nigel had absolutely no intention of giving up any of his rights'.[68] Lawson admits to 'holding fast to the hallowed Treasury doctrine that taxation is a matter for the Chancellor [alone]', but argues that he was not merely engaged in a 'defence of my own turf': there was an 'overwhelming practical case for keeping the two systems apart'. This case was subsequently set out in a Green Paper, *The Reform of Personal Taxation*, which Lawson presented in March 1986.[69] Lawson's refusal to agree to a joint Treasury–DHSS study group thus had the effect of defending the Treasury's monopoly over the authorship of Government papers that deal with taxation. I infer that it *does* demonstrate an interest on his part in defending his own turf.

Thatcher too evidently had a number of strongly held 'policy preferences' which she had a personal stake in promoting: the abolition of SERPS and the introduction of compulsory occupational and personal pensions; the 20 per cent compulsory domestic rates contribution for people on Income Support; and the reduction of public spending, but not by targeting Child Benefit. All of these except the first made a mark on policy.

Process

The chronological landmarks in this case divide the process into eight stages.

1 Up to and including the commissioning of the reviews: this stage includes the registering of 'issues' by Fowler, Lawson and Thatcher.
2 Up to and including the Wilton Park conference: the review teams at work (some overlap with stage 1, the reviews having been set up at different times).
3 Up to and including the publication of the Green Paper: MISC 111 at work.
4 Period set aside for responses to the Green Paper.
5 Up to and including the publication of the White Paper and tabling of the Bill in Parliament: consideration of responses to the Green Paper, drafting or redrafting of the White Paper and Bill (possibly some overlap with stage 4, if drafting began before that stage had been concluded).
6 Up to and including Royal Assent: the Parliamentary process.
7 Up to and including the Act taking effect: the making (and subsequent amending) of Regulations and directions; public expenditure decisions; setting of benefit levels.
8 The Act in force: further amendments to Regulations.

From the fact that in stage 1 four separate reviews were commissioned, we might infer that there was more than one issue, i.e. more than one imperative and related set of perceptions, and the White Paper's listing of five 'clear and fundamental defects' is consistent with this. Each defect is rooted in certain perceptions, and the (common) imperative is clearly stated: '[The] Government's duty is to act.' Fowler also records feeling strongly that something needed to be done about occupational pensions, his feelings arising out of his parents' and his own personal experiences. This imperative was thus a very personal one. Fowler was also under pressure from Lawson to reduce expenditure on social security: this constituted an acutely felt imperative.

During stage 1, Fowler evolved the strategy of setting up reviews. He set up the first, on provision for retirement, after the conference on pensions, open to the press, at the DHSS headquarters in September 1983. At this conference he encountered 'almost universal consternation' in response to his support for 'portable' pensions that workers could take with them when they moved from one job to another.[70] Fowler doesn't say precisely *why* he chose to set up the inquiry/review, but he writes: '[My] aim was to ensure an expansion in provision [of occupational pensions].' He adds that under the inquiry's scrutiny, the pensions industry 'had to justify, under cross-examination, its policies. Opponents of changing the rules on early leavers found it difficult to sustain their case.'[71] I infer that it was Fowler's intention to demonstrate this publicly, and that he saw the inquiry as a means of exerting pressure on pensions companies. He makes it clear that he already had firm intentions, so for him the focus of the inquiry – and thus of the rationale that it was expected to produce – was not *whether* changes should be made but *what* changes should be made.

The terms of reference for the pensions inquiry included state pensions as well as occupational ones (see Box 7.3), although on Fowler's account when announcing its setting up he described it as 'an inquiry into occupational pensions'.[72] We know that Lawson had a continuing concern that inquiries of this kind might create pressures for further spending (see Chapter 8), but since Fowler's aim was to ensure that people could have 'what they regarded as their own pension',[73] he would presumably have argued that if the industry could be induced to reform itself, much of the long-term financial burden of pensions on the state would be transferred to the private sector, consonant with the Chancellor's desire to save money and the Prime Minister's desire for a further attack on 'welfare dependency'. The inclusion of a junior Treasury minister in the inquiry team would have safeguarded 'Treasury interests' (the inclusion of ministers from two other departments would have 'balanced' those interests), and non-publication of the inquiry's report would also have been consistent with the Treasury's desire to keep control should any pressures for additional spending materialize.

Fowler says nothing in his memoirs about the setting up of the Housing Benefit Review. But that was a 'safe' enterprise in the sense that it was directed at the activities of local authorities rather than central government – evidently safe enough for the chair to be entrusted to someone other than a minister and for its report to be published. And fulfilment of its terms of reference – to ensure that the scheme was as simple as possible and concentrated help on those most in need – could be expected to save the Exchequer money.

As to the other two reviews, from Fowler's account they were prompted by what he saw as the success of the pensions inquiry:

> Rather than having the whole of the public and the press against us, we gained support . . . Surely, I thought, if we can do this with pensions can we not do the same with social security? . . . I recognized that all would not be plain sailing. Changing supplementary and housing benefit would be more contentious than reforming occupational pensions. Nevertheless, I felt that an open inquiry should be the aim.
>
> My resolve to set up an inquiry into the social security system was strengthened by one other important factor. Like every other Secretary of State who has ever been in charge of social security, I was under pressure from the Treasury.[74]

Unfortunately Fowler doesn't say any more about how the inquiry/review would help him to resist pressure from the Treasury. Nor do we know how the Chancellor and his officials felt about it, although Lawson successfully insisted that taxation should be excluded from the reviews' terms of reference.[75] Nor were the reports of the reviews published (although we do not know whether or not this was a Treasury stipulation). Having each of the two social security reviews chaired by DHSS ministers might have been thought to guarantee some control over recommendations: as mentioned above, we know that there was some sense among witnesses that the public hearings were being controlled. But it appears that Fowler anticipated that the reviews would mobilize support for him in his conviction that 'the priority for the 1990s should be families with children',[76] just as the pensions inquiry had mobilized support for his proposal on occupational pensions.

Stage 2 – the review teams at work – offered the opportunity to individuals and groups outside government to contribute their views on the defects of the existing social security system, in the shape of information on the workings of the system, the consequences for the people on the receiving end, and proposals for improving the system. The review teams appear to have played a 'gate-keeping' role: some people who gave oral evidence felt that their minds were closed on certain topics. Unfortunately for us as observers, the reports of three of the review teams were not published, so we cannot make our own judgements as to whether all submissions were faithfully considered and reported.

At the beginning of stage 3, the setting up of Cabinet committee MISC 111 on the social security reforms was a matter of routine. That the Prime Minister decided to chair it herself is an indication that she attached some importance to it (as with E(LF) in the poll tax case and with the Cabinet committees that worked on the education and housing proposals for legislation in early 1987). The main 'players' within MISC 111 were Fowler, Lawson and Thatcher, Fowler being by far the most junior of the three.

The members of MISC 111 appear to have accepted at the outset that reforms were necessary. From the clues available to us, it seems that the original bundle of issues was resolved into three: the issue of what should be done about SERPS; the issue of what should be done to reform the structure of the other parts of the social security system; and the issue of how money should be shifted within the system, i.e. which benefits should be reduced if others were to be increased or maintained at their existing levels.

To this complex of issues were added the personal aims of the three main participants, which seem to have been reflected in the dynamics of the interaction between them. Lawson was pressing Fowler to reduce social security expenditure. So for Fowler to achieve his aim of a cost-neutral outcome and fend off Lawson he needed Thatcher's support. But she had aims of her own, notably to make private provision of pensions compulsory,[77] and to compel everyone, even social security claimants, to pay at least 20 per cent of their domestic rates bill. It is conceivable that Fowler was led to support these aims by the strength of the arguments for them, but this seems unlikely: Lawson writes that Fowler himself did not originally put forward the proposal for compulsory private pensions (and it was not among Fowler's Wilton Park objectives, as he records them) but went along with it because he was 'anxious to see the back of SERPS',[78] while the domestic rates proposal was inconsistent with Fowler's aim of targeting help on those in greatest need. I conclude that a factor in Fowler's endorsement of Thatcher's proposals was that he needed her support against the Chancellor.

What may have happened, to judge by the content of the Green Paper, was that MISC 111 concentrated in its work on the two issues of the future of SERPS and the reform of the structure of the other parts of the social security system. As regards the latter, this would have had two important consequences, which presumably were well understood by ministers and officials.

First, it allowed the Treasury and the DHSS to put aside their differences over addressing the relationship between taxation and social security: they had a common interest in establishing a structure that allowed expenditure to be controlled overall and rationed: any conflict over setting benefit levels could be deferred for the time being. Second, it meant that when the Green Paper was published, groups defending the interests of claimants would be hampered in arguing against the general structural proposals on the grounds that they would have harmful effects, since the effects on individual claimants and families would not be known, even in general terms, until it was clear how money would be shifted among the different benefits and until Regulations and directions had been published. (These effects wouldn't be known precisely until claimants began to experience the new system. The Government did eventually produce illustrative figures showing the effects of the changes, but only when the White Paper was published, in a technical annexe to it.[79])

Stage 3 concluded with the publishing of MISC 111's conclusions as a Green Paper. The extent to which the Government was committed to its proposals has been discussed above. Publishing them made clear the direction which the Government wished policy to take, but doing so in a Green Paper rather than a White one would allow more time for any disagreements between ministers to be resolved and make it easier to retreat from specific proposals without too much 'loss of face'. It would also provide an opportunity either to get the pensions industry and employers accustomed to the inevitability of changes, or to come to terms with a refusal on their part to do so. Lawson, whose opposition to compulsory private pensions had been overruled by Thatcher, evidently anticipated that employers would be strongly opposed to the costs that occupational pensions would impose on business (the fact that they opposed it, he wrote later, 'caused me no surprise'[80]) and approved of publication of the proposals with 'Green Paper status' for this reason. The *opportunity* for holding a further consultation stage would have existed if it had already been decided that the Bill would not be tabled in Parliament until after Christmas.

Stage 4 of the process was a stage of sending views – information and judgements – to the DHSS. More than 7000 written responses to the Green Paper were submitted. As we have seen, a survey of a sample of 60 organizations (which did not include left-wing political parties or organizations) revealed overwhelming hostility to the proposals for ending SERPS, setting up the discretionary Social Fund, lower rates of Income Support for people under 25, compulsory payment of 20 per cent of domestic rates bills, and cuts in the total expenditure on Housing Benefit. These responses, unlike the submissions made to the review teams, were 'tailored' to the specific proposals in the Green Paper.

Consideration of the responses to the Green Paper was part of stage 5 of the process. Those concerned in this stage – including the reconvened MISC 111 – appear to have performed a gate-keeping role, looking critically at the various suggestions put forward and exercising their discretion as to whether to accept them or not. Adler argues that 'If the Government had taken the public response to its Green Paper seriously, it would have had no option but to abandon its chosen approach to the reform of social security.'[81] However, the White

Paper demonstrated that the Government saw the purpose of the 'consultation' as merely

> to ensure that no points of legitimate public concern were overlooked in preparing for change. The responsibility of the Government is to look critically at the various suggestions put forward and to evaluate the substance of the arguments behind them. Public consultation has produced a number of valuable suggestions which the Government has accepted.[82]

Evidently the Government did not feel obliged to treat the responses to the Green Paper as if they were the product of a kind of referendum. However, in the chapter on income-related benefits, a number of points were acknowledged as valid, and the proposals modified to take account of them, while others were met with unchallengeable formula like 'The Government are not persuaded that . . .' and 'The Government remain of the view that . . .'. With regard to the proposed Social Fund, however, many respondents had not been 'ready to recognise the shortcomings of the present system nor to examine carefully the new approach',[83] and their objections in principle were not discussed.

As we have seen, the biggest change was in relation to the proposed abandonment of SERPS, where there was opposition from Lawson within the Government and from pension companies outside it. Fowler refers to the pensions industry waging a 'campaign' against his proposals: evidently he felt under pressure from this campaign.[84] Some other proposals were modified. The publishing of the White Paper committed the Government to the new and modified proposals.

The tabling of a government public Bill is necessarily preceded by the drawing up of instructions to Parliamentary Counsel, who then go on to draft the Bill: these stages commonly take some months for a complex Bill such as this. If, as Lawson says, it was only in mid-October that MISC 111 decided that SERPS would be retained, but in a less costly form, it is possible that a good deal of officials' and Parliamentary draftsmen's work after that date was concentrated on SERPS. So the scope for reappraising and modifying the other proposals after mid-September, the deadline for responding to the Green Paper, will have been correspondingly limited. In effect, the administrative resources necessary to carry out reappraisal and modification may have been pre-empted by the SERPS issue. This is consistent with the fact that numerous further amendments were made after the Bill was tabled.

The White Paper, like its Green predecessor, dealt with the structure of the proposed new system, but went into more detail than the Green Paper. It and the Bill which ushered in stage 6 of the process set out firm legislative intentions to which the Government were correspondingly committed. Alternatives had been considered and rejected. In the House of Commons Opposition attempts to amend the Bill were resisted and, with the aid of the Government's majority, defeated. However, as we have seen, the Lords made three amendments to the Bill, of which the Government accepted one (providing for the payment of Family Credit by cash order to the mother rather than through the pay packet), removed the second but made a small concession, and removed the third but gave an undertaking to take the concerns expressed into account later.

Fowler justified the 'U-turn' on the method of paying Family Credit on the grounds that it was what 'a range of people inside and outside the House of Commons, including Emma Nicholson, then the Women's Vice-Chairman of the Conservative Party, wanted'.[85] Given that the Cabinet had expressed and reiterated clear reasons for payment through the pay packet, and had already passed up opportunities to modify that proposal and so were evidently heavily committed to it, its eventual acceptance of the Lords' amendment is consistent with heavy pressure having been exerted on a susceptible Government by Nicholson and others. Baroness Trumpington, the Government social security spokesperson in the Lords, made it clear that 'others' had had access to the Government. While the Lords Committee stage was in progress, discussions had been held

> with the Confederation of British Industry, National Federation of Self-Employed and Small Businesses, the Equal Opportunities Commission and the Women's National Commission . . . [It] would not be right to impose a change of this sort, particularly if the immediate cost was undue additional work for employers, particularly small employers, who have to operate the system.[86]

Stages 7 and 8, following Royal Assent to the Social Security Act, saw the making of Regulations, the issuing of directions, and various public expenditure decisions, all affecting the levels of benefits and people's eligibility to receive them. Some changes were subsequently made, in a manifest response to the pressure exerted after 11 April 1988 by Conservative backbench MPs when the impact of the new system on those affected began to become apparent. From the fact that the improvements (such as transitional arrangements) proved on close examination to be less in amount and to benefit fewer people than appeared to be the case when announced by the new Secretary of State, John Moore, to the House of Commons, it seems reasonable to infer that the motivation behind them was primarily to allay the pressure, rather than genuinely to offset the burden on the people most disadvantaged by the changes.

We don't have any evidence as to when and how the Government formed a commitment to promulgating those particular Regulations, issuing those particular directions, and taking those particular expenditure decisions, that it eventually did. It may be that at the time that the Bill was tabled, little work on Regulations and directions had been done: the immediate pressure was to get the Bill drafted, and the Regulations appear to have been drawn up in some haste, which is consistent with them being formulated as the deadline for *their* publication approached.

Power structure

We have seen that certain ingredients of the rationale underlying the Act and subsequent measures were contributed by particular individuals and groups.

Likewise, the interests of certain individuals and groups but not others were observed to make a mark on the reforms. To what extent did these effects reflect the positions of these individuals and groups in the power structure?

At the beginning of stage 1, we find Fowler in his 'starting position', as it were. By virtue of being Secretary of State for Social Services, he had structural links to the Prime Minister (as a member of the Cabinet and owing his position to her); to the Chancellor (on whom as Secretary of State he depended in part for funds for his department's purposes, and to whom he was in practice under an obligation to account for the funds allocated to the DHSS); to his advisers on the Social Security Advisory Committee; to his Permanent Secretary and other senior officials; through them to the officials who administered the social security system; through those officials to the local housing authorities, who dispensed Housing Benefit; and through all of these to the claimants and other beneficiaries of social security.

In stage 1, the setting-up of the reviews involved the exercise by Fowler of a 'power to do', presumably with the consent of the Prime Minister and Chancellor. Their setting-up amounted to the creation of pieces of temporary institutional structure: *ad hoc* teams, to be disbanded when they had done their work. In stage 2, when the review teams were at work, they constituted a communication link to organizations (and some individuals) concerned with social security matters, out in the wider political system. It was, however, a one-way communication channel: information was solicited from these outsiders, but they were not told what measures ministers had it in mind to take. Moreover, the review teams were in a 'gate-keeper' position, with a discretion that they could exercise: they had some latitude in deciding which views should be passed on and which ignored, or treated as irrelevant, or forwarded with approbation or with critical comments. Once it was decided that the reports of those chaired by ministers would not be published, their discretion was not fettered by an obligation to account publicly for how they had represented evidence to them.

At the beginning of stage 3, Thatcher, in causing the Cabinet committee MISC 111 to be set up, and chairing it herself, was exercising a prime ministerial power to do this. As with the review teams, the effect was to create a piece of temporary institutional structure. The central members, by virtue of the Cabinet posts that they occupied, were Thatcher, Lawson and Fowler. We have already noted Fowler's structural dependence on Thatcher and Lawson; he now acquired an *issue-based* dependence on them as well by virtue of the fact that he wished to make changes to the social security system and depended on them for their support if he was to succeed.

In stage 4, the period set aside for responses to the Green Paper, a communication channel was once again established to Fowler and the DHSS from any organization or individual that wished to take advantage of it. This time they knew what structural reforms the Government was proposing – although very little was said about finance and benefit levels – and there was no review team acting as gate-keeper. We need to distinguish between different categories of respondents. Two in particular are significant. One category comprised organizations concerned with the welfare of social security claimants and beneficiaries. Although Fowler presents himself as having become convinced that the priority for the 1990s should be families with children,[87] and Lawson describes the case for switching priority to those families and away from the elderly as being an article of DHSS 'departmental faith, where officials had been exposed to years of effective lobbying by that most professional of all social security pressure groups, the Child Poverty Action Group',[88] this group does not appear to have had privileged access to Fowler, nor to have possessed any behind-the-scenes means of bringing pressure to bear on him without the assistance of others.

In contrast, it appears that members of the other category, firms and organizations in the pensions 'industry', and employers represented by the Confederation of British Industry and the Engineering Employers' Federation, *were* able to and did express their views and exert pressure. The consequences are apparent in stage 5 of the process, when the comments on the Green Paper were considered and the White Paper and Bill drafted. Fowler, as we saw, felt it was too risky to go ahead with abolishing SERPS and imposing compulsory occupational pensions 'without the support of the providers of the pensions, of the companies who were going to help finance them or of the Treasury itself . . . I could be tripped up at any stage'.[89]

Given that in the seclusion of MISC 111 Thatcher, with Fowler's support, had overruled Lawson in opting for the abolition of SERPS and the imposing of compulsory occupational pensions, the intervention of the pensions industry and employers appears to have been crucial in bringing about the abandonment of the compulsory scheme. Moreover, it appears to have been *pressure*, and not merely the conveying of views, that was crucial. From the fact that Thatcher (described by Fowler as 'the last person to reopen decisions already taken'[90]) gave way and from Fowler's references to campaigning and moving against him, I infer that he and Thatcher were not merely aware of what these bodies were saying but also felt under pressure from them. One evident lever, existing by virtue of the particular issue of pensions, was his *dependence* on the pensions industry to 'deliver the goods'. Another lever that could be deployed – this a structure-based one – was his dependence on his party in the House of Commons for support in getting his Bill passed. Despite the overwhelming Conservative majority,[91] it 'was going to be a major battle and there were plenty of press predictions that the radical changes would cost us the next general election'.[92] Moreover, he would have to carry with him – and hence depended on – the one-third or so of Conservative MPs who had backgrounds in business (including commerce and insurance). Their support might not be forthcoming if they both feared losing their seats and – with their close connections to the pensions industry and employers – felt the policy to be misguided. Dependence on the electorate was evidently also a factor here. A less visible connection existed by virtue of the fact that large industrial employers and firms involved in life assurance and pensions were (and are) major contributors to Conservative Party funds. As regards the latter, an investigation by Labour MP George Howarth revealed that in the year 1992–3 Legal and General

Assurance gave £40,000, Sun Alliance gave £50,000 and Hambros gave £53,000; General Accident and Fire and Life Association also donated.[93] Interestingly, the General Manager (Finance) of Legal and General Assurance (Stewart Lyon) was a member of the first review team that Fowler set up, and chaired – the Inquiry into Provision for Retirement – and the Chairman of Hambro Life (Mark Weinberg) was a member of that team's sub-group on personal pensions. Although we do not know whether pressure was applied behind the scenes, or precisely what went on in Fowler's mind (although he makes it clear that he paid a great deal of attention to weighing up support), the existence of this structural dependence on the pensions industry for contributions to party funds and of connections of personal acquaintance, together with the industry's interest in not having to implement compulsory occupational pensions, are consistent with Fowler and Thatcher giving in to pressure and abandoning the proposal. Even if pressure had not been exerted overtly, they would have been aware of the importance of not alienating their financial backers (doing so would not have raised their reputation in the party), and would have made sure that they had a clear appreciation of the industry's point of view.

In stage 6, the Parliamentary process, we can learn something of the power structure from the different fates of the three Lords' amendments to the Bill. We can infer from the Commons' overturning of the amendment to delete the 20 per cent compulsory payment towards domestic rates – a matter of principle to Thatcher – that ministers felt under no automatic obligation to accept Lords' amendments. On the right of appeal against Social Fund decisions, where no additional expenditure or sacrifice of principle was involved, we can perhaps infer from the concession that was made that some degree of obligation was felt: it would be tactful to indicate that *some* attention was paid to their Lordships' deliberations. As for the U-turn on the payment of Family Credit, if ministers judged it sensible not to alienate its women supporters inside and outside the Commons, and especially if they shared Fowler's view that they depended on the support of backbenchers to get this 'highly controversial Bill' through the House of Commons,[94] this would have given those supporters a lever that they could use to exert pressure on the Government.

In stage 7, as coming-into-force day approached, the process of making Regulations went ahead. In March 1987, in what proved to be the run-up to the June 1987 general election, the DHSS published a draft Social Fund Manual, which was sent to a small number of organizations and to the Social Security Advisory Committee (SSAC), which also circulated it, for their comments.[95] Its principles and recommended practices came under strong criticism from the concerned organizations. However, these were largely ignored by the Government – still led by Thatcher but now reshuffled – when it went ahead after the election. Although the SSAC had a statutory link to the new Secretary of State for Social Services, the latter's interest in demonstrating his 'Thatcherite' credentials[96] evidently lessened his susceptibility to any pressure that the SSAC might have been able to exert. Insofar as the SSAC had a lever at its disposal, it could not be used to exert sufficient pressure to dislodge Moore from his intention.

In contrast, in stage 8 complaints by their constituents to backbench Conservative MPs produced an immediate relaxation of the Housing Benefit eligibility criteria. The Government's sensitivity to its dependence on support from its backbench MPs, and its interest in retaining that support, provided the backbenchers with a lever that could be used to exert a significant amount of pressure on the Government.

The structural elements involved in the process changed from stage to stage. To some extent this was beyond the Government's control. For example, it could not prevent the House of Commons and the House of Lords from being involved in the formal legislative stage. Nor could it insulate itself from pension companies and employers, because of its dependence on them for cooperation in operating pension schemes and, I suggest, for contributions to party funds. But the Government *was* able to control the involvement of groups on which it did not have such a dependence, notably those which made up the Social Security Consortium. In allowing them to make representations to the review teams, albeit not without constraints when they were made orally, face-to-face, and to comment on the Green Paper and draft Social Fund Manual, it was creating a communication channel (one-way in the case of the reviews) but not accepting any obligation to heed what was said and so not offering any lever by which pressure might be exerted.

There is an interesting point here about the nature of dependence. A minister who accepts a moral obligation to help people in 'genuine' or 'real' need, to whom it is important to have endorsement for his or her policies from, say, charitable bodies with no political affiliations, and who finds it embarrassing when those policies are publicly criticized, effectively places in those bodies' hands a lever which can be used to exert pressure on him or her. In contrast, a minister who asserts that availability of resources must take priority over meeting any but the 'greatest' of needs, to whom it is immaterial whether his policies are approved of or not by charitable bodies, who accordingly is not dependent on them to give such approval, and who is so 'thick-skinned' in such circumstances that the feeling of being embarrassed does not lie within his or her emotional repertoire, will not be susceptible to pressure from such sources, and so will not be offering them a lever by means of which they can exert pressure on him or her. (In the language of interests, he or she has no interest in seeking endorsement from independent sources or in avoiding embarrassment.) The existence of such a lever, therefore, depends – at least in part – on the personal characteristics of the minister evoked by those circumstances.

Thatcher's position as Prime Minister, at the centre of the structure, is consistent with the compulsory 20 per cent domestic rates contribution finding its way into the Green Paper and then the legislation. However, the partial offsetting of that duty by the increase of Income Support rates is consistent with her and the Government's dependence on backbenchers for support and, in the run-up to a general election, on the electorate for being returned to power. And the abandoning of the proposal to abolish SERPS and impose compulsory occupational or personal pensions, which had appeared in the Green Paper largely at her insistence, is consistent with the dependences already referred to on pension companies and employers.

Lawson's position as Chancellor of the Exchequer, with its special 'powers to do' in the domains of public expenditure and taxation, reinforced in the former case by the presence in the Cabinet of the Chief Secretary to the Treasury, is at first sight consistent with the abandoning of the pensions proposal, the blocking of Fowler's proposal for a joint Treasury–DHSS study group on the links between the tax and social security systems, the making of stringent cuts in the Housing Benefit allocation, the freezing of Child Benefit, and the low (compared with previous provision) budget for the discretionary Social Fund. But Lawson's position was not consistent with his failure to secure a £2 billion reduction in the social security allocation or with the original inclusion in the Green Paper of the pensions proposal. We need to distinguish between issues over which he obtained Thatcher's support and those over which he did not. In the former case, the two of them formed an unbeatable combination: in the latter, either Lawson lost (over the £2 billion reduction and the original pensions proposal) or he triumphed only when he was allied to a strongly placed group outside, as with pension companies and employers in overturning the original pensions proposal.

Of the three main participants, Fowler was in the weakest position. (His preoccupation with securing support, both inside and outside government, is consistent with his having realized this.) Since his stance over several issues brought him into conflict with Lawson, and since, in structural terms, the boundary between his social security domain and Lawson's taxation domain was a 'fuzzy' and contested one, he was accordingly very dependent on Thatcher for her support over these. Where he got his way, it was over issues where his objectives and hers coincided.

Fowler's successor, John Moore, although occupying the same formal position, appears to have had a different informal relationship with Thatcher. He was not in the position of seeking support for policies (the Act had already been on the statute book for nearly a year) but, on Lawson's account, sought to show himself more Thatcherite than Fowler – and thereby, we can speculate, to earn Thatcher's approval and show that her trust in him was well founded. This dependence for approval (self-interest plus the 'patronage' relationship) appears to have directly resulted in budgetary allocations being lower than they would otherwise have been. As Lawson puts it, '[it] soon became clear that the problem with John Moore was not the normal one of overbidding, but the fact [that] he had not asked for enough.'[97]

Conclusions

As in the manifesto case, we have observed a number of issues identified separately at first and then brought together and treated as a 'bundle' – a 'rational' response given that all were Fowler's responsibility and that if funds for one were to be safeguarded or increased, savings would have to be found from the others. Although the approach was presented in the Green Paper as a 'rational-comprehensive' one, we have seen that it grew incrementally into a wide-ranging inquiry rather than being designed at the outset as one. And although Fowler and his officials ostensibly set out to derive proposals from objectives, the approach in the White Paper was one of remedying specific defects, and Fowler's attempt to get the social security and taxation systems looked at together had been rebuffed by Lawson.

As presented in the Green and White Papers, the proposals were addressed to real-world considerations, but we have seen that they were also responses to the interests of certain individuals and groups. Fowler, Thatcher and Lawson had their personal stakes, and were sensitive to the interests of the pensions industry and those who had the ear of leading women in the Conservative Party. Each took advantage of his or her particular position in the structure as it assumed importance at different stages of the process: Fowler in the drafting of the proposals that went to MISC 111; Thatcher in the chair of that committee, as it considered and approved the Green Paper proposals; Lawson at various points when his agreement was sought; others during the Parliamentary stage of the process.

It is very clear in this case that 'the Government' cannot be regarded as 'monolithic'. Ministers pursued their own interests, not only substantive (where they had a personal stake in the substance of policy) but also procedural, notably as revealed by Lawson's defence of the Chancellor's prerogative over matters of taxation. Fowler, as the junior member of the leading trio, had to adopt a more flexible approach than Thatcher and Lawson: to use a nautical metaphor, they were like 'icebergs' which he had to navigate his way round. Reluctant to commit himself to proposals without being sure of his support, he supported Thatcher's personal proposals and found support from her against Lawson's pressures, at the same time finding some common ground with Lawson in aiming to create a controllable structure. And finding support from neither in his attempts to provide some protection for Housing Benefit,[98] he conceded larger cuts than he was originally prepared to accept. He seems to have been disinclined to proceed with a proposal unless he could be sure in advance of support from those who were in a position to block it, however great he judged the likely benefits for the 'consumers' of policy to be.

The replacement of Fowler by Moore after the 1987 general election, nine months before the Act came into effect, demonstrates the importance of *who* occupies a particular post. Unlike Fowler, Moore appears to have had no objectives for social security other than to reduce expenditure on it: he duly failed, as Lawson saw it, to bid for a sufficient amount.

In contrast to the poll tax case, people outside government had some access to ministers at an early stage of the process, in the shape of the four reviews, and were later able to comment on the proposals in the Green Paper. But the review teams appeared reluctant to 'take on board' some of the evidence submitted, and some of the proposals of the campaigning groups, notably the call for a substantial increase in Child Benefit, were so unrealistic that we might conclude that there was a gulf of comprehension between them and ministers.

The two sides had different perceptions, and subscribed to different theories and value judgements: in effect they saw the world differently and spoke different languages. Communication at that stage was not helped by the groups' ignorance of the changes that ministers had in mind to make (e.g. the possibility of abolishing SERPS and imposing compulsory occupational pensions was not put forward for consideration by the pensions inquiry).

The campaigning groups were at a further disadvantage during the reviews, because the reviews concentrated on the *structure* of the social security system: submissions which described the experiences of claimants but did not relate them to the structure were thus beside the point. Even after the Green Paper was published, the emphasis was still on structure, and ministers were able to ignore submissions based (inevitably) on speculations about how the Social Fund would operate. And even after the Act was on the statute book, the Government evaded criticism by not publishing the 'impact tables' until October 1987, after the general election in June of that year. Even then, they were presented in a form which enabled ministers to claim that only one in eight of all claimants would be worse off. It was only when the consequences for individual claimants became clear with the coming into force of the Act on 11 April 1988 that protests on behalf of claimants, expressed to MPs and in the media, had an effect, and then only in relation to Housing Benefit.

The Government's dependence on its backbenchers in Parliament, especially as the 1987 general election approached, and on pension companies and employers for the implementation of pension reforms, enabled those sources to exert effective pressure on the Government over the issues that concerned them. There were no equivalent levers available to the Social Security Consortium and its constituent organizations, or to the statutory Social Security Advisory Committee, although they were able to publish critical reports. Only those who supported the retention of Child Benefit in non-targeted form were effective, and then by virtue of the support they had from certain Conservative MPs and party activists.

Chapter eight

THE TREASURY VERSUS THE SPENDING DEPARTMENTS: THE ANNUAL SPENDING ROUND

Introduction

Every year there takes place within British government what is known as the 'annual spending round'. The outcome of it is a set of 'expenditure plans', which are presented to the House of Commons in November by the Chancellor of the Exchequer. In recent years these have taken the form of figures showing the total amount of spending planned for the approaching financial year (i.e. the year beginning on 1 April next) and the two following years. This 'planning total' is broken down into so much per department or departmental field of activity, and also includes an amount for the Reserve.[1]

The annual spending round involves an on-going interaction between the 'spending departments' and the Treasury, at both official and ministerial levels. In this chapter I examine this interaction, again using the four perspectives employed in previous chapters. This does not require a detailed analysis of policies and measures like those presented in previous chapters, but it does require a careful look at how the figures are arrived at. Relevant evidence is to be found in the ministerial memoirs of Nigel Lawson[2] (he was Financial Secretary to the Treasury 1979–81 and Chancellor of the Exchequer 1983–9) and of other Cabinet ministers of the Thatcher era, notably Kenneth Baker.[3] Barbara Castle's diaries for 1974–6, when she was Secretary of State for Social Services, have some 'bits of the jigsaw' not found elsewhere.[4] Leo Pliatzky's books *Getting and Spending*[5] and *The Treasury under Mrs Thatcher*[6] give us an analysis as well as some raw evidence from the civil servant's point of view (Pliatzky had 27 years' experience in the Treasury, rising to the grade of Second Permanent Secretary). Andrew Likierman, author of *Public Expenditure: Who Really Controls It and How*,[7] has observed the process at close quarters in the capacity of adviser to the House of Commons Treasury and Civil Service Select Committee, and his book

---

Box 8.1   The annual spending round in the mid-to-late 1980s

January	White Paper published for the three-year period beginning 1 April next. Public Expenditure Survey Committee (PESC) begins review of previous round.
March	PESC decides timetable, etc. Treasury tells 'spending departments' what economic assumptions ('guidelines') to plan on.
April	Officials in the Treasury and spending departments agree 'baselines' (adjusted figures from the latest Public Expenditure White Paper). Officials and ministers in the spending departments prepare and agree proposals for future spending.
May	Spending departments submit details of their proposals to the Treasury. Treasury officials quiz departmental officials on justification, value for money, etc.
June	Spending departments submit formal 'bids' for money for the programmes they wish to carry out. Treasury officials and principal finance officers discuss these bids. PESC then assembles them into a report to the Chief Secretary to the Treasury. The Chief Secretary has 'exhaustive discussion within the Treasury with the Chancellor and senior officials', then agrees with the Prime Minister the recommendations that he will put to Cabinet.
June/July	Meeting of the Cabinet. The Chief Secretary makes recommendations for public expenditure totals for the three years under consideration. Chancellor spells out taxation implications of alternatives. Cabinet takes 'decisions' on totals, possibly leaving some flexibility. 'Bilateral' discussions between the Chief Secretary and 'spending ministers' begin.
September	Bilaterals resume after the summer holidays.
October	Party conference. The 'Star Chamber' meets if required, and makes recommendations to Cabinet if no settlement is reached.
November	The final public expenditure Cabinet meeting. The Chancellor delivers the Autumn Statement.

---

does a valuable job in bringing materials from many sources together. And Heclo and Wildavsky, in their book *The Private Government of Public Money*,[8] cite some illuminating excerpts from their interviews. (As Americans they received exceptionally good access to officials, but on the condition that their book did not identify participants and policy issues: as a consequence their 'story line' is not easy to follow.) Young and Sloman's *But Chancellor: an Inquiry into the Treasury*[9] has some interesting comments from Treasury and other officials, made in radio broadcasts in the winter of 1982–3. Contemporary newspaper reports are also invaluable, both for the most recent developments and for 'leaked' letters and memoranda.

Evidence from these sources needs to be 'quarried' and marshalled in a way that is appropriate to the subject matter. We are dealing here not with a single issue, like the poll tax, or a bundle of issues, but a recurring cycle of activities. I have therefore taken as my framework the basic events and activities in a 'typical' annual spending round of the mid-to-late 1980s: these are shown in Box 8.1, which was assembled by taking Likierman's model of the planning cycle[10] as a starting point and modifying it in the light of ministers' accounts of what had actually happened when they themselves took part. I then combed the sources looking for material relating to successive steps in the sequence. I have also incorporated some material from recent years where it appears characteristic of what happened previously. This material is assembled and presented following the sequence of the cycle rather than in year order (so, for example, evidence from 1988 on an early stage comes before evidence from 1983 on a late one).

A technical note

'Public expenditure' is a technical term. Precisely what should count as public expenditure is a matter of definition. The Government's official definition has frequently changed from year to year since the mid-1970s. We do not need to go into the detail of the different definitions, although it is worth noting that the choice of definition has often been criticized as being based on reasons other than logic. Until 1976 the definition had been laid down by Treasury officials. Denis Healey, the then Chancellor, suspects that they had chosen a definition which would deliberately overstate public spending in order to put pressure on a Government that was reluctant to cut it. (The definition was also out of line with that used by other countries.[11]) Nigel Lawson chose to treat the proceeds of privatization – sales of national assets – as negative public expenditure, justifying this accounting device on the grounds that since purchases of assets added to public expenditure, it was entirely consistent that sales of assets should reduce it:[12] critics pointed out that the result was to give a false (but favourable to the Government) impression of the extent to which the Chancellor had succeeded in controlling actual spending.[13]

From 1982–3 to 1989–90 expenditure plans were published annually, first in outline form in the Autumn Statement delivered by the Chancellor of the Exchequer to the House of Commons in November, and then in more detail in the Public Expenditure White Paper the following January. Since then there has been a period of transition, with first the White Paper and then the Autumn Statement being superseded. At the time of writing the arrangements are that the Chancellor presents to the House of Commons a combined Financial Statement and Budget Report at around the end of November, and the following spring each department publishes in a single document its annual report and a detailed description of its own expenditure plans. In the mid-to-late 1980s and early 1990s the plans took the form of figures for planned spending in the approaching financial year (i.e. the year beginning on the next 1 April) and the two following years.

The annual spending round

Placing ourselves back in the mid-to-late 1980s, we find the process more or less following the timetable shown in Box 8.1. In January, around the time of publication of the White Paper containing detailed plans for the year due to begin in three months or so, work starts on the following November's Autumn Statement and the subsequent White Paper, which will cover the three years beginning on 1 April in the following year, 15 months hence. (For example, work began in January 1988 for the year 1989–90, and – in less detail – the years 1990–1 and 1991–2. Outline figures for 1989–90 and 1990–1 had already been published in the 1987 Autumn Statement and the January 1988 White Paper.)

The early part of the spending round is handled by the Public Expenditure Survey Committee (PESC), an interdepartmental committee of civil servants: principal finance officers (usually deputy secretary grade) from the 'spending departments' with a senior Treasury official in the chair. PESC carries out a review (or 'post-mortem', as Likierman puts it[14]) of how well the previous year's work has turned out, including whether the actual spending in the current year is likely to overshoot or fall short of what was planned. It also decides what the timetable for the current spending round should be, which topics should be given particular attention and what kind of information is required.[15]

The process is not carried out in isolation from what is going on in the 'real world'. Rising unemployment creates rising numbers of people legally entitled to social security benefits: whatever the take-up of these, under the existing legislation central government is under a legal obligation, and hence committed, to paying them. In January 1991 the latest unemployment figure of 1.847 million was reported to have 'wrecked the Treasury assumption of 1.75 million for 1991/92, forcing ministers to plan for higher benefit payments than anticipated . . . Ministers are now estimating that unemployment could easily reach 2 million before it falls back again'.[16] The public spending implications of such information cannot be ignored simply because they arrive at an inconvenient time.

In March the Treasury sends to the spending departments its assumptions and forecasts about economic developments affecting public expenditure.[17] These are based not only on the judgements of Treasury 'experts': as Sir Douglas Wass (Permanent Secretary at the Treasury 1974–83) told Young and Sloman, in some areas

there is room for judgement as to whether the right assumption has been made. And in those areas ministers may express scepticism or doubt about particular assumptions, may say, 'Well, wouldn't it be . . . isn't it more likely to be, this?' And we'd talk about the possibility that it would be this rather than that, and may change the forecast somewhat.[18]

In other words, Treasury ministers may choose the assumptions – about inflation, for example – that suit their political aims or public statements.

When the process begins, the outline figures from the previous year's work provide a 'baseline', but they are reviewed in the light of any discrepancies between the plans for the current year (1987–8 in the above example) and the latest forecast of the likely 'outturn' (what spending will actually be) for that year. Pliatzky tells us it is normal for spending departments to try to get the figures changed in their favour. They may argue that actual inflation has been running above the allowance made for it, or that there have been new developments since the last White Paper. Or it may be claimed that the baseline figures will be inadequate 'for carrying out government policy'.[19] This, of course, is where disputes can arise over what 'government policy' actually *is*.

Baseline figures are significant not only for 'year 1' – the first year now being planned for – and 'year 2', but also for the new 'year 3', for which there are no baseline figures to be brought forward from the previous Autumn Statement and White Paper. According to Pliatzky, 'The gap is filled by projecting departmental programmes forward into the extra year on the basis of a formula for which the Treasury has obtained Cabinet approval as part of the ground rules for the exercise.' Such a formula might be to uprate the year 2 baseline figures roughly in line with, or slightly below, the prospective rate of inflation.[20]

All this suggests a very 'incremental' approach, with spending allocations simply being extrapolated forward from one year to the next, so that once a programme is 'in PESC', the only argument is about the size of the change, or 'increment'. The House of Commons was, however, told in 1986 by the then Chief Secretary, John MacGregor, that the Government did

> ensure that a number of areas are fundamentally reviewed each year. These reviews will ask: is this programme essential, does it have to be carried out in the public sector, have its objectives kept pace with changing circumstances, and can these objectives be achieved more economically?[21]

The Treasury, of course, would prefer decrements to increments, even where no fundamental review is carried out. In 1993 it came to light that Treasury officials had in February sent a memorandum to spending departments asking them to calculate the effects of cuts of 2.5 and 5 per cent in their 'budgets' (allocations) for 1994–5: 'Whitehall sources' insisted that the Treasury circular was standard practice at this stage in the fiscal year,[22] and 'Downing Street' was reported as insisting that the letter was 'routine'.[23] So such a request seems to have been made in previous years too. Indeed, Heclo and Wildavsky describe the strategy and the classic counter to it, the 'sore thumb' technique, which consists of suggesting for cuts programmes which ministers won't want to hit because of the political consequences – something to which there is a manifesto commitment, for example.[24]

Treasury officials also inspect outturns with a view to identifying particular expenditures that are growing unexpectedly fast. (Recent examples have been nursery education in 1990, invalidity benefit in 1992, the NHS drugs bill in 1993, Housing Benefit and benefits for 16- and 17-year-olds in 1994.) Evidently rapid growth is a criterion for the fundamental review referred to by Mac-Gregor. The onus is then on the department to find a way of economizing. (The Treasury may make its own suggestions.)

The Chancellor may add to the pressure. In April 1990, the then Chancellor, John Major, was reported to have told the Cabinet, with the Prime Minister's backing, that the autumn spending negotiations between the Treasury and the other departments would be the toughest for years:

> He fears the Government risks fighting the next election with inflation at an unacceptably high level – it is expected to approach 10 per cent this month – and has implied that if spending is not controlled, income tax may have to rise next year. Ministers say they have never known the Treasury to dig in against spending bids . . . so far in advance.[25]

Once the baselines are agreed (in April), the contest between the Treasury and the spending departments begins in earnest. Senior Treasury officials, who are the ones closest to ministers, seek to 'hold the line' – the 'planning total' (the aggregate of all public expenditure, however defined). If any spending department wants more money for a particular programme, the onus is on its officials to make its case. It may be found in four ways: by switching money from other programmes of its own; by cuts in the spending of other departments; by raising the planning total, and thus increasing the amount needing to be found by taxation and/or borrowing; or from the reserve. As Pliatzky says, 'The planning total for each future year always includes a large reserve. The further away the year, the larger the reserve allowed for in that year's plans.' As that year approaches, part of the reserve is allocated to meet unforeseen demands and additional bids.[26]

However, in the first instance the civil servants in the spending departments have to put their cases to the Treasury. It is the younger, middle-ranking and junior Treasury officials who deal with them. But they are heavily outnumbered by the officials in the spending departments and do not have the latter's depth of knowledge of the subject matter. Young and Sloman were told by the assistant secretary then in charge of monitoring spending on social security:

> In my job there are ten of us altogether – that's including clerical support – dealing with the entire spending on the staff and benefit side of the Department of Health and Social Security. Now it stands to reason that there's quite a lot of what the department does that we don't actually see and that we don't know about. Overall the system should ensure that public expenditure is planned according to faintly rational principles . . . But there are quite large areas of departmental spending on which the Treasury is not expert, cannot – by nature of what it is and how many we are – be expert on everything that's done.[27]

Young and Sloman found that Treasury officials are enjoined to avoid getting 'immersed too much in the merits of any particular policy': essentially their technique is to question and challenge proposals, and to see whether they are compatible with the department's already agreed public expenditure pro- gramme and with the policy of the Government as a whole. So they probe arguments, ferret out inconsistencies, ask questions like 'Do you consider that this can be justified if we have to add one penny in the pound to the standard rate of income tax?', and try to encourage spending departments to strive towards value for money. As the principal dealing with spending on higher education put it, 'We're interested not only in whether it costs x million pounds, but what that x million pounds is intended to do, and you can't have a sensible discussion about a proposal unless you do that.'[28] This, then, is rather more than simply keeping the totality of public spending down.

The recently retired Permanent Secretary at the Ministry of Defence did accept that over a small proportion of his department's budget there was an argument with the Treasury: 'It's a test of manliness, I suppose, as to who's the strongest, who's going to last out the longest.'[29] In another radio programme, a former 'high-flyer' in the MoD said:

One of the things that bothered me was the way that Whitehall plays it as a game rather than trying to arrive at the best possible decision in the national interest. I can illustrate that by an occasion when we made a bit of an error [in a calculation] and it wasn't until publication that we realized what we'd done. And when I talked to my Treasury opposite number the reply was 'Ah, I wondered if you'd spot that'.[30]

The Permanent Secretary of the DHSS would not publicly admit to Young and Sloman that his department and the Treasury had conflicting interests:

Far from it being an adversarial relationship, I see it as a continuing, constructive dialogue . . . If I thought that any of my staff here were suppressing or editing information passing between this department and the Treasury, I would be very angry about it, because it wouldn't in the long run be in the interest of the department. Certainly it wouldn't be in the interest of this department's ministers, nor of the many different clientele whom we exist to serve, because sooner or later something would go wrong, as a result of having only a partial awareness in the Treasury of what it is that we're doing.[31]

In the spending departments, it is the principal finance officers who are the 'middlemen' – the 'fixers'. It is they who seek to make 'deals' and find bases for agreement between the departments and the Treasury. Heclo and Wildavsky found that they need to gain the trust of Treasury officials and to be prepared to see the Treasury point of view, and say where necessary: 'The department and minister will be difficult, but I will support it.' Thus it is expected that they will make 'a fresh and individual offering rather than defensively parroting [their] departmental case'.[32]

Does a sense of duty towards its clientele – social security claimants – lead the DHSS (now the Department of Social Security) into conflict with the Treasury, with its motivation to keep public spending down? A report in *The Guardian* in June 1994, headed 'Treasury plan to curb youth hardship bill', and said to be based on correspondence between the Treasury and the DSS (and going into detail in a way which corroborates this), contained indications that the relationship can indeed be adversarial. The issue was the position of 16- and 17-year-olds since the implementation in 1988 of the social security reforms. As we saw in Chapter 7, they had no general right to claim Income Support, but they were eligible for discretionary payments of £27.50 or £36.15 a week if they could demonstrate severe hardship, e.g. they had suffered abuse or had no option but to live apart from their parents. The number of young people applying for these payments increased by 23 per cent in 1993–4 to 141,644, while the number of successful applications rose by 30 per cent to 123,745 – a success rate of more than 87 per cent.

> Correspondence from the Treasury shows that officials think the hardship scheme has been too lax . . . [They] have told the DSS that the bill for so-called 'severe hardship' cases has been rising too fast . . . [They] have proposed that the Department check with parents when a young person claims to have been thrown out, while social workers should be brought in to verify the stories of claimants who say they have been abused.

The DSS was said to have questioned the Treasury's figures, but accepted that the true figures were higher than expected. This it attributed to

> the Employment Service's 'consistent failure' to honour the Government's guarantee of a youth training place for all who seek one: ' . . . the result has been that more and more cases, living in low-income homes [or] estranged from their family, have been forced to claim' . . . In correspondence seen by *The Guardian*, a senior department official has warned the Treasury: 'I am sure you will be sensitive to the criticisms that could be levelled against the Department and ministers if just one case could be proved that the Department forced an abused child back into the clutches of an abuser' . . . Rejecting any tightening of controls 'already regarded as too severe', [he] said the Treasury's proposals would be costly and counter-productive. Social workers would be likely to side with claimants, while checking with parents on estrangement could leave the Government exposed to judicial review over its failure on the training guarantee . . .
> The correspondence shows that a Treasury team, preparing for the annual departmental [public expenditure] negotiations, visited in April the unit in Glasgow then responsible for all hardship claims. Responsibility has since passed to local benefit offices – further fuelling Treasury anxiety.[33]

By some time in June, the proposals have undergone sufficient scrutiny and testing for the spending departments to crystallize them into formal 'bids', which are now submitted to the Treasury. There may be further discussion, and then the bids from all the departments, in their final form, are put together by PESC into a report, from officials, to the minister concerned, the Chief Secretary to the Treasury. This report, Likierman tells us, forms the basis of the recommendations that the Chief Secretary puts to the Cabinet at their end-of-July meeting, which 'decides' the levels of total public expenditure for what are now the next three financial years.[34] According to Lawson, however, the Chief Secretary has 'exhaustive discussion within the Treasury with the Chancellor and senior officials', after which he agrees his recommendations with the Prime Minister: there is then a meeting of the Cabinet in *early* July, 'at which the Chief Secretary [presents] a paper setting out in stern and measured tones the current public expenditure picture and trends' and recommending expenditure totals for the three years. There is also a paper from the Chancellor setting out the general economic context, spelling out the tax consequences of alternative spending decisions, and calling on colleagues to agree to the Chief Secretary's recommendations. 'With varying degrees of enthusiasm, they . . . do so.'[35]

We need to look carefully at Likierman's word 'decides'. What does it actually mean in this context? Lawson tells us that in the early years of the Thatcher government, the Chief Secretary's recommendation would be in terms of a precise cash total derived from the previous year's White Paper.

This . . . proved too rigid . . . I eventually decided to switch to a double-barrelled guideline which permitted an adequate but not excessive degree of flexibility – something like 'as close as possible to the previously published planning total, and certainly a further decline in General Government Expenditure as a percentage of GDP'.[36]

So the decision does not represent an irrevocable commitment to a highly specific figure: it is not 'set in concrete'. *The Guardian* reported that the formula agreed by the Cabinet in July 1990 was indeed a flexible one:

It was agreed that strict control of public expenditure must be maintained by sticking as closely as possible to the planning totals set out in the [January] 1990 White Paper with the aim of keeping the ratio of public spending, excluding privatization proceeds, to Gross Domestic Product on a downward path.[37]

After the Cabinet meeting, 'bilateral discussions' between the Chief Secretary and the spending ministers usually begin. In exceptional situations they may begin much earlier. In 1990 'hard bargaining' was said to be about to take place at the beginning of June between Chris Patten, Secretary of State for the Environment, and Norman Lamont, Chief Secretary, over the former's bid for an extra £3 billion to reduce poll tax (Community Charge) bills in 1991–2. The additional money, to be used in grants to local authorities, was to be announced in July, immediately before the summer recess of Parliament. 'There is enormous pressure to send the back-benchers off to their constituencies with something in their pockets', a source said.[38]

Barbara Castle's diaries for 1974 give us something of the feel of bilateral negotiations at that time and the role of the Principal Finance Officer in them. It seems to be the case that officials continued to be active even after ministers had become involved:

10 July. Dick Bourton [Deputy Secretary and Principal Finance Officer at the DHSS] had managed to get Treasury to cough up £47 million to offset price rises in the NHS and thus avoid the threatened reduction of services . . . [He asked me to] tell Parliamentary Secretary [David Owen] to leave these things to him as [Owen] had nearly upset the apple-cart by going direct to the Chief Secretary. These things were far better left to officials, as it had been necessary to twist the rules.[39]

23 August. Next to PESC. Bourton said he thought he might get another £100 million for the NHS, though he had conceded that [the cost of a mobility allowance for disabled people] should be taken out of it . . . I can see that officials' hearts are not in my battle to get more money . . . I suspect that they thoroughly sympathize with the Treasury's traditional retrenchment attitude to public expenditure.[40]

3 September. [Meeting with the Chancellor (Denis Healey), Chief Secretary (Joel Barnett) and two Treasury officials (Baldwin and Widdup), plus DHSS junior ministers and officials]. Denis . . . drew up an agenda of items for us to deal with. I interrupted to say, 'You have left out the housewives' disablement benefit.' 'Oh, no, that's agreed,' replied Denis. I looked at my officials, who have been bringing me messages, ostensibly from the Chancellor, to the effect that he couldn't accept any commitment to a disabled housewives' benefit and, if I didn't fall immediately into line, he would take the whole thing into Cabinet (where I . . . shall have few allies in my efforts to pre-empt some of the PESC discussions). 'But I thought you had reservations, Chancellor,' I said sweetly . . . Denis looked puzzled. Joel shrugged: 'We reached agreement.' Widdup then protruded his head reluctantly to admit that he had been the author of the diktats. 'You haven't seen this yet, Chancellor,' he said.[41]

28 October. Dick Bourton . . . told me . . . he had got another £30 million for the NHS next year, but it was to be non-recurring. Nonetheless this, together with a few other things, meant that . . . I had in fact got the additional £100 million for which I was pressing . . . Part of the deal was, of course, to be that I accepted the offer and would not argue the matter any more in Cabinet . . . [If] I were to question the offer in any way, it would be withdrawn . . . (Philip [Permanent Secretary, DHSS] keeps coming to me and saying how marvellous Dick is at getting more than our share out of the Treasury and how wise it is to leave him alone to get on with it.)[42]

Interestingly, Alan Clark (then Parliamentary Under-Secretary of State at the Department of Employment) records receiving a similar warning in September

1983 from his Private Secretary: 'It's not really a good idea to get the wrong side of Fred.'[43]

The bilaterals, having resumed in September, continue up to and usually during the party conference in October. Lawson tells us that it was very rare for agreement with any spending minister to be reached after one bilateral. There would invariably be a second and, if it was likely to prove productive, a third. As he saw it, 'It was a matter of virility for some spending ministers, egged on by their officials, to put in bids well above anything remotely consistent with the overall envelope agreed by Cabinet.'[44]

During the party conference the broadsheet newspapers have often contained leaked accounts of goings-on in the Chief Secretary's hotel room. In 1990 an internal memorandum to Kenneth Clarke, Secretary of State for Health, from one of his senior officials, was leaked to the Labour Party and the press. According to press reports, it showed that Clarke had put in a bid for about £26.3 billion, including, on the advice of his officials, 'an overall negotiating margin' of £800 to £900 million (i.e. his 'bottom line' was £25.5 or £25.4 billion). He had then volunteered to the Chief Secretary, Norman Lamont, to cut his bid by £172 million, but Lamont had asked for more. The memorandum suggested to Clarke that while he would want to protect his main patients' services, he would 'otherwise want to make a fair response. Since then Treasury officials have conveyed to us that the Chief Secretary would interpret a total bid reduction in the range of £500 to £600 million as "constructive" and likely to get a response in kind.' It also suggested that Clarke reply to Lamont that he was asking for cuts which 'represent considerable sacrifices and risks over the financing of my programmes', and was seeking a settlement so tough on health education and other centrally financed services that it would 'undercut our commitments or damage our credibility on key policies in the coming year', but that he should raise his offer of cuts to £431 million. This would include a reduction in extra spending on community care from £50 million to £4 million and a cut of £234 million in spending on drugs, said to be made possible because information that family doctors had been given on the cost of their prescribing against that of other doctors had reduced the rise in the drugs bill. The memorandum warned against a further cut, saying that the figure must be 'publicly defensible' and must 'not undermine this important cost saving initiative'. Clarke was reported as having 'visibly blushed' when it was put to him at a press conference that he would be forced to accept his bottom line, which had now been revealed to the Treasury. He declined to say whether the draft letter to the Chief Secretary had actually been sent, but said: 'I deliberately put in for generous bids' (which is not inconsistent with Lawson's impression). When the Autumn Statement was published four weeks later, it showed an allocation to Health of £25.08 billion, some £300 or £400 million below Clarke's 'bottom line'.[45]

If the bilaterals don't result in agreement between Chief Secretary and departmental minister, there are basically three options.[46] One is for the Chancellor to have a private meeting with the minister, with no officials present, to agree a compromise acceptable to both. The second, likely to be used when there are 'both large sums and major policy issues involved', is for the Prime Minister, Chancellor, Chief Secretary and minister to meet and try to reach agreement. The third option (in the period 1982–92) is to activate the 'Star Chamber', an *ad hoc* Cabinet committee set up by Thatcher, whose task is to adjudicate on the outstanding issues.

Both the first and second options were employed in the 1988 spending round, which Lawson describes as 'satisfactorily uneventful until very near the end, when there were two hiccups'. One concerned Nicholas Ridley, who, as Environment Secretary, refused to settle his housing budget with John Major, then Chief Secretary. Their dispute would normally have been resolved in the Star Chamber, but, according to Lawson, 'both of them were anxious to avoid this. John was proud that he had [achieved] a good result in the 1987 spending round without recourse to Star Chamber. He was determined to maintain his record if he possibly could.' On Ridley's side the problem was different. White-law had suffered a stroke in December 1987 and subsequently resigned his Cabinet post. The Prime Minister had given the job of chairing the Star Chamber to Cecil Parkinson:

> A number of colleagues . . . could not adjust to the idea of having Cecil sitting in judgement over them. All of these had settled bilaterally, except Nick . . . I saw Nick privately . . . We went over his programme together, and I offered him a number of modest concessions – which I had discussed with John in advance. We soon reached what was from the Treasury's point of view a very satisfactory agreement on all the outstanding issues.[47]

The other hiccup was over Child Benefit, which was paid 'indiscriminately' to all families with children. In 1987, for the first time, this had been 'frozen' in cash terms, i.e. not uprated to take account of inflation. The 'Treasury's position' was that help should be concentrated on the poorest families via the means-tested Family Credit, but, Lawson writes, 'it was not until 1987 that the DHSS had, in John Moore, a Secretary of State sufficiently in favour of selectivity to accept it. John defended the decision very effectively at the despatch box, and there was no serious back-bench revolt', despite the Press describing the freeze as 'a defeat for John Moore at the hands of the Treasury'.[48]

In 1988 the Chancellor and Chief Secretary sought a further freeze in Child Benefit, plus a further large increase in Family Credit. But in July 1988 the Prime Minister had decided to split the DHSS in two: when this was done Moore had been given the junior post of the two, Social Security rather than Health. Lawson writes: 'Feeling his political position on the slide, and knowing full well how a further Child Benefit freeze would be interpreted by the media, he became determined to resist it, and unwisely let this be known to the Press.' (We don't have Moore's account of this.) Moore, Lawson says, also told the Chief Whip that unless Child Benefit were increased he would resign his post, reiterating this stance at a meeting with Thatcher, Lawson and Major. The following morning, however, he had a private meeting with Lawson. According to Lawson:

his mood had changed . . . he clearly did not wish to resign, and was looking for a way out . . . I offered him something for the poorer, older, pensioners as a way out. He rejected it, insisting that it was child poverty that the argument was all about. I then offered him what the official Treasury had had in mind all along – a freeze in Child Benefit, but extra money for Family Credit. This he accepted.[49]

The third option for resolving outstanding disagreements between Chief Secretary and spending minister has been the 'Star Chamber', an *ad hoc* Cabinet committee which was first set up in 1982, under the chairmanship of William Whitelaw (later Lord Whitelaw), who was Deputy Prime Minister besides holding other Cabinet posts. The Star Chamber would also comprise the Chief Secretary, the Chief Whip and four other ministers, 'ideally three public spending hawks and one public spending dove, thus ensuring that while both wings of the Cabinet and the Party were represented, the balance was sound', as Lawson puts it.[50] Mostly the other ministers were themselves spending ministers who had already settled:

Membership . . . was . . . quite sought after, partly because it was enjoyable in itself to sit in judgement on one's colleagues. Thus I could sometimes persuade a colleague to settle early with the incentive that, if he did, he would be asked to go on the Star Chamber.[51]

The experience of facing the Star Chamber has been described by Kenneth Baker.[52] On becoming Environment Secretary in September 1985, in succession to Patrick Jenkin, he found himself faced with the issue of the Department's public expenditure bid for 1986–7, and especially the amount for new building, maintenance and repair of public sector housing. In 1984–5 this had amounted to £1850 million.

For 1986–7 the Treasury wanted me to accept £1200 million. They were oblivious to the fact that I would soon have to publish a report . . . which revealed that the backlog of repairs amounted to £20 billion . . . The report was political dynamite, as homelessness was increasing by 20,000 a year and about 3000 people were going into bed-and-breakfast accommodation.

Baker was unable to reach a settlement with the Chief Secretary. On 24 October he appeared before the Star Chamber. It consisted of Willie Whitelaw, Norman Tebbit and three other ministers: Leon Brittan, John Biffen and Nicholas Edwards. Baker gives his personal account of the meeting:

Willie straightaway offered an increase of £100 million for 1986–7 and £200 million in each succeeding year. That was quite impossible, for it meant I would have had to acknowledge publicly that the housing programme would be cut by about £400 million. Then the others piled in. Leon acted as the prosecuting barrister – sharp, sarcastic, critical, forensic stuff . . . Norman Tebbit [was] bullying and abrasive, openly critical of public sector housing. At one stage I lost my temper . . . and I said: 'I will not accept your argument nor will any of my ministers.' There was a deathly pause and Nick Edwards tried to smooth things over. John Biffen was the most sympathetic and tried to explore ways of bridging the gap. Willie Whitelaw [said] the Cabinet 'could cut their generous offer or even withdraw it altogether'.

During the meeting Norman Tebbit sent him a note reminding him that if he didn't settle but pursued the issue to Cabinet, and was the only minister to do so, it would be his programme that would have to be 'squeezed to meet the overall target. I can assure you that your 21 colleagues will be unlikely to cut their programmes to bail you out.'

After this meeting Baker had to make a short visit to the USA. While he was away one of his junior ministers telephoned to say that the Chief Whip had 'sounded him out' to see how strongly he supported Baker. On his return Baker went to see Whitelaw, who told him: 'You must settle outside Cabinet', and increased his previous offer by £100 million. The offer was raised further during the discussion but not accepted by Baker, whose 'bottom line' was a total of £600 million.

The following day (5 November) Baker asked to see the Prime Minister, but was refused: she was, he says, not prepared to act as an appeal court while Star Chamber was sitting. That day he was again summoned before the Star Chamber: Tebbit and Brittan 'were offensive once again' and the offer was raised yet again but again Baker declined. The next morning (6 November) Baker met the Chief Secretary, John MacGregor. 'John said he was prepared to move the Treasury's position and I said I was prepared to accept a [total of £500 million]. We agreed on these figures.' Baker recounts that friends congratulated him afterwards, and that the Chief Whip was reported to have said 'I had played it brilliantly, as I had got more than anyone expected by going to the Star Chamber'.

What we aren't told is how much of the extra £500 million for the public sector housing programme was found from elsewhere within Environment's own budget. Baker himself adds that 'one of the consequences of this settlement was that the Urban Programme directed at the inner cities had to be cut back from £338 million to £317 million for 1986–7. I was very disappointed with this.'[53]

Where was the Chancellor while all this was going on? Interestingly, Lawson, the then Chancellor, says nothing at all of this episode, merely commenting: 'The 1985 expenditure round was in the end uneventful – which means it went well.' He was helped by the drop in inflation in the second half of 1985 and by being able to hold defence spending down to zero real growth. We can perhaps infer that what was a central issue to Baker – whom Lawson refers to as 'an indiscriminate big spender' – and to the Star Chamber was not so crucial to the Chancellor, who left it to the Chief Secretary and the Star Chamber to deal with.[54]

If, exceptionally, there are any issues which the Star Chamber is unable to resolve, they will be dealt with at the final event in the process, the public expenditure Cabinet meeting in the first half of November. Lawson recalls only two such occasions, both in 1984: 'a little extra money' was secured for the housing programme, and on the other matter the Star Chamber's suggested figure was upheld.[55]

Lawson also writes that before the meeting he and the Chief Secretary would see friendly colleagues to make sure that they were happy with the papers circulated. He would also see the Prime Minister alone to discuss the sequence in which she called ministers to speak:

> It was important to open and close the discussions with comments from ministers who were dependable on public expenditure, leaving the less sound colleagues sandwiched in the middle – but not in a bunch, otherwise there was the risk of momentum building up . . . The one colleague who could be guaranteed to be unsound was Peter Walker: it was useful to have his contribution immediately followed by one from Norman Tebbit.[56]

Lawson tells us that he always kept a few cards up his sleeve, such as estimates of debt interest and the size of the Reserve. 'But clearly it was not in my interest to make any of these unrealistic.'[57]

Finally the Cabinet would formally take the public expenditure decisions, and a few days later these would be outlined by the Chancellor in his Autumn Statement.

Sometimes the figures in the Autumn Statement were higher than had been anticipated. Lawson writes:

> I was obliged to announce in the Autumn Statement of November 1986 a Planning Total (excluding privatization) for 1987–88 some £5 billion higher in cash terms than the figure previously published. This was intensely embarrassing to me, to John [MacGregor, the Chief Secretary], and to our officials alike, and inevitably led to the accusation that I was engaging in a pre-election public spending bonanza. In fact the previously published figure had once again been unrealistic; and the figure for which we settled represented only a minuscule real increase over the previous year.[58]

However, Pliatzky suggests that the accusation may have been justified. He points out that 'the White Paper of January 1987 . . . stated that, as compared with the last White Paper, extra funds had been allocated to the Government's priority services, including health [and] education.' The approach of an election, in his opinion, 'must have some effect on the political climate in which decisions are taken'.[59] More recent events seem to bear this out. Economics editor David Smith argues:

> In the long run-up to the 1992 election, spending was first boosted in 1990 because the Government originally planned to go to the country in 1991. When the election was delayed until 1992, the process was repeated. 'We had two pre-election public spending rounds', says one senior Treasury official, 'and the second was more generous than the first.'[60]

In most years the Autumn Statement will be the end of the Government's decision-making process, save for its elaboration into the White Paper. But in 1984 Sir Keith Joseph, Secretary of State for Education and Science, had agreed with the Chief Secretary that an increase in universities' science research budgets should be financed by abolishing the minimum student maintenance grant (which was paid to all students, however well-off their parents) and by charging better-off parents a means-tested contribution towards the tuition fee as well. Both Lawson and Thatcher had known about it, but it had been 'buried away in the papers' and not specifically mentioned at the November meeting. 'When the Autumn Statement was published, along with the usual departmental press releases filling out the details, all hell broke loose.'[61] Joseph was summoned to appear before the Conservative backbench Education Committee on 4 December. More than 250 backbenchers were present, most of them 'baying for blood'. Thirty-three MPs spoke at the meeting: 30 of them criticized him, some in very strong terms.[62] The following day in the House of Commons he announced the withdrawal of the proposal to charge a contribution towards tuition fees.

Lawson comments:

> I proposed to him that we should stand firm on the abolition of the minimum grant but . . . drop the idea of seeking a parental contribution towards tuition fees. This would leave a shortfall of some £20 million [in 1985–6], which I suggested we should split 50:50 . . . I would give him an extra £10 million from the Reserve and he would reduce the proposed . . . increase in the science budget by £10 million. Keith agreed, and this did the trick. The revolt simmered down to containable proportions.

He adds that the real problem was that the people who would have been hurt by the proposed changes weren't the poor, who were fully protected, or the rich, who could easily afford them, but the people in between: 'They were the people who comprised the bulk of the Party activists in the constituencies and, in particular, the local Party officers.'[63]

We see, then, that the Autumn Statement need not be the end of that phase of public expenditure decision making: pressure from the Government's own backbenchers can bring about a marginal change in what has thus far been decided.

Morrison Halcrow, in his biography of Keith Joseph, writes that he was unusual among ministers for accepting a 'no' from the Treasury in the bilateral negotiations. Unlike other ministers, who are said to have subscribed to the principle of cutting public expenditure but fought hard for money for their own department, he declined to play 'the Whitehall game' of asking for more than he really wanted and then letting himself be negotiated down. Halcrow records: 'Several times during his years at Education the Treasury were astonished when he accepted a *No* which other ministers would have regarded only as a first stage in a negotiating process.'[64]

For the Autumn Statement to serve as a means of keeping expenditure down – i.e. to be something that the Government can sensibly commit itself to – it must be based on realistic assumptions. Following the 1984 Statement, it rapidly became apparent to Lawson that the totals published for 1985–6 and subsequent years 'had been based on unrealistic assumptions and were thus far too low'. He persuaded the Prime Minister that the least bad course was to increase the Reserve for each of those years. 'It was profoundly embarrassing.'[65] Two years later, in 1986, when Lawson announced in the Autumn Statement a planning total some £5 billion higher in cash terms than the figure previously published, because that figure had been 'unrealistic', this too was 'intensely embarrassing'.[66] While rebutting the accusation that he was engaging in a pre-election public spending bonanza, he nevertheless 'felt it sensible to change the presentation of the Government's public expenditure objective', in the process redefining that objective, as mentioned above.[67]

It is worth noting at this point the most recent developments in the public expenditure process. In 1992 a new Cabinet committee on Public Expenditure (EDX) was set up, chaired by the Chancellor and including the Chief Secretary. (Other members were the Home Secretary, the President of the Board of Trade, the Leaders of the House of Commons and House of Lords, and the Chancellor of the Duchy of Lancaster, giving a total of five non-spending ministers to two spending ones). In 1993, the summer meeting of the Cabinet took place on 17 June. It set spending ceilings for 1994–5 and the immediately following years and issued a brief to EDX: 'EDX has been asked to make proposals to Cabinet in the autumn about the allocation of spending within these totals, taking account of the Government's priorities and of competing claims on available resources.'[68] As before, the Chief Secretary then held bilateral meetings with spending ministers, but instead of concluding agreements himself in successive rounds of negotiation, he then reported to EDX, presumably highlighting areas of disagreement. Spending ministers then appeared before EDX to argue their cases, before the committee made its recommendations to Cabinet. Next, at a meeting of the Cabinet on 28 October 1993, they had the opportunity to challenge those recommendations and argue against any proposed cuts before the Cabinet took its final decisions.[69] So under the new system the Chief Secretary is relieved of much of the burden of negotiating with the spending departments: seven members of Cabinet rather than he alone are pressing to maintain the ceiling decided in June. (In 1994 Chief Secretary Jonathan Aitken appeared from press reports to be devoting his efforts – unsuccessfully as it turned out – chiefly to the cutting of Housing Benefit for council tenants who had spare bedrooms.[70]) And the *ad hoc* Star Chamber is no longer needed since its task is performed by EDX.

What is Parliament's role in the process? The Autumn Statement (nowadays the Financial Statement and Budget Report) is presented to the House of Commons and debated. The Treasury and Civil Service Select Committee holds an enquiry into the plans as a whole, and the 'departmental' select committees enquire into and report on the spending plans of the respective departments. The House of Commons is also formally responsible for authorizing the actual expenditure, through the system of 'Estimates': these are detailed requests for authorization drawn up by the spending departments, approved by Treasury ministers and presented to the House. They too are submitted to select committees, who pick out items for enquiry, some of which are later debated by the House as a whole on one of the three Estimates Days set aside in each session for the purpose. But MPs use these occasions to raise issues, or make ministers and officials aware of feelings, rather than to change the spending decisions already taken. Likierman, who devotes a chapter of his book to Parliament's role in the process, concludes that 'the crucial spending decisions still take place in the political back-rooms and in the deals ministers strike with each other in the [PESC] process'.[71]

Control of public expenditure is not merely a matter of making plans, setting limits and authorizing spending. The actual spending of sums above a certain limit has to be approved by the Treasury, which also monitors the progress of each department's spending through the year. And circumstances always arise during the financial year that necessitate extra allocations and supplementary estimates. For spending departments, there are particular problems towards the end of the year, when the possibility of overspending or underspending in certain fields arises.[72] We have seen that overspending has been strongly discouraged. Indeed, the whole system is constructed around the goal of putting a ceiling on expenditure, and for a department to seek supplementary estimates from the House of Commons without the justification of a change in circumstances that could not have been anticipated has meant 'disgrace and trouble': 'You're considered sloppy by the Treasury.'[73] Anxiety not to overspend may have contributed to the frequency with which departments have found that they were in danger of *underspending*.

The rule until recently was that money not used by the end of the year had to be returned to the Treasury. (There is now some relaxation in respect of major projects, where it may be difficult to get actual spending to follow the timetable exactly, and since 1993–4 departments have been able to carry forward all underspends on running costs to add to provision in a later year.[74]) This rule gave officials an incentive not to underspend if they could help it, especially as there was the risk 'that the Treasury will not be willing to give so much money the next time round'.[75] So we find departments looking anxiously for ways of spending money as 1 April approaches. Alan Clark relates being told by worried officials at the Department of Employment in September 1983: '[It] looks as if there is going to be a shortfall as our overall provision is £408 million and at present we are going to be pushed to get expenditure over £335–360 million.'[76] 'Shortfall' meant a shortage not of money but of things to spend money on! On suggesting that this was surely a matter for congratulation because the Government was dedicated to reducing public expenditure, Clark was told: 'It's important to get as close as possible to last year's provision in order to have a firm base from which to argue for increases this year.'[77] A month later the Department of the Environment asked local housing authorities to submit bids for extra spending totalling £1 billion before the end of the financial year.[78] The money went largely to those who had had the foresight to lay in a store of non-priority 'short notice' projects, on which spare resources could be utilized – 'burned off' – towards the end of the financial year: these were not necessarily the ones where 'housing need' was greatest.[79]

By way of a postscript, it is worth noting that at all times of the year Lawson and Treasury officials went to considerable lengths to prevent the arising of demands for increased public spending. 'The one constant belief at the heart of the Treasury . . . is its mission to stand firm against the desire of politicians of all parties and the rest of Whitehall to devise new ways of increasing government spending.'[80] Thatcher was said to take a similar view. Baker writes: 'One of her greatest anxieties was the creation of bodies she believed would then become demanders for more state funding.'[81] When Lawson returned to the Treasury as Chancellor in June 1983, he put a stop to the publication of a Green Paper on public expenditure that was based on a trawl of the spending departments' own estimates of what they would need to spend in the year ahead. 'It seemed to me painfully obvious that public exposure of the various departments' spending aspirations would make savings harder, not easier, to achieve.'[82] He was also opposed to giving freedom to local authorities to spend as they wished the proceeds of the sale of council houses, partly on the grounds that it gave them 'an opportunity to increase their spending in a particular year to a level which could not subsequently be maintained without substantially increased Exchequer assistance'.[83] And he was opposed to switching support from the elderly to families with children, on the grounds that 'any upsurge of popular feeling about pensioner hardship was bound to lead to renewed pressure for a general increase in the basic state pension'.[84]

We can get some idea of what it is like to be on the receiving end of Treasury pressure when there is no principal finance officer acting as mediator from the experience of David Donnison, who from 1975 to 1980 was Chairman of the Supplementary Benefits Commission (a body of non-civil servants within the Department of Health and Social Security with responsibility for the system of discretionary social security benefits). Donnison instigated the publishing of annual reports by the Commission, but this would inevitably draw attention to hardship in a way that would constitute a claim for extra resources, and had been opposed by the Treasury. And when the Treasury, together with other departments, was sent the draft annual report for 1975, it

> sent the longest list of comments and objections, many of them couched in tones of rather supercilious distaste. 'I am surprised', said the Treasury official in question during a final telephone conversation, 'that civil servants should be associated with such stuff. It's like something out of *New Society* – a magazine I fortunately do not have to read.'[85]

Donnison gives other examples of the Treasury exerting pressure, complete with 'rather supercilious distaste', to suppress reports or modify them so they could not easily be used as campaigning material.[86]

The policy

Once again, to identify 'policy' we need to look for commitment. In this case we need to ask: what was it that (a) the Cabinet collectively, and (b) individual ministers, were committed to at different points in the annual spending round?

Although every decision, such as that reached by a spending department's ministers and officials on what 'bid' to submit to the Treasury, creates commitment on their part, of particular significance are the Cabinet's decision in July on the 'grand total' of public expenditure for each of the three years under consideration (especially for the impending year, for which it is most strongly committed), and its decision in November on the totals for individual departments – their spending plans.

In what sense do these figures represent 'policy'? What commitments, on whose part, do they denote? For ministers and officials in the 'spending departments' they represent plans, statements of intention, so they denote a commitment to spend the monies made available on the purposes described (subject to any hidden thoughts about keeping open the possibility of diverting money earmarked for lower-priority purposes to higher-priority use), and to spend all of it. The money has been strenuously fought for and justified, and underspending has to be convincingly explained if it is not to cast doubt on the justification and to be used by the Treasury as grounds for cutting next year's allocation.

For ministers and officials in the Treasury, the figures represent ceilings, limits to expenditure, and their commitment is to seeing that these limits are not exceeded. (Below these ceilings, spending departments have a mandate for the expenditure.) This is also true of the Government as a whole, because the figures constitute objectives to which the Government is collectively committed, whether in absolute terms (e.g. to stabilize public spending: the Thatcher Government's first Public Expenditure White Paper in November 1979 stated that 'the Government's economic strategy must be to stabilise public spending for the time being'[87]) or in relation to other factors (e.g. 'to ensure that public expenditure takes a steadily smaller share of our national income', as the 1987 Conservative manifesto put it). The figures may also represent the realization of the Government's policy in another sense. For example, a Cabinet decision to switch resources from one field to another over a period of time will be reflected in the departmental spending totals while the changeover takes place.

Rationale

Means and ends.   To what extent were the overall totals and the departmental spending plans derived logically from objectives and constraints? From the standpoint of the Chancellor and the Chief Secretary and Treasury officials, the purpose of having spending plans is to *control* the spending of money. Setting a precise figure for a given year is a way of achieving that objective, a means to that end. The objective of ministers and officials in the spending departments is to get such figures agreed for their own department as will give them a mandate for the actual spending of money; that actual spending is a means to the further end of achieving certain objectives in the real world and the world of government and politics.

Since 1979, 'control of spending' has been defined by the Chancellor in different ways. At first, the objective was to reduce public spending in real terms; it was then replaced (in 1983–4) by the objective of holding it steady in real terms; this in turn was replaced (in autumn 1986) by the objective of having public expenditure decline over a period as a share of GDP. (The lack of specificity of this objective allowed the Government to increase spending in the run-up to a general election without infringing it.) Such objectives themselves clearly reflect the belief – held particularly strongly, as an article of faith, by successive Chancellors and Chief Secretaries – that public spending ought to be held down, whether in absolute or in relative terms, as far as possible. But the changes reflect the Government's learning over the years, through a process of trial and error, what the limits were to acting on that belief: what was 'realistic'[88] and what was not. Setting precise figures for a given year was thus not a matter solely of deriving them from the ultimate objective: constraints were an important determining factor too. The fact that Lawson chose to adopt a fresh objective when he discovered that the old one could not be achieved reflects the impact of perceptions of the real world – the ageing of the population, the development of costly technologies and rising unemployment – as well as 'the lobbying of vested interests'[89] and the Government's obligation to pay social security benefits to the unemployed. The totals were thus the product of a rationale, but the mechanism was one of choice within very limiting constraints, deriving both from the real world and from the world of government and politics.

The spending plans are made up of components of different kinds. In particular there is the component rolled forward as part of an on-going programme already 'in PESC'. There is also the component that is present to meet statutory and other obligations. Both these components can be calculated (e.g. by extrapolation) from the existing situation, so at first sight they are the products of a rationale. But some essential ingredients of these calculations are assumptions and forecasts (e.g. about future levels of inflation and unemployment) and we have seen that ministers' expressions of scepticism or doubt were able to enter into them, at least in the early years, with the figures receiving a certain amount of 'political massage', as Young and Sloman put it.[90]

Considerations. By definition, financial considerations – to do with the costs of departmental programmes – were pre-eminent in the formation of spending plans. The interesting question is: what part did real-world considerations play? At a 'global' level, the whole purpose of public spending is to do good for the people, to achieve real-world objectives. In practice, spending involves making choices, and when we look at the case made for spending on a particular programme rather than others, or the justification put forward after a decision has been taken, we find that not only were real-world considerations present: political considerations were invariably present too. Manifesto commitments, political 'indefensibility', the possibility of judicial review, protecting the Chancellor's position and avoiding embarrassment are examples we have encountered.

Interests

Before we can get sensible answers to the question of whose interests made a mark on policy, in the shape of the July decisions and the spending plans, we need to have some idea of whose interests, and what kinds of interests, were in contention. It is evident that the active participants in the process had institutional/political interests, which made considerable marks on policy. But we also need to ask what mark was made by the interests of consumers – the people on the 'receiving end' of government policies and measures.

The Prime Minister and the Cabinet. In her memoirs Thatcher says little or nothing about the annual spending round after 1983. Seemingly she was content to leave it to Lawson and whoever was Chief Secretary at the time, and to the Star Chamber if it was convened. (We have already noted her refusal to see Baker about his dispute over the housing budget while the Star Chamber was sitting.) Her role was to meet the Chief Secretary in June/July and agree his recommendations (we don't know whether she ever insisted on amendments), then to chair the crucial meetings of the Cabinet in July and again in November. The Prime Minister and the Cabinet collectively had conflicting interests: on the one hand, in holding public expenditure down and seeing that the July 'ceiling' was not exceeded; on the other, in being able to claim credit, in the Party's next general election manifesto, for 'increased spending' on health, education etc., and in defending themselves against accusations that they were running those services down. Thatcher also had a personal interest in spending on her 'pet projects' (such as Housing Action Trusts, as we have seen in earlier chapters): however, the forgoing of tax revenue through the use of tax allowances to encourage recourse to the private market for pensions and health care was not counted as 'spending'.

The Chancellor. What interests did the Chancellor have? It is clear that the holding down of spending totals and allocations reflects not only an intellectual belief on Lawson's part that that was the right thing to do, but also his *interest* in doing so, in that he identified himself with that belief and acquired a stake in securing its implementation. He also appears to have had a parallel interest in winning the 'game' against spending ministers, judging by the relish with which he describes the tactics that he employed and the considerable satisfaction that he evinces when relating how he contrived to get spending ministers to settle for less than they had wanted, and prevented demands for expenditure from surfacing. Public declaration of his intention strengthened his commitment to it and thereby gave him an even greater interest in achieving this end.

Lawson also had a strong interest, as his memoirs make very evident, in avoiding embarrassment, such as the embarrassment that comes with publicly setting targets and then failing to reach them: in 1985 this was 'profoundly embarrassing',[91] in 1986 it was 'intensely embarrassing'.[92] Better to change targets, or make them flexible – even if they are articles of faith – than to be seen to fail to reach them (a case of rationality and political interest coinciding). There is some support here for Heclo and Wildavsky's conclusion: 'Avoiding embarrassment to ministers in public, and particularly in the House of Commons, is one of the driving forces throughout British government.'[93] So the flexibility of the target appears to have been consistent with the Government's and the Chancellor's interest in avoiding embarrassment.

The connection between the 'publicness' of the failure to achieve such a target and the embarrassment that it causes is evident in Lawson's concern with 'presentation'.[94] Embarrassment is lessened if a change of target can be presented as a 'refinement', rather than an admission of failure.

The Chief Secretary.   The Chief Secretary to the Treasury shares many of the Chancellor's interests in terms of holding down expenditure and winning the battle with the spending ministers. The pride that John Major took (according to Lawson) in securing agreement on spending bids without needing to activate the Star Chamber suggests that in his negotiations he had a personal interest in bringing about that (procedural) outcome.

Treasury officials.   The Treasury has the reputation of being a 'high-powered' department, and unusually among departments around three-quarters of senior officials have higher degrees.[95] While its formal organization is hierarchical, business is conducted relatively informally, with discussion papers circulated among people at all levels, each of whom can add comments which others read. This, and the apparent playing down of 'old school' connections,[96] seems consistent with a strong socialization process continually taking place. Certainly Treasury officials appear to have a strong *esprit de corps*[97] and sense of their own identity. Pliatzky refers to the Treasury as if it were a corporate body or even a person: 'the Treasury believed . . .'; 'Treasury policies'; 'the Treasury . . . floated the idea'; 'the Treasury itself must form its judgment'.[98] Such language does not assign any distinctive role to ministers, which suggests that they don't occupy a significant place in Pliatzky's mental picture of the Treasury. Lawson recollects Pliatzky describing the Treasury to him as 'the praetorian guard' (a description which cannot conceivably include ministers). 'A good phrase, true, and how they see themselves', adds Lawson.[99]

All this would be entirely consistent with Treasury officials sending spending ministers 'peremptory' messages rejecting their bids in the Chancellor's name but without his knowledge, and with the disdain manifested in the communications to Donnison at the Supplementary Benefits Commission. (A leaked internal memorandum from the Permanent Secretary to his staff in 1994 was reported as warning them against being 'arrogant'.[100])

The interests of Treasury officials and their mission of holding down Government spending in the face of demands from the spending departments seem to have given them a number of specific motivations. For example, securing a switch from 'indiscriminate and untaxed Child Benefit' to the means-tested Family Credit for poorer families became, according to Lawson, a 'long-standing ambition'.[101] So that switch was not merely intellectually desirable, but a goal that officials had a personal stake in achieving: it would bring them personal satisfaction and credit among their peers. Such an interest is also consistent with the zeal shown in detecting and resisting potential new expenditures and upturns in spending on existing policies (rather like the zeal of the fireman for dousing flames).

Ministers and officials in the 'spending departments'.   The Government, as we have seen, has a dual interest in holding public expenditure down and at the same time claiming credit for 'increased spending' in certain social policy fields when an election approaches. In other words, it has an interest in both eating its cake and having it. This conflict of interest is institutionalized in the formalities of the spending round, which set Treasury ministers against spending ministers.

Ministers and officials in the spending departments have been portrayed by Thatcher,[102] Lawson and others as having a strong interest in defending if not increasing their allocation and share of public expenditure. For officials it can be a test of 'manliness' not to be beaten by the Treasury,[103] and ministers record their satisfaction at doing well ('My cuts were the smallest'[104]) and congratulations received on getting more money by going to the Star Chamber.[105] Heclo and Wildavsky were told that it was important to a minister's reputation and 'credibility' to be seen to be fighting for his or her department.[106] So here is a personal interest in being seen to do well; precisely what the money would be spent on, and whether that purpose would be affected by the extra finance allocated, may be secondary. Heclo and Wildavsky relate the words of a 'combative' spending minister:

> I remember time and time again I would go through a heartbreaking battle for money and come back to the officials and say 'at least I got half, and now what has to go?' And time and again the permanent secretary would say that we really did not need all this expenditure for this or that item. Everyone does this.[107]

Not all spending ministers enagage the Treasury in active combat. Some – notably during the Thatcher era – consciously identified with the aim not of spending but of cutting or restraining public expenditure: Keith Joseph is the most conspicuous example. 'Spending officials' may do the same, to judge by Barbara Castle's experience in 1974.

Spending ministers, like the Chancellor and the Government as a whole, have an interest in embarrassment avoidance. John Moore's embarrassment at staying in office and defending a continued freeze of Child Benefit, and the damage to his reputation, were the greater for his having let it be known to the press (if Lawson's account is accurate) that he would resist such a freeze – an illustration of the role that can be played by the media in policy making. The senior DSS official who warned the Treasury of the criticisms that could be levelled against the Department and ministers if in just one case it could be proved that the Department forced an abused child back into the clutches of an abuser, was basing his argument on ministers' and officials' interest in not being publicly criticized over such a case.

A different kind of personal interest stemmed from Nicholas Ridley's antagonism to Cecil Parkinson, which motivated him to avoid having Parkinson, as chairman of the Star Chamber, sit in judgement on his spending bid for housing.

Backbench MPs. Backbench MPs were not assigned a formal part in the process. This ran the risk that backbench pressure might build up and intrude very late, and we have seen that the interest of middle-class parents of children in higher education in resisting parental contributions towards tuition fees made a significant mark in 1984, after Joseph had been attacked by backbenchers who had espoused that interest.

Pressure and interest groups.   Pressure and interest groups did not play a discernible part in the annual spending round, unlike the Budget, before which Lawson would have a chart constructed 'showing which outside groups were in favour of which particular changes', and would invite a small number of 'sufficiently important' organizations to present their views in person.[108] It is as though the 'decision space' – the scope for decisions – was fully taken up by departmental interests when it came to public expenditure.

Consumer interests.   Outside observers like ourselves, looking at the expenditure allocation in any particular Autumn Statement, will usually not be able to detect the impact of consumer interests or of the institutional/political interests of ministers and officials. It is only from accounts of what went on during the process or after it that we can infer such an impact. The case of parental contributions to tuition fees is one such example. Another is the resolution of Ridley's housing budget without recourse to the Star Chamber. When Lawson describes the outcome of his discussions with Ridley as 'a very satisfactory agreement' from the Treasury's point of view, it is clear that Ridley did not defend the housing allocation with as much determination as he might otherwise have done. In other words, his personal interest, founded on nothing more than his feelings about Parkinson, took priority over the consumer interest of those who would have benefited from a higher allocation to housing, and who consequently lost out. (It could be said, though, that their loss allowed a gain for other consumers who would otherwise have got less, or for taxpayers who would otherwise have paid more.) And Joseph's failure to take on a personal interest in maximizing or sustaining education's share of spending is consistent with the underfunding of education during his period of office (evidenced by Baker's judgement on taking over from him at the DES that there was an urgent need for repairs to school buildings and for books and equipment for the introduction of the GCSE examination in secondary schools: Baker obtained an immediate injection of £20 million for the latter purpose[109]). We might suspect, therefore, that the consumer interest of secondary school pupils suffered through the absence of an institutional interest allied to it.

Other consumer interests that don't make a mark on policy, or make a lesser mark than they otherwise would, are those that fail to be voiced because reports, enquiries etc. might give rise to pressures and demands for increased public spending, or because spending ministers don't get the chance to speak up in Cabinet. Suppressing the pressures and demands implies suppressing or preventing the collection of information about how people are faring in the real world.

It appears that consumer interests don't make a mark on policy unless there are institutional/political interests calling for that same mark, i.e. unless those consumer interests are allied to institutional or political interests and pressure is exerted on behalf of them, as happened in the case of student loans in 1984, for example. The DSS official who was defending the hardship scheme for 16- and 17-year-olds in his letter to the Treasury was hinting at such an alliance when he referred to the risk of public criticism and of 'exposure' to judicial review in the courts. In the light of his warning, if Treasury officials went ahead with their attack they would carry the blame for any disaster: he was thus seeking to persuade them that it was in their interests not to go ahead.

We must be careful lest through focusing on institutional and poitical interests we come to think that it is only these that motivate ministers and officials, that it is only spending – or, alternatively, holding down expenditure – for its own sake in which ministers and officials in 'spending departments' have an interest. Some evidently do have genuine sympathy for particular groups.

Process

Why have an annual spending round at all? The imperative for it is provided by the institutional necessities of having a public spending programme, of keeping spending in line with the resources to be made available and of monitoring the growth of committed expenditure and anything that might threaten the balance between spending and resources. It is an imperative felt most strongly by Treasury ministers and officials. Once the process is under way, many of the events that take place – every agreement that is reached (whether between officials in the spending departments and their Treasury opposite numbers over 'baselines' and 'what government policy is', or between the Chief Secretary and individual ministers in the 'bilaterals'), every formal decision of the Cabinet, every public announcement or 'leak' about the Treasury's stance on spending or about a minister's determination to resist a cut or freeze – involve the creating or reinforcing or registering of a commitment. In particular, an important element of the Treasury strategy in holding down public spending is to get the Cabinet committed to a public expenditure ceiling at its meeting in July, before its precise implications become apparent and pressures to safeguard the affected programmes are applied. When the Chancellor, Chief Secretary and Treasury officials 'dig in against spending bids', and secure the Prime Minister's backing, they are all committing themselves to imposing a ceiling on the total of those bids. Committing themselves can actually be part of the strategy: when they say publicly, 'We simply can't give you any more', or words to that effect, they are making it difficult for themselves to back down without loss of face.

The significance of the July meeting is that the overall issue is transformed from one over which spending departments are competing against the Treasury into one over which they are competing against one another – not only for money, but also not to be the last one to 'settle', having to go into the Star Chamber with the programme that would have to be 'squeezed to meet the overall target', as Tebbit is said to have put it.[110]

Inherited commitments and external events, and their pre-empting effects, provide the constraints within which the game is played. Rising unemployment creates a rising demand on the social security budget, which in the short term the Government has no alternative but to meet; manifesto commitments and inflation put up the costs of running the National Health Service, as do technological innovations and increasing numbers of elderly people; and most education, health and personal social services 'have to be' kept running, they can't be abruptly terminated. All of these create pressures for spending: they are the source of what Pliatzky calls 'the force of circumstances'.[111]

Power structure

The relevant power structure changes from stage to stage in the process, being dominated by officials in the early stages and by ministers in the later ones. But throughout, the power structure is centralized, with the Treasury at the centre having radial communication links to the spending departments. These run via the Treasury's teams devoted to particular spending departments and the principal finance officers with whom they negotiate. The spending departments are preoccupied with their own plans, they do not link up with one another except that principal finance officers meet those from other departments on PESC. Essentially the other departments are their competitors: each has an interest in gaining funds for its own departmental purposes from a limited 'cake'. Insofar as the Treasury dominates the process and the decisions taken, its capacity to do so appears to derive more from its centrality in the communication network, the negotiating skills of its members (very clever people working as a team) and the fact that the spending departments are 'compartmentalized' – shut off from one another – than from any detailed knowledge of policies and measures and their impact. As Pliatzky reminds us, the Treasury is isolated from the real world and 'a rather cloistered institution', even by the standards of the Bank of England. The 'Treasury sees itself as a small beleaguered citadel of financial prudence, surrounded by spendthrift predators and surviving only by its wits and tireless vigilance'.[112]

What forms do the linkages between the Treasury and spending departments take? Evidently they constitute communication channels, but they also incorporate dependences and obligations. The Treasury is dependent on spending departments for information, but there is an obligation on the principal finance officers to supply it. They have to keep their 'credibility' with the Treasury, and continually demonstrate their trustworthiness. Principal finance officers also take back to their own departments information about the respective strengths of other departments' cases and the pressures behind them, and their estimate of the likelihood that the Treasury will exert pressure for economies on their own departments.[113]

As the July meeting of the Cabinet approaches, the linkage between Chancellor and Prime Minister takes on importance. It appears to be essential for the setting of an overall target and holding firmly to it that the Chancellor and the

Prime Minister should be in agreement throughout. There is still the radial pattern with the Treasury at the centre and spending departments at the rim, but the connections are now between ministers, with the Chief Secretary to the Treasury holding 'bilateral' negotiations with the spending ministers. He reports back to the Chancellor, who keeps the Prime Minister informed and can convey back her views. It appears that the Prime Minister remains apart from the negotiating machinery: if a spending department were able to enlist her support it would manifestly damage the authority of the Chief Secretary and Chancellor.

The considerable impact of the Chancellor's views on the spending total (as long as he has the Prime Minister's support) reflects a structure in which his position is central and those of the spending ministers are peripheral. It also reflects his 'powers to do', which incorporate a significant degree of autonomy, as evidenced by Lawson's reference to keeping a few cards up his sleeve: the Chancellor retains discretion over the use of the Reserve, and can make unofficial promises of favourable treatment next year.

Note too that the role of both Star Chamber and the November Cabinet was not to take decisions from the perspective of government as a whole (e.g. considering all the fields of social policy together rather than individually) but to exert pressure on ministers who had not yet settled. There was in fact no arena in which decisions were made in the light of an *overview* of government policies, in which, say, decisions about housing, health and social services were taken together, as logically it could be argued that they should: community care requires attention to be paid to the housing of people who would otherwise be in institutions, as well as to their social care. Instead there were 'fragmented decisions', and this reflects the fragmented structure of those who were involved in determining the spending plans. (What the precise allocations were, of course, also reflected the strategies adopted by the various participants, e.g. Baker's success in adopting the high-risk strategy of taking his claim to the Star Chamber.)

Finally, we have encountered once more the important power of the Prime Minister to create structures: Thatcher set up the Star Chamber, Major abolished it and set up Cabinet committee EDX, with a consequent reduction in the domain of the Chief Secretary. And Lawson has described what appears to be another significant power of the Prime Minister, namely the power to determine the procedure at Cabinet meetings, in this case the sequence in which ministers are called to speak.

Conclusions

The deciding of public spending plans poses some unique problems in government policy making. Spending plans must, by their nature, incorporate implicit or explicit decisions about priorities between policies or departments or fields of policy: this is a more abstract and complex task than registering an issue and developing concrete proposals to deal with it.

In one respect the policy-making process followed a similar approach to others we have observed, namely in starting by identifying 'givens', or constraints, which in this case were chiefly commitments carried forward from previous years. It was thus rational in the sense of ensuring that whatever decisions were taken would be consistent with those commitments. In other respects, however, it was very different, notably in the fragmentation of the process, with Treasury ministers and officials engaging in simultaneous, compartmentalized negotiations with those of the spending departments. This pattern itself reflected the compartmentalized, departmental structure of government, which was reinforced by the following of a procedure that gave departments competing interests by setting a limit to the total funds available and forcing them to compete against one another for these funds. (In practice, every department could usually count on receiving a certain amount; strictly speaking, the competition was for funds above that level.)

Is it possible for the reconciling of the competing bids from spending ministers to be done rationally? Lawson refers to the main job of the Star Chamber as being that of 'weighing up the relative merits of the cases put by different spending ministers, and allocating the sum that remained . . . between them'.[114] However, Whitelaw, who chaired the Star Chamber on a number of occasions, felt that it 'is not in a position to judge priorities between departments'.[115] And Lawson himself underlines that weighing merits is a political act:

> It is argued that there ought to be an explicit and rational method for deciding priorities between rival claims on the public purse. Unfortunately there is no such science upon which we can draw . . . How, for example, do you decide objectively between building a new hospital, recruiting more policemen, increasing British Rail's investment programme or providing the local authorities with more money to spend on schools? . . . Attempts to use [cost benefit] to make comparisons *between* sectors are in practice a waste of time . . . [The] political market place is the only known method of making choices between different types of collective spending, or between the collective and private variety.[116]

Baker, however, makes the point that even in terms of political priorities there was, in his experience, no 'real balancing':

> Ministers collectively were simply not allowed to discuss an overall strategy or to determine priorities as between one area of expenditure and another. All that mattered was that the expenditure level pushed through Cabinet the previous July was met at all costs . . . The issue became not the priorities of spending but the importance of protecting the Chancellor's position.[117]

In other words, when the Star Chamber met, the dominant consideration was the Chancellor's commitment to enforcing the expenditure ceiling set in the previous July: the financial consideration was heavily reinforced by a political one. And the matter was resolved, unless it was to go to the Cabinet, by the exerting of pressure.

The subsequent setting up of Cabinet committee EDX seems to be an attempt to meet Baker's point. It allows those ministers who are members of it to form a collective view as to whether, for example, road building has had a generous allocation in recent years and should now undergo a lean period while funds are diverted to meet increasing pressures for spending on health care. While Lawson's argument that there is no objective way of choosing between competing programmes is, it seems to me, irrefutable, EDX does allow for spending decisions to be taken on the basis of an overall view of the Government's spending programmes rather than 'trials of strength' between individual spending ministers and the Chief Secretary or the Star Chamber. However, given that the majority of spending ministers are not members of EDX, it could be an overall view that continues to be dominated by 'the importance of protecting the Chancellor's position'.

*Chapter
nine*
EUROPEAN SOCIAL POLICY AND THE UK: THE SOCIAL CHARTER AND THE PROTECTION OF WOMEN WORKERS

Introduction

This chapter takes as a case study a 'stream' of policies and measures: the 1989 'Social Charter' of the European Community (now the European Union); the ensuing 'Social Charter Action Programme'; the 1992 European Directive on the protection of women workers who are pregnant or have recently given birth or are breastfeeding; and the Trade Union Reform and Employment Rights Act 1993 and other measures that incorporated the provisions of the Directive into the law of the UK. It examines how the vague aspirations expressed in the Social Charter, which the UK Government opposed and Margaret Thatcher refused to sign, nevertheless came to be 'translated' into very specific provisions in the legislation of the United Kingdom.

This case study provides an interesting contrast with the preceding ones, in that it deals with policy making by supranational and intergovernmental bodies, and accordingly with structures and procedures very different from those we have already encountered. It makes use of extracts from the documents themselves and from drafts, reports, explanatory memoranda and legal judgments, as well as relevant material from government and parliamentary sources in the UK and Europe, and reports in the media.

The story

Background. In 1972, at their 'summit' meeting in Paris, the (then nine) heads of state or government agreed that they 'attached as much importance to vigorous action in the social field as to achievement of economic union'. In 1973 the Council of Ministers resolved to support the introduction of a Social Action

Programme for 1974–6, a move which was welcomed by the European Commission as a first step towards 'the ultimate goal of European Social Union'.[1] During the 1970s and 1980s many Directives and other measures were adopted, especially in the fields of equal treatment for men and women, and health and safety in the workplace.

In May 1988, Jacques Delors, President of the Commission, in a speech to the European Trade Union Confederation, promised that the Commission would address the social aspects of the Community.[2] A year later, in May 1989, the Commission published a 'preliminary draft' of a proposed 'Community Charter of fundamental social rights'.[3] (For the chronology, see Box 9.1.) It was followed in October 1989 by a 'draft'[4] with the same title. Two months later, on 9 December 1989, at a meeting of the European Council in Strasbourg, the heads of state or government of 11 of the 12 member states (the UK dissenting) formally adopted a further modified text as a 'declaration constituting the "Community Charter of the Fundamental Social Rights of Workers" '.[5] This declaration has come to be known as the 'Social Charter'. It declares that workers, men and women, elderly persons, disabled persons etc. 'shall have' or 'must have' certain rights or entitlements. Besides the addition of the words 'of workers' to the title of the drafts, the words 'worker' and 'workers' were substituted for 'citizen' and 'citizens' in several places.

The Social Charter. In the text adopted at Strasbourg, the declaration itself is preceded by a preamble, which sets out a number of aspirations. For example:

- 'Whereas . . . the European Council of Madrid considered that, in the context of the establishment of the single European market, the same importance must be attached to the social aspects as to the economic aspects and whereas, therefore, they must be developed in a balanced manner'.
- 'Whereas the completion of the internal market is the most effective means of creating employment and ensuring maximum well-being in the Community; whereas employment development and creation must be given first priority in the completion of the internal market'. (This was somewhat less tentative than the draft, which ran: 'the completion of the internal market presents major opportunities for growth and job creation' and 'one of the priority objectives in the economic and social field is to promote employment and to combat unemployment'.)
- 'Whereas the social consensus contributes to the strengthening of the competitiveness of undertakings, of the economy as a whole and to the creation of employment'.
- 'Whereas, in order to ensure equal treatment, it is important to combat every form of discrimination, including discrimination on grounds of sex, colour, race, opinions and beliefs, and whereas, in a spirit of solidarity, it is important to combat social exclusion'.

The declaration itself is presented under a number of headings: 'freedom of movement; employment and remuneration; improvement of living and working conditions; social protection; freedom of association and collective bargaining; vocational training; equal treatment for men and women; information,

---

Box 9.1 Chronology: the Directive on the protection of women workers

29 May 1989	Commission publishes a preliminary draft 'Community Charter of fundamental social rights'.
27 September 1989	Commission adopts (modified) draft.
9 December 1989	Heads of state or government of 11 of the 12 member states formally adopt a further modified text as the 'Social Charter'. Commission immediately publishes an 'Action Programme' for the implementation of the Charter, with general proposals for Directives and other measures.
17 October 1990	Commission submits to the Council of Labour and Social Affairs Ministers a draft directive 'concerning the protection at work of pregnant women or women who have recently given birth'.
20 November 1990	Economic and Social Committee approves the draft.
12 December 1990	European Parliament (first reading) approves the draft but proposes amendments.
3 January 1991	Commission submits a modified draft to the Council of Ministers.
19 December 1991	Council of Ministers formally approves a 'common position' reaches agreement on draft directive: UK abstains in the vote.
December 1991	Treaty on European Union agreed at Maastricht. UK 'opts out' of the 'Agreement on social policy' (the 'social chapter') annexed to it.
13 May 1992	European Parliament adopts the 'common position' subject to 17 amendments.
10 June 1992	Commission submits further amended draft directive. Not accepted by Council of Ministers.
19 October 1992	Council formally adopts Directive 92/85/EEC.
1 July 1993	Trade Union Reform and Employment Rights Bill 1993, incorporating the provisions of the Directive, receives Royal Assent.
February 1994	UK Government announces changes to maternity benefits.
1 April 1994	Relevant provisions of the 1993 Act come into effect.
1 October 1994	Changes to UK maternity benefits come into effect.

---

consultation and participation of workers; health protection and safety at the workplace; protection of children and adolescents; elderly persons; disabled persons'. (In the preliminary draft and the draft many of these headings had appeared as a *'right to . . .'*, e.g. 'Right to freedom of movement'.) In each section is to be found a mixture of exhortations and assertions of 'rights', employing the words 'must', 'shall' and 'should'. Examples are:

- 'According to the arrangements applying in each country: Every worker of the European Community shall have a right to adequate social protection and shall . . . enjoy an adequate level of social security benefits. Persons who have been unable either to enter or re-enter the labour market and have no means of subsistence must be able to receive sufficient resources and social assistance in keeping with their particular situation.'
- 'Equal treatment for men and women must be assured. Equal opportunities . . . must be developed. To this end, action should be intensified to ensure the implementation of the principle of equality between men and women as regards in particular access to employment, remuneration, working conditions, social protection, education, vocational training and career development. Measures should also be developed enabling men and women to reconcile their occupational and family obligations.'
- 'Every worker must enjoy satisfactory health and safety conditions in his working environment.'

The declaration concludes with a section on 'Implementation of the Charter'. This changed considerably between the draft and the final, adopted version. The draft, if adopted, would have invited the Commission 'to pursue . . . its present activities in the social domain' and instructed it 'to present . . . an action programme'. The declaration as adopted was worded very differently. A paragraph was added: 'It is more particularly the responsibility of *the Member States in accordance with national practices* . . . to guarantee the fundamental social rights in this Charter and to implement the social measures' (italics added). The Commission was now invited to submit only 'initiatives which fall within its powers', with a view to implementing only 'those rights which come within the Community's area of competence'. The invitation to present an action programme was deleted.

The Social Charter Action Programme.   Anticipating an instruction to present an action programme, as included in the draft Charter, the Commission had already prepared one – an 'Action Programme relating to the implementation of the Community Charter of Basic Social Rights for Workers'[6] – and promptly published it, even though the instruction to that effect contained in the draft had been removed. Among the actions proposed were:

- proposing a Directive on the protection (in the *health and safety* sense) of pregnant women at work;
- drawing up a Recommendation setting out a code of good conduct on the protection (in the *job security* sense) of women workers in pregnancy and maternity.

The first was justified in the document by pointing to the measures previously promoted and currently being discussed by the Commission, and arguing: 'These various measures have not taken sufficient account of the specific problems of pregnant women. This shortcoming should therefore be remedied by the Council by means of minimum requirements at Community level.' The second was justified as follows:

In the 12 Member States . . . there are at present 52 million working women for whom adequate protection in the case of pregnancy and maternity represents an important objective.

Job security is a vital factor in achieving equal opportunities between women and men in working life: recruitment opportunities, protection against dismissal, and maintaining of employment and accrued rights in the case of pregnancy and maternity have implications for the propensity of girls to undergo training and further training and as regards the birth rate. If women consider that pregnancy weakens their chances at work, they will be less inclined to have children, and if they want to have children, they risk forgoing opportunities for appropriate training. As a result, women will continue to be largely employed in low-level jobs. If they wish both to have a career and have children, they will have to overcome many difficulties.

In the light of current demographic trends and the search for greater competitiveness with a view to [the introduction of the single market in 1992] it is essential to make better use of skills and therefore of women workers. Women have in fact an ever increasing role to play in the economy. The workplace must therefore be adapted to . . . allow women to carry out both their work and maternal responsibilities.

Although the UK was not a signatory to the Social Charter, UK representatives evidently did not demur from taking part in the formulation and adoption of the Action Programme's initiatives. In a letter published in *The Guardian* in December 1991, Michael Howard, Secretary of State for Employment, claimed that the UK Government had

taken a full and active part in all of the negotiations over the last two years, and significant progress has been made in the social action programme. Since autumn last year 18 of the 32 measures published so far have been agreed . . . The substantial majority of these measures are binding legislation and agreements on action in key areas such as health and safety, free movement of labour, training and equal opportunities. Almost all have been agreed by a unanimous vote.[7]

(The UK Government has consistently referred to the Social Charter Action Programme as 'the social action programme',[8] as in this letter.)

The draft directive.   Exercising its exclusive 'right of initiative' under the EEC Treaty, in October 1990 the Commission submitted to the Council of Ministers a draft directive 'concerning the protection at work of pregnant women or women who have recently given birth'[9]. Copies also went to the Economic and Social Committee, which approved it unanimously, and to the European Parliament, which debated it in December 1990 and issued a formal Opinion approving it but asking for certain amendments. In January 1991 the Commission submitted a modified draft to the Council.[10] Both the draft and the modified draft contained provisions regarding job security as well as health and safety. The preamble of both documents referred to paragraph 19 of the Social Charter, citing its stipulations that 'every worker must enjoy satisfactory health and safety conditions in his working environment' and that 'appropriate measures must be taken with a view to achieving further harmonization of conditions in this area while maintaining the improvements made', and to the Action Programme's aim of proposing a Directive on the protection (in the health and safety sense) of pregnant women workers. However, the other aim, of drawing up a Recommendation setting out a code of good conduct on the protection (in the job security sense) of women workers in pregnancy and maternity, was not mentioned.

Under the modified draft directive, member states would have to take the measures necessary

- to ensure that their health and safety authorities evaluated the impact on pregnancy of the activities in which pregnant women were engaged and communicated them to employers and workers;
- to ensure that women's working conditions and/or hours were adapted, or a change to alternative work was allowed, when their activity endangered their health and safety, but with no change to their pay or employment rights;
- to ensure that women were excused night work for at least eight weeks before the expected date of childbirth and for a total of at least 16 weeks altogether;
- to ensure that women were granted an uninterrupted period of at least 14 weeks' maternity leave on full pay or a corresponding allowance; member states could grant a longer period, but the pay for the entire period would have to be at least 80 per cent of salary; periods of sickness during maternity leave would count towards the 14-week entitlement unless the sickness was not related to the pregnancy (it was not specified that a woman would have to have worked a minimum period of service to qualify);
- to ensure that pregnant workers were granted an 'obligatory period' of paid leave covering at least the two weeks prior to the expected date of childbirth, and did not lose pay for attending antenatal medical examinations if such examinations could take place only during working hours;
- to make it illegal to dismiss women covered by the Directive for reasons connected with their condition from the beginning of their pregnancy until the end of their maternity leave.

In putting forward this proposal, the Commission relied, as stated in the preamble, on Article 118a of the EEC Treaty (the Treaty of Rome, as amended by the Single European Act). This runs:

1 Member States shall pay particular attention to encouraging improvements, especially in the working environment, as regards the health and safety of workers, and shall set as their objective the harmonization of conditions in this area, while maintaining the improvements made.
2 In order to help achieve [this objective], the Council [of Ministers], *acting by a qualified majority* on a proposal from the Commission, in cooperation with the European Parliament and after consulting the Economic and Social

Committee, shall adopt, by means of Directives, minimum requirements for gradual implementation, having regard to the conditions and technical rules obtaining in each of the Member States (my italics).

The Commission was thus relying on the health and safety provisions of the EEC Treaty for a measure that dealt also with pay and job security. This gave rise to considerable dissension among the national governments and between the Council and the Commission. The UK Government in particular objected strongly to the inclusion in the proposed Directive of employment and social security matters. In the EEC Treaty (as amended), these matters are dealt with under Article 100 and Article 235 respectively, both of which require a *unanimous* vote for a measure to be adopted rather than a qualified majority. (Under 'qualified majority voting', a proposal will be adopted even if it is opposed by two of the largest states – France, Germany, Italy and the UK – so long as the others vote for it.) As Eric Forth (then Parliamentary Under-Secretary of State, Department of Employment) explained to the European Communities Committee of the House of Lords in May 1991, the Government's view was that

> the inclusion of social policy provisions in this health and safety directive amounts to an abuse of the Treaty. It is an attempt by the Commission to extend qualified majority voting into the social area . . . [We could support] a directive that dealt solely with health and safety matters but . . . are very unhappy about what I would call the social security and pay provisions.

This view, he said, was shared by other governments. Moreover the proposal went much further than was 'necessary on health and safety grounds', and there was no scientific or medical justification for some of the prohibitions proposed (e.g. on night work). The proposed directive would have the effect of substantially increasing the cost to employers of employing pregnant women, and this would provide a disincentive for employers to recruit women of child-bearing age.[11]

This last point gave rise to some disagreement. The Commission argued, without making any attempt at quantification, that the proposal would – in the long term if not the short – have a beneficial effect on efficiency:

> By rendering working conditions more healthy for female workers, the competitiveness of undertakings will be improved in the long-term, to the extent [that] human potential can be utilized in a more rational and responsible fashion. Viewed in this fashion, the short-term cost of the measure envisaged seems even smaller . . . From the macro economic perspective and taking all factors into account, the present proposal will be advantageous to employers to the extent that female labour will become more and more necessary, and must therefore be encouraged by measures of this nature.

On the other hand, according to the UK Department of Employment, 'the total costs of implementing the health and safety provisions might amount to £10 million or more, and would probably outweigh the benefits', and implementing the maternity pay provision and extending pregnant employees' right to return to their post would probably cost £400–500 million a year and £100–150 million a year respectively.[12]

On 6 November 1991, under the Netherlands Presidency, the Council of Labour and Social Affairs Ministers, on which the UK representative was Michael Howard, Secretary of State for Employment, discussed the modified draft Directive and reached a 'political agreement' on it in a further modified form. (The UK abstained in the vote, to register its view that the Directive should not have been promoted under Article 118a of the EEC Treaty.[13]) In this form it was adopted as the 'common position' of the Labour and Social Affairs Council on 19 December 1991.

The 'common position' draft provided for significantly less protection than the modified draft would have done. It deleted the obligation on member states that their health and safety authorities should carry out a general assessment of hazards to pregnant and breastfeeding women, substituting a requirement that guidelines on such hazards be drawn up by the Commission in consultation with member states and its own advisory committee. It removed women's entitlement to be excused night work. During maternity leave full pay would be maintained or an allowance paid, but this need be no more than national sickness benefit. There was now a qualifying period for eligibility for this benefit of 12 months of employment.

Under the 'cooperation procedure', the 'common position' draft Directive was then considered by the European Parliament, together with a critical comment on it from the Commission.[14] On 14 May 1992 the European Parliament endorsed the 'common position' subject to a number of amendments, including one which would have provided for maternity benefit to be paid at 80 per cent of salary.[15] The Commission backed this and certain other amendments, and a period of discussion between the Commission and the Committee of Permanent Representatives ensued. This culminated on 19 October 1992, when, under the presidency of the UK, the Council of Labour and Social Affairs Ministers eventually adopted Council Directive 92/85/EEC on the introduction of measures to encourage improvements in the safety and health at work of pregnant workers and workers who have recently given birth or are breastfeeding.

The Directive. The Directive *was* adopted under Article 118a, dealing with health and safety, of the EEC Treaty. It incorporated some of the amendments which had been proposed by the European Parliament and backed by the Commission, including stronger sanctions against dismissal during pregnancy or maternity leave, but the Council rejected the proposal that maternity benefit should be paid at 80 per cent of salary in favour of linking it to sickness benefit. (The Directive also expressly stated that the reference to sickness benefit was for purely technical reasons, and was not intended in any way to imply that pregnancy and childbirth be equated with sickness.) A press release from the Commission described the Directive as 'an inadequate response to the proposals of the Commission and the requests of the European Parliament, particularly with regard to night work and the level of maternity benefits'. It did not 'fully meet the expectations of the workers concerned' and took little account of 'some significant amendments' proposed by the Parliament. Nevertheless, many of the original provisions remained, and the Directive *would* improve the situation of women workers in certain member states.[16] In particular

- Women would maintain their employment rights while taking maternity leave, which was 'undoubtedly a step forward in the UK'.
- The qualifying period for maternity benefits was reduced to one year, which was 'particularly advantageous to women workers in the UK, where it had been necessary to have worked for the same employer for two years (or five years in the case of part-time work) to qualify for maternity benefits at the higher rate'.
- Women would be entitled to antenatal medical examinations in working time without loss of pay, which was a step forward in four countries.
- It would be illegal to dismiss a pregnant woman for reasons connected with her condition, irrespective of her length of service and the size of the company, which was a notable improvement in the UK and elsewhere.
- Countries with levels of protection higher than those specified would not be permitted to take advantage of the Directive to lower their standards.

As we can see, the UK Government had not succeeded in getting the legal basis of the Directive altered, or in dividing 'social security and pay provisions' from those to do with health and safety. And the references to improvements and advantages in the UK are to do with employment rights, maternity leave and benefits, and job security: none of those measures is to do directly with health and safety. Nevertheless, the UK Government, together with others, had succeeded in limiting maternity benefits, restrictions on night work, and duties that would be imposed on national health and safety agencies.

It now remained for each member state to comply with the Directive by bringing into force the necessary 'laws, regulations and administrative provisions'. In the UK some of the most important provisions of the Directive were incorporated into the Trade Union Reform and Employment Rights Bill, which was tabled in Parliament in November 1992 and received its Royal Assent on 1 July 1993. The Act's provisions, covering the right to maternity leave, the right to return to work, and rights if dismissed or suspended from work on maternity grounds, came into effect on 1 April 1994. As to levels of maternity benefit, the Government announced in February 1994 that as from October 1994 the lower rate of Statutory Maternity Pay would be increased from £48.80 to £52.50 per week; the two-year qualifying rule for the higher rate would be abolished (any woman who had worked for the same employer for 26 weeks and whose earnings were above the lower earnings limit for paying National Insurance contributions would get 90 per cent of her average earnings for the first six weeks of her maternity pay period followed by 12 weeks at the flat rate); and the majority of working women would be free to start their maternity pay period at any time from the eleventh week before their expected week of confinement until their baby's birth without loss of benefit.[17]

Once a Directive has been translated into national law, the possibility arises that an employee who feels that he or she is being denied rights conferred by it will take their complaint to the courts. National courts are required to give effect to Community law ('It is an established principle of membership of the Community that in case of conflict Community law takes precedence over national law'[18]), and in a number of instances national courts have called on the European Court of Justice (ECJ) to interpret the provisions of directives. Of particular interest is the case of *Landsorganisationen i Danmark* v *Ny Mølle Kro*.[19] Part of the judgment reads: 'It follows from the preamble . . . that the purpose of the directive is . . .' On this precedent, if the (ECJ) today were called upon to interpret the Directive on working women in pregnancy and maternity, the preamble of which referred to the adoption of the Charter and to paragraph 19 in particular, it would if it wished be able to infer the purpose of the Directive from such references. The unspecific aspirations and assertions of the Charter might then come to have considerable significance (although the fact that the Charter was not signed by all 12 heads of state or government could perhaps be taken by the judges to detract from its significance).

The Maastricht Treaty.   At the same time that work and negotiations were proceeding on the proposals of the Social Charter Action Programme, so was the drafting of the Treaty on European Union, which was agreed at Maastricht in December 1991. (It came into force in 1992 when all the signatory states had ratified it.) Annexed to the Treaty is a 'Protocol on social policy', to which in turn is annexed an 'Agreement on social policy' (also known as the 'social chapter') concluded between all the member states except the United Kingdom. Article 1 of the Agreement runs:

> The Community and the Member States shall have as their objectives the promotion of employment, improved living and working conditions, proper social protection, dialogue between management and labour, the development of human resources with a view to lasting high employment and the combating of exclusion. To this end the Community and Member States shall implement measures . . .

The 'opt-outs' secured by the UK Government on social policy and on moving to the third stage of economic and monetary union were a matter of some satisfaction to the Prime Minister, John Major, who returned from Maastricht proclaiming 'Game, set and match for Britain'.[20] How was this triumph achieved? According to former Labour Foreign Secretary Denis Healey, crucial support for John Major on the social policy opt-out came from Chancellor Kohl of Germany in return for Major supporting Kohl on the recognition of Croatia as a sovereign state.[21] Kohl's support for Major is directly corroborated by contemporary newspaper reports, which also attest to Kohl's wish for support in resisting a French procedural proposal that would have considerably delayed the recognition of Croatia.[22]

Despite the UK's opt-out, it will continue to be possible, in some of the fields covered by the Social Charter, for the Council of Ministers to adopt Directives and Recommendations that will apply in the UK. This is because the provisions of earlier Treaties, under which a number of Directives stemming from the Charter have already been adopted, remain largely unchanged. We may note too that although the Protocol noted the wish of 11 member states 'to continue along the path laid down in the 1989 Social Charter' and had adopted the 'Agreement on social policy' to this end, the Agreement is appreciably narrower than the Charter. This comes about because the subjects of freedom of movement for workers – and for citizens – and vocational training appear not in the Agreement but in the very body of the Maastricht Treaty.[23] Thus the United Kingdom, when it ratified the Treaty, did become bound by some further provisions in the spirit of the Social Charter from which it had dissented.

The policy and measures

Once the Social Charter had been proclaimed, who was committed by it, to what were they committed and how strongly? The Charter is described in the Directive's preamble as having been adopted at the Strasbourg European Council by the heads of state or government of 11 member states. Even if the declaration had been unanimous, we must be cautious in attributing commitment to the Council as one would to a collective body, since it is essentially intergovernmental rather than supragovernmental – a forum where the governments of the member states are represented, each bringing its own national interests rather than sharing a single European one. Can we say what the 11 signatories were committed to? It appears that their endorsement put them in a position where it was difficult for their national governments to oppose on principle proposals put forward by the Commission that could convincingly be represented as furthering the aspirations of the Charter: to this extent they were under a commitment to the furthering of those aspirations.

Also committed to furthering those aspirations was the European Commission, which *had* been operating as a collective body, under the active lead of its president, Jacques Delors. The strength of its commitment can be judged by the effort that Commissioners had evidently put into preparing and consulting over the sequence of drafts, and into preparing the Social Charter Action Programme even before the Social Charter had been endorsed.

As for the Directive and the Trade Union Reform and Employment Rights Act 1993, their status is unambiguous: they are legislative measures, of the Community and of the UK respectively.

Rationale

Means and ends.   When we look for the rationale underlying the Social Charter we find some obscurity and inconsistency. The reasoning, as set out in the preamble, uses terms – notably 'social aspects' and 'social consensus' – which are quite unspecific (in the English language, at least); it is inconsistent as between the economic and the social, in that economic objectives come first ('employment development and creation must be given first priority'), but social objectives do not come second ('the same importance must be attached to the social aspects as to the economic aspects'); and it enunciates a theory about job creation in a manner which suggests that it is above debate, although changes between the preliminary draft and the final version show clearly that they *were* debated. When challenged by the UK Government, the Commission cited productive efficiency as a further objective, but in very general terms, and it was unable to persuade a majority of national governments that there was medical and scientific justification for accepting that the objective of improving or safeguarding the health of pregnant women would be attained by banning them from night work. The UK Government, the House of Lords Select Committee on the European Communities was told, '[agreed] fully that there must be high standards of health and safety at work in the Community for pregnant women and women who have just given birth',[24] but its caveat that proposals for achieving that aim must be 'sensible and practical', which is open to widely differing interpretations, underlined the scope that existed for disagreement.

Measures on behalf of women workers who were pregnant or had recently given birth were first put forward by the Commission in the Social Charter Action Programme, under the heading of 'Equal treatment for men and women'. This heading in itself implies that equal treatment was one objective, but two others were specifically mentioned. First, safeguarding health and safety was a desirable objective in its own right. Second, improving the efficiency of the economy, in terms both of achieving greater competitiveness and of making the best use of the resource that women and their skills represented, was likewise a valued end in itself.

Interestingly, the more aspirational objectives of achieving equal treatment of men and women, and 'greater competitiveness', did not feature in the preamble to the Directive or in the Commission's press release. (In the Directive itself, the objectives set out are all to do with the well-being of the women who would benefit.) Their omission is consistent with the policy proposals not actually having been derived from them: it also directs our attention to the possibility that other considerations besides these real-world objectives, and/or interests of various kinds, played a part in the Commission's reasoning and in the individual and collective reasoning of the members of the Council of Labour and Social Affairs Ministers.

Considerations. The reasoning contained in the Social Charter Action Programme stresses real-world considerations, to do with the personal, social and economic implications of the position of women in the labour market. Likewise the UK Government cited the cost to employers, and the disincentive to recruiting women of child-bearing age, as grounds for opposing the draft directive. It also, unlike the Commission, produced quantitative estimates of the costs of implementing it. But political considerations too appear to have played a significant, if not dominant, part. As well as the interests of the various parties (discussed below), considerations of support seem to have been crucial, since among the Council Ministers, the proponents of the draft Directive needed the support of enough other members to gain a qualified majority and thus ensure its adoption. Seen from the Commission's standpoint, as Mrs Vasso Papandreou, then European Commissioner with special responsibility for employment, industrial relations and social affairs, told the European Parliament, in considering what amendments to propose to the Labour and Social Affairs Council she felt constrained to give priority to the political consideration of whether they had 'some chance of being accepted by the Council', in preference to the real-world consideration that they would constitute an improvement for women over the Council's already adopted common position.[25] Thus the content of the measure reflected not only some intellectual justification but also the availability of support from the national governments. For the proponents of the draft, accepting a less-than-desirable provision was the price that had to be paid for that support. This view was also held by some British Labour MEPs who were reported in October 1992 as arguing that it was important to establish EC legislation: once established, it could then be improved. 'Despite its serious limitations, [the Directive] offers real improvement for a large number of British working women whose maternity protection is the poorest in the community.'[26]

From the viewpoint of Ministers, there may also have been the presentational consideration that they could not let themselves be seen as opponents of women's rights, especially when that meant yielding the 'moral high ground' to the Commission, which had the support of many MEPs.

Interests

Consumer interests.   We have seen in various Commission documents the perception that the population of the Community includes particular groups, together with implicit or explicit acknowledgements that a particular group has a valid *claim* to action on its behalf. Thus, in the Social Charter Action Programme we find it argued that women (albeit women in general) had a valid *claim* to action on their behalf, by virtue of: (a) the Community subscribing to the principle of equal opportunities as between women and men: women had a *right* to equal treatment; (b) the fact that pregnant women encountered 'specific problems' and women wishing to have both a career and children faced 'many difficulties': effectively, the Community should be under an obligation to help them; and (c) the fact that as many as 52 million women had an interest in the matter. The Directive was much more specific as to what action was in the interests of women workers who were pregnant or breastfeeding, notably as regards employment rights, maternity leave and benefits, and job security.

Political/institutional interests.   From subsequent events, it appears that those members of the Commission who were most involved had some strong motivations for promoting a Directive that covered job and social security together with health and safety. Among them was the motivation to claim credit for improving the situation of women workers (as witness the press release that it issued on the adoption of the Directive) and thereby gaining their goodwill and support; to establish the precedent of legislating on job and social security under the qualified majority voting procedure governing health and safety measures, which would deny a veto over future social and job security pro-posals to a minority of only one or two national governments; to gain the personal satisfaction of seeing an initiative come to fruition; and presumably to gain the altruistic satisfaction of achieving something worthwhile on behalf of people whom they saw as having a valid claim for legislation on their behalf. In other words, Commissioners seem to have had political/institutional interests in claiming credit as social benefactors, in recruiting a 'constituency' of suppor-ters and well-wishers, and in making it easier to get their proposals adopted by the Council of Ministers. A further interest, deriving from their structural position rather than the particular issue, was in bringing about a greater degree of uniformity – or harmonization – of provision for women workers among the countries of the Community: the wording of the draft Directive shows that such harmonization was treated as a self-evident good by the Commission.

So far as we know, the Commission acted as a collective body. Although the lead appears to have been taken by the President and the Commissioner for employment, industrial relations and social affairs, there are no public indica-tions that any of their colleagues dissented from their approach, i.e. that there was any conflict of interests. In contrast, the Council of Labour and Social Affairs Ministers acted collectively only at the point when it adopted the Dir-ective. Prior to that it was effectively an arena in which conflicting interests were articulated by representatives of national governments.

In the UK, some ministers, if not all, saw their Government as having an interest in being seen as 'good Europeans' and constructive participants in decision making (which presumably made it more likely that they would be consulted at an early stage, and less likely that they would turn up to meetings to find the other participants already agreed on the line to take), as witness Howard's public insistence that the UK Government had been taking 'a full and active part in all of the negotiations over the last two years [on] the social action programme'. Ministers also had an interest in defending what they saw as their national interests, and to claim credit for doing so, as witness the UK Government's refusal to sign the Social Charter or agree to be bound by the provisions of the social chapter of the Maastricht Treaty, and Major's tri-umphant 'Game, set and match to Britain'. The UK Government also appears to have been motivated when the occasion arose to avoid the embarrassment inherent in being seen attempting to be both good Europeans and defenders of the national interest simultaneously, as witness its continual referring to the Social Charter Action Programme as 'the social action programme'. A majority of national governments, not only that of the UK, were evidently strongly motivated to defend their own existing powers and autonomy when these seemed threatened, supporting the 'subsidiarity' clause of the Maastricht Treaty and attaching the condition 'according to the arrangements applying in each country' to the Commission's proposals. Those with high standards of social protection had an interest in high standards being enforced in other countries, so that industries in those other countries did not have the advantage of the lower costs that went with lower standards. And the governments that occupied the Presidency appear to have been motivated to claim 'achievements' at the conclusion of the summit meetings. The corresponding interests, then, were those in being at the centre of decision making and avoiding embarrassment (if you were British), and defending their national autonomy.

Overall, it appears that the provisions of the Charter and Directive are consistent with being compromises between conflicting interests – among national governments, between national governments and the Commission. Can we actually find any compromising going on in the course of the process?

Process

Issues.   Why was there a Social Charter at all? There was nothing to stop the Commission going ahead, exercising its sole right of initiative, to produce an action programme of draft directives, Recommendations etc. without troubling to draw up a Charter at all. But in its aspirational content and its presentation the draft resembles the Conservative 1987 election manifesto, and there are indications that the imperative was similar: to recruit popular support, in this case to offset the Commission's disadvantage *vis-à-vis* the national governments of being unelected; and to make progress towards 'a social Europe', an enterprise in which the 'social partners', employers and trade unions, would have an incentive to cooperate. Possibly the personal political ambitions of the Commission president, Jacques Delors, who was later to be regarded as a socialist candidate for the French presidency, were also a factor in his thinking. He and his colleagues evidently envisaged promoting and gaining endorsement for the Charter as a deliberate strategy for getting 'social policy' Directives and Recommendations adopted.

What to do about the draft Charter was evidently an issue for the national governments. The obligation to respond constituted an imperative for them, as we can see by the changes made to the draft before it was formally adopted as the Charter proper by 11 of the 12 members of the Strasbourg European Council. Evidently a majority preferred to see rights conferred upon workers rather than citizens in general (i.e. rather than upon non-workers as well as workers), and a majority were reluctant to see the Commission's powers extended at the expense of their own autonomy. Evidence of this is the deleting of the invitation to the Commission 'to pursue . . . its present activities in the social domain' and the instruction to it to present an action programme, and the addition of the paragraph stressing the responsibility of the member states, rather than the Commission, 'to guarantee the fundamental social rights in [the] Charter and to implement the social measures'.

Commitment.   Because the Council of Labour and Social Affairs Ministers was the sole body with the power to confer legislative status on a proposed

Directive, yet was informally junior to the European Council (since the latter was composed of heads of state or government while the former was composed of rank-and-file members of their governments) it is the growth of commitment on the part of those two bodies to which we must pay attention here.

With the adopting and publishing of the Charter, the 11 heads of state or government acquired a 'contingent' commitment to acquiescing in future proposals that manifestly conformed to the principles and exhortations set down in it. (Their reluctance to endorse the invitation to the Commission to produce an action programme is consistent with their anticipating that they, and thus their national governments, would be so committed, with consequent limitations to their freedom of choice regarding new measures.)

Having secured this contingent commitment, the Commission now faced the issue of how to secure the commitment of the Council of Ministers, and hence of national governments, to concrete proposals. In the Social Charter Action Programme, the Commission had committed *itself* to proposing a Directive on the protection (in the health and safety sense) of pregnant women at work, and to drawing up a Recommendation setting out a code of good conduct on the protection (in the job security sense) of women workers in pregnancy and maternity. Of these, the proposed Recommendation seems to have been the more problematic, although Recommendations are not legally binding: we can infer this from the trouble taken to justify it in the Action Programme and from the fact that the idea of a Recommendation was not proceeded with. For it to be adopted a unanimous vote in its favour would be required, and this was unlikely to be forthcoming, since the UK Government was certain to oppose it. It seems, therefore, to have been a matter of deliberate strategy on the Commission's part to incorporate the job security provisions of the proposed Recommendation in the proposed Directive instead and to promote that proposed Directive under the qualified majority voting procedure appropriate to a health and safety measure, and see what happened.

Once the Commission had put forward the draft directive, the national governments were faced with the issue of how to respond. It seems to have been an awkward issue for the UK Government in particular. On the one hand it contested the validity of incorporating social and job security provisions in a health and safety directive, an approach which threatened its autonomy in this field, and it was opposed to a measure which ministers saw as imposing costs on employers and making them reluctant to employ women. On the other hand, it wished to demonstrate its credentials as 'good Europeans' and to ensure that it was not excluded from the decision-making process, and ministers cannot have been unaware that large numbers of women, each with the vote, would be affected by it. In choosing to go ahead with incorporating the provisions of the Directive in the law of the UK, with ministers doing no more than complain, and not taking (or letting the Commission take) the matter to the European Court of Justice (ECJ), it too appears to have been employing a strategy: work closely with other national governments, and try to weaken the Directive as much as possible, rather than opt for confrontation and risk the possibility that the ECJ might rule against it and that its partners might exclude it from decision making in the future. Ministers may also have been advised that there was a possibility that the UK's existing maternity pay arrangements – in particular, the lengthy qualifying periods of employment – would be held by the ECJ to constitute unfair competition in the single market. They may have been advised too that in any litigation the Commission would be able to point to the endorsement of the Charter as justifying the more specific proposals contained in the Directive. The ECJ had already shown itself to be prepared, when litigation arose, to infer the purpose of a Directive from its preamble, and the preamble of the Directive on women workers in pregnancy and maternity made explicit reference to the Charter (as well as to the Action Programme).

We know from Eric Forth's testimony to the House of Lords Select Committee on the European Communities[27] that the process of reaching agreement on the 'common position', the penultimate form of the Directive, took the form of negotiation within the Labour and Social Affairs Council over its various elements. Discussions also took place at official level, among officials from the member states. Successive presidencies (Luxembourg, followed by the Netherlands), keen to reach agreement, tabled new texts to see whether they would find support as bases for compromise. In effect, alliances were formed and deals were done over particular elements of the bundle of proposals. The UK Government cited its credentials: 'Our record on the implementation of directives that are already agreed in social areas is second to none'[28] and stressed its support for those clauses which 'would materially contribute to the improvement of health and safety'. The outcome was, to put it colloquially, that it 'won some and lost some', and its defeats appear to be the price that it paid for its victories. The adoption of the common position ratified these deals. Given the considerable effort that had gone into achieving that common position, there was evidently significant commitment to it on the part of the Council and its members. To abandon one element could incur the penalty of the whole 'package' falling apart. The Council was then pressed by the Commission and European Parliament to accept amendments: in the Directive's final version, adopted while the UK held the presidency, most of these amendments were rejected, which is consistent with the existence of strong commitment. Some concessions were made, however, despite no new reasoning being put forward, from which we may conclude that some pressure was indeed felt by the Council and presidency.

On this evidence as to the process, I conclude that the Directive is indeed appropriately seen as a compromise between conflicting interests. I conclude too that the 'consumer' interest of working women made a mark on the measure through being allied to the political/institutional interests of the Commission, some national governments, and some members of the European Parliament.

Power structure

The fact that the Social Charter and Directive came into existence at all seems to reflect the central position of their initiators, the President of the

Commission and his colleagues, and their 'ratifiers', the European Council and the Council of Labour and Social Affairs Ministers respectively. The fact that the detail of the Directive bore the marks of many participants seems to reflect both the division of powers among the Commission and the Council of Ministers and the intergovernmental nature of the latter. Unlike, say, the members of the British Cabinet, the Labour and Social Affairs Ministers are not bound together by obligations of collective responsibility, or the common interest and mutual dependence born of being members of the same Parliamentary party. Their main linkages are to their national governments, and each acts as advocate of, and negotiator on behalf of, their national interest as it is seen by their government.

As regards linkages of dependence and obligation, the Commission manifestly depended on the Council of Ministers for giving legislative effect to its proposals, something that it could not do itself. In the case of the protection of women workers, it sought to lessen this dependence by basing its proposal on the qualified majority voting provisions of the Treaties, so it could dispense with the support of one or two members. To gain acceptance for its proposed Directive, it accordingly had to design it to be in the interests of, and thus likely to gain support from, at least some of the national governments. When the Council met, therefore, those members with something to gain from the proposal (from countries where social and job security were better) were already supporters of it.

We do not know whether the Ministers felt that they could not simply ignore proposals from the Commission, especially when, as in this case, it allied itself with the European Parliament and the Economic and Social Committee, and represented itself as speaking for the large number of women, i.e. electors, who stood to gain from it. Or whether they appreciated that their governments depended for the successful pursuit of their interests on maintaining a good working relationship with the body that initiates legislative proposals, and that when their government occupied the presidency it would also depend on the Commission in a practical way for assistance in achieving 'deals'. Likewise there is only scanty evidence that the UK Government acted in constant awareness of its dependence on and obligations to organized groups (e.g. employers, trade unions) and its electorate. Although the Commission claimed that the proposal had been put together after consultations with 'government experts and social partners' (employers and trade unions), 'whose comments were taken into account to the extent possible'[29] – possibly an indication that the unelected Commission, with no constituency of its own, was attempting to construct one[30] – the UK Government's objections were not supported in this way. Rather they were objections on principle, to the coupling of social and job security measures with health and safety ones, and to the lack of justification for imposing restrictions on the employment of women and financial and administrative burdens on employers, public authorities and the taxpayer. We have, I think, circumstantial evidence that the intergovernmental structure of the law-making body, the Council of Labour and Social Affairs Ministers, is conducive to decisions being taken on the basis of somewhat abstract considerations and the trading of support rather than an assessment of the likely impact on specific social and economic groups.

Conclusions

An important conclusion to be drawn from this case study is to do with the role of the Social Charter. Kleinman and Piachaud have dismissed its references to social protection as nothing more than aspirations that 'lack any substance',[31] but this judgement ignores its significance for subsequent events. This significance is, I suggest, fourfold. First, its adoption by 11 of the 12 heads of state or government established publicly that there was a consensus among them on the desirability of 'social' measures, and created a contingent commitment on their part to subsequently accept concrete proposals that conformed to it. Second, its adoption provided a mandate for the Commission to propose concrete proposals. Third, its adoption created expectations among other bodies that such proposals would be forthcoming, expectations that the Commission was able to encourage by publishing the Social Charter Action Programme. And fourth, its existence subsequently allowed reference to be made to it in the preambles to the ensuing Directives, so the Courts may be able to refer to it to infer the purpose of those Directives. In effect, the adoption of the Social Charter amounted to establishing a 'policy bridgehead'. It 'paved the way' for the concrete proposals and measures that followed it. Another bridgehead will have been established if the Directive on the protection of women workers sets a precedent for legislating on certain social and job security provisions under the health and safety 'rubric', so they can be passed by a qualified majority vote as opposed to an unanimous one.

In this light, the role of the Social Charter can be seen to have been much more a political one than an intellectual one. Largely as the Commission and its allies among the heads of state or government intended, it paved the way for the measures that followed it. In its content, the Directive that ensued bore, like the Social Charter, marks of the special interests of the governments of the member states, notably in defending their autonomy. But it also reflected what were seen as the valid and legitimate claims of groups within the population, in this case women workers who were pregnant or had recently given birth.

Kleinman and Piachaud, on the basis of their examination of the Social Charter, conclude that the European Community 'lacks any coherent, consistent or comprehensive social philosophy or policy'. Evidently they themselves make the value judgement that this is something that the EC/EU *ought* to have. But arguably, given the political reality that Directives and Recommendations, like Treaties and indeed the Social Charter, are negotiated over and ultimately adopted by the intergovernmental Council of Ministers, we cannot realistically expect them to embody a single, consistent set of motives or philosophy. They will reflect bargains and compromises. As in the case of the Directive on the protection of women workers, governments that currently make high levels of provision will try, usually with the support of the Commission, to get the others to raise their levels; the others will try to retain the advantages that go with low levels; and the government that holds the presidency will try to find a compromise. Sometimes the outcome will be arrived at by linking the issue with others, possibly fortuitous, such as the issue of the recognition of Croatia which arose when the Maastricht Treaty was being finalized, allowing Major – by supporting Kohl on this issue – to gain crucial German support for the UK's opt-out from the Agreement on social policy.

It is, I suggest, particularly unrealistic in the European context to expect a policy bridgehead to be marked by coherence, consistency and comprehensiveness. By its nature, because it is aimed at disrupting the status quo, it has to be opportunistic, exploiting differences of view, and taking advantage of conflicts between vested interests. Its proponents must find allies, and ways of defeating or reaching compromises with enemies. It may be only when the policy bridgehead has been established, and has itself become part of the status quo , and the process has begun of pulling policies in related fields into line with it, that there is scope for considerations of coherence, consistency and comprehensiveness to enter into policy making.

Chapter ten

CONCLUSIONS: THE MECHANISMS OF POLICY MAKING

Introduction

In the case studies, we have encountered a variety of mechanisms – 'ways of doing things' – through which policies and measures come into being. In this final chapter, I summarize what we have found out about them. I examine first personal mechanisms, which are revealed primarily by viewing policies and measures as the product of a rationale and a selective response to interests, and then mechanisms involving interaction among people: these are revealed when we bring all four perspectives together. Finally I draw some conclusions about the machinery of government in the UK and about the forms taken by some UK social policies and measures since the mid-1980s.

Rationale

The mechanisms encountered when we view policy as the product of a rationale are essentially intellectual ones, to do with ways of thinking and reasoning. A rationale exists in the mind of an individual, and in this section I deal with individual reasoning mechanisms. Although Government publications use expressions like 'the Government believe . . .', we should not assume that all members of it share the same rationale. We have seen that different ministers come to policy making with different considerations uppermost in their minds: the implied collective single mind is a fiction. (The agreeing or collective endorsing of a rationale – for the purposes of publication, for example – is an interactive mechanism, and I deal with it below in the section on 'process'.)

Reasoning from objectives. The language of objectives seems to be used without inhibition in Green and White Papers and other official documents, and in politicians' memoirs, with the implicit suggestion that a 'choosing policy to satisfy objectives' mechanism has been employed, a variant of the 'rational actor' model employed by academic writers. But on closer inspection we find that many of those objectives – for example, as articulated by Thatcher and Fowler – took the form of unspecific aspirations, such as 'improving account-ability', abolishing 'welfare dependency', or tackling 'real need', all of which were so self-evidently 'a good thing' that they couldn't readily be opposed, but which were so imprecise that they left open a wide range of possibilities for action. The same was true of the aspirations in the European Social Charter. And, in practice, even where a number of alternative courses of action were identified, the selection was not made by evaluating options on a common set of criteria (the mechanism said to be employed by the classic 'rational actor' seeking the optimum solution). It seems to have been characteristic of this way of working that the rationale that developed centred on proposals rather than objectives, the question was: What is the best course of action to take? rather than: What should the objectives be? Indeed, when objectives were expressed as vague aspirations, impossible to oppose, that left only proposals to argue about.

Remedying defects.   Besides the language of 'objectives', we have found much use of terms such as 'defects', 'issues', 'shortcomings' and 'problems', which seem to convey a more authentic description of what goes on in the minds of politicians and officials (and those hybrids between the two, European Com-missioners), to judge by the techniques employed. For example, even where reasoning has been presented as taking the form of aiming to attain specific objectives, uppermost in their minds were the 'problems with the old system', as Thatcher puts it,[1] together with beliefs about how policies and measures 'caused' these effects and who was 'to blame'. When it came to making policy, what they saw themselves as doing was *remedying defects*. The intellectual mech-anism for doing this entailed identifying the 'defects of the existing system'; identifying – from whatever sources were available – possible alternative mea-sures; and assessing each alternative in the light of its likely contribution to remedying those defects, together with whatever other particular outcomes were seen as following from it.

Moving in a direction.   Another characteristic of all the case studies is that minis-ters and European Commissioners saw themselves as moving in a *direction, to-wards* the situation to which they aspired, rather than aiming to attain a specified, clearly defined goal or objective. (This feature is also not captured by the 'rational actor' model.) This may have followed partly from adopting a remedial approach, partly from the fact of planning for a future which could not be known in every respect, and partly from the fact that political and practical limitations to what could be achieved would become known only in the course of the process. Politicians and officials seem to have been well aware that policies which would be given effect in Acts of Parliament would do no more than provide for the setting up of systems or structures, and the modifying of existing arrays of powers, rights and duties, and the obligations and dependences that went with them. What happened subsequently would depend on what finance was made available to the new and existing bodies, on how the staff of those bodies exercised the powers and discretion that they found themselves with, and on the extent to which people accepted and became accustomed to the immediate changes etc. The Government could not *determine*, by designing legislation, what the precise outcomes would be.

But even if outcomes were perceived only distinctly, Thatcher and her advisers and ministers were aware that some measures, once introduced, would not easily be reversed – the sale of Council houses, for example – and that others could be introduced incrementally. As Thatcher puts it, 'Through the assisted places scheme and the rights of parental choice of school under our 1980 Parents' Charter we were moving some way towards [a straightforward education voucher scheme] without mentioning the word "voucher". In the 1988 Education Reform Act we now made further strides in that direction.'[2] Machiavelli's dictum that 'one change always leaves a toothing-stone for the next'[3] seems to have been well understood.

Reasoning from constraints. Where several options had been identified, one procedure employed – most conspicuously in the poll tax case – was to identify the particular advantages and disadvantages attendant on each one, and then to 'whittle down' the list of options by reference to disadvantages, especially those in the form of constraints, like 'X would have the effect that . . . and this would be intolerable'. This was literally a procedure of successive elimination.

We have also seen that a proposal could be 'ruled out' or 'ruled in' not only on the basis of what were seen as its likely outcomes but also on the basis of its own characteristics, as when a proposal was ruled out as 'unacceptable' (e.g. because 'the public would never accept it') without enquiring into what its consequences would be, or ruled in because it was seen as conforming to a requirement and thus as 'good in its own right' (e.g. because it entailed reducing the autonomy of local authorities). Thatcher describes the procedure that she adopted in the manifesto case as precisely one of 'ruling out and ruling in'.

Addressing dilemmas. All the above mechanisms can be effective at revealing *dilemmas*. In the assessing of alternative proposals crucial dilemmas may become apparent – for example, 'How do we help the neediest without being unfair to those who have avoided need by being thrifty?' or 'Which is the lesser of the two evils, keeping high levels of housing subsidies or increasing the amount paid out in Housing Benefit?' It is perhaps a significant characteristic of social policy issues in general that they present policy makers with dilemmas. (To describe policy making purely in terms of achieving goals and objectives is to overlook this characteristic entirely.) And in turn a characteristic of dilemmas is that the conflicts between value judgements that they entail is liable to be resolved by the bringing to bear of political/institutional interests.

Assessing risk. Given that policy making involves designing measures to be implemented in the future by other people not under the Government's total control, in circumstances that are far from wholly predictable, and with unpredictable effects in terms of the behaviour of the people on the 'receiving end', one might expect policy makers to be sensitive to the risk that the outcomes of implementing the measures might not be what they expected. In fact we have seen remarkably little assessing of risk in the five case studies. Although the use of skeleton Acts of Parliament would allow some flexibility when unforeseen events actually materialized, this does not appear to have been the prime motivation behind such legislation. Uncertainty as to outcomes was dealt with by pretending that there was certainty. Calculations of risk appear to have been applied only to the risk of not having sufficient support to get one's proposals adopted, exemplified in Fowler's fear that he 'could be tripped up at any stage'.[4]

Subconscious mechanisms. There is evidence of a variety of subconscious mechanisms at work in the minds of politicians and officials. We have seen that many different considerations may be present in someone's mind – some 'in the forefront', with an imperative that they be taken account of; others at 'the back'. There may also be a time effect, with some considerations starting off in the forefront but being progressively relegated to the back. The consideration that 'people need to become accustomed gradually to the poll tax' was an important one while the Green Paper was in preparation, but was subsequently relegated to the background as fresh political and practical considerations were borne in on those concerned. We have seen too that some information, projections and views can be 'refused entry' to the rationale, in a way that seems to denote subconscious mechanisms at work, if they are inconsistent with existing preconceptions, beliefs and commitments – the mechanism known by psychologists as 'cognitive dissonance'.[5] (We have seen how Thatcher was unable to 'take on board' Lawson's May 1985 projection of the likely consequences of adopting the poll tax proposals.)

The considerations and 'ingredients' of various kinds (perceptions, theories, ideas and value judgements) that make up a rationale seem to draw on a chaotic mass of raw material. From ministerial memoirs, we see that it may incorporate impressions left by personal experiences and anecdotes related by others, as well as images and metaphors and self-justifications. Seemingly some quite complex psychological mechanisms are at work here, involving the construction and 'cementing together' of a rationale out of a great assortment of elements, although from observations of 'cognitive dissonance reduction' it does appear that one such mechanism involves selecting ingredients that form a mutually consistent whole and rejecting possible ingredients that do not 'fit'.

Interests

The mechanisms encountered when we view policy as a selective response to interests are essentially to do with *feeling* as opposed to reasoning. The policy maker is implicitly seen as an 'emotional actor' rather than a 'rational actor'. The interests of different individuals and groups make their mark on policies and measures via 'personal' mechanisms, such as experiencing the feeling that 'something must be done' or making moral judgements, and via interactions among participants, as when pressure is exerted. This section deals with personal mechanisms: interactive mechanisms are dealt with under that heading below.

Registering issues.   Although the case study approach adopted in this book is one that selects issues for study – i.e. the approach itself focuses on issues – there is plenty of evidence that in their daily work, ministers and officials engaged with a stream of what they registered as 'issues'. Issue-registering mechanisms create a conjunction of perceptions and imperative.[6] We have seen that everyone who registered an issue not only had perceptions of the situation facing them but also experienced an *imperative*, a feeling that impelled them to '*do* something' about that situation. They thereby acquired a political/ institutional *interest* in doing something about it.

The interest that was integral to an imperative could be evoked through a variety of mechanisms. Some of these were interactive, involving the exerting of pressure, or a requirement to respond to initiatives from other bodies or people (e.g. the European Commission or a Private Member's Bill). Interests were also evoked by forthcoming events in the political calendar, such as a general election (we have noted the interests of Thatcher and her colleagues, in the context of the 1987 election, in advancing 'new and well-worked-out re-forms' showing that they weren't 'stale and running out of ideas') or party conference (Baker, Fowler and Lawson were all keen to announce measures at, and be acclaimed by, their party's annual conference in October).

Responding to issues.   We have encountered a wide variety of self-interests in the form of political/institutional interests on the part of ministers and officials, and these appear to have made significant marks on policies and measures in the course of responding to issues. Among politicians, we have seen interests in fulfilling a personal mission (both Thatcher and Ridley appear to have had a personal stake in diminishing the powers, autonomy and domains of local authorities[7]); in successfully piloting Bills through Parliament (Fowler, Baker); in keeping to targets (Lawson); in avoiding embarrassment (Lawson, Fowler, Howard); in 'carrying' backbench MPs and party activists with her (Thatcher); in gaining the Prime Minister's favour (Baker, Waldegrave); in demonstrating independence of thought, and perhaps of the Prime Minister too (Baker); in guarding their reputation (Lawson, as an opponent of using tax allowances to encourage virtuous behaviour); in preventing pressures for expenditure from surfacing (Lawson); and in demonstrating ability (Major, in getting the annual spending round settled without recourse to the Star Chamber). In the public spending case, we also have (according to Lawson) the personal interest of Ridley in not having to appear before the Star Chamber under the chairman-ship of Cecil Parkinson. And in the case of the social security reforms we have encountered the vested interest of Lawson as Chancellor in defending his prerogative – autonomy – where matters of taxation and National Insurance were concerned.

As for officials, although our evidence is limited, we have examples of inter-ests in having a challenging task to carry out, in being able to exercise autonomy in how they do their work (this may be manifested in a preference for broad terms of reference or in 'shutting out' others who might bring pressure to bear on them, as the poll tax study team did), or in bringing their work to fruition in a way that would gain them credit. Seeking to get as much money as they can from the Treasury does not necessarily denote an interest in 'budget-maximizing' for its own sake: finding themselves in a 'game' with the Treasury seems inevitably to give them an interest in winning, while a desire to maximize the funds obtained would again be consistent with an interest in maximizing their autonomy when it came to deciding how they should be spent. An interest in 'looking after' the material interests of their department's clients would also be met by such autonomy. And the arguments deployed to protect departmental spending, citing the embarrassment for ministers that might result from cuts, suggest that some officials might see others (if not themselves) as having an interest in protecting ministers from such embarrassment.

By what mechanisms were such interests created? They are the interests of people who occupied a particular place in the formal structure of government. They are also interests that were evoked by the particular issue, the particular imperative (e.g. the imminence of a general election), and the particular procedure adopted or structure created, as when setting up a committee or study team, and assigning it a task, created an interest on the part of most of its members in carrying out the task successfully. Sometimes they were evoked by a particular opportunity, for personal advancement and/or to do good, as they saw it. The mechanism by which they were evoked was not necessarily the same for any two individuals: they involved the 'emotional actor' and hence an individual's particular 'subpersonalities', although those who had risen through the same political party or civil service may have some characteristics in common, whether qualifying them for entry at the outset of their career or acquired by socialization subsequently. But it would not be surprising if that mechanism involved mentally picturing the task completed, hearing the plaudits, and feeling the well-being associated with them. (Likewise, picturing failure may induce negative feelings, such as fear and anxiety.) It may be that the significant powers of a Prime Minister include the capacity to bring about the conjuncture not only of person, position and task but also of such visions of success and reward.

Responding to pressure. Personal mechanisms were also involved in responding to pressure exerted by others. When pressure was successfully exerted, discomfort was experienced by the person 'on the receiving end': one way of removing that discomfort was to do what the pressurizer wanted, to accede to his or her interests. We have some clues about the nature of the psychological mechanism that gives rise to the discomfort. From accounts of Thatcher's 'handbagging' in Cabinet committees, which appears to have taken the form of treating grown men like schoolboys, and the embarrassment caused to those who witnessed it as well as those who suffered it, the mechanism may have involved creating a discrepancy between self-image, of dignity and respect, and reality, viz. indignity and disrespect; and/or creating an inner conflict, perhaps between two subpersonalities, e.g. the day-to-day confident wielder of power and an evoked small child who can never get anything right; and/or by conditioning a subpersonality which will identify with 'the oppressor' and overrule other, resistant, subpersonalities. Evidently conflict, like inconsistency, is uncomfortable to live with. The way in which Fowler rationalized his defeats – his proposals didn't deserve to 'make it'; if he couldn't get the proposals past Thatcher and his colleagues, he was unlikely to convince the public – seems consistent with his having identified himself with 'the oppressor'.

Empathizing.   We have seen several examples of ministers expressing sympathy towards a group of 'consumers' of policy – Thatcher with widows in the poll tax case, Fowler with people 'trapped' in their jobs by their pension arrangements. The mechanism here seems to be one of *empathizing* or identifying with those concerned, imagining yourself in their situation and experiencing their feelings 'at second hand'. Thatcher and Fowler appear to have done more than merely register information about the plight of others: it 'resonated' with them and evoked feelings and images in them: as a consequence they were sympathetic to what they felt were the interests of those people. The experiences of other people, however, did not affect them in the same way. Different mechanisms were involved. (Maybe different 'subpersonalities' were invoked.) As a corollary, Thatcher in particular seems to have acquired an antipathy to those whom she saw as 'causing' the plight of those with whom she empathized, as witness the strong antagonism which she expressed towards 'left-wing' local authorities.

Making moral judgements.   The mechanism here is essentially evaluative, involving the application of what we colloquially describe as a 'sense of fairness', of justice, of 'right and wrong'. We have seen that when a minister described a situation or a proposal as 'unfair' or 'unjust', commonly his or her emotions had been aroused; for example, they were *angered* by what they saw as an injustice or unfairness. (Emotions may be feigned, of course, and we often encounter a proposal described as 'fair' or 'unfair' for what are evidently presentational purposes: in our political culture, if the label 'fair' can be successfully associated with a policy – as in 'fair rents' – it is assumed that the electorate will accept it more readily.) We can recognize the exercise of moral judgements by the use of language which praises or condemns, as in distinguishing the deserving from the undeserving, and the conscientious citizen from 'the skilled claimant' and others who take advantage of their position or of state provision. The deserving and meritorious were implicitly regarded as having a legitimate claim upon the state, for provision or special consideration of some kind: in contrast the 'undeserving poor', whom Thatcher saw as associated with the development of a 'dependency culture', found among people 'who had simply lost the will or habit of work and self-improvement', had no legitimate claim on the state. Their irresponsibility had to incur some penalty, or irresponsibility would 'become the norm'. 'Need' too was taken to signify a legitimate claim upon the state for assistance, although the unspecific terminology – 'real need', 'genuine need' and 'areas of greatest need, notably low-income families with children' – had the effect that it was difficult to see who qualified for membership of the 'need group'.

Conflicts of interests. Policy makers were faced with dilemmas not only when formulating a rationale: they also faced dilemmas in the sense of having to resolve conflicts among interests, whether consumer interests or political/ institutional ones. A variety of different mechanisms could be adopted to handle these: 'taking sides'; ascertaining what support different interests had among the public; treating certain interests as pre-eminent and as imposing constraints ('We cannot do X because we have not got support'); finding a compromise; increasing the size of the 'cake', so there was enough for those that matter; qualifying proposals by giving assurances, and so on. Sometimes dilemmas could be suppressed by following procedures that concealed interests or made it easy to ignore them, such as refraining from carrying out and publishing a 'gainers and losers' exercise; expressing proposals and objectives vaguely; concentrating on the structures of new or reformed systems rather than on the detail of how they will work. All these had the effect of making it difficult for people to see how their interests would be affected. An attempt may be made to stigmatize certain groups in the eyes of the public, which would allow ministers to ignore their interests in the safe expectation that those interests will not have support and sympathy among the electorate.

Interactive mechanisms

When we examine the way in which people interact with one another in the course of bringing policies and measures into being, we find that process and structure are inseparable. Accordingly I discuss both in this section.

Setting up structures and procedures. When an issue arose which captured the Prime Minister's attention, a common response was to set up an *ad hoc* piece of structure, appoint people to positions in it, and assign them their task and the procedure that they were to follow (e.g. to whom they were to report). Examples are party policy groups, Cabinet committees (which the Prime Minister can chair, if he or she wishes), special teams of officials, and one-off meetings at Chequers or Downing Street. Sometimes use was made of an existing piece of structure, by appointing to a post an individual chosen to carry out a particular task (as when Baker was appointed Education Secretary).

Setting up an *ad hoc* body or appointing a certain individual to a post has been seen to have wider ramifications. Social mechanisms came into play, as those appointed created their own informal networks of communication and interdependence (as Baker did on becoming Education Secretary) and as members of a newly set up body 'gelled' into an exclusive 'club', or an inner group of committed members was formed, or disaffected members found themselves isolated. (All evidently occurred in the poll tax case.) Over public spending issues, social mechanisms could not be depended on to overcome the cleavage between Treasury and spending ministers. Social mechanisms were set up over particular issues in the European context too, as the representatives of the national governments set up informal coalitions and alliances. And once a 'deal' has been done, it creates a social and psychological bond between members. Once 'the eleven' had put their signatures to the Social Charter and the UK Government had dissented, the latter was on its own, outside their circle. This new structure gave UK ministers a strong interest in re-establishing their credentials as willing, full participants in Community affairs.

Formation of structures by procedures. We can see too that some procedures effectively formed structures. The Treasury's conduct of the annual spending round created cleavages between spending departments. Likewise the formal procedure for making an Act of Parliament rendered ministers dependent on their backbenchers for support in the form of their votes. And the qualified majority voting procedures of the European Union Council of Ministers rendered the government of a member state dependent on the support of other governments for achieving the result it sought.

Using structures and procedures. We have seen that formal and informal procedures constitute mechanisms which can be taken advantage of by politicians and officials. In the UK, constitutional law-making procedures permitted the Prime Minister to use the strategy of committing herself or himself to securing the adoption of a proposal even before it reaches Parliament, by making public announcements of intention, by securing a mandate by party acclaim (before the likely impact is understood), by investing scarce resources in drafting legislation, and by pre-empting alternatives by virtue of the time used up. The formal legislative procedures also allowed the Government to adopt the strategy of 'uncoupling' some decisions from others, as with 'framework' or 'skeleton' legislation which delegates powers to ministers: this makes it more difficult for opponents to demonstrate persuasively that the effects of the legislation would be harmful. The Government is also able to take advantage of the fact that legislative decisions are only loosely coupled with decisions about public expenditure, so that a Bill comes before Parliament – as in the poll tax and social security cases – in the absence of the spending commitments that would enable MPs to gauge the likely financial consequences.

In the case of the annual spending round, the conventional procedure splits decision making into two (the 'uncoupling' of decisions again) with ministers collectively committing themselves at the June/July Cabinet meeting to expenditure ceilings for the three years ahead, and only subsequently, at its November meeting, deciding the totals for individual departments. Between the meetings, the fact that spending ministers negotiate individually with the Treasury inhibits them from forming coalitions among themselves and revealing their 'hands' to one another. (And the Star Chamber set ministers who had already 'settled' against those who hadn't.) Effectively the whole structure and procedure amount to a mechanism by which Treasury ministers are able to maximize the pressure they can exert on supplicant ministers.

In the manifesto case, the *ad hoc* structures and procedures set up by Thatcher, with the policy groups effectively reporting to her alone, amounted to a mechanism – under her control – for ruling certain proposals out and others in. And the Chequers seminar in the poll tax case provided her with the opportunity to commit herself to the proposal in front of an audience of her Cabinet colleagues, and, witnessed by most of the other ministers present, to give a mandate to the studies team to continue their work on developing the poll tax. The next, *ad hoc*, procedural decision was to publish the Government's proposals in the form of a Green Paper, ostensibly tentative but in fact demonstrating and by its publication strengthening the Government's commitment to presenting legislative proposals based on it.

In the social security case, Fowler, a middle-ranking minister, made use of the *ad hoc* procedure which he set up to consult widely, seeking a consensus where one could be found but also demonstrating that doing nothing was not an option. This procedure gave him some help in anticipating criticisms from his colleagues to the effect that his proposals would not be feasible or would not command support: it also enabled him to select from among the representations those that supported his proposals and to develop arguments to counter those that did not.

In the European case the structure had strongly radial elements. Over the Social Charter one set of linkages ran from the European Council and the Council of Ministers at the centre to the governments of the member states, via those governments' ministerial representatives. Another set ran from the Commission to national governments. In addition there was the network of central bodies, dominated at that stage by the Commission and the Council of Ministers. Within that structure, for Delors and his fellow Commissioners, the *ad hoc* procedure of getting the European Council to endorse the Social Charter constituted a strategy for securing a mandate to prepare and submit an Action Programme and a contingent commitment from the governments of the member states to acquiescing in the proposals that would result. Once endorsed, the Charter would provide that mandate, serving as a 'policy bridgehead', a 'peg' on which more specific proposals could be 'hung'. When no invitation was forthcoming, they took the procedural decision to submit their already prepared Action Programme nevertheless. A further *ad hoc* procedural decision was evidently taken at some point to combine the proposed directive on health and safety and the proposed recommendation on job and social security into a single proposed directive. The formal legislative procedure, within a structure involving the European Parliament too, would then be used to secure its adoption, greatly assisted by the formal (albeit legally untested) use of the qualified majority vote procedure and the rotating presidency, a system which mostly gives the government occupying it an interest in being able to claim achievements at the end of its six months in office.

We can view the Commission's procedure over the Social Charter, and Thatcher's procedures over education vouchers and SERPS, as essentially strategies, using the available mechanisms, for formulating proposals in aspirational terms and 'navigating them' through the power structure: they acquired specificity and commitment on the way, as they progressed towards legislative measures and eventual action. So the objectives were initially 'open-ended' but became specific in the course of the process. Similarly, when Lawson pressed Fowler for a promise of £2 billion in savings from the social security review, he appears to have done so not with that specific objective in mind but with the aim of getting as much as he could. Whether they intend to or are forced to, governments effectively adopt strategies rather than concrete objectives. Certainly the stating of an objective may form part of a strategy – like Lawson's demand for £2 billion savings – but to regard the failure to achieve such an objective as a failure of implementation is, I suggest, to misunderstand how government works and relates to society and the wider political system. Likewise, to complain that the Government has 'moved the goalposts' is to miss the point that one of the never-ending tasks of government is to find out where goalposts may safely and appropriately be put.

Communicating views and exerting pressure.   Groups outside government that seek to make a mark on government policies and measures rely on establishing linkages either to ministers – whether directly, or via advisers, officials or MPs, or via the media – or to officials, especially officials who are working on issues that concern them. Essentially they seek to create communication channels and, if possible, levers – or make use of already existing ones – by which at the very least they can communicate their views if not also exert pressure to which ministers are susceptible.

Some people have privileged access to ministers. In the case of the social security reforms, the representatives of the pensions industry who were invited to serve on the Inquiry into Provision for Retirement, had privileged access to the Minister (who chaired it) and the opportunity to operate a 'gatekeeper' mechanism so far as evidence from other bodies was concerned. We may infer that the Conservative Party's dependence on some of the companies involved for contributions to Party funds placed those companies in a privileged position in the sense of having their views carefully considered, although care will be taken not to provide grounds for any suggestion that the Government's favours have been purchased by their contributions. Some companies may have had access to ministers via the backbench Conservative MPs whom they retained as consultants/advisers. And the Government would depend on pensions companies, and on employers generally, for cooperation in realizing its intentions regarding occupational pensions and SERPS. As Fowler makes clear, he could not afford to alienate them. Interestingly, the Institute of Directors 'in general . . . finds the British government very open'.[8]

In other cases we find a 'standing' obligation to heed the views of party activists and MPs' constituents, especially at 'set-piece' events like annual party conferences. Party officers may act as intermediaries: women's organizations with access to the then Women's Vice-Chairman of the Conservative Party made effective use of that connection to press their case over Child Benefit. Members of the electorate who wrote to their MPs or joined in public protests about the poll tax also made their opinions felt. And privileged access may be afforded to people who are seen as capable of producing useful ideas and analyses, as exemplified by the invitations to members of right-wing 'think-tanks' to No. 10 Downing Street in the manifesto case. They also had contacts with Baker and the No. 10 Policy Unit, and their publications were read by ministers and advisers. Their contributions appear to have made a mark on policy despite the fact that they were not in a position to exert pressure on ministers.

For other people and groups, the linkage took the form of a communication channel, *available only when ministers and officials allowed*. In the poll tax case, local authority associations and professional bodies had no links to the DoE studies team or DoE ministers while E(LF) was at work, and the social security reviews provided access for a limited period only. In that case, very few of the suggestions put forward by CPAG and other 'poverty lobby' groups made a visible mark on the bundle of policies set out in the Green Paper. One element in this result may have been that the Government did not depend in any way on these groups, and ministers appear to have felt no obligation to heed their views. But another element may have been that they used the opportunity of access, when they had it, to advocate a rationale that was fundamentally inconsistent with ministers' perceptions and value judgements: its emphases on fiscal equity, no means-testing, redistribution of resources, and increased spending on Housing Benefit, and its opposition to a 'no-cost' review, were diametrically opposed to those of ministers: there was no meeting of minds. They were indeed talking different languages, as became very apparent from the oral sessions held by the review teams. It seems that a communication channel requires mutual understanding and a common language between the parties if it is to function as a communication *mechanism*.

Identifying the scope for choice. How much scope for choice do ministers have? To what extent do realities – Pliatzky's 'force of circumstances' – allow room for manoeuvre? We have seen that ministers characteristically face dilemmas, a situation which allows more choice than if there were an obvious single optimum course of action. Moreover, a variety of theories were available to anyone wishing to explain such phenomena as the decline of private renting or low standards in schools, and ministers were able to choose whichever they preferred. Likewise a variety of theories were available for calculating the likely real-world outcomes of proposals, as in the case of the draft directive on the protection of women workers: both supporters and opponents could find a theory to justify their stance.

There was also considerable latitude for Thatcher and her ministers where financial considerations were concerned. Although the reduction of public expenditure might be expected to have constituted a major objective for Thatcher and her ministers, and indeed did so where social security expenditure was concerned, it was not evident in her readiness to spend large sums on public services in the run-up to the 1987 general election, to make 'huge sums of money' available for spending on untried Housing Action Trusts, to allow the public purse to incur huge sums in setting up the Community Charge, and to forgo tax revenue by giving tax allowances to encourage 'virtuous' recourse to the private market for health care, pensions and housing. We might conclude that consistency was not necessarily important to ministers, or that Thatcher felt free to choose in which fields the reduction of public spending would be a priority.

It seems possible too for considerations of practical feasibility to impose little constraint on the choice of policies and measures – as in the poll tax case, where the collection problems created for local authorities were considerable, and magnified by last-minute instructions from the DoE. This is consistent with an attitude of 'let's move in the direction we want and deal with the problems as we encounter them', as seen in the Thatcher governments' increasing reliance on 'framework' or 'skeleton' legislation.

Moreover, because policy is to do with future action, policy justifications must necessarily rest upon guesses, assumptions and extrapolations from the present. These are all inherently susceptible to being influenced by political considerations, subjectively held (as in the public expenditure case). Even over population forecasts and their implications for pensions, a field in which there is a great deal of technical expertise, there is scope for pessimistic and optimistic interpretations and assumptions, and thus scope for employing value judgements and images in coming to conclusions. To some extent, then, politicians were able to operate a mechanism of choosing what constraints they were prepared to accept.

Making choices: compromising, bargaining and voting. Individuals make choices throughout the process of creating and synthesizing an internally consistent rationale – in admitting or keeping out particular considerations, assigning priorities etc. – and in responding or not responding to particular interests, up to the point at which a single course of action has been seized on as the best. Although interests will previously have 'fed in' to the rationale via value judgements, at this point rationale and interests *must* come together, even if it involves intellect overruling feelings, or vice versa. If only a single individual is involved, this can take place inside his or her head. Where many people are involved, however, matters are more complicated.

As an example of the simplest case, involving two participants, we have the disagreement between Thatcher and Lawson over tax relief on mortgage interest. We have seen that Thatcher wished to increase it, Lawson to reduce it. Their respective rationales were very different. They had different objectives, different calculations of the likely outcomes of perceived alternatives, and applied different constraints; different considerations were uppermost in their minds; and they were operating on different perceptions, theories and value judgements. No meeting of minds, in terms of amalgamating their rationales into a single one, took place: the compromise on which they agreed, and which was enshrined in the very unspecific manifesto commitment to 'keep the present system', entailed nothing more than keeping the door open for the preference of either to be adopted at a later date. The formal structure (Prime Minister and Chancellor, with their respective well-recognized domains and linkages) and the informal one (long-standing colleagues in Cabinet, Government and Party; neighbours in Downing Street; meeting over work matters from day to day and accordingly needing to maintain a civilized working relationship; and both recognizing that in alliance with each other they were in practice better able to 'get their way' in Cabinet than if they were on 'opposite sides') provided a variety of levers that they could use to exert pressure on each other to agree with what they proposed: they also provided certain *inhibitions* to the use of those levers. In the case of tax relief on mortgage interest, the outcome reflected a kind of 'balance of power' between them, but over the use of tax relief to encourage private health insurance Thatcher forced an embarrassing concession from Lawson, while over the proposal to introduce a poll tax she effectively overruled him, with the support of other members of the Cabinet. Over the issue of introducing compulsory occupational and personal pensions, however, with the support of the pensions industry and employers' groups, he defeated her. These four different outcomes illustrate the difficulty of finding safe generalizations in this field.

Where a number of participants are involved, as in the European Council of Ministers or the House of Commons, voting procedures are customarily employed. The vote formally creates commitment to the policy or measure adopted. But formal votes are likely to be preceded by informal negotiating and the reaching of bargains. Significant in this process is the disaggregating of the proposal into a 'bundle' of proposals, and the trading of support for different elements of the bundle. The currency, then is support: 'I'll give you my support over X if you'll give me your support over Y.' The trading of support may also involve linking proposals that are completely unrelated: 'I'll give you my support over your opting out from the social policy provisions of the Maastricht treaty if you'll give me your support over recognizing Croatia.'

Commitment, mandate and pre-empting. Commitment, mandate and pre-empting appear to be integral to the mechanisms by which a choice becomes a decision, a proposal becomes a policy, and a policy is 'translated' into a measure. Commitment in particular was important in all five cases studied. In putting a case to their colleagues, reaching agreements, taking decisions, making public announcements, and publishing manifesto promises and proposals in Green as well as White Papers, Thatcher and her ministers committed themselves to future actions and measures, and thereby ruled out others. The significance of commitment appears to be well appreciated by ministers, officials and other participants in policy making: in the manifesto case the compromises reached where there was disagreement between Thatcher and other ministers took the form of agreeing not to commit the Government more strongly to one alternative rather than another. Commitments created early in the process governed the scope for subsequent decisions: in the case of the annual spending round this was precisely what they were intended to do. The existence of commitment also constituted an obstacle to taking further information and views into account, particularly in the poll tax case, although it was not necessarily an insuperable obstacle, as various 'U-turns' demonstrate (see below). Mandate effectively allowed the DoE studies team to work up the poll tax proposals in seclusion and the European Commission to formulate measures that would give effect to the Social Charter. The European Court of Justice evidently feels it has a mandate, in resolving cases that turn on inferring the purpose of a Directive, to take account of the content of its preamble, and this may allow it to infer the Directive's purpose from references to the Charter. Even though the Charter wasn't signed by the heads of state or government of all the member states, the Council of Ministers, in adopting the Directive, endorsed references to the Charter in its preamble.

Procedures that create commitments can simultaneously have a pre-empting effect, when the obstacle to going back on a decision is not only psychological and social but practical: if it would involve repeating steps taken earlier, further expenditure of scarce resources, or merely disruption and delay, or 'there simply isn't time', it may be ruled out as infeasible. In all sequences of decisions (e.g. framework legislation, public spending), the earlier ones have a pre-empting effect when the time comes to take the later ones.

Commitment, mandate and pre-empting all have implications for future action. They amount to 'policy bridgeheads' into the future, governing in advance what government will do. To borrow Sandberg's phrase, to create commitments is to 'colonize the future'.[9]

'U-turns'.   Publicly, Thatcher made a feature of her adherence to decisions she had taken: 'The lady's not for turning.'[10] Despite this, and despite the obstacles to reversing policy that commitment, mandate and pre-empting in particular cases constitute, we have seen some instances of U-turns: the poll tax (both the abandonment of the tax within two years of its introduction, after Thatcher's departure, and the earlier abandoning of dual running), the social security reforms (the abandoning of the proposal to abolish SERPS and replace it by compulsory occupational and personal pensions, and of the proposal to pay Family Credit through the pay-packet, as well as the last-minute change to the savings disregard for Housing Benefit) and the 1983–4 spending round (the abandoning of Sir Keith Joseph's proposal to institute a parental contribution towards students' tuition fees).

The common factor in these U-turns was *pressure*, especially pressure exerted by Conservative backbench MPs. MPs themselves were under pressure – from their constituents, or from interest and campaigning groups – as well as acting out of a desire to do good and/or the fear of losing their seats. Particular circumstances – a leadership election, a flood of letters from constituents, low standing in public opinion polls, a mood of rebelliousness and mobilizing of backbench groups – evidently enhanced ministers' susceptibility to pressures that at other times they might have resisted.

'Public discourse'.   We have seen that politicians and officials pay a great deal of attention to the 'presentation' of policies, in their election manifesto and in Green and White Papers. The making of public statements forms part of several mechanisms. The public announcement of intentions registers and creates commitment, and helps to persuade other people that the intentions *will* be acted on. In relation to specific issues, ministers seek through other public

pronouncements to establish and gain public acceptance for – among other things – the justifications and claims of legitimacy that they choose to put forward for their policies and measures; their view that blame for certain situations lies with other bodies, not themselves; and their stigmatizing judgements of certain groups as undeserving. Insofar as the media assist or hinder them in their endeavours, their activities too form part of the mechanism: they serve as a means of communication between the Government and the public.

But opposition parties and interest and campaigning groups try to use the media to contest the Government's presentation. Reporters and editors, paying varying heed to the views of their medium's owners, investigate and (necessarily selectively) report and interpret these and the Government's contributions to 'public discourse'. If, sometimes with the assistance of individuals within government (politicians or officials) who 'leak' documents that reveal that all is not as the Government says, they discover and reveal discrepancies between what ministers have said or done in the privacy of Whitehall and what they have said or done in the public domain, ministers come under pressure to explain themselves, and may suffer considerable embarrassment and loss of 'face' or 'credibility' as a result.

Reflections on the machinery of government

In the literature on the government of the UK, the powers and relationships of the constituent bodies are customarily examined in a way that focuses on their structural position. What do we see if we focus on their interaction over *issues*?

Powers of the Prime Minister. We have observed that in relation to issues the occupant of the post of Prime Minister possesses a number of significant capacities and 'powers to do' besides those that appear in conventional lists. They include

- The capacity to utter commands that other people feel obliged to obey.
- The capacity to cause *ad hoc* structures, such as meetings, committees and working groups, to be set up. She or he can effectively decide their terms of reference, who shall be invited or be a member and who excluded, and place herself or himself in the chair or a central 'gate-keeping' position.
- The capacity to exert pressure, notably exercised by Thatcher in the Cabinet committee setting.
- The capacity to generate commitment, obtain mandates and pre-empt possible courses of action, e.g. by formulating statements of intention which are publicly announced as 'policy', or by taking 'authoritative' decisions, which other people treat as binding.

The Prime Minister and other ministers. The rate of ministerial turnover in the Thatcher era is frequently criticized, both by ex-ministers and by academics, on the grounds that it is not conducive to good or skilful management. We have already noted, however, that Thatcher was very alert to *issues*, and made a number of ministerial appointments on the basis of that person's qualifications for tackling a particular issue or task. As the issue or task was completed and overtaken by others – e.g. when the issue of the content of the legislation had been resolved, and replaced by the issue of finance – the minister might be replaced by one keener on imposing public expenditure cuts. Whether this is reprehensible or not is a matter for debate. It could be argued that Government ministers *ought* to be concerned with contentious issues, whether of their own making or not, and that other, non-contentious matters can be perfectly well left to officials under the supervision of the minister.

What is the relationship between the Prime Minister and ministers who have been appointed to handle issues? The conventional view is that ministers are heavily *dependent* on the Prime Minister for staying in post and for career advancement, and that this gives the PM a lever to exert pressure on the minister to do his or her bidding. There is some evidence of this. In the poll tax case Jenkin fully appreciated that the PM's support was 'crucial' if another review of local government finance was to be launched, and the interest of Baker and Waldegrave in gaining the PM's acceptance and favour rendered them dependent on her. Fowler depended on Thatcher for support in rebuffing Lawson's attempt to cut the social security budget. But we have seen in the manifesto and poll tax cases that once the appointment has been made, it is the Prime Minister who depends on the minister to carry out the task assigned to him or her, especially as a recently appointed minister cannot be dismissed without giving the impression that an error of judgement had been made in making the appointment. Moreover, some recent appointees may make their own, different, judgement of what is desirable and feasible, and/or may wish to demonstrate that they are their 'own man' or woman and not merely an instrument of the PM, as seems to have been true of Baker when he was Education Secretary. The effect of the PM's dependence on the minister will be that the latter's views cannot be ignored. To some extent the Prime Minister can lessen his or her dependence on the minister by relying on the No. 10 Policy Unit and outsiders, but for thinking through the detail of the necessary legislation, drawing up the brief for the Parliamentary draughtsmen and liaising with them, and taking the Bill smoothly through its Parliamentary stages it will be necessary to enlist the active support of the minister and his or her officials.

The Prime Minister's relationship with the Chancellor of the Exchequer is a special one, involving mutual dependence over issues that involve both legislative and spending decisions. Because these are taken separately and through different machinery, with the Chancellor, Chief Secretary and Treasury officials able to dominate the latter, the PM is very dependent on the Chancellor for cooperation in allocating expenditure for reforms or other schemes which the PM favours. On public expenditure issues generally, the Chancellor depends on the PM for support – perhaps in the shape of refusing to intervene on a spending minister's side – over issues that bring him into conflict with spending ministers, if he feels that the traditional prerogative of the Chancellor is threatened and wishes to defend it. Where PM and Chancellor are in dispute, the importance of preserving the relationship between them will be a factor – if not the overriding one – to be taken into account.

The use of ad hoc *Cabinet committees and ministerial meetings.* Cabinet committees are said to be necessitated by the sheer volume and complexity of government business. Are they nothing more than an aid to efficient decision making? We have seen that the system allowed Thatcher to choose particular issues for her special attention. She could set up a committee on that issue, chair it and put pressure on her colleagues to endorse proposals that she favoured. Evidently it was important that they should do so, which seems to imply that *she* depended on *them*: she needed them to endorse her ideas so that they could go to Cabinet carrying a commitment, as agreed policy. As for *ad hoc* ministerial meetings such as those at Chequers, they did not have the status of Cabinet committees and could not take decisions that would be binding on the Cabinet, but Thatcher evidently felt able to take away from them a mandate to develop her proposals further. Again, then, she depended on her colleagues for endorsement, but her style on these occasions, as at meetings of Cabinet committees, appears to have assisted her to obtain it.

The Treasury and the spending departments. According to Coxall and Robins: 'What is particularly notable about the British decision-making process is the power of the Treasury to influence the policy proposed in every other ministry through its control over departmental spending.'[11] Issues bringing the Treasury and the spending departments into conflict arise when there are proposals for new measures that will have to be paid for, and in the normal course of the annual spending round, when Treasury officials and ministers may 'make an issue' of an area of expenditure that is conspicuous by its size or rate of growth, or simply exert pressure for cuts in projected expenditure. Although the Treasury is customarily regarded as pre-eminent among government departments, that reputation seems to derive largely from its centrality and the cleverness and diligently cultivated elitism of its officials. Where public spending in the social policy fields is concerned, Treasury officials have 'power without responsibility'. They possess the capacity to exert pressure (although this is limited by their dependence for information on the spending departments) but their interests are only in holding down the total and in winning the 'game' against the spending department over the ground – the issue – they have chosen.

Although the procedure for deciding spending plans favours the Treasury, it is not a foregone conclusion that the Treasury will 'win' over a particular issue. The outcome in a particular case depends heavily on the capacity of a spending minister to resist exerted pressure, whether in bilateral negotiations or Cabinet committee, and on the political considerations raised by the issue. The need to be able to claim that more money is being spent on the National Health Service as a general election approaches, the wish to avoid provoking a backbench revolt or being overruled by the Prime Minister, and the desire to escape blame and embarrassing publicity in the media are only some of the political considerations that may, as we have seen, 'outrank' financial ones.

The Government, the House of Commons and the wider political system. Relationships between the Government and its backbench MPs in the House of

Commons are customarily discussed in terms of the kinds of activity that engage both, such as the legislative process and scrutiny of the executive by departmental select committees. The poll tax and social security cases both involved legislation, and both illustrate the crucial role of the Government's own backbenchers, whose support was necessary to the Government winning the necessary votes. The interaction between them and ministers over these particular issues took place against a background of continuing interaction over a large number of issues. Ministers cannot afford to take their backbenchers for granted. When the Government's majority is small, it is of course important to ensure that backbenchers turn up and vote; but even when the majority is large there is the possibility of a rebellion. Essentially, then, ministers wish to 'carry' their backbench MPs with them, and an important role of the Whips is to keep ministers informed of feeling on the backbenches, as well as ensuring that MPs support the Government in votes and debates. The on-going relationship is one where loyalty is nurtured by attentiveness.

But this relationship between ministers and backbenchers does not exist in a vacuum. When an issue like the poll tax or social security reforms arises, there are many linkages extending out into the wider political system, so the minister–backbencher linkages are part of a much wider network. Backbench rebellions took place or were threatened when MPs felt they were speaking for their own (literally) or a wider constituency on whom they were dependent: people who lost as a result of the introduction of the poll tax, the pensions industry, women who opposed payment of Family Credit through the pay packet instead of to the mother, parents who would have to pay the fees of their children in higher education. Once again, an issue-based perspective gives us a different picture of the phenomenon.

The form of social policy

In the five case studies, we have seen that real-world considerations left considerable scope for choice in the determining of policies and measures. The content of measures has been determined by a variety of other considerations – notably political and ideological – and by a variety of events and activities, notably the exerting of pressure, both from within government and upon it from outside. Contemporary accounts of policy making in the mid-to-late 1980s depict a system that 'ran on pressure', in the sense that the exerting of pressure was a prominent part of the dynamic interaction between participants. When it came from the Prime Minister, that pressure was put behind social policy proposals that were rooted in a rationale incorporating theories about welfare dependency and the 'culture of the underclass' and political considerations to do with avoiding blame and placing it elsewhere. If we look for a common value behind the policies and measures we have observed, a unifying perspective with which they were all consistent, we don't find it in espousal of the 'free market', or centralization or decentralization. We find instead feelings of hostility towards those individuals and groups whom Thatcher saw as *taking advantage* of their position.

The world as she saw it seems to have been peopled partly by the advantage-takers, partly by other individuals and groups who were their victims. Local authorities were taking advantage of business rate-payers; local education authorities and teachers were taking advantage of their positions to promote left-wing ideology; families with working sons living at home were taking advantage of the property-based rates system and the widow on her own next door; the irresponsible, welfare-dependent members of the 'underclass' were taking advantage of the state and of deserving, 'responsible' members of society. The beauty, if that is the appropriate word, of the value-laden theories of the 'underclass' and 'welfare dependency' is that they enabled people who might otherwise be considered victims to be portrayed as advantage-takers, living off others – 'scroungers', in popular parlance, people who were 'working the system', even when it was the system that had transformed them into welfare dependants by forcing up the rents of their council houses and flats and as a consequence compelling them to claim Housing Benefit. It was the responsible, 'our people', who were the victims.

Thatcher's writings make clear her aggressive feelings and hostility to those who were 'working the system'. Her interest – the 'mission' that motivated her – lay in righting the wrong that was being done. And to do this, she in turn 'worked the system', in this case the governmental and political system, first by using the existing linkages, and *ad hoc* ones which she created, to exert pressure to 'get her way'. On top of what might once have been described as an 'old boy network' was superimposed another, more centralized, issue-related set of networks which were mechanisms for the exerting of pressure: Cabinet committees chaired by herself were a prime example.

But she also worked that system to create other systems in its own image. Her Governments made use of the policy instruments available to it – in particular, legislative measures, spending plans and organizational structuring – to create in the social policy fields *systems for exerting pressure*. The poll tax system was a mechanism for bringing pressure to bear on local authorities to cut their expenditure, by virtue of creating hardship for the poor and not-quite-poor when the Government-prescribed Standard Spending Assessment level of spending was exceeded. A system of local authority finance that involves giving authorities more freedom to spend less is, if it works as intended, a system for blaming them for cuts in services when central funding is reduced: the principle is that their interest in avoiding blame will create pressure to make better use of their resources. Withdrawal of housing subsidies to local authorities and 'ring-fencing' of housing revenue accounts forces rents up and thereby puts pressure on tenants to buy or to leave. Tenants are put under pressure to agree to their estates being handed over to Housing Action Trusts by denying them funds for improvement unless they do. Giving Social Fund officers in local areas cash-limited budgets places them – and not the Secretary of State for Social Security – under pressure to deny one applicant in order to help another. The underclass are to be 'dragged back into the ranks of responsible society': evidently pressure is the mechanism here too. One would not necessarily wish to defend the fabric of relationships between the citizen and the state as it existed prior to 1979, any more than one would wish to defend old boy net-works within the world of government and politics. But perhaps there are better ways of structuring relationships between the citizen and the state than as mechanisms for exerting pressure.

NOTES AND REFERENCES

Chapter 1 Introduction

1 Not such a paradox as it may at first sight seem: a generalization about generalizations is a meta-generalization, in a different class from them and therefore not comparable with them. For a similar conclusion to mine see S. de Smith and R. Brazier (1989) *Constitutional and Administrative Law*, 6th edn (Harmondsworth: Penguin), p. 170.

Chapter 2 The policy-making machinery

1 For a broader overview than is possible in this chapter, browse through the latest edition of S. de Smith and R. Brazier, *Constitutional and Administrative Law* (Harmondsworth: Penguin). Texts like B. Jones *et al.* (1994) *Politics UK*, 2nd edn (Hemel Hempstead: Harvester Wheatsheaf), and to a lesser extent B. Coxall and L. Robins (1994) *Contemporary British Politics*, 2nd edn (Basingstoke: Macmillan), contain some useful nuts-and-bolts material.
2 *Hansard* is the official verbatim report of the proceedings of the House of Commons and the House of Lords. References to it are sometimes expressed as HC Deb. or HL Deb. for 'House of Commons Debates' and 'House of Lords Debates' respectively.
3 *Dod's Parliamentary Companion* is published annually by Dod's Parliamentary Companion Ltd, Hurst Green, Etchingham, East Sussex.
4 *Vacher's Parliamentary Companion* is published quarterly by Vacher's Publications, 113 High Street, Berkhamsted, Herts.
5 *BBC-Vacher's Biographical Guide* is published annually by Vacher's Publications (see note 4).
6 Cabinet committees are listed in *Dod's Parliamentary Companion* (see note 2), *Vacher's Parliamentary Companion* (see note 3) and *The Whitehall Companion*, published annually by Dod's Publishing and Research Ltd, 31a St James's Square, London SW1.

7 The document *Standing Orders of the House of Commons* is published by Her Majesty's Stationery Office (HMSO) as a House of Commons Paper.
8 A comprehensive survey of central departments and their staffs and related organizations is contained in *The Whitehall Companion* (see note 6). See also *Civil Service Yearbook*, published annually by HMSO.
9 Departmental reports are currently published in March each year by HMSO.
10 The 'core' government departments (Treasury, Cabinet Office etc.) and the headquarters of the functional departments are known collectively as 'Whitehall'. Only a few are situated on Whitehall itself, the street in central London that connects Parliament Square and Trafalgar Square.
11 *The Whitehall Companion*, p. 830.
12 B. Donoughue (1987) *Prime Minister* (London: Jonathan Cape) describes arrangements as they were in 1974–9: they appear to have changed little if at all since that period.
13 A very useful text on this subject is N. Nugent (1994) *The Government and Politics of the European Union*, 3rd edn (Basingstoke: Macmillan). For a comprehensive survey of EU institutions and their staffs, see *The European Companion*, published annually by Dod's Publishing and Research Ltd (see note 6), and *Vacher's European Companion*, published quarterly by Vacher's Publications (see note 4).
14 Prior to the 1994 European elections, the UK had 81 out of 518 MEPs.

Chapter 3 'Policy' and 'social policy'

1 Foreword to *The Conservative Manifesto 1992*. London: Conservative Central Office.
2 M. Thatcher (1993) *The Downing Street Years*, p. 281. London: HarperCollins.
3 *The Conservative Manifesto 1987*, p. 63. London: Conservative Central Office.
4 *The Conservative Manifesto 1979*, pp. 27–8. London: Conservative Central Office.
5 *The Conservative Manifesto 1987*, *op. cit.*, p. 47.
6 *Ibid.*, p. 12.
7 *The Conservative Manifesto 1992*, *op. cit.*, p. 17.
8 *Ibid.*, p. 29.
9 Cm 214 (1987) *Housing: The Government's Proposals* (White Paper). London: HMSO.
10 Lord Howe, formerly Geoffrey Howe (Chancellor of the Exchequer 1979–83, Foreign Secretary 1983–9), interviewed on *The World at One*, BBC Radio 4, 3 February 1993.
11 Thatcher, *op. cit.*, p. 604.
12 L. Pliatzky (1989) *The Treasury under Mrs Thatcher*, p. 57. Oxford: Basil Blackwell.
13 House of Commons Social Security Committee (1993) *The Operation of the Child Support Act*, HC69, Session 1993–4, p. vii. London: HMSO.
14 HC Deb., 18 April 1989, Written Answers, col. 131.
15 M. Linklater and D. Leigh (1986) *Not with Honour*, p. 99. London: Sphere.
16 Cm 2213 (1993) *Social Security: Departmental Report*. London: HMSO.
17 Cm 2513 (1994) *Social Security: Departmental Report*, p. 29. London: HMSO.
18 H. Heclo and A. Wildavsky (1974) *The Private Government of Public Money*, pp. 217–19, 346–8. London: Macmillan.
19 Thatcher, *op. cit.*, p. 281.
20 See The Hansard Society Commission (1993) *Making the Law*, pp. 64–7. London: The Hansard Society for Parliamentary Government.
21 See Chapter 9.
22 See Chapter 8.
23 Department of Health (1991) *The Patient's Charter*. London: HMSO.
24 Ofsted, (Office for Standards in Education) is a non-ministerial central government department set up under the Education (Schools) Act 1992.

25 *The Independent*, 18 January 1990.
26 Cm 1264 (1990) *Children Come First* (White Paper). London: HMSO.
27 House of Commons Social Security Committee, *op. cit.*, p. x.
28 C. Ham and M. Hill (1993) *The Policy Process in the Modern Capitalist State*, 2nd edn, p. 11. Hemel Hempstead: Harvester Wheatsheaf.
29 P. Hall *et al.* (1975) *Change, Choice and Conflict in Social Policy*, p. 308. London: Heinemann.
30 *Ibid.*, p. 289.
31 T. H. Marshall (1965) *Social Policy*, p. 9. London: Hutchinson.
32 B. Rodgers *et al.* (1979) *The Study of Social Policy: a Comparative Approach*, p. 6. London: Allen and Unwin.
33 C. Jones (1985) *Patterns of Social Policy*, p. 16. London: Tavistock.
34 M. Kleinman and D. Piachaud (1993) European social policy, *Journal of European Social Policy*, 3(1), 1–19.
35 Central Policy Review Staff (1975) *A Joint Framework for Social Policies*, pp. 2–3. London: HMSO.
36 A. Walker, Letter to the Editor, *The Guardian*, 19 March 1988.
37 M. Hill (1980) *Understanding Social Policy*, p. 1. Oxford: Basil Blackwell and Martin Robertson.
38 Thatcher, *op. cit.*, p. 278.
39 R. M. Titmuss (1963) *Essays on 'the Welfare State'*, pp. 50–3. London: Allen and Unwin.
40 K. Banting (1979) *Poverty, Politics and Policy*, p. 11. London: Macmillan.
41 J. Le Grand *et al.* (1992) *The Economics of Social Problems*, 3rd edn, p. 32. Basingstoke: Macmillan.

Chapter 4 Approaches and methods

1 P. Hall *et al.* (1975) *Change, Choice and Conflict in Social Policy*, pp. 16–17. London: Heinemann.
2 N. Barr (1993) *The Economics of the Welfare State*, 2nd edn, p. 379. London: Weidenfeld and Nicolson.
3 D. Donnison *et al.* (1975) *Social Policy and Administration Revisited*, Chapter 12. London: George Allen and Unwin.
4 J. Greenaway *et al.* (1992) *Deciding Factors in British Politics*, p. 212. London: Routledge.
5 *Ibid.*
6 J. Carrier and I. Kendall (1977) The development of welfare states: the production of plausible accounts, *Journal of Social Policy*, 6(3): 271–290; P. Dunleavy (1981) *The Politics of Mass Housing in Britain 1945–1975*, p. 199. Oxford: Clarendon; M. Adler (1988) Lending a deaf ear: the Government's response to consultation on the reform of social security, in R. Davidson and P. White (eds) *Information and Government*. Edinburgh: Edinburgh University Press; and more.
7 For examples see Hall *et al.*, *op. cit.*; K. G. Banting (1979) *Poverty, Politics and Policy*. London: Macmillan; Donnison *et al.*, *op. cit.*
8 W. H. Newton-Smith (1981) *The Rationality of Science*, p. 234. London: Routledge & Kegan Paul.
9 P. H. Levin (1960) 'The structure and growth of reaction products formed on metal and other surfaces, particularly by oxidation', unpublished PhD thesis, University of London.
10 *Ibid.*, p. 130.
11 In Hall *et al.*, *op. cit.*, p. 375.
12 See Banting, *op. cit.*, and D. Fraser (1984) *The Evolution of the British Welfare State*, 2nd edn. Basingstoke: Macmillan, for examples.

13 M. Bulmer *et al.* (eds) (1989) *The Goals of Social Policy*. London: Unwin Hyman.
14 T. Wilson and D. Wilson (eds) (1991) *The State and Social Welfare: the Objectives of Policy*. Harlow: Longman.
15 J. Hills (1993) *The Future of Welfare: a Guide to the Debate*, pp. 4, 15. York: Joseph Rowntree Foundation.
16 Barr, *op. cit.*, p. 379.
17 Cmnd 4728 (1971) *Fair Deal for Housing*; Cm 214 (1987) *Housing: the Government's Proposals*. London: HMSO.
18 Cmnd 6851 (1977) *Housing Policy: a Consultative Document*. London: HMSO.
19 J. Le Grand *et al.* (1992) *The Economics of Social Problems*, 3rd edn, p. 3. Basingstoke: Macmillan.
20 N. Lawson (1992) *The View from No. 11*, p. 616. London: Bantam: 'Our objective has to be to see that . . . the NHS provides health care as efficiently and effectively as possible.'
21 This model is expounded in J. Tinbergen (1956) *Economic Policy: Principles and Design*. Amsterdam: North Holland Publishing Company; and criticized in D. Braybrooke and C. E. Lindblom (1963) *A Strategy of Decision*. New York: Free Press of Glencoe.
22 J. G. March and H. A. Simon (1958) *Organizations*, pp. 140–1. New York: Wiley.
23 M. Thatcher (1993) *The Downing Street Years*, pp. 590–2. London: HarperCollins.
24 See note 17.
25 As Barr does: see note 2.
26 The term is used by L. Pliatzky (1987) in The macro choice, in A. Gillie *et al.* (eds) *Politics and Economic Policy*. London: Hodder and Stoughton.
27 T. Blackstone and W. Plowden (1988) *Inside the Think Tank*, p. 127. London: Heinemann.
28 J. Edwards and R. Batley (1978) *The Politics of Positive Discrimination*, p. 52. London: Tavistock.
29 *The Independent*, 18 January 1990; Cm 1264 (1990) *Children Come First* (White Paper). London: HMSO; House of Commons Social Security Committee (1993) *The Operation of the Child Support Act*, HC69, Session 1993–4, p. x. London: HMSO.
30 Thatcher, *op. cit.*, p. 590.
31 S. Hogg (1995) Opening up the stuff of politics, *The Independent*, 26 September.
32 W. E. Connolly (1983) *The Terms of Political Discourse*, pp. 62–76. Oxford: Martin Robertson.
33 P. Saunders (1980) *Urban Politics*, pp. 45–8. Harmondsworth: Penguin.
34 See P. Dunleavy (1991) *Democracy, Bureaucracy and Public Choice*. Hemel Hempstead: Harvester Wheatsheaf, for a critical survey.
35 K. Baker (1993) *The Turbulent Years*, p. 114. London: Faber and Faber.
36 Lord Bridges (1964) Whitehall and Beyond, *The Listener*, 25 June. Cited in R. G. S. Brown (1970) *The Administrative Process in Britain*. London: Methuen.
37 Lawson, *op. cit.*, pp. 572, 575.
38 L. Festinger (1957) *A Theory of Cognitive Dissonance*. Evanston, IL: Row, Peterson.
39 H. Eckstein (1956) Planning: a case study, *Political Studies*, 4(1), 46–60 (reprinted in R. Rose (ed.) (1969) *Policy-making in Britain*. London: Macmillan.
40 P. H. Levin (1976) *Government and the Planning Process*, pp. 26–8. London: Allen and Unwin.
41 N. Korman and H. Simons (1978) Hospital closures, in Royal Commission on the National Health Service, *The Working of the National Health Service*, Research Paper Number 1. London: HMSO.
42 B. Ingham (1991) *Kill the Messenger*, p. 243. London: Fontana.
43 Banting, *op. cit.*, p. 10; F. N. Forman (1991) *Mastering British Politics*, 2nd edn, p. 226. Basingstoke: Macmillan; B. W. Hogwood and L. A. Gunn (1984) *Policy Analysis for the Real World*, p. 4. Oxford: Oxford University Press; B. Jones *et al.* (1994) *Politics UK*, 2nd edn, p. 537. Hemel Hempstead: Harvester Wheatsheaf.

44 On implementation theory, see C. Ham and M. Hill (1993) *The Policy Process in the Modern Capitalist State*, 2nd edn. Hemel Hempstead: Harvester Wheatsheaf; M. Hill (ed.) (1993) *The Policy Process: a Reader*. Hemel Hempstead: Harvester Wheatsheaf.
45 See recent departmental reports of the Department of Health.
46 Banting, *op. cit.*, pp. 150–1.
47 D. Hencke (1978) *Colleges in Crisis*, pp. 116–17. Harmondsworth: Penguin.
48 N. Ridley (1992) *My Style of Government*, p. 3. London: Fontana.
49 B. Donoughue (1987) *Prime Minister*, p. 6. London: Jonathan Cape.
50 J. P. Mackintosh (1977) *The British Cabinet*, 3rd edn, p. 143. London: Stevens.
51 G. W. Jones (1985) The Prime Minister's power, in A. King (ed.) *The British Prime Minister*, 2nd edn, pp. 195–220. Basingstoke: Macmillan.
52 Jones *et al.*, *op. cit.*, pp. 6, 401.
53 S. Lukes (1974) *Power: a Radical View*, p. 34. London: Macmillan.
54 D. H. Wrong (1979) *Power: Its Forms, Bases and Uses*, pp. 2, 22. Oxford: Blackwell.
55 R. Hadley and D. Forster (1993) *Doctors as Managers*, p. xi. Harlow: Longman.
56 Lawson, *op. cit.*, pp. 616–17.
57 According to one of the meanings given in the *Collins English Dictionary*.
58 Lord Bridges (1964) *The Treasury*, pp. 35–6. London: Allen and Unwin.
59 H. Heclo and A. Wildavsky (1974) *The Private Government of Public Money*, pp. 134–8. London: Macmillan.
60 F. Greenstein (1987) *Personality and Politics*, new edn, p. 173. Princeton, NJ: Princeton University Press.
61 G. Allport (1937) *Personality*. New York: Holt. Cited by Greenstein, *op. cit.*, p. 3.
62 See J. Rowan (1990) *Subpersonalities*. London: Routledge; also R. Ornstein (1986) *Multimind*. London: Macmillan.

Chapter 5 Formulating intentions: housing and education in the Conservative 1987 election manifesto

1 The Hansard Society Commission (1993) *Making the Law*, p. 164. London: The Hansard Society for Parliamentary Government.
2 H. Young and A. Sloman (1982) *No, Minister: an Inquiry into the Civil Service*, p. 22. London: BBC.
3 L. Pliatzky (1989) *The Treasury under Mrs Thatcher*, p. 48. Oxford: Basil Blackwell.
4 M. Thatcher (1993) *The Downing Street Years*, p. 570. London: HarperCollins.
5 *The Independent*, 25 January 1993.
6 S. de Smith and R. Brazier (1989) *Constitutional and Administrative Law*, 6th edn, p. 93. Harmondsworth: Penguin.
7 *The Conservative Manifesto 1987*. London: Conservative Central Office.
8 Thatcher, *op. cit.*, p. 572.
9 H. Young (1989) *One of Us*, p. 503. London: Macmillan. See also N. Lawson (1992) *The View from No. 11*, p. 315. London: Bantam. I return to this subject in Chapter 8.
10 Thatcher, *op. cit.*, p. 563.
11 *Ibid.*, p. 574.
12 *Ibid.*, pp. 565–6.
13 *Ibid.*, p. 568.
14 K. Baker (1993) *The Turbulent Years*, pp. 181–2.
15 Thatcher, *op. cit.*, p. 566.
16 *Ibid.*, p. 570.
17 *Ibid.*
18 *Ibid.*, pp. 571–2.
19 D. Butler and D. Kavanagh (1988) *The British General Election of 1987*, p. 44. Basingstoke: Macmillan.

20 Thatcher, *op. cit.*, p. 571.
21 See Lawson, *op. cit.*, p. 609; N. Ridley (1992) *'My Style of Government'*, p. 93. London: Fontana; Thatcher, *op. cit.*, p. 594. There was a similar sub-committee on the housing proposals.
22 Lawson, *op. cit.*, pp. 609–10.
23 Ridley, *op. cit.*, p. 94.
24 Baker, *op. cit.*, p. 194.
25 *Ibid.*, p. 222.
26 *Ibid.*, p. 221.
27 *Ibid.*, p. 192.
28 Thatcher, *op. cit.*, p. 572.
29 *Ibid.*, p. 574.
30 Ridley, *op. cit.*, p. 94.
31 N. Tebbit (1989) *Upwardly Mobile*, p. 330. London: Futura.
32 Lord Young (1990) *The Enterprise Years*, p. 197. London: Headline.
33 Thatcher, *op. cit.*, pp. 574–5; Lawson, *op. cit.*, p. 694.
34 N. Fowler (1991) *Ministers Decide*, p. 278. London: Chapmans.
35 *Ibid.*; Lawson, *op. cit.*, p. 696.
36 Baker, *op. cit.*, pp. 194–5; Lawson, *op. cit.*, p. 696.
37 C. Chitty (1989) *Towards a New Education System: the Victory of the New Right*, p. 219. Lewes: Falmer.
38 Thatcher, *op. cit.*, p. 600.
39 *Ibid.*
40 Ridley, *op. cit.*, pp. 86–7.
41 Thatcher, *op. cit.*, p. 600.
42 *Ibid.*
43 *Ibid.*, p. 601.
44 *Ibid.*, p. 605.
45 Connoisseurs of housing tenure will note that the state was not to stop prescribing what forms of housing tenure there could be.
46 Ridley, *op. cit.*, p. 88. The first rent control legislation of the twentieth century was actually the Rent and Mortgage Interest (War Restrictions) Act 1915.
47 Thatcher, *op. cit.*, p. 599.
48 See Cmnd 6851 (1977) *Housing Policy: a Consultative Document*, and Technical Volume, Part III, Chapter 9. London: HMSO.
49 Other factors were involved. Notably, since 1919 there had also appeared many alternative places for investment, besides putting money into housing to rent. The moral is: beware the single-cause explanation.
50 Lawson, *op. cit.*, p. 443. In the 1988 budget Lawson did, however, include an amendment to the Business Expansion Scheme to include within its scope, for five years only, the provision of accommodation for private rental. Evidently he recognized the strength of Ridley's case.
51 Ridley, *op. cit.*, pp. 86–8.
52 Thatcher, *op. cit.*, pp. 600–1.
53 *Ibid.*, p. 571.
54 *Ibid.*, p. 572.
55 Thatcher, *op. cit.*, p. 599.
56 Ridley, *op. cit.*, pp. 87–8.
57 *Ibid.*, pp. 88–9.
58 *Ibid.*, p. 88.
59 Thatcher, *op. cit.*, p. 603; Ridley, *op. cit.*, p. 90.
60 Thatcher, *op. cit.*, p. 599.
61 *Ibid.*

62 Lawson, *op. cit.*, p. 617.
63 *Ibid.*, p. 600.
64 *Ibid.*, p. 570.
65 *Ibid.*, pp. 681, 696.
66 Ridley, *op. cit.*, p. 88.
67 Thatcher, *op. cit.*, pp. 600–1; Ridley, *op. cit.*, pp. 88–9.
68 Thatcher, *op. cit.*, p. 672.
69 Lawson, *op. cit.*, p. 686.
70 *Ibid.*, p.681; Thatcher, *op. cit.*, p. 566.
71 Ridley, *op. cit.*, p. 28.
72 Thatcher, *op. cit.*, pp. 602–6.
73 *Ibid.*, p. 603.
74 *Ibid.*, p. 590.
75 Baker, *op. cit.*, p. 168.
76 See Box 5.3 Extracts from the Conservative 1987 election manifesto: education.
77 Thatcher, *op. cit.*, pp. 590–1.
78 *Ibid.*, p. 593.
79 Baker, *op. cit.*, pp. 190–1.
80 *Ibid.*, pp. 192–3.
81 Thatcher, *op. cit.*, p. 592.
82 Baker, *op. cit.*, pp. 211–12.
83 Ridley, *op. cit.*, pp. 92–3.
84 Thatcher, *op. cit.*, p. 591.
85 *Ibid.*, p. 592.
86 *Ibid.*
87 Ridley, *op. cit.*, p. 93.
88 See Chitty, *op. cit.*, and C. Chitty (1992) *The Education System Transformed*. Manchester: Baseline.
89 Thatcher, *op. cit.*, p. 592.
90 *Ibid.*, pp. 591, 592, 593.
91 Baker, *op. cit.*, p. 221.
92 Thatcher, *op. cit.*, p. 593.
93 *Ibid.*, p. 592.
94 Baker, *op. cit.*, p. 191.
95 Thatcher, *op. cit.*, p. 590.
96 *Ibid.*, p. 570.
97 See Lawson, *op. cit.*, p. 609; Ridley, *op. cit.*, p. 93; Thatcher, *op. cit.*, p. 594.
98 Baker, *op. cit.*, p. 192.
99 Chitty (1992), *op. cit.*, p. 31.
100 Baker, *op. cit.*, p. 169.
101 Lawson, *op. cit.*, p. 609.
102 Thatcher, *op. cit.*, p. 592.
103 Ridley, *op. cit.*, p. 89.

Chapter 6   The dependence of the Prime Minister: the 'poll tax' saga

1 M. Thatcher (1993) *The Downing Street Years*. London: HarperCollins.
2 N. Lawson (1992) *The View from No. 11*. London: Bantam.
3 K. Baker (1993) *The Turbulent Years*. London: Faber and Faber.
4 N. Ridley (1992) *'My Style of Government'*. London: Fontana.
5 D. Butler, A. Adonis and T. Travers (1994) *Failure in British Government: the Politics of the Poll Tax*. Oxford: Oxford University Press.

6 M. Crick and A. Van Klaveren (1991) Mrs Thatcher's greatest blunder, *Contemporary Record*, 5(3), 397–416.

7 Thatcher, *op. cit*, p. 644.

8 Cmnd 8449 (1981) *Alternatives to Domestic Rates* (Green Paper). London: HMSO.

9 Cmnd 9008 (1983) *Rates* (White Paper). London: HMSO.

10 Thatcher, *op. cit*, p. 646.

11 *Ibid.*; Jenkin, in *A Tax Too Far*, Channel Four, March 1993.

12 Thatcher, *op. cit*, p. 646.

13 Baker, *op. cit.*, p. 114; Thatcher, *op. cit*, p. 646; Crick and Van Klaveren, *op. cit.*, p. 401.

14 Thatcher, *op. cit.*, p. 646.

15 *Ibid.*

16 Butler *et al.*, *op. cit.*, p. 47. Baker idiosyncratically refers to the studies team as the 'review group' and writes incorrectly that it 'involved, of course, other government departments'. He also claims 'It was chaired by me but the work was coordinated by William Waldegrave.' Baker, *op. cit.*, p. 115.

17 Crick and Van Klaveren, *op. cit.*, p. 403.

18 Thatcher, *op. cit*, p. 647.

19 *Ibid.*

20 *Sunday Times*, 1 April 1990.

21 Lawson, *op. cit.*, pp. 570–1.

22 Crick and Van Klaveren, *op. cit.*, p. 410.

23 Butler *et al.*, *op. cit.*, p. 73.

24 Baker, *op. cit.*, p. 122; see also Crick and Van Klaveren, *op. cit.*, p. 409.

25 Thatcher, *op. cit.*, p. 648.

26 Baker, *op. cit.*, p. 123.

27 Butler *et al.*, *op. cit.*, p. 79.

28 *Ibid.*, p. 80.

29 Baker, *op. cit.*, p. 122; Lawson, *op. cit.*, p. 561.

30 Lawson, *op. cit.*, p. 574.

31 Baker, *op. cit.*, p. 125.

32 Thatcher, *op. cit.*, p. 650.

33 Baker, *op. cit.*, p. 125.

34 Lawson, *op. cit.*, p. 576.

35 Cmnd 9714 (1986) *Paying for Local Government*. London: HMSO.

36 Butler *et al.*, *op. cit.*, pp. 101–3; Thatcher, *op. cit.*, p. 652.

37 Butler *et al.*, *op. cit.*, p. 103.

38 Thatcher, *op. cit.*, p. 652.

39 *Ibid.*

40. Ridley, *op. cit.*, p. 125.

41 Thatcher, *op. cit.*, p. 653.

42 After a Bill has been tabled in the House of Commons and its principles debated (at Second Reading), it is in most cases referred to a Standing Committee for detailed consideration. When the Committee stage has been completed, it returns to the floor of the House for further debate – the Report Stage. The Third Reading debate and vote follow immediately.

43 Butler *et al.*, *op. cit.*, p. 118.

44 *Ibid.*, p. 119.

45 *Ibid.*, p. 120.

46 Baker, *op. cit.*, pp. 131–2.

47 *Ibid.*

48 On the working of the SSA system, see Audit Commission (1993) *Passing the Bucks*: The Impact of Standard Spending Assessments on Economy, Efficiency and Effectiveness. 2 vols. London: Audit Commission.

49 Thatcher, *op. cit.*, p. 656.
50 Baker, *op. cit.*, p. 133; *The Guardian*, 2 March 1990.
51 *The Independent*, 7 November 1989.
52 *The Independent*, 24 January 1990.
53 Butler *et al.*, *op. cit.*, pp. 145, 157.
54 *Ibid.*, p. 157.
55 Under the Social Security Act 1986: see Chapter 7.
56 Butler *et al.*, *op. cit.*, p. 158.
57 *Ibid.*, pp. 180, 289.
58 *Ibid.*, p. 150.
59 *The Guardian*, 2 March 1990.
60 Butler *et al.*, *op. cit.*, p. 151.
61 Baker, *op. cit.*, p. 134.
62 Baker, *op. cit.*, p. 138.
63 Lawson, *op. cit.*, p. 621.
64 Cmnd 9714, *op. cit.*, p. 76.
65 *Ibid.*, p. 5.
66 *Ibid.*, p. 9.
67 *Ibid.*, p. 10.
68 *Ibid.*, pp. 19–24.
69 *Ibid.*, pp. 19, 24.
70 Thatcher, *op. cit.*, p. 643.
71 *Ibid.*, p. 644.
72 *Ibid.*, p. 643.
73 *Ibid.*, p. 645.
74 *Ibid.*
75 *Ibid.*, p. 646.
76 *Ibid.*, p. 644.
77 *Ibid.*, pp. 644, 647, 645.
78 Baker, *op. cit.*, pp. 117–18.
79 Thatcher, *op. cit*, pp. 648–9.
80 Baker, *op. cit.*, p. 123.
81 Baker, *op. cit.*, p. 122.
82 Cmnd 9714, *op. cit.*, p. 25.
83 *Ibid.*, pp. 103–7.
84 Lawson, *op. cit.*, p. 574.
85 Thatcher, *op. cit.*, p. 652.
86 *The Guardian*, 28 July 1987.
87 Thatcher, *op. cit.*, p. 659.
88 Baker, *op. cit.*, p. 126.
89 Lawson, *op. cit.*, p. 576.
90 Butler *et al.*, *op. cit.*, p. 108.
91 *Ibid.*, p. 97.
92 Thatcher, *op. cit.*, p. 652.
93 *Ibid.*, p. 653.
94 *Ibid.*, p. 627.
95 *Ibid.*, p. 627.
96 *Ibid.*, pp. 658–9.
97 Butler *et al.*, *op. cit.*, p. 111.
98 Thatcher, *op. cit.*, p. 660.
99 *Ibid.*, p. 644.
100 Butler *et al.*, *op. cit.*, p. 74.
101 Lawson, *op. cit.*, p. 584.

102 *Ibid.*, p. 576.
103 Crick and Van Klaveren, *op. cit.*, p. 404.
104 Butler *et al.*, *op. cit.*, pp. 211–15.
105 Crick and Van Klaveren, *op. cit.*, p. 406.
106 Butler *et al.*, *op. cit.*, p. 82.
107 *Ibid.*, pp. 53–4.
108 Thatcher, *op. cit.*, p. 652.
109 *Ibid.*, p. 648.
110 Lawson, *op. cit.*, p. 576; Butler *et al.*, *op. cit.*, p. 75.
111 Lawson, *op. cit.*, p. 577.
112 Thatcher, *op. cit*, p. 652; Butler *et al.*, *op. cit.*, p. 110.
113 Butler *et al.*, *op. cit.*, p. 71.
114 Thatcher, *op. cit.*, p. 667.
115 *Ibid.*, p. 658.
116 Cmnd 9714, *op. cit.*, p. 105.
117 G. Howe (1994) *Conflict of Loyalty*, pp. 520, 548, 602–3.
118 *Ibid.*, p. 580.
119 Thatcher, *op. cit.*, pp. 650–1.
120 Butler *et al.*, *op. cit.*, pp. 209–18.
121 P. Hennessy (1989) *Whitehall*, p. 483. London: Secker and Warburg.
122 Butler *et al.*, *op. cit.*, p. 84.
123 D. Mason (1985) *Revising the Rating System*. London: Adam Smith Institute.
124 Baker, *op. cit.*, p. 119.
125 G. Howe, *op. cit.*, pp. 520, 548, 602–3.
126 N. Fowler (1991) *Ministers Decide*, p. 120. London: Chapmans.
127 Lawson, *op. cit.*, p. 583.
128 *Ibid.*, p. 584.
129 Baker, *op. cit.*, pp. 131–2.
130 Thatcher, *op. cit.*, p. 654.
131 Butler *et al.*, *op. cit.*, p. 139.
132 *Ibid.*, p. 143.
133 *The Guardian*, 18 November 1989.
134 Butler *et al.*, *op. cit.*, pp. 142–3 (italics in the original).
135 Lawson, *op. cit.*, p. 574.
136 Butler *et al.*, *op. cit.*, p. 142.
137 Thatcher, *op. cit.*, p. 659.
138 See Secretary of State for the Environment (1990) *The Revenue Support Grant Distribution Report (England)*, House of Commons Paper 049. London: HMSO; Audit Commission (1993) *Passing the Bucks: The Impact of Standard Spending Assessments on Economy, Efficiency and Effectiveness*. London: Audit Commission.
139 Audit Commission (1993) *Passing the Bucks . . .* , Vol. 1, p. 19. London: Audit Commission.
140 *The Independent*, 6 April 1990.
141 Audit Commission, *op. cit.*, p. 19.
142 *Ibid.*, p. 4.
143 Audit Commission (1993) *Passing the Bucks . . .* , Vol. 2, p. 8. London: Audit Commission.
144 J. G. March and H. A. Simon (1958) *Organizations*, p. 139. New York: Wiley.
145 Cmnd 9714, *op. cit.*, p. 24.
146 Thatcher, *op. cit.*, p. 659.
147 Baker, *op. cit.*, pp. 129, 126.
148 Thatcher, *op. cit.*, p. 661.
149 *Ibid.*, p. 659.

150 Butler *et al.*, *op. cit.*, p. 82.
151 Thatcher, *op. cit.*, pp. 658–9.

Chapter 7 Consultation and pressure: reforming social security in the mid-1980s

1 N. Fowler (1991) *Ministers Decide*, p. 278. London: Chapmans.
2 N. Lawson (1992) *The View from No. 11*, p. 609. London: Bantam.
3 K. Andrews and J. Jacobs (1990) *Punishing the Poor: Poverty under Thatcher*. London: Macmillan.
4 M. Adler (1988) Lending a deaf ear: the Government's response to consultation on the reform of social security, in R. Davidson and P. White (eds) *Information and Government*. Edinburgh: Edinburgh University Press.
5 A.I. Ogus, E.M. Barendt *et al.* (1988) *The Law of Social Security*, 3rd edn. London: Butterworth.
6 *Ibid.*, p. 414; D. Donnison (1982) *The Politics of Poverty*. Oxford: Martin Robertson; Cmnd 7773 (1979) *Reform of the Supplementary Benefits Scheme* (White Paper). London: HMSO.
7 P. Kemp (1984) *The Cost of Chaos*, SHAC Research Report No 8. London: SHAC.
8 Reproduced from Cmnd 9519 (1985) *Reform of Social Security: Background Papers* (Green Paper, Volume 3). London: HMSO.
9 This is an extract from Fowler's statement to the House of Commons on 2 April 1984, outlining the proposed review process. HC Deb., 2 April 1984, cols 652–60.
10 Those who gave evidence to the reviews (except to that on Housing Benefit) are listed in Cmnd 9519, *op. cit.*, pp. 131–8.
11 Besides Thatcher, Lawson and Fowler, other members may have been the Leaders of the House of Commons and the House of Lords, and the Secretaries of State for Employment, the Environment, Trade and Industry, Scotland and Wales.
12 Fowler, *op. cit.*, p. 213.
13 *Ibid.*, pp. 216–17.
14 Cmnd 9517 (1985) *Reform of Social Security* (Green Paper, Volume 1). London: HMSO.
15 Cmnd 9520 (1985) *Housing Benefit Review*. London: HMSO.
16 House of Commons Select Committee on Social Services (1985) *The Government's Green Paper 'Reform of Social Security'*, HC451, 17 July 1985. London: HMSO.
17 Cmnd 9691 (1985) *Reform of Social Security: Programme for Action* (White Paper), p. 2. London: HMSO.
18 A. Hadjipateras (1985) Against the Green Paper: a survey of responses, *London Advice Services Alliance Review*, No. 8, November.
19 Cmnd 9691. See note 17.
20 *Ibid.*
21 Fowler, *op. cit.*, p. 223.
22 Lawson, *op. cit.*, p. 594.
23 Andrews and Jacobs, *op. cit.*, p. 249. The Consortium's members included Age Concern, Child Poverty Action Group, Disability Alliance, Mind, National Council for One Parent Families, National Association of Citizens' Advice Bureaux, Association of County Councils and British Association of Social Workers.
24 Lord Glenarthur (Parliamentary Under-Secretary of State, DHSS) to the House of Lords. HL Deb., 15 May 1987.
25 Under the 'affirmative resolution' procedure, Regulations must be formally approved by both Houses of Parliament before they can come into force, but Parliament cannot amend them, only pass them or not pass them.
26 Child Poverty Action Group, in The Hansard Society Commission (1993) *Making the Law*, pp. 64–7. London: The Hansard Society for Parliamentary Government.

27 Andrews and Jacobs, *op. cit.*, p. 255.
28 DHSS (1987) *Impact of the Reformed Structure of Income-related Benefits*. London: DHSS.
29 Andrews and Jacobs, *op. cit.*, pp. 59–65.
30 Ogus and Barendt, *op. cit.*, p. 513.
31 Andrews and Jacobs, *op. cit.*, p. 259.
32 *Ibid.*
33 Cmnd 9517, *op. cit.*, p. 47.
34 Cmnd 9517, *op. cit.*, Preface and p. 45.
35 *Ibid.*, p. 45.
36 Fowler, *op. cit.*, p. 209.
37 Cmnd 9517, *op. cit.*, pp. 1–3.
38 Cmnd 9691, *op. cit.*, p. 1.
39 *Ibid.*, p. 2.
40 Fowler, *op. cit.*, p. 212; Cmnd 9517, *op. cit.*, p. 2; Cmnd 9691, *op. cit.*, p. 1.
41 Cmnd 9517, *op. cit.*, p. 46.
42 *Ibid.*, p. 29.
43 Cmnd 9691, *op. cit.*, p. 31.
44 M. Thatcher (1993) *The Downing Street Years*, p. 631. London: HarperCollins.
45 Cmnd 9517, *op. cit.*, p. 29.
46 Cmnd 9691, *op. cit.*, p. 31.
47 *Ibid.*, p. 33.
48 Fowler, *op. cit.*, p. 213.
49 Cmnd 9691, *op. cit.*, p. 12.
50 Cmnd 9517, *op. cit.*, p. 45; Cmnd 9691, *op. cit.*, p. 10.
51 Fowler, *op. cit.*, p. 213.
52 Cmnd 9517, *op. cit.*, p. 46.
53 Cmnd 9691, *op. cit.*, p. 12.
54 Fowler, *op. cit.*, p. 222.
55 Adler, *op. cit.*, p. 173.
56 Andrews and Jacobs, *op. cit.*, pp. 46–8.
57 *Ibid.*
58 Lawson, *op. cit.*, p. 594.
59 See Adler, *op. cit.*, p. 183.
60 Cmnd 9517, *op. cit.*, p. 31.
61 Fowler, *op. cit.*, pp. 206–7.
62 Cmd 6404 (1942) *Social Insurance and Allied Services*. London: HMSO.
63 Fowler, *op. cit.*, p. 208.
64 *The Guardian*, 16 April 1988, cited by Andrews and Jacobs, *op. cit.*, p. 49.
65 Lawson, *op. cit.*, pp. 614, 720.
66 Fowler, *op. cit.*, pp. 223–4.
67 *Ibid.*, p. 213.
68 *Ibid.*, p. 209.
69 Lawson, *op. cit.*, p. 596.
70 Fowler, *op. cit.*, p. 204.
71 *Ibid.*, p. 205.
72 *Ibid.*, p. 204.
73 *Ibid.*
74 *Ibid.*, pp. 205–6.
75 Lawson, *op. cit.*, p. 596; Fowler, *op. cit.*, p. 209.
76 Fowler, *op. cit.*, p. 209.
77 Lawson, *op. cit.*, pp. 590–2.
78 *Ibid.*, pp. 590, 592.
79 DHSS (1985) *Reform of Social Security: Technical Annex*. London: HMSO.

80 Lawson, *op. cit.*, p. 592.
81 Adler, *op. cit.*, p. 175.
82 Cmnd 9691, *op. cit.*, p. 2.
83 *Ibid.*, p. 38.
84 Fowler, *op. cit.*, p. 222.
85 *Ibid.*
86 HL Deb., 23 June 1986, Session 1985–86, vol. 477, cols. 40–1.
87 Fowler, *op. cit.*, p. 209.
88 Lawson, *op. cit.*, p. 594.
89 Fowler, *op. cit.*, p. 222.
90 *Ibid.*, p. 220.
91 The Conservatives had an overall majority at the 1983 general election of 145.
92 Fowler, *op. cit.*, p. 223.
93 S. Baxter (1993) The sleaze at the heart of Tory Britain, *New Statesman and Society*, 1 October 1993. This article was based on G. Howarth (1993) *Quangos and Political Donations to the Tory Party*. Knowsley: Knowsley North Constituency Labour Party.
94 Fowler, *op. cit.*, p. 223.
95 Andrews and Jacobs, *op. cit.*, p. 244.
96 Lawson, *op. cit.*, p. 720.
97 *Ibid.*
98 Although Thatcher was later prepared to countenance an increase if it allowed a reduction in housing subsidies to local authorities, as we saw in Chapter 5.

Chapter 8   The Treasury versus the spending departments: the annual spending round

1 See for example Cmnd 9702-I (1986) *The Government's Expenditure Plans 1986–87 to 1988–89* (White Paper, Volume I). London: HMSO.
2 N. Lawson (1992) *The View from No. 11*. London: Bantam.
3 K. Baker (1993) *The Turbulent Years*. London: Faber and Faber.
4 B. Castle (1980) *The Castle Diaries 1974–76*. London: Weidenfeld and Nicolson.
5 L. Pliatzky (1982) *Getting and Spending*. Oxford: Basil Blackwell.
6 L. Pliatzky (1989) *The Treasury under Mrs Thatcher*. Oxford: Basil Blackwell.
7 A. Likierman (1988) *Public Expenditure: Who Really Controls It and How.* Harmondsworth: Penguin.
8 H. Heclo and A. Wildavsky (1974) *The Private Government of Public Money*. London: Macmillan (new edition, but no new research, published in 1981).
9 H. Young and A. Sloman (1984) *But Chancellor: an Inquiry into the Treasury*. London: BBC.
10 Likierman, *op. cit.*, p. 40.
11 D. Healey (1989) *The Time of my Life*, pp. 401–2. London: Michael Joseph.
12 HC Deb., 6 December 1984, col. 525, cited by Likierman, *op. cit.*, p. 9.
13 Likierman, *op. cit.*, p. 9.
14 *Ibid.*, p. 40.
15 *Ibid.*, p. 41.
16 D. Hencke, Rising cost of jobless brings tough choice for Chancellor, *The Guardian*, 28 January 1991.
17 Likierman, *op. cit.*, p. 41.
18 Young and Sloman, *op. cit.*, p. 71.
19 Pliatzky (1989), *op. cit.*, p. 42.
20 *Ibid.*, p. 43.
21 HC Deb., 20 February 1986, col. 507; cited by Likierman, *op. cit.*, pp. 41–2.

22 P. Wintour and B. Laurance, Treasury memo reveals £12bn cuts, Brown says, *The Guardian*, 22 February 1993.
23 A. Grice, Treasury seeks £12bn cut in government spending, *The Sunday Times*, 21 February 1993.
24 Heclo and Wildavsky, *op. cit.*, pp. 91–2.
25 D. Smith, Major warns of spending squeeze, *The Sunday Times*, 22 April 1990.
26 Pliatzky (1989), *op. cit.*, p. 44.
27 Young and Sloman, *op. cit.*, p. 49.
28 *Ibid.*, p. 45.
29 *Ibid.*, p. 47.
30 P. Hennessy (1989) *Whitehall*, p. 678. London: Secker and Warburg.
31 Young and Sloman, *op. cit.*, pp. 50–1.
32 Heclo and Wildavsky, *op. cit.*, pp. 85–7.
33 D. Brindle, Treasury plan to curb youth hardship bill, *The Guardian*, 2 June 1994.
34 Likierman, *op. cit.*, p. 42.
35 Lawson, *op. cit.*, p. 288.
36 *Ibid.*, p. 288.
37 A. Travis and D. Hencke, Ministers bust cash barriers, *The Guardian*, 5 October 1990.
38 C. Brown, Tories prepare to bargain over £3bn to ease poll tax, *The Independent*, 30 May 1990.
39 B. Castle, *op. cit.*, p. 143.
40 *Ibid.*, p. 169.
41 *Ibid.*, pp. 171–2.
42 *Ibid.*, p. 203.
43 A. Clark (1993) *Diaries*, p. 40. London: Weidenfeld and Nicolson.
44 Lawson, *op. cit.*, pp. 288–9.
45 C. Brown, NHS spending memo leaked, *The Independent*, 11 October 1990; N. Timmins, Clarke spending round strategy exposed by leak, *The Independent*, 11 October 1990; M. White, Leaked paper puts squeeze on Clarke, *The Guardian*, 11 October 1990; C. Brown, Thatcher calls talks on education cash, *The Independent*, 17 October 1990.
46 Lawson, *op. cit.*, p. 289.
47 *Ibid.*, pp. 724–5.
48 *Ibid.*, p. 725.
49 *Ibid.*, pp. 725–7.
50 *Ibid.*, p. 290.
51 *Ibid.*, p. 291.
52 K. Baker (1993) *The Turbulent Years*, pp. 142–6. London: Faber and Faber.
53 *Ibid.*, p. 146.
54 Lawson, *op. cit.*, p. 312.
55 *Ibid.*, p. 292.
56 *Ibid.*, p. 292.
57 *Ibid.*
58 *Ibid.*, p. 315.
59 Pliatzky (1989), *op. cit.*, p. 32.
60 D. Smith, Broken promises, *The Sunday Times*, 10 April 1994.
61 Lawson, *op. cit.*, p. 309.
62 Morrison Halcrow (1989) *Keith Joseph: a Single Mind*, p. 182. Basingstoke: Macmillan.
63 Lawson, *op. cit.*, p. 309.
64 Halcrow, *op. cit.*, pp. 174–5.
65 Lawson, *op. cit.*, p. 311.
66 *Ibid.*, p. 315.
67 *Ibid.*

68. C. Brown, Clarke team sharpens the axe, *The Independent*, 18 June 1993.
69 J. Sherman, Cuts victims take their grievances to Cabinet, *The Times*, 28 October 1993.
70 P. Wintour, Cash cut threat for tenants with room to spare, *The Guardian*, 2 November 1994.
71 Likierman, *op. cit.*, p. 164.
72 Heclo and Wildavsky, *op. cit.*, pp. 103–18; Likierman, *op. cit.*, pp. 79–89.
73 Heclo and Wildavsky, *op. cit.*, p. 107.
74 *Financial Times*, 30 November 1994.
75 Heclo and Wildavsky, *op. cit.*, p. 106.
76 Clark, *op. cit.*, p. 40.
77 *Ibid.*
78 Young and Sloman, *op. cit.*, p. 57.
79 P. Leather (1983) Housing (dis?)investment programmes, *Policy and Politics*, 11(2).
80 Lawson, *op. cit.*, p. 26.
81 Baker, *op. cit.*, p. 236.
82 Lawson, *op. cit.*, p. 304.
83 *Ibid.*, p. 567.
84 *Ibid.*, p. 595.
85 D. Donnison (1982) *The Politics of Poverty*, p. 58. Oxford: Martin Robertson.
86 *Ibid.*, pp. 146, 149.
87 Cited by Pliatzky (1989), *op. cit.*, p. 29.
88 Lawson, *op. cit.*, p. 315.
89 *Ibid.*, p. 306.
90 Young and Sloman, *op. cit.*, p. 129.
91 Lawson, *op. cit.*, p. 311.
92 *Ibid.*, p. 315.
93 Heclo and Wildavsky, *op. cit.*, p. 15.
94 See Lawson, *op. cit.*, pp. 297, 367, 479, 689, for some references to matters of presentation.
95 These data can be found in the potted biographies in *BBC-Vacher's Biographical Guide* and *The Whitehall Companion*. (For publishers and their addresses, see notes to Chapter 2.)
96 *Ibid.*
97 Pliatzky (1989), *op. cit.*, p. 160.
98 *Ibid.*, pp. 155, 23, 30, 81.
99 Lawson, *op. cit.*, pp. 25–6. According to *Collins English Dictionary*, the Praetorian Guard was the bodyguard of the Roman emperors. It existed from 27 BC to AD 312 and was noted for its political corruption. This may not have been the feature that Pliatzky and Lawson had in mind.
100 D. Hencke, Treasury 'interference' put under scrutiny, *The Guardian*, 25 April 1994.
101 Lawson, *op. cit.*, p. 720.
102 M. Thatcher (1993) *The Downing Street Years*, p. 54. London: HarperCollins.
103 Young and Sloman, *op. cit.*, p. 47.
104 Castle, *op. cit.*, p. 653.
105 Baker, *op. cit.*, p. 146.
106 Heclo and Wildavsky, *op. cit.*, pp. 136–7.
107 *Ibid.*, p. 197.
108 Lawson, *op. cit.*, p. 317.
109 Baker, *op. cit.*, p. 169.
110 *Ibid.*, p. 143.
111 Pliatzky (1989), *op. cit.*, p. 48.
112 *Ibid.*, pp. 159–61.

113 *Ibid.*, p. 16.
114 Lawson, *op. cit.*, p. 290.
115 W. Whitelaw (1990) *The Whitelaw Memoirs*, p. 330. London: Headline.
116 Lawson, *op. cit.*, p. 302.
117 Baker, *op. cit.*, p. 145.

Chapter 9   European social policy and the UK: the Social Charter and the protection of women workers

1 C. Brewster and P. Teague (1989) *European Community Social Policy: Its Impact on the UK*, p. 6. London: Institute of Personnel Management.
2 A. Byre (1992) *EC Social Policy and 1992: Laws, Cases and Materials*, p. 4. Deventer: Kluwer.
3 COM(89)248 final.
4 COM(89)471 final.
5 It is reprinted, together with the preliminary draft and draft, in *Social Europe*, 1/90.
6 COM(89)568 final. This too has been reprinted in *Social Europe*, 1/90.
7 *The Guardian*, 9 December 1991.
8 See House of Commons Employment Committee, *The European Social Charter: Government Reply to the Fourth Report of the Committee in Session 1990–91*, HC Paper 676, Third Special Report of Session 1990–91, HMSO 1991.
9 COM(90)406) final.
10 COM(90)692 final.
11 House of Lords Select Committee on the European Communities, *Protection at Work of Pregnant Women and Women Who Have Recently Given Birth, and Child Care*, HL Paper 11, Second Report of Session 1991–92, HMSO 1991: Minutes of Evidence, pp. 2–3.
12 *Ibid.*, Report, pp. 8, 18.
13 *Ibid.*, pp. 44–5.
14 SEC(91)2398 final.
15 *Official Journal of the European Communities*, No. 3–418: Debates of the European Parliament, 1992–93 Session, Report of proceedings from 11 to 15 May 1992, pp. 39–44, 52–3.
16 Press Release IP(92)832.
17 Cm 2513 (1994) *Social Security Departmental Report*, p. 26. London: HMSO.
18 M. Zander (1989) *The Law-making Process*, 3rd edn, p. 388. London: Weidenfeld and Nicolson. The leading case is that of *Van Gend en Loos* (Case 26/62 [1963] ECR 1)).
19 European Court of Justice, Case 287/86, reprinted in Byre, *op. cit.*, pp. 69–75.
20 EC leaders strike treaty deal, *The Independent*, 11 December 1991.
21 *The World This Weekend*, BBC Radio 4, 18 April 1993.
22 France's 'grande idée' for Europe, *The Independent*, 10 December 1991.
23 Article G(9)–(13).
24 House of Lords Select Committee on the European Communities, *op. cit.*, pp. 2–3.
25 *Official Journal of the European Communities, op. cit.*, pp. 41–2.
26 J. Wolf, Deadlock may kill EC maternity law, *The Guardian*, 8 October 1992.
27 House of Lords Select Committee on the European Communities, *op. cit.*, pp. 2–3.
28 *Ibid.*, p. 3.
29 *Ibid.*, Report, p. 18.
30 Cf. N. Nugent (1994) *The Government and Politics of the European Union*, pp. 259–61. Basingstoke: Macmillan.
31 M. Kleinman and D. Piachaud (1993) European social policy: conceptions and choices, *Journal of European Social Policy*, 3(1), 1–19.

Chapter 10   Conclusions: the mechanisms of policy making

1 M. Thatcher (1993) *The Downing Street Years*, p. 642. London: HarperCollins.
2 *Ibid.*, p. 591.
3 N. Machiavelli, in the English translation by G. Bull (1981) *The Prince*, p. 34. Harmondsworth: Penguin. A 'toothing-stone' is described by the translator as 'a projection at the end of a wall to provide for its continuation'.
4 N. Fowler (1991) *Ministers Decide*, p. 222. London: Chapmans.
5 L. Festinger (1957) *A Theory of Cognitive Dissonance*. Evanston, IL: Row, Peterson.
6 The conjunction of perceptions and imperative has parallels with Banting's 'awareness' ('How are policy-makers made aware of the existence of the situation?') and 'salience' ('Why is the situation judged to be a 'problem' and sufficiently important to be acted on?'), but he treats them as 'phases', i.e. not occurring in conjunction. K.G. Banting (1979) *Poverty, Politics and Policy*, p. 10. London: Macmillan.
7 Thatcher's attitude was summed up by Bernard Ingham, her Chief Press Secretary throughout her period in office: 'She never liked local government.' A Tax too Far, Despatches, Channel Four, 10 March 1993.
8 The Hansard Society Commission (1993) *Making the Law*, p. 256. London: The Hansard Society for Parliamentary Government.
9 A. Sandberg (1976) *The Limits to Democratic Planning*, p. 111. Stockholm: LiberFörlag.
10 Thatcher, *op. cit.*, p. 122.
11 B. Coxall and L. Robins (1994) *Contemporary British Politics*, 2nd edn, p. 355. Basingstoke: Macmillan.

INDEX